REVELATION STUDY

MUNCIA WALLS

INTRODUCTION
A REVEALING

The word Revelation is from the Greek word "apocalupsis." So, we have the word, "apocalypse," by which the book is often referred. It is from the verb "Apocalupto," which means "to unveil;" from apo "away from," and kalumma, "a veil." So, Apocalupsis means a taking away of a veil, as when a statue is unveiled, so that what is behind, or underneath, may be seen.

The book of Revelation is a prophecy book. It is not a history book! It does not record the past - it reveals the future. It makes this claim in the title, and some four times in the concluding chapter; 22:7, 10, 18, 19. There has been - and there will be - no new revelations since it was written by John.

SATAN HATES THE BOOK

We can say that while Satan hates all the Bible, he probably hates the book of Genesis and the book of Revelation the most. Genesis reveals Satan's introduction of sin into the world and thus bring about the fall of mankind. In Revelation, we are informed of his ultimate doom and defeat. So, we find Satan attacking the authenticity of Genesis and warning people to stay away from the book of Revelation.

SIGNS AND SYMBOLS

We will find more signs and symbols in the book of Revelation than in any other book of the Bible.

They are either explained there where they are found, or in some other place in the Word of God. To fully benefit from the message which is contained in the book of Revelation one must have an understanding of the book of Daniel. These two books go hand-in-hand with one another in unfolding for us the events which transpire in the last days.

The prophet Daniel was told to "*seal up*" the words of his prophecy until the "time of the end." Not the "end of time," but the end of the times of the Gentiles. The "*time of the end*." But John was told to "*seal not*" the sayings of the book of Revelation; (Daniel 12:4,9; Revelation 22:10).

The symbolism of the book of Revelation reveals that it was written for a special class of people; those who are acquainted with the Word of God, and who have spiritual discernment. It was not written for the carnally minded reader. Note Deuteronomy 29:29.

The book of Revelation was written to reveal the purpose of God as to the earth, and the nations which dwell upon the earth. It being the last prophecy of the Word of God, we would expect it to sum up all previous prophecy; and as the previous prophecy had to do with the Church, with Israel, and with the nations, we should expect this last prophecy to give us the final word as to them. That is what it does. We may find the Church in the beginning of the book. We may find Israel in the middle of the book. And we may find the Nations at the end of the book. We can as well notice these three divisions in the city which John saw coming down from God out of heaven; The foundation of the city has the names of the Apostles inscribed in them, which speaks of the Church. The twelve gates to the city have the names of the tribes of Israel inscribed in them, which speaks of Israel. And then we find the saved Nations walking in the light of the city.

JEWISH

A glance through the book and we readily note that the book is primarily Jewish. This can be seen in its "signs," and the many symbols found in it. Such as the Tabernacle, the Ark, the Altar, the Trumpets, and Plagues, and the sealing of the 144,000 of Israel. It is Jewish, because God, in it, after the Church has been taken out, deals again with Israel, and in chapters six to nineteen, He reveals what shall take place during the last - or 70th - week of Daniel's seventy weeks which he spoke to us about in chapter nine of the book of Daniel.

While it is evident that those involved in the events which transpire during those last seven years will include others besides the Jew, it is also evident that the Jews are the primary characters who are involved in this period.

It would not seem proper to notice these Jewish symbols that are found so clearly noted in this book and not realize that they must have some significance to the people of Israel.

INTERPRETATIONS

There are some five schools of interpretation of the book of Revelation;

1. The Preterist School. They are those who insist that the Revelation was fulfilled in the struggles of the Jews and early Christians and in the conquests of Greece and Rome. That the book applies specifically to the problems and persecutions of the early church existing at the time of its writing.

2. The Historical School. This school of thought contends that the events symbolically described by the Lord in the book represent the chronological order of historical events since the time of John to the time of the coming again of Jesus Christ to establish His kingdom on this earth. They are being progressively fulfilled as time marches by - with the vast majority of them having already been fulfilled.

3. The Cyclic School. They seek to combine the chronological interpretations of the past - present - and future schools of thought, by noting a cyclic repetition of similar prophetic events.

4. The Idealistic School. They make no attempt to relate the events described in Revelation to any historical events at all; past, present or future. They treat the book as a series of parables or allegories which are designed to encourage troubled believers that eventually good will triumph over evil.

5. The Futurist School. Although there are some differences in their ranks, they generally contend that from chapter four forward the book is future-tense in its meaning. That the prophecies after chapter four are yet to be fulfilled.

It is our opinion that the book of Revelation should be studied in the Futurist sense. That the events which are revealed in the book are primarily FUTURE events.

The final years which lie ahead will be filled with exciting - active - events such as this world and the human race has never witnessed before.

FIRST AND LAST

The comparison between the first and the last books of the Bible are very interesting. The first depicts for us the introduction of God to mankind; as well as man being introduced to God. The last book depicts the ultimate introduction of God to man - and man to God, when God shall return in the person of Jesus Christ to put down all evil and bring an end to the open rebellion among creation. Man will be made aware of the fact that it is God who rules in the kingdoms of men. Especially will this be a startling revelation to the man of sin as he is toppled from his throne at the time of Armageddon. Also, we find that at least four times in the book of Revelation there is a reference made to the creation of the world - or the record of Genesis; 4:11; 10:6; 13:8; 14:7.

The prophecy which we find in the book of Genesis concerning the conflict between the seed of the woman and the serpent is found in great detail in chapter 12 of the Revelation.

The first rebel - Nimrod - is found in the book of Genesis. His counterpart, or anti-type, is found in the book of Revelation, along with his ultimate doom.

Also, many of the things which we find brought upon the world in the Genesis account, due to the fall of man, is found removed in the Revelation:

• Cursed ground, 3:17 Curse removed, 22:3

• Sorrow on mankind, 3:17 No more sorrow, 21:4

• Satan, opposer of man, 3:15 Satan cast out, 20:10

• Tree of life out of reach, 3:24 Tree available, 22:14

• Promised Redeemer, 3:15 Redeemer comes, 5:9,10; 19:11.

These are just a few of the many comparisons which may be found in the two books.

While no book of the Bible should be shunned; especially do we find that this book of Revelation should not be shunned. While it is true that it's many signs and symbols make it a more difficult book to understand, it is not like reading the Sermon on the Mount, but nonetheless, it is a book which should be read and studied because it is talking about OUR FUTURE!

The book reveals the ultimate triumph of God and all that is good over the Devil and all that is evil.

WHEN?

One of the big debates found among the teachers of the book of

Revelation is just when will the rapture take place. We could probably divide the debaters into three main camps;

1. Pre-Tribulationist's. Those who contend that the Church will be taken out before the tribulation begins. The tribulation being that period which will last some seven years, and oft times referred to as Daniel's seventieth week.

2. Mid-Tribulationist's. Those who feel that the Church will endure at least one half of the seven-year period of trouble which will come on the world. That the Lord will call the Church out in the middle of the week before the last half - the Great Tribulation - begins. Which they contend is God's wrath.

3. Post-Tribulationist's. They contend that the Church will endure this time of trouble which shall come upon the earth. That it will only be at the end of this dark tribulation that the Lord will come and call His Church up to meet Him in the air.

THE BOOK TELLS US

The way the book is written answers the question for us as to just when the Lord will come His Church. A careful examination of the book reveals that the first few chapters deal primarily with the Church.

Chapters two and three are devoted entirely to letters written to seven of the Churches of Asia. These are probably representative churches. The conditions which existed in these churches are also evident in various ages through which the Church travels. Culminating with the Laodicean Church and the luke-warm condition with an increase of riches. Such a condition which certainly speaks very loudly of the present conditions which we find the Church world in today.

Following this line of thought, we come to chapter four in which we find a voice like a trumpet calling John up to heaven. What a vivid description which is employed here, and which seems to speak so clearly to us of Rapture Morn!

Chapter five seems like a pause in the discourse as John shares with us his vision of the Lamb who was slain and who only was found worthy to open the seven-sealed book which would reveal the events which would transpire during the last seven years of man's day.

And then, beginning with chapter six, we are introduced to those dark events and times which shall come upon this earth. The language which is employed after chapter four is so Jewish oriented that it could apply to no other people. There is no mention made of the Church any more after chapter four as being involved in the events which are taking place on the earth at that time.

The very fact that the Church is obviously missing at this time, and the Jewish people are so evident, that the Church has been removed prior to chapter six and the opening of the seals which brings the days of tribulation to the world, seems to be an indication that the tribulation is not for the Church but for Israel.

SEVENNESS

Another thing of interest and importance is the "seven-ness" of the book. Notice some of the seven's which are to be found in the book of Revelation;

- 1. Seven Churches; 1:4, 11,20
- 2. Seven spirits; 1:4; 3: 1; 4:5; 5:6
- 3. Seven candlesticks; 1:12
- 4. Seven stars; 1:16
- 5. Seven lambs; 4:5
- 6. Seven seals; 5:1
- 7. Seven horns; 5:6
- 8. Seven eyes; 5:6
- 9. Seven angels; 8:2,6
- 10. Seven trumpets; 8:2,6
- 11. Seven thunders; 10:3,4
- 12. Seven thousand; 11:13
- 13. Seven heads; 12:3; 13:1
- 14. Seven crowns; 12:3
- 15. Seven angels; 15:1 ,6,7
- 16. Seven plagues; 15:1
- 17. Seven vials; 15:7

- 18. Seven mountains; 17:9

- 19. Seven kings: 17:10,11

Now I don't think this is something which should be taken just for granted. The unusual amount of "sevens" could hardly be called accidental! In fact, there are more sevens to be found in the book of Revelation than are found in the rest of the entire New Testament!

Now we point out that these are merely the places where the numeral "7" is employed. There are other places where the number seven is also employed, not the actual use of the number seven, but the number of times it is found. Like the seven beatitudes for instance of; 1:3; 14:13; 16:15; 19:9; 20:6; 22:7; 22:14.

• There are also seven "I AM's" of Jesus Christ to be found in the book.

This use of the numeral seven adds to the significance of the book of Revelation. Most all agree the number seven speaks of fullness; perfection; and completeness. It is the number which God employed to signify completeness, or perfection. We find this in the very first book, Genesis. We do not read very far until we come upon the reference to the seventh day - which spoke of completeness.

So, the book of Revelation speaks of completeness; it speaks of perfection. It informs us of how God will bring an end to sin and the problems which beset mankind. It informs us that God will bring His creation, the faithful, to a glorious end of perfection and completeness.

While the Bible begins in that first book with Paradise LOST - it closes with last book revealing that Paradise will be REGAINED at last!

Another unique thing about this book is John's use of the term "I" which he employed some 70 times or more in this book. This is unusual for John as we do not find him employing this term at all in his gospel account.

• What an interesting study!

JOHN ... The Beloved Disciple

John, along with James, was a son of Zebedee and Salome. He was a fisherman of Galilee. His family were partners with another set of brothers: Peter and Andrew, as fishermen of Galilee.

John was a disciple of John the Baptist before becoming a follower of Jesus Christ.

Upon committing himself to become a disciple of Jesus he became closely involved with Jesus and His ministry. He, along with Peter and James, became the inner circle which Jesus took with Him at special times.

They were there at the raising of Jairus' daughter, Mark 5:3-7. They were present at the transfiguration of Jesus, Matthew 17. When Jesus went to the garden of Gethsemane prior to His arrest, it was these three who were taken deeper into the garden with Jesus and who were closer to Him during that vigil of prayer.

John and Peter were the first Apostles to visit the garden tomb where Jesus had been laid after death. He, along with Peter, were involved in the healing of the lame man at the beautiful gate of the temple. He accompanied Peter, the man with the keys, to Samaria so that they too might receive the Holy Ghost. He, along with Peter and James, were spoken of as "pillars" of the Church in Jerusalem.

It is said that he owned a house in Jerusalem and that it was probably in his home that the interview with Nicodemus took place.

It was probably John who was referred to as the disciple whom Jesus loved.

As Jesus hung on the cross He committed the keeping of Mary, His mother, into the hands of John. It is believed that John later moved to Ephesus, where he also moved Mary, and where she would later die.

Eusebius wrote in Chapter 18:1-5: "It is said that in this persecution the apostle and evangelist John, who was still alive, was condemned to dwell on the island of Patmos in consequence of his testimony to the divine word. Irenaeus, in the fifth book of his work Against Heresies, where he discusses the number of the name of Antichrist which is given in the so-called Apocalypse of John, speaks as follows concerning him: "If it were necessary for his name to be

Proclaimed openly at the present time, it would have been declared by him who saw the revelation. For it was seen not long ago, but almost in our own generation, at the end of the reign of Domitian." To such a degree, indeed, did the teaching of our faith flourish at that time that even those writers who were far from our religion did not hesitate to mention in their histories the persecution and the martyrdoms which took place during it... "

Then Eusebius wrote in 23:1-4a: "At that time the apostle and evangelist John, the one whom Jesus loved, was still living in Asia, and governing the churches of that region, having returned after the death of Domitian from his exile on the island. And that he was still alive at that time may be established by the testimony of two witnesses. They should be trustworthy who have maintained the orthodoxy of the Church; and such indeed were Irenaeus and Clement of Alexandria. The former in the second book of his work Against Heresies, writes as follows. And all the elders that associated with John the disciple of the Lord in Asia bear witness that John delivered it to them. For he remained among them until the time of Trajan."

Tertullian wrote that John was with Peter in Rome and for a time was in danger of his life. The legend is that he was submitted to the torture of being boiled in oil but was delivered miraculously. This story does not seem to have much foundation in historical fact, but the Church of San Giovanni in Olio seems to have been built on the spot in Rome to honor the Apostle's escape.

Jerome wrote: "In the fourteenth year then after Nero, Domitian having raised a second persecution, he was banished to the island of Patmos, and wrote the Apocalypse, on which Justin Martyr and Irenaeus afterwards wrote commentaries. But Domitian having been put to death and his acts, on account of his excessive cruelty having been annulled by the senate, he returned to Ephesus under Nerva Pertlnax and continuing there until the time of the emperor Trajan, founded and built churches throughout all Asia, and, worn out by old age, died in the sixty-eighth year after our Lord's passion and was buried near the same city."

CHAPTER ONE

Verse 1:

The Revelation of Jesus Christ, which God gave unto him, to shew unto his servants things which must shortly come to pass; and he sent and signified {it} by his angel unto his servant John:

The Revelation of Jesus Christ, which God gave unto Him... The title of this interesting book should be just what we find in verse one; *"The revelation of Jesus Christ."* Not the revelation of Saint John the divine. It is the revelation which was given to John. But it is not John's revelation.

Verse 2:

Who bare record of the word of God, and of the testimony of Jesus Christ, and of all things that he saw.

While John was chosen to be the writer of this book, he was not the author. The author was the Lord Jesus Christ Himself. John merely recorded the things which he saw and was told to write. Twice in the book we find John stating that the contents of the book were revealed to him by an angel; 1:1; 22:8.

The Book of Revelation is the only book of the New Testament to which Jesus gives His endorsement and affixes His own signature. He states at its close; *"I Jesus have sent mine angel to testify unto you these things in the churches,"* (22:16).

This book is the only book among the sixty-six in which we find a blessing pronounced upon those who read it:

Verse 3:

Blessed {is} he that readeth, and they that hear the words of this prophecy, and keep those things which are written therein: for the time {is} at hand.

BLESSED... This statement pronounces an endorsement upon the book to begin with. The only book of the sixty-six in which we have such an announcement placed upon those who read this book.

While many shun not only the studying of this book, but also even the reading of it. The argument is that no one understands the book, so, we should not confuse our minds by reading it.

It is felt that John expected this book to be read publicly to the people; much like we have Ezra reading the Law to the people upon returning to Jerusalem and re-building their temple; Nehemiah 8:1-3.

<u>**Verse 4:**</u>

John to the seven churches which are in Asia: Grace be unto you, and peace, from him which is, and which was, and which is to come; and from the seven Spirits which are before his throne.

We have already made reference to the use of the numeral 7 in the Revelation. This is the first Place that we come upon the number, but we will come across it many times more before we get through the entire book.

John uses the term "I heard" some twenty-eight times in the book - which is four sevens. He also stated "*I saw*" (or some similar term like, "I looked," "I beheld," which are all from the same Greek word), some forty-nine times - which is seven sevens.

John's salutation is similar to what we find Paul employing in his epistles.

John introduces us to the One who "*is, and which was, and which is to come.*" The ever-existing Eternal One. The one whom the writer of Hebrews wrote; "*Jesus Christ the same yesterday* (which was), *and today* (which is), *and for ever* (which is to come)."

And from the seven Spirits which are before the throne... The ancient Jews said the "Angels which were first created ministered before Him. II And some feel that this has reference to those angels.

However, notice the salutation is FROM the seven Spirits as well. Grace and peace can come only through the One who is the Prince of Peace and the giver of grace. Probably this has reference to the Spirit of God which comes forth from the throne of God to bless and fill the heart of the believer.

Again, seven speaks of completeness or perfection. The Spirit which proceeds from God from His throne is sufficient to bring those to whom the Spirit ministers to perfection and completeness in God.

Certainly, it is only the Spirit which can bring this into our life. And it is the Spirit which ministers grace and peace to the people of God. We do not find where any angel has been commissioned to do this.

The prophet Isaiah spoke of the seven divine attributes which are manifested through our Lord Jesus Christ (11:2); Spirit of the LORD, wisdom, understanding, counsel, might, knowledge, and fear of the LORD.

Verse 5:

And from Jesus Christ, who is the faithful witness, and the first begotten of the dead, and the prince of the kings of the earth. Unto him that loved us, and washed us from our sins in his own blood.

First of all, there are three things which catch our attention in this verse. It speaks of Jesus Christ as:

• 1. The One who is the faithful witness;

• 2. The first begotten of the dead;

• 3. The Prince of the kings of the earth.

This book portrays to us Jesus Christ in His threefold role of Prophet, Priest, King.

As Prophet, He was the faithful witness on the earth. As Priest, He offered His own blood on heaven's mercy seat for our sins, and today He stands in heaven as our High Priest through whom we may make intercession.

As Prince of the kings He shall someday return to this earth and put down all authority which is contrary to His will, and to Him, and He shall reign as King of kings and Lord of lords. While kings may not bow the knee before Him in acknowledging His lordship now, the time will come when they shall do so.

This book, like every other book in the Bible, reveals the Lord Jesus Christ to us. He is the central character of the entire Bible.

We also come upon three other things which stand out in this verse and the first clause of the next verse:

• 1. He loved us;

• 2. He washed us;

• 3. He hath made us kings.

This love is not only revealed to us through the scriptures, but it is also evident to us today as well.

He loved us when He went to Calvary in our stead. He took our sins and carried them to Calvary. No wonder the writer wrote; "Greater love hath no man than this, that a man lay down his life for his friends" (John 15:13). He loved us in spite of ourselves. In spite of what we were. In spite of our own unworthiness - He loved us. As the song writer said; "He looked beyond my faults and saw my needs."

- That was love. That was the love of Jesus Christ.

If we could see ourselves in our loathsomeness we could then more fully appreciate that love which took our Savior to Calvary and which held Him there while He paid the demands for our redemption. If we could realize the awesomeness of that love that reached down to where we were in our sins and degradations, then we could be more appreciative of that love. It was nothing on our part which brought us up out of the miry clay - out of that horrible pit - to stand on the solid rock. No, it was not our worthiness - it was His. It was not anything we did - it was what He did!

John also said He washed us from our sins in His blood. Only the blood can wash away my sins. Only the blood can make me whole again. How despicable we must have looked in our filthiness of sin; How repulsive we must have appeared to a holy and pure God. To any other eyes we must have looked helpless; but not to His eyes. In His mercy, He picked us up and washed us until ALL the filth of sin was removed from our life.

Not only did He wash us till we were clean - the filth of sin which He washed away from our life was also removed for ever from our presence. Never again will we witness the sins which at one time held us bound. As far as the east is from the west is how far the Psalmist described the distance to which our sins are removed from us. And who among us can measure that immeasurable distance?

Verse 6:

And hath made us kings and priests unto God and his Father; to him be glory and dominion for ever and ever. Amen.

Again, it is nothing which we do that brings about this wonderful privilege. It is He who hath made us! We in no way could make ourselves. Nothing we can do. No manner of sacrifice that we make will suffice. No amount of money which we may give to the Church will suffice. Only God bestows upon those whom He chooses this honorable position of glory.

So, then, we have John exclaiming "To Him be glory and dominion for ever and ever. Amen." He alone is worthy of praise and honor.

There is no way that we with our finite minds can fully grasp or comprehend all that lies in store for those who willingly walk with the Lord in this life. Paul himself spoke of how we look through a dark glass being in the flesh (1Corinthians 13:12). We must wait, he said, until *that which is perfect is come* to know *as we are known.* We only see in part at the best while in this life and in this world. We anxiously await that day when we shall be changed from this body of temporariness to a body of glory and eternity. In that day, we shall reign with Him. In that day, we shall rise above the conflicts and bondages of this world.

Verse 7:

Behold, He cometh with clouds; and every eye shall see him, and they also which pierced him: and all kindreds of the earth shall wail because of him. Even so, Amen.

The soldier stood at the base of the cross and smote his chest stating, "Surely this was the Son of God." His decision was a little late. He had already assisted in hanging Him on that cross. What feelings will overwhelm those who have through the years rejected Jesus Christ as Savior and Lord, and then stand one day in His divine presence!

AND ALL KINDREDS OF THE EARTH SHALL WAIL BECAUSE OF HIM

This must be speaking of the time when He returns to this earth in judgment. When He comes the first time for His Church and calls her up into the heavens, there will be rejoicing among that number who know that thrilling experience. No one will be found wailing among that number who will know rapture and glorification. But when He returns to this earth to bring judgment and righteousness, then men will seek to hide their face from him. Then there will be wailing as men realize their awful doom.

Like the soldier at the base of the cross though, they will only realize their folly after it is too late!

BEHOLD. HE COMETH

The hope of every child of God is this glorious promise that Jesus Christ is returning. He is coming again to this earth. This is the theme of both the Old and the New Testament. His coming is announced in the beginning of the Revelation (1:7), and it is again announced in the middle (11:15-18), and then at the end of the Revelation (22:20). In fact, the last words we have recorded that Jesus spoke was the He was coming back again (22:20).

EVERY EYE SHALL SEE HIM

This may not take place all at one time, but sooner or later, every eye shall see Him, and every knee shall bow before Him (Philippians 2:9-11).

Every eye that is prepared shall see Him when He appears in the clouds for His church. Every eye of every saint shall be upon their beloved Savior when the trump of God shall call us to His side.

Verse 8:

I am Alpha and Omega, the beginning and the ending, saith the Lord, which is, and which was, and which is to come, the Almighty.

Jesus is saying in this statement that He is God! Alpha and Omega are the beginning and ending letters of the Greek alphabet. Jesus is saying I am the A and the Z!

Reading this verse for what it is saying removes all doubt from our mind as to who Jesus Christ is. It is impossible to read this verse for what is said here, and take the words just as they are spoken, and not realize that Jesus Christ is God!

The claim to being Alpha and Omega is also found in chapter 21:6 and 22:13. Here it is evident that Jesus is the spokesman. When we turn to chapter twenty-one, though, we find that the speaker there is God. If they are not one and the same, one of them is making a false claim! There is no way that two could claim to be Alpha and Omega, the beginning and the ending.

To add to the significance of this verse we find Jesus concludes by stating that He was *"the Almighty."* Again, there is no way that two or more could claim to possess almightiness! There can be but one Almighty!

This term Almighty is also found employed in the Old Testament in

Genesis 17:1. There God is speaking to Abraham and He informs Abraham that He is "El Shaddai," Almighty God. Thus, the God of the Old Testament is found making the same claim to the aged apostle John in the New Testament, the only thing, we recognize Him now as Jesus Christ. It is the same Spokesman in both places!

This verse and statement by Jesus is the first of some seven "I AM's" of Revelation.

The Greek word employed by Jesus here in stating that He is the Almighty is "pantokrator." It means "The One of all power." Jesus had already informed us in Matthew 28:18 that all power was His.

A little matter of simple deduction makes us to know that the One who was speaking this day to John was the One who alone possessed Omnipotence, Omniscience, and Omnipresence. The One who alone could make such a claim as Being Almighty. If He possesses all power then it only stands to reason if there was any other person before Him in the Godhead, they would be without the same power. For Jesus possesses ALL POWER! He alone is ALMIGHTY!

Verse 9:

I John who also am your brother, and companion in tribulation, and in the kingdom and patience of Jesus Christ, was in the isle that is called Patmos, for the Word of God, and for the testimony of Jesus Christ

Here John gives a brief history of himself. He identifies with those to whom he is addressing his letters. Just what kind of personal relationship he had with these seven churches to whom he wrote these letters, we do not know. But he identifies with them as their Brother, and companion.

John knew the problems of tribulation. He had been banned to this desolate Island because he had been found guilty of preaching Jesus Christ. He could identify WITH them.

It is easy to write to the churches in South America, or Africa, and exhort them in the Lord. But how much more impressive would our words be if we had walked in their steps for a while. How much more could we bless them if we had endured some of their hardships for a while. This John could do. His words must have had lasting effect.

Verse 10:

I was in the Spirit on the Lord's day, and heard behind me a great voice, as of a trumpet.

There are differing opinions as to just what is meant here by the apostle in his reference to *the Lord's day*... Some contend that he was speaking of Sunday, the day they say the Lord was seen alive after His resurrection for the first time. Others contend that John was speaking of the Day of the Lord. Or, that period of time when the judgments of Christ will fall upon man in the last days. To this we would enquire, If this is what John had in mind, why didn't he use that kind of expression; "the day of the Lord," instead of the term we find him employing?

Now we know from the scriptures that the Church gathered together on the first day of the week, which, of course, would be on Sunday. But the term Lord's Day is not found employed during those occasions. It is years later that men begin to refer to Sunday as being the Lord's Day. Possibly John was the first one to employ this term as referring to that day when his blessed Lord was seen alive victorious over death and hell and the grave.

On the other hand, after the obvious suffering that John has been through, and then being banned to this Island in the Aegean Sea, it is possible that John could have lost track of the days of the week. It is possible he did not even know what day of the week it was. That to him this expression could have meant, any day is the Lord's Day when you are in the Spirit.

John said he heard behind him a great voice, as of a trumpet. John, remember, is on a barren island, banned there for the message which he loved and preached. Spending time in prayer and meditation, he hears the voice of his Lord and Master. What a feeling must have come over John to know that Jesus had come down from glory to visit with His beloved apostle on this barren island. Now while it has been some sixty years or so since John last saw his Lord, and last heard His voice, do you think that John had forgotten what His voice sounded like? I believe John recognized that voice.

Verse 11:

Saying, I am Alpha and Omega, the first and the last: and, What thou seest write in a book, and send it unto the seven churches which are in Asia; unto Ephesus, and unto Smyrna, and unto Pergamos, and unto Thyatira, and unto Sardis, and unto Philadelphia, and unto Laodicea.

Again, John hears the words I am Alpha and Omega. This time, however, the voice is speaking directly to him.

John is here given instructions to write a book about what he is about to see. He is told to send this book to the seven churches of Asia. The churches are listed one by one for John. We know from history there were more than seven churches in that area of Asia at that time, but the Lord directs John to write only to these seven.

As we shall point out in our study of the next chapter, these letters to these seven churches no doubt stand as letters that are also directed to the church of this hour. There is a message in each of them for us today as well.

Verse 12:

And I turned to see the voice that spake with me. And being turned, I saw seven golden candlesticks

What John saw must have filled his heart and mind with awe and thrilling feelings. For as he turned, he saw his Lord in His glorified form. The first reference, however, is to seven golden candlesticks. We know from verse twenty that the seven golden candlesticks represent the churches to whom John is to address his letters. So, John sees, first of all, the Church in her glory. He sees the Church first. If the Church fails to manifest the Lord through her activities; through her worship; then she has failed in her purpose of being on this earth.

The Church is to manifest the Lord Jesus Christ to the world in which it exists. The Church is to be an extension of the Lord Jesus Christ. She must be His voice in a world of confusion and chaos.

Verse 13:

And in the midst of the seven candlesticks one like unto the Son of man, clothed with a garment down to the foot, and girt about the paps with a golden girdle

Oh, that that which John witnessed would always be true. Would that the Lord would always be seen in the midst of the church. If this can be said of the church where we attend and worship the Lord, there will be no problem with being identified by Him when He comes.

Jesus had promised that after His leaving them wherever "two or three" of them would gather together in my name, there am I in the midst of them. It is the Lord's delight to dwell in the midst of His people. In the Tabernacle the Lord instructed Moses to have an Ark made with a Mercy Seat to cover it with. The mercy seat was to be made from pure gold. A cherubim was to be made on each end of the mercy seat. They were to be so situated as to be "looking" toward one another and down toward the ark which contained the law of God. The Lord also informed Moses and Israel, that He would meet with them there, *from above the mercy seat, from between the two cherubims which are upon the ark of testimony* (Exodus 25 :22). The ark occupied the inner-most area of the Tabernacle. It was in the Holy of Holies. The Tabernacle in turn was pitched in the midst of all the camps of Israel. The twelve tribes were each assigned a position around the Tabernacle to camp. In this we can see the wonderful figure of that day when the Lord - our Ark and Mercy Seat - would dwell in the "midst" of the Church.

Verse 14:

His head and his hairs were white like wool, as white as snow; and his eyes were as a flame.

Although Jesus had twelve apostles who walked close to Him for about three years; and three of them even closer to Him than the rest during His ministry, we have no accurate record of just what our Lord looked like. The many pictures which are seen today in so many ways do Him an injustice. We do not know whether He was short or tall. We do not have any of His features described by either of the four Gospel writers. We are not to know Him for what He looked like, we are to know Him for who He is!

The reference by John to the Lord as having hair that was "white like wool," reminds us of the vision which Daniel saw (7:9), *The Ancient of days did sit, whose garment was white as snow, and the hair of His head like the pure wool.*

It is of interest that John saw the Lord with hair as wool, and that Daniel also saw the Lord with hair as wool. In fact, Daniel referred to Him as *Ancient of days*. Solomon said; *The hoary head is a crown of glory*, (Proverbs 16:31).

And His eyes were as a flame of fire... John is not seeing the Lord in mercy. John is not seeing the Lord as Savior. John is seeing the Lord as the One who is getting ready to bring judgment upon a world who has rejected Him as their Lord.

There was a time when those eyes wept over a people with love and compassion (Luke 19:41). Now, the world over which He wept has rejected His call of mercy. There remains but one alternative - JUDGMENT!

Verse 15:

And his feet like unto fine brass, as if they burned in a furnace; and his voice as the sound of many waters

In this verse, the feet which had been pierced with spikes when He was placed on the cross at Calvary, are now seen as f they were burned in a furnace. Certainly, He is the One who stated: *I have trodden the winepress alone* (Isaiah 63:3).

We know that in the Old Testament Tabernacle typology brass spoke of judgment. The altar on which the animals were sacrificed was a brazen altar. It spoke of judgment. The Lord is coming in judgment - not in mercy - to the world which John is writing to in Revelation.

That voice which spoke the troubled sea to sleep; that voice which comforted the restless during His ministry; that voice which spoke the world into existence; that same voice is now speaking, and John says it sounds like the sound of many waters. That doesn't sound like expressions of peace to those whom He is speaking to.

Verses 16,17:

And he had in his right hand seven stars: and out of his mouth went a sharp two-edged sword: and his countenance was as the sun shineth in his strength.

And when I saw him, I fell at his feet as dead. And he laid his right hand upon me, saying unto me, Fear not; I am the first and the last.

The seven stars are the seven angels of the churches in Asia. They are "held" in the hand of the Lord. If this does have reference to the pastors of these churches - and every church - then what a comfort to know that they are in the hand of the Lord Jesus!

The reference to the sharp two-edged sword is a reference to the

Word of God. This is pointed out in Hebrews 4:12, where there we find the Word of God spoken of as *sharper than any two-edged sword.*

This is also expressed in Ephesians 6:17, regarding the weapons and armor that the child of God may don in his warfare with the enemy. It is the Word of God which gives life to the obedient - and bring judgment to the disobedient.

The first reaction of John upon witnessing this vision of His Lord was to fall down at His feet in a faint. The vision is overwhelming to the apostle - and would be to us as well.

Verse 18:

I am he that liveth, and was dead; and, behold, I am alive for evermore, Amen; and have the keys of hell and of death

Jesus again employs the term "I AM."

This is a very interesting as well as important verse of scripture. Notice that Jesus here states that He *has the keys of hell (hades) and of death.* While science debates just what life is - when it begins and when it ends - Jesus plainly states that He is in possession of life. I am He that liveth.

Not only is the Lord the possessor of life for evermore, but He also possesses the keys to hades - or hell - and to death itself. When Jesus died on Calvary, they placed His body in the garden tomb of Joseph, but only His body was placed in that tomb. He, that is, His Spirit, had left the body and entered the region of the dead. Paul informs us that he "descended first into the lower parts of the earth,"

(Ephesians 4:9). Peter, in speaking of the Lord's death, and referring to the prophecy of David, said, *He seeing this before spake of the resurrection of Christ, that His soul was not left in hades, neither his flesh did see corruption* (Acts 2:31).

Since that day hades has never been the same! Since that time death has never been the same! Jesus conquered death and hades. Now, those who die in Christ have no fear of the beyond, knowing that Jesus has been there before us and has conquered the unknown. Now, when the child of God dies, there is no trip for the soul to hades. Now when the child of God dies, he goes to be with the Lord.

<u>Verse 19:</u>

Write the things which thou hast seen, and the things which are, and the things which shall be hereafter

Having beheld this wondrous vision, John is now told to write. And here we have the divisions of the Revelation as given to John. *"The things which thou hast seen."* Possibly the events which took place in the days of John; or the Apostolic age of the first century. As well as the vision he has just described for us of His Lord. *"The things which are."* The things which John was the address his seven letters about to the seven churches of Asia. Things which would affect no doubt the entire church age.

The things which shall be hereafter... You will note that this same phrase is employed in 4:1 and seems to be referring to those things which shall transpire from Revelation four on through the rest of the book. The last phrase is literally, *The things which shall be after* these things. Which is no doubt referring to the events that would follow chapters two and three.

The greater part of the book involved in these three divisions would be that period which is referred to as the things which shall be hereafter. This as well emphasizes the fact that the book of Revelation is a prophecy book. The events which take place during the church age comprises only two chapters; two and three. While the events which shall take place during that seven-year period of tribulation takes up chapters six through nineteen.

<u>Verse 20:</u>

The mystery of the seven stars which thou sawest in my right hand, and the seven golden candlesticks. The seven stars are the angels of the seven churches: and the seven candlesticks which thou sawest are the seven churches

Here the Lord identifies for John what the "stars" and the "candlesticks" are which he saw. The stars are the angels of the seven churches, and the candlesticks are the churches.

The term "angels" has brought about quite a bit of discussion as to just what the Lord was having reference to. Probably the majority feel that the reference is to the "Pastor" of the churches. Taking the word, "angel" which has a meaning of "messenger," and applying it to the man of God who is the messenger of the local church.

There is, however, another way of looking at this phrase. For one thing, if the Lord meant Pastor of the church, why didn't He just say Pastor, or Elder? Some will contend, possibly, that His referring to the pastor as an angel to the church complies with the rest of the book which is written in signs and symbols.

Henry Morris, in his book, The Revelation Record, had this to say about this verse: "If 'angel' means 'pastor' here, it is used with this meaning here and nowhere else. If the Lord meant the pastors of the churches, why did He not say 'pastors?' Or why did He not say 'elders,' a term which is used in the New Testament as essentially synonymous with 'pastors,' and which is later used twelve times in Revelation.

"Instead, He spoke of the angels of the churches, and this term is used sixty-seven other times in Revelation, in none of which could the meaning possibly be that of 'pastors.' The principle of a natural, literal interpretation seems to require us to understand here that true churches of the Lord have individual angels assigned for their guidance and watch-care.

"This fact is hardly surprising in view of the innumerable company of angels (Hebrews 12:22) and their assigned function as ministering spirits to those who are heirs of salvation (Hebrews 1:14). Individual believers have angels assigned to them (Matthew 18:10; Acts 12:15). Angels are present in the assemblies during their services (1Corinthians 11:10) and are intensely interested in their progress (1Corinthians 4:9; Ephesians 3:10; 1Timothy 3:16; 5:21; Hebrews 13:2; 1Peter 1:12).

"Admittedly, the concept of an angel of God assigned to each church and in some degree, responsible for the effectiveness of its ministry is one which is largely unrecognized among Christians. Nevertheless, this seems to be the teaching of the Lord's words here. The symbolism is also appropriate to angels. Stars are frequently identified with angels in scripture, especially here in Revelation (9:1,11; 12:3-9).

"Thus the letters to the churches were indeed addressed to the church and to their members and ministers, but they were somehow to be transmitted through their angels. Pastors, elders, deacons, teachers - all may change from time to time as the membership changes. But the individual church itself goes on, sometimes continuing over many generations, and its angel continues with it. Though its members may not be able to see him or communicate with him, he is there, and the very knowledge of his protecting and ministering presence should be a source of encouragement and purification in all its activities."

Well, whoever the stars are, it is to them that John addresses his seven letters.

CHAPTER TWO

• **Ephesus - First Love Left**

Verse 1:

Unto the angel of the church at Ephesus write; These things saith he that holdeth the seven stars in his right hand, who walketh in the midst of the seven golden candlesticks

Angel is taken from the Greek word "aggelos." The phrase is employed in the Bible in referring to both angelic beings and men. The word means messenger. It is to be noted that when John had been given the revelation, and had faithfully recorded it, that he fell down before the feet "of the angel which shewed me these things" (22:8). But this "angel" told him not to do it, "*For I am thy fellowservant, and of thy brethren the prophets.*" (22:9) From this, as well as other passages, we may conclude that the Lord employed His saints as well as angelic beings to deliver His message to His people.

He that holdeth the seven stars in His right hand... The seven stars are the seven pastors - or angels - of these seven churches to whom John is addressing his letters (1:20). If this is a reference to the pastor of the church, then we conclude that the ministry is not only the "hand of God" (1Peter 5:6) in the land, it is also "in" the hand of God. While the ministry should not be subjected to giving account to some board or group of men in the local assembly when it comes to his ministry, he must keep in mind that he will give account to God!

• *Who walketh in the midst of the seven golden candlesticks*

The candlesticks are the churches. Here we see the Lord walking in the midst of the church at Ephesus. The position which the Lord desires to have with all assemblies. It is worthy of note here in our beginning study of these seven churches that the Lord is walking in the midst of the first one, while as we get to the last church, Laodicea, He is found on the outside, knocking for admittance into that church!

Verse 2:

I know thy works, and thy labor, and thy patience, and how thou canst not bear them which are evil: and thou hast tried them which say they are apostles, and are not, and hast found them liars:

The All-seeing eye of God knows our works. The Lord begins with the good, commendable, things that He can say about this church. He commends them for their good works. From this we may learn what the Lord looks at in the local assembly; Works - Labor - Patience - a zeal for truth. The church cannot be passive and be pleasing to the Lord. There must be some activity around the church.

There can be no place for compromise in the church today just as there could not be in that first century. There are those who will come in sheep's clothing, but inwardly they are ravening wolves, seeking only to bring harm to the flock. The pastor and local assembly must guard against these invaders.

The church at Ephesus was commended for their zeal in keeping out those who professed to be apostles but were not.

Verse 3:

And hast borne, and hast patience, and for my name's sake hast labored, and hast not fainted. The Lord commends this church for seven things which He found favorable to the church:

• 1. Patience -

• 2. Refused to accept those who were evil -

• 3. Exposed the false apostles -

• 4. Carried burdens -

• 5. Had patience for the Name of the lord -

• 6. labored -

• 7. Had not fainted.

For all the good things, which the Lord commended this church, there was one thing which He found unacceptable about them. They had left their first love.

Verse 4:

Nevertheless I have somewhat against thee, because thou hast left thy first love.

Considering all the church at Ephesus had going for them, and that there was mentioned only this one thing which the Lord found against them, human reasoning would say, "Why not overlook this one thing, considering there are so many good things about her!"

That the Lord did enumerate all the good things about Ephesus and then rebuked her for leaving her first love, emphasizes to us the importance which God places on complete devotion, and especially our first love.

Much has been said and written about just what this first love of Ephesus was that the Lord was speaking about. There has been many different opinions mentioned as to just what it was. Considering the beginning of this church at Ephesus will help us determine just what the Lord is referring to here in His rebuke.

Ephesus was a highly favored church. Paul had firmly laid the foundation of this church. He had some assistance from Aquila and his wife Prescilla (Acts 18:19-28). The Jews had given ear to the word of this great apostle of the Lord. Apollos, upon hearing the fullness of the truth, added his eloquent voice to the truth at Ephesus. Later Paul spent three months, disputing in the synagogue *"and persuading the things concerning the kingdom of God"* (Acts 19:8). After some of the people hardened their hearts to this message, he continued to preach and teach in the school of Tyrannus for some two years. It was here that special miracles were wrought by the hands of Paul (Acts 19:9-12). The result of Paul's preaching and the miracles had such an effect on the people of Ephesus that many of them brought their libraries of valuable books on magic, valued at fifty-thousand pieces of silver, and burned them. The record states; "so mightily grew the word of God and prevailed."

The Ephesians were given to idolatry. Silversmiths made their living making statues to the goddess of the Ephesians, Diana. A people so steeped in this type of tradition, a people who had been witnesses of such divine miracles among them, a people who were so willing to divorce themselves of their past idolatrous ways, a people who were willing to destroy valuable material in order to please the Lord, were surely blessed of the Lord. It is with this background behind them that the Lord speaks to them now about this love which they had left. It would have been a love of devotion to the will of God to separate themselves from such a past and walk in the will of God.

The works for which the Lord commended the church at Ephesus were works which were seen on the surface. Things which one could readily see that they were committed to doing. But this which the Lord rebuked them for - *"thou hast left thy first love"* was an inner virtue. The Lord probes deeper than the surface.

It is evident from this that the most important thing in the eyes of God is love. Love for God. Love for truth. Love for others. All our works which we may boast about are futile unless they are built upon love.

What does it matter if we build a cathedral if it is not filled with love? What does it matter that we eloquently fight for the truth if our heart is not filled with love? What difference does it make if we give our body to the stake if we are not motivated by love?

The maintenance of the testimony of the church depends upon love for Christ Jesus, to whom the church belongs!

Verse 5:

Remember therefore from whence thou art fallen, and repent, and do the first works; or else I will come unto thee quickly, and will remove thy candlestick out of his place, except thou repent.

We are admonished to "*forget the past*" (Philippians 3: 13), and here, to "*remember.*" If we are talking about the past life of sin and shame, then one should forget this. If one is talking about the mistakes, errors, and blunders, then it would be wise to forget them. But if one is talking about the past memories of blessings from heaven; of walking in the sunshine of His warmth; of basking in His divine glory; of the time when we forsook everything to follow His steps, then it is good to remember. Let us never forget that devotion which brought us to an altar of repentance and dedication. Let us never permit that love which burned in our hearts for God and His word in the beginning to leave us.

THOU ART FALLEN... Ephesus was a church. Ephesus had been baptized in Jesus' Name and filled with the Holy Ghost. Ephesus was recognized in the eyes of God as one of His local assemblies, yet, He speaks of her as having fallen. Leaving this first love had resulted in her falling from her position before God.

AND REPENT... Thank God that there is an opportunity to repent (1John 2:1). It is best not to sin!

This is the ideal! But when those times come to us - and they will! - when we become aware of the error of our ways, how comforting it is to know that there is One who does care and will offer a space to repent.

AND DO THE FIRST WORKS... Remember that God is speaking to the church. He is speaking to saints. He is telling saints to do their first works. The first works they did as saints in the church of Ephesus. This statement has nothing to do with returning to do again something we did BEFORE we became a child of God. This statement does not give license to re-baptism.

The works we did upon first coming to God: loving truth; witnessing to the world of friends and fellow-workers; embracing the Word of God; doing those things which bring praise and honor to the Name of the Lord. We can have a tendency to drift from things spiritual into things carnal. We can become engrossed in material things, in things that may help keep the church building functioning without keeping the spiritual man functioning. Involved in the mechanics without being involved in the spiritual aspect of the work of God. The mechanics must be carried on; the material matters must be kept in order; but not at the expense of leaving the spiritual matters.

OR ELSE I WILL COME UNTO THEE... There is no other alternative. We either repent and get things back on course with God, or we will lose out with God. There can be no middle-of-the-road with God.

AND WILL REMOVE THY CANDLESTICK... Again, the candlestick is the church. How many local churches have had "Ichabod" written over their door by the Lord without them really realizing it?

They continue functioning religiously. They continue singing the same songs; expressing the same dry, dead, sermons from the pulpit and testimonies from the pew; but the Spirit of the Lord has long ago departed.

It is not the building that the Lord is talking about removing. The building can remain and yet have the light removed from it as far as God is concerned.

In an age of materialism and permissiveness, there have been local congregations which have left the zeal and love of God far behind long ago. There are many local assemblies which some years ago were examples of holiness and godly zeal, which today look nothing like their previous generations.

While this is true of the nominal world churches, it is sad to see similar things happen to the Apostolic Church as well. When we replace the move of the Spirit of God; the power of worship; the anointing of the Holy Ghost, and the guidance of the Spirit, for our own ingenuities, we are becoming like Ephesus. Book knowledge can never take the place of Spirit knowledge. Education can never replace anointing. A talent show must never replace true worship in Spirit and truth.

Verse 6:

But this thou hast, that thou hatest the deeds of the Nicolaitans, which I also hate.

The Lord again commends the church at Ephesus for her stand against the *deeds of the Nicolaitans*.

We will be studying more about the Nicolaitans when we get to the Church of Pergamos.

Verse 7:

He that hath an ear, let him hear what the Spirit saith unto the churches; To him that overcometh will I give to eat of the tree of life, which is in the midst of the paradise of God.

Here the Lord brings His message to a personal basis. *"He that hath an ear, let him hear."* When we stand before the Lord and His judgment seat, it will be for ourselves. It will matter little what state or city or church we were a part of on that day. The thing that will matter is how we stand there for our own record. The local church may stray from the will and ways of God. The local pastor may quit preaching the Word of God in its fullness. He may begin to compromise and permit anything and anyone to be accepted. And the church may go along with such actions on the part of the pastor without raising one finger of objection, but this does not excuse me! It will not excuse my responsibility before God.

Just because the church and the pastor have closed their ears to the voice of God does not mean that I have to. If the church grows cold and walks away from God, this does not mean that I have to follow them.

TO HIM THAT OVERCOMETH... It is an individual matter. It is not to the church that overcometh now, but to the individual who overcomes.

Knowing what awaits those who will be faithful to the Lord should encourage everyone to resist to the last every temptation to surrender to evil's embrace. "The tree of Life" beckons to those who will be faithful!

PARADISE OF GOD

R F Horton wrote: "The paradise of God can no more be determined locally than the original Garden of Eden. It is no more invisible than visible. It belongs to a region of another kind of experience than that of the senses. A paradise of God - we shall get the meaning of it by being of it. Let us repeat it to ourselves day and night for a week: 'The tree of life, which is in the paradise of God.' The meaning of it will begin to clear itself without effort. It is a state, a condition of experience which is closely connected with Jesus. It is not in a particular locality; it is in Him, or, rather, He is in it. It is a place where His thought has become the atmosphere and His life the life."

The Paradise of God is surely that place and condition where everything and everyone will be perfect. Just right! It will be Eden all over again - with one exception! - No serpent will ever be able to spoil that new paradise of God!

COMPARISONS

This is the first church and we compare it with the first mystery of Matthew 13, which was concerning the Sower who went forth to sow. Ephesus was the first church. Referring to that first church period when the message was first "sown" into the world. In many places the message was like newly sown seed. This seems to compare with that period of time during the first century as the apostles went forth, sowing the seed of the Word, which would establish the church in the world.

In this first century, we see that Christ is walking in the "midst" of His church. Probably no other period of time has the church witnessed such a manifestation of the power of the Spirit as this first century.

SMYRNA - THE PERSECUTED CHURCH

Verse 8:

And unto the angel of the church in Smyrna write; These things saith the first and the last, which was dead, and is alive;

The salutation to this church from the Lord is according to the character of the church. It is of interest to notice that the Lord addresses Himself to this church as, the first and the last, which was dead, and is alive. This is very appropriate for this church was in "tribulation and poverty." In their persecution they receive encouragement as the Lord appears to those persecuted as the One who had conquered death. He had robbed death of its sting, and the grave of its victory. In this they could find consolation and trust. For if He who conquered death and the grave was among them, they could trust in His strength to carry them through even death.

Verse 9:

I know thy works, and tribulation, and poverty, (but thou art rich) and {I know} the blasphemy of them which say they are Jews, and are not, but {are} the synagogue of Satan.

Smyrna was known as the persecuted church. It stands out as the church which felt the sting of the persecutor's whip more than any of the other churches.

Significantly the name Smyrna comes to us from the word "myrrh." Myrrh is mentioned in the scriptures in connection with the embalming of the dead. In order for myrrh to give off its fragrance it has to be crushed. In this we see the connection with the troubles through which the church must pass as ordained by the Lord. Smyrna would feel the crush of the Roman heel as it persecuted this church period even to death. Yet, as it always has, when it is crushed the church gave off sweet fragrance and refused to lie down and die. Instead of stopping the church, it spread that much more.

It is when we are under "fire" that we show our true colors. It is no problem to walk with God in the midst of the church and while the sun is shining all around us. But let the dark clouds hover near, let the darkness of trouble and problems come around, then we really find out what we have got in our heart.

The statement which the Lord makes concerning the church; *"I know thy poverty (but thou art rich),"* must no doubt have reference to spiritual richness. This is not the same statement which the Lord makes against the church of the Laodiceans (3:17,18). Smyrna was a poor church and also a very persecuted church. Yet they also manifested a rich spirit. They were possessors of great riches which awaited them at the end of their faithfulness.

JEWS WHO ARE NOT JEWS

There were only two of the seven churches against which the Lord did not bring any condemnation: Smyrna and Philadelphia. It is interesting that in only these two churches we have reference to those who called themselves Jews, whom the Lord said were not, but were of the synagogue of Satan.

Just exactly what the Lord has in mind here we are not for sure. One commentator stated: "... referring to the Judaizing movement that came into the church in the early centuries. It was the leaven of Galatianism which has never been wholly judged, and which made astonishing progress in the second and third centuries." (Ironside)

Adam Clarke stated: "There were persons there who professed Judaism, and had a synagogue in the place, and professed to worship the true God; but they had no genuine religion, and they served the devil rather than God. They applied the sacred name to an unholy thing: and this is one meaning of the word blasphemy in this book."

There have always been - since the church began - those who were not sincere in their worship and walk with God (Acts 5 for example). These cause more harm to the cause of Christ than good. Even in our own day there are those who are not sincere in their worship of God. They do so by pretense. They are religious for political advantage, for social advantage, for tax advantage, etc.

Verse 10:

Fear none of those things which thou shalt suffer: behold, the devil shall cast {some} of you into prison, that ye may be tried; and ye shall have tribulation ten days: be thou faithful unto death, and I will give thee a crown of life.

If this church was the second period in the "church age," then this church period would follow that of Ephesus - the church who lost her first love. A condition which the Lord would no doubt chastise the church for. In the church age of Smyrna, we could see that chastisement taking place possibly.

Pentecost is now receding into the past. It is now history and the church has settled down from the excitement of those first few years of revival. The newness has worn off. The excitement has waned as well. Now the church has settled down and is faced with some problems which shall call for true faith to see them through. And they will make it!

TRIBULATION TEN DAYS... This has been taken by many to have reference to the ten emperors of Rome which persecuted the church so bitterly: Nero - Domitian - Trajan - Marcus Aurelius - Severus - Decius - Valerian - Aurelian - Diocletian, and Constantine. Diocletian, we are told, was the worst emperor under which the church suffered. That the last ten years under Diocletian were the worst persecution the church had suffered.

Another view of this statement is that the term ten days has no reference to these ten edicts given by these ten different emperors, but rather has symbolic meaning to indicate a complete testing, or trial to the limit. Jacob had his wages changed ten times (Genesis 31:7,14). The plagues upon Egypt were ten in number. Israel was given ten commandments to try them fully. Job complained to his friends, *"These ten times have ye reproached me."* So, we get the thought that the church at Smyrna was to be fully tested in the furnace of affliction.

However, one may interpret this statement by the Lord, there is the promise held out to the faithful of a *"crown of life,"* to those who will be faithful to death. This is the martyr's crown, and there will no doubt be many who will be wearing this crown someday.

Verse 11:

He that hath an ear, let him hear what the Spirit saith unto the churches; He that overcometh shall not be hurt of the second death.

This is a very appropriate remark to make to the church which would face more persecution and death than any of the other seven churches, possibly. While they - many of them at least - would face death in their faithfulness, they would never have to be concerned about that second death which would last eternally. While no one desires to die, especially through some cruel way at the hands of some persecutors, we do have the consolation that dying one time is much better than having to face death that second time, which will last eternally.

COMPARISONS

This is the second church, which we compare with the second mystery of Matthew 13. This mystery was concerning the wheat and tares. Some enemy sowed tares among the wheat while the owner of the field slept. Upon seeing the tares the servants asked if they could uproot the tares from among the wheat. The wise householder instructed them to not do this as they would uproot some of the wheat in the process. Leave them alone, he said, and the separation would take place at the time of the harvest.

The church at Smyrna was faced with those among them who claimed to be part of them, when in reality they were not. They were called "*the synagogue of Satan.*" The promise to this church was a crown of life if they would be faithful to death. The end will show whose are His. Our concern should be faithfulness.

This church seems to compare with that period of time when after the death of the apostles, false prophets moved in among the church, as Paul warned they would do (Acts 20:29), as well as John. The church faced bitter persecution during this period of time, which culminated with the rise of Constantine to the throne of Rome, which brought about a temporary end to the persecution, as he professed conversion himself.

PERGAMOS - MARRIED

Verse 12:

And to the angel of the church in Pergamos write; These things saith he which hath the sharp sword with two edges;

According to Webster's Dictionary the suffix "gam" or "gamo," is Greek for "marriage" from the term "gamos" which, some feel, implies bigamy. The prefix "per" means, "by, through, or throughout." So, Pergamos could mean "throughout marriage."

Because of this many Bible scholars have concluded that Pergamos represented that church period during the time of Constantine, who wedded church with the state. Making from this an un-holy union, which resulted in chaos for the true church.

Now there was a church in Pergamos in the time of John to whom he addressed this letter. But the conditions which existed in the church are so indicative of the conditions existing during the years Constantine brought about the union of Church with State.

At the same time, the message to this church - as well as the message to every church - stands out as a message to any period through which the church has journeyed on her way to that City. There is a message for us in every letter.

SHARP SWORD WITH TWO EDGES... Significantly, the Lord is identified to the church at Pergamos as the One who holds the sharp sword with two edges. This has direct reference to the Word of God (Hebrews 4:12). Pergamos is the first church, thus far, in which we witness the spirit of compromise. So, it is appropriate that the Lord be identified to them as the One who holds the Word of God in His hand. That which should never be compromised, regardless of the influence exerted against us, is the Word of God.

Verse 13:

I know thy works, and where thou dwellest, {even} where Satan's seat {is}: and thou holdest fast my name, and hast not denied my faith, even in those days wherein Antipas {was} my faithful martyr, who was slain among you, where Satan dwelleth.

There are three things for which this church is commended by the Lord:

1. Where thou dwellest... even where Satan's seat is. The fact that this church dwelt in such a place, and yet many among them held true to the Word of God, is commendable. The church found herself faced with some great odds when the emperor, Constantine, brought about the unholy union of church and state. His purpose in doing this was political - not religious altogether! Although he claimed to have a conversion, in reality he was interested in strengthening his empire and power over the people.

2. Holdest fast my name... While most historians in writing their history of the church take it through the church of Rome, through the council of Nicea. It just did not happen that way at all. The result of the council of Nice was that the doctrine of the Trinity was accepted and became the message of the new religious system headed now by Rome. All who opposed this doctrine - and there were many who did - were faced with bitter persecution and yet were still holding fast to the Name of Jesus Christ, preaching baptism in His Name.

3. Hast not denied my faith... It would have been easier - and more popular - to have gone along with the crowd during that period. It is always easier to go along with the crowd! But the easy way is not the right way. This church was commended for her stand for the truth in the face of such opposition.

Notice the wording of the commendation, *"hast not denied MY faith."* It is not the beliefs or convictions of the people at Pergamos that the Lord is speaking about; but rather HIS faith. His teaching. His truth, which they had not denied.

The term *"Satan's seat,"* is Satan's throne. He reigns from this place at this time. Some are of the opinion that when persecution caused the priest-king of the Chaldean Mysteries to flee from before his enemy he came to Pergamos and settled. And that doing this, Satan shifted his capital of operations from Babylon to Pergamos.

Whatever the true interpretation may be, it is evident that Satan is very active in this world, and obviously was especially present in Pergamos. Sometimes one may refer to him as being in hell, but he is not contained there yet!

IN THOSE DAYS WHEREIN ANTIPAS... We have no record as to just who this faithful man was. There is no mention of him anywhere else that we could find. This does tell us that even Pergamos was faced with persecution which brought death to some just as in Smyrna. While Smyrna seemed to have faced persecution more than any other church, there still were those who died for the truth in other periods as well.

Dr Ironside, in his commentary on this church, states that it was during this period that the church (Rome) began to preach that the Lord was not coming again right away. Before the days of Constantine, the church was looking for the Lord to return. That was their expectation and hope. The message of Rome was that Constantine's empire was the empire of Christ. That Christ had come in the spirit of Constantine's empire.

It was only several years later when men begin to break away from Rome's bondage, that the message of the Lord's return was once again renewed in people's heart. And it is in our day that this hope bums even brighter in the hearts of the people of God.

Verse 14:

But I have a few things against thee, because thou hast there them that hold the doctrine of Balaam, who taught Balac to cast a stumblingblock before the children of Israel, to eat things sacrificed unto idols, and to commit fornication.

This indictment, which falls upon most of the churches to which John wrote, is brought against this church as well. It is great that Pergamos had not denied the faith. It is great that they had *held fast to the name of Jesus;* especially in a time when Constantine and Rome were introducing the pagan trinity into the religious world. It was great that they were doing this when they were dwelling right where Satan had his throne established. BUT, it is not enough to just have some good marks on our side when at the same time we permit things to enter among us which are not right in the eyes of God. We may be so busy fighting off things which attack us outwardly, that we fail to see those things which are working against us from within.

Our biggest enemy today is not the taverns and hell-holes of this world. It is not the brewery. It is not the gambling dens. It is from within that we have most of our troubles. It is from within that the enemy is busy today. If he can weaken the structure from within, he knows it will eventually fall.

THE DOCTRINE OF BALAAM... This character, hired to curse Israel as they wandered across the wilderness, is referred to in two other places in the New Testament in reference to;

• 1. "The way of Balaam," (2Peter 2:15).

• 2. "The error of Balaam," (Jude 11).

Now, here, we have reference to *"the doctrine of Balaam."*

The *"error of Balaam"* could speak of his thinking that by looking at Israel from different viewpoints he could bring a word from God to curse them, and thus make himself a little richer. That God possibly changes his mind, so he asks Him the second time as to whether he should go after the servants of Balak. God will never bring a curse upon those whom He has blessed. God does not change His mind as we mortals do!

The *"doctrine of Balaam"* could speak of his teaching Balak how he could bring a curse upon Israel by encouraging them to engage in corrupt practices with the Moabitish women.

The "*way of Balaam*" could refer to his readiness to seek payment for his services, seeking selfish gain by using his office of prophet.

It is true that the church at Pergamos was not filled with such a doctrine, but there were those there who taught this doctrine. Those who were guilty of this practice. Because of this the Lord spoke out against them. While we may not be guilty of committing an act of sin ourselves, if we condone it when we could do otherwise, we stand guilty before God. In this respect the man of God who is pastor of the local assembly should be careful of the things which are permitted to continue in the church. If they are wrong in the eyes of God, then he too can stand guilty before God!

Verse 15:

So hast thou also them that hold the doctrine of the Nicolaitans, which thing I hate.

As if the doctrine of Balaam was not enough against this church, they are also rebuked for permitting this doctrine to exist in the church as well.

It is interesting to note that the Church at Ephesus hated the "deeds of the Nicolaitans," while the people at Pergamos seemed to tolerate them. In the church at Pergamos it is no longer "*deeds*" which the Lord speaks out against; now it is the "*doctrine of the Nicolaitans*" which the Lord condemns. How subtle the enemy is with his methods of approach. At first it may be something simple - just "deeds;" but they will have a tendency, if permitted to grow, to become "doctrines."

Who were the Nicolaitans? This has been a question which has been tossed around by many for some time. Some have taken the word apart; "nikao," which means to "conquer," and "laos," which refers to the "people." Taking these meanings, some have concluded that this refers to the forming of the priestly order of the Catholic Church in which the people were degraded and the priests exalted above the people.

There is another interesting connection to be considered with this word. We are told that the word "*Balaam*" in Hebrew has substantially the same meaning as "*Nicolas*" does in the Greek.

"Nicolas" is the person, we are informed, whom these Nicolaitans were following. Supposedly this means "one who conquers (or one who lords it over) the people." It would seem then that the doctrine of the Nicolaitans must have been some form of heresy which would result in bringing the people of God into spiritual bondage. When Rome brought about the wedding of Church with the State of Rome, she certainly did bring about a spiritual bondage to her people. An unholy alliance was thus formed which resulted in many people becoming lost in Romish-paganish practices which continues to this day, binding the souls of people.

Verse 16:

Repent; or else I will come unto thee quickly, and will fight against them with the sword of my mouth.

There can be but one cure for sin, and that is repentance! A complete turning from sin and turning to God. Nothing short of this will be accepted by the Lord.

One interesting thing in this verse should be pointed out here. Notice in this warning from the Lord, the entire church is not guilty before God. God, in warning that He would come if they did not repent, states; "I will come unto thee quickly, and will fight against them." It is not against "*thee*," but against "*them*."

The judgment of God will fall upon all who are guilty. And yet the call of repentance is issued to the entire church, as the church is responsible for what she has permitted to take place among her.

Verse 17:

He that hath an ear, let him hear what the Spirit saith unto the churches; To him that overcometh will I give to eat of the hidden manna, and will give him a white stone, and in the stone a new name written, which no man knoweth saving he that receiveth {it}.

To those who will overcome the promise of eating of "*hidden manna*" is given. What a contrast this is to verse fourteen which speaks of them who "*eat things offered to idols*."

Manna was what Israel was fed in the wilderness. As long as they ate the manna there was not a feeble one among them. As long as the child of God eats of the "*Bread of life*," we too will enjoy health and strength in the Spirit.

A WHITE STONE... The white stone signifies one is approved of God. When one received a new name given to them by the Lord, it carried with it a great blessing. Those who receive this stone with a new name will receive something of great value.

COMPARISONS

It was during this period in church history that Rome introduced into the religious world many pagan customs which she had borrowed from the Babylonian-Chaldean Mysteries. In doing so she brought spiritual fornication to the people who accepted this dogma.

When the Devil found that his efforts at bringing persecution to the church from the outside was only resulting in more people embracing the truth, he switched his tactics and began to work from the inside. He donned the guise of religion to continue his onslaught against the people of God. Only the faithful withstood him.

This compares with the third mystery of Matthew thirteen. The parable of the Mustard Seed. The mustard seed may be sown with other seeds, but it will never mix with the other seeds. It will always remain mustard. It will never cross with any other seed. And this seed which God planted in the earth has grown until it has become "the greatest among" the religious institutions of the world. Not the greatest in number - but the greatest in quality!

THYATIRA

Verse 18:

And unto the angel of the church in Thyatira write; These things saith the Son of God, who hath his eyes like unto a flame of fire, and his feet {are} like fine brass;

There are two things which stand out in this salutation upon which emphasis should be placed:

• 1. The Lord's referring to Himself as "*the Son of God.*"

• 2. The Lord's being identified to this church as the One "*who hath eyes like unto a flame of fire, and his feet are like fine brass.*"

SON OF GOD... It is significant that this is the only place in the entire book of Revelation that the Lord refers to Himself in this manner. Here He is identified by name as the Son of God. Placing this church in that period which followed the period covered by

Constantine's wedding church with state - which period saw the church of Rome holding full sway by force over the religious world - then we better realize the significance of this name by which the Lord identifies Himself here.

One thing which Rome has accomplished through her determined efforts is to indoctrinate the religious world into accepting her theory of Jesus Christ and the godhead. In fact, the very first Council which convened in Nicea was for the purpose of settling the issue as to who Jesus Christ is. The role which He plays in the godhead. After this Council was concluded the Rome-influenced religious world adopted the theory of the trinity - which Rome had borrowed from paganism in order (it appears) to appease the pagans and help swell the ranks of the church.

The next Council held in Constantinople, called by Theodosius the Great, was to further define and settle the doctrine of the trinity.

The third Council held at Ephesus in 431, during the time of Theodosius II, was to dispute still more the doctrine of the trinity and the person of Christ.

The fourth Council also gathered in Ephesus at the request of Eutyches. This Council, held in 449, under the direction of Dioscorus, bishop of Alexandria, was also to continue to debate the issue concerning Jesus Christ.

So, the issue which continued to stir the religious world of that day - as well as this day - was one concerning the Lord Jesus Christ and His deity. The violence of some of these meetings has prompted the title "Assembly of Robbers" to be given to them. After these Councils, the true Church only felt greater persecution and oppression by those who adopted the dogma of the trinity.

It is an evident teaching that the Church of Rome does not recognize Jesus Christ in His rightful place. It has been their purpose since Nicea to degrade Him. Hence, we have this title in the salutation to this church which, many feel, represented this era of time.

With diabolical cleverness, the Romish heresy systematically presents Jesus Christ, not as the Son of God, but as the Son of Mary. In all its doctrine, in all its ceremonies, in all its liturgy and books of devotion, the false church of Rome, with most consummate and Satanic craft, and with most deadly purpose, exalts Mary. They make her to be the mediator between God and man.

EYES LIKE UNTO A FLAME... What a message is contained in this statement! How interesting to have the combination of these two symbols here together. The eyes of the Lord are in every place.

Eyes which see every evil practice of man. These are not eyes of mercy and compassion which so many were privileged to see during the Lord's ministry on this earth. These are eyes of fire! The fires of judgment and wrath.

FEET LIKE FINE BRASS... Just as His eyes behold the words of man and speak of wrath, here

we see His feet are of fine brass which also speak of judgment and wrath. Brass in the Old Testament typology spoke of judgment, the brazen altar, for instance. Here the Lord is depicted as the One who sees every wicked move which evil men make, and He will trample them in judgment.

This age is especially faced with the judgments of God because of the effects which this period has upon the work of God in the world.

Verse 19:

I know thy works, and charity, and service, and faith, and thy patience, and thy works; and the last to be more than the first,

Even in such a dark period as this the church had those who were active in the work of the Lord. In fact, it has always been that during times of persecution the true soldiers of the cross will excel. There is an abundance of evidence that the Church of Jesus Christ was very much alive during this period: proclaiming the message of Pentecost. (Some would have us to think that the church died during this period and was brought gradually back to life, beginning with Martin Luther. But that is just not the way it was at all!)

AND CHARITY... There is a need of love in a time when everyone around is cold with indifference. During this period, there were those who manifested the love of God.

AND SERVICE... Or, "ministry," which service is speaking about. The mouth of the preacher was never stopped from preaching Acts 2:38.

AND FAITH... Whether we consider personal faith, or THE faith, both would certainly apply here. It took someone who had faith in themselves and their Lord to stand in these days. And THE faith - the doctrine - was certainly proclaimed among the people during this time.

THY PATIENCE... What endurance the people of the Name manifested during this period of persecution!

The work of the church increased during these dark days instead of decreasing.

<u>Verse 20:</u>

Notwithstanding I have a few things against thee, because thou sufferest that woman Jezebel, which calleth herself a prophetess, to teach and to seduce my servants to commit fornication, and to eat things sacrificed unto idols ..

There are those who strongly feel that the words "a few things," were not in the original letter. Considering that the Lord takes more space to speak out against this matter of wrong in this church than the others, it would seem that He did not consider it merely a "few" things.

JEZEBEL... The name "Jezebel" rings a bell. Even the name sounds evil and wicked to our ears. Mr Lockyer, in his book, The Women Of The Bible, refers to her as "The woman who was a She-devil." He is referring to the Jezebel of the Old Testament, the only other Jezebel mentioned in the Bible. The name Jezebel carries with it such a stigma of evil that it is associated with the name Judas. Both stand out as names which speak of evil and wickedness. The name implies everything which is sinful and ungodlike. Jezebel in the Old Testament was the daughter of Ethbaal, king of the Zidonians. Why Ahab, king of Israel, would choose to marry such a woman is one of the puzzles of Biblical history. Both the Old Testament Jezebel and the New Testament character must represent the same thing. It is possible there really was a woman in the church in Thyatira by the name of Jezebel, although we shudder to think that anyone would name their daughter after such a character! At the same time this name must stand as a representation of wickedness which prevailed during this period of church history.

COMPARISONS OF JEZEBELS

1. Jezebel must have possessed a commanding personality. The Old Testament character does not have it said of her that she was attractive. There is no mention of any female qualities which would infer that she was a beautiful woman. Yet she did command attention!

2. During the time that Ahab and Jezebel reigned - for she most certainly shared in his reign - Baalism became the state religion. It was into this period that the prophet Elijah came and challenged - and defeated - the prophets of Baal on Mount Carmel.

3. Ahab was nothing more than a puppet in her hand. What she wanted she got. That spineless character is found whimpering in the background while Jezebel gets her way. Nothing seemed to stand in her way when she sat out to get what she wanted. Nothing, that is, except the prophet Elijah!

4. It was Jezebel whom the Bible said, "painted her face." Edith Deen wrote of sixteenth century England; "Painting the face was accepted as prima-facie evidence that a woman had loose morals. Certainly, no woman's name in history has become so commonly accepted as a synonym for wickedness."

5. The death which Jezebel died was anything but befitting a queen. She died a horrible death - being thrown from the tower window with her body and blood splattering over the pavement below.

ROME

What a comparison lies between the Jezebel of the Old Testament and that Jezebel in Thyatira!

1. By very brute force the church of Rome commands attention. During the dark days of persecution, many thousands of people died under the heel of Rome because they would not accept her dogmas. And yet with her bloody history she remains a strong and influential force in the world.

2. Jezebel brought Baal worship into Israel. Her New Testament counterpart, the church of Rome, mimics her actions. Becoming established in the land after the council of Nicea, and after this the acceptance of the Papal authority, Rome began to introduce pagan customs into the religious world. Because of the heathen which

dominated Rome's empire, she saw the opportunity through the church to gain them. Heathen temples were taken over by Rome.

Without changing the structure, the religion of Rome moved in. Idols which decorated the walls of the heathen temples merely had their names changed from that of some heathen deity to that of one of the apostles or some "Christian" name. The ceremonies of Rome are so associated with pagan rites and traditions that there remains little - if any - difference between that of religious Rome and pagan Rome.

In the book A Story in Stone, Baalbek, the author states; "When Aramaic was the current language of the country, Baal's consort was called Atargatis, and the son, Adon. Following Alexander's invasion these names were Hellenized and Baal was called Zeus or Helios; Atargatis became known as Aphrodite; and Adon the son, Hermes. With the advent of the Romans, Latin became the official language and the names were Latinized: Helios became Jupiter Heliopolitanus; Aphrodite, Venus; and Hermes, who was a metamorphic character, appeared now as Dionysos. Contrary to what might be imagined, the mere changing of names was not accompanied by any responding change of the traditional Phoenician cult and rites. The deities retained their unaltered original Phoenician character through the Greek and Roman era."

It is evident that when pagan Rome became religious Rome, this practice continued. Heathen temples taken over by Rome for the church continued to house the same statues of the heathen gods; they merely changed their names.

After the acceptance of the papacy, Rome began to dominate the lives of everyone she could. It was after this that the pagan customs began to enter the religious world.

- Image Worship - Fourth century
- The Confessional - Fifth century
- Purgatory - Fifth century
- Transubstantiation - Ninth century
- Immaculate Conception - Twelfth century

As well as many others. The practices borrowed directly from paganism, along with many more too numerous to list, were adopted into the religious world by the Catholic Church and forced upon the people.

3. Just as that ancient Jezebel controlled her weak husband, Ahab, even so did the church of Rome bend the vacillating religious hierarchy of the day to her wishes.

4. Just as ancient Jezebel was noted for her painted face and ungodly appearance, her counterpart on this side of the cross likewise is one which is worldly. Drunkenness, gambling, and immoral practices prevail in this religious system.

5. Jezebel of the Old Testament died a horrible death. The New Testament Jezebel is likewise headed for a horrible death.

Verse 21:

And I gave her space to repent of her fornication; and she repented not.

The mercies of God were extended to this idolatrous church, giving her an opportunity to repent of her wicked ways.

To change her course. This she did not do, and she will not do.

Verse 22:

Behold, I will cast her into a bed, and them that commit adultery with her into great tribulation, except they repent of their deeds.

This statement is not speaking of a bed of ease and comfort. No, it speaks of just the opposite. The "bed" of which the Lord speaks is one of trouble and unrest. She may ride high for the time being with all her pomp and splendor, but the time will come when she shall be brought down.

There are many who feel that Revelation 17:16 is speaking of that time when Rome - and all other religious systems which join forces with her at that time - shall be destroyed by the hands of those whom she thought would help her to supreme glory.

There are different opinions as to just what the Lord means here in His reference to "*tribulation.*"

Some feel it may have reference to the trouble which she has had among Communist nations - which would be debatable. Others feel that it has reference to the great tribulation of the last days.

Verse 23:

And I will kill her children with death; and all the churches shall know that I am he which searcheth the reins and hearts: and I will give unto everyone of you according to your works.

There is one thing which Rome loves to be recognized as being, and that is that she is a "*mother*." She is proud to inform the world that she is the "*mother*" church. If she is a mother, then it stands to reason that she has children. Her children would be all those who embrace her teachings. While all her children may not look just exactly like their mother, if they cling to "mother's" ways they are identified with her nonetheless. Much has been said in history about Martin Luther's break from the church of Rome, thus beginning the Reformation period, as it is termed. But there is one terrible mistake Luther made - and consequently others which followed in Luther's wake - and that is he did not divorce himself completely from mother's apron strings! Many of the dogmas of Rome were brought over into Luther's religion with him. There is not a big difference between Luther's followers and Rome. Other religions which formed since Luther's time have been guilty of the same error. Throughout all of them one may find the erroneous dogma of the trinity. All who continue to be identified with Rome shall also share with her in the judgment which God will bring upon them.

Verse 24:

But unto you I say, and unto the rest in Thyatira, as many as have not this doctrine, and which have not known the depths of Satan, as they speak; I will put upon you none other burden.

There has never been a time so dark but what there were those who preached and practiced the message of the apostles and Acts 2:38. Everyone was not accepting this dogma of Rome during this period, regardless of the pressures which were put upon them.

History bears out that the true church of Jesus Christ, those who embraced Acts 2:38, has prevailed throughout history. There never was a time - there never will be a time - when the Church did not have a voice.

Verse 25:

But that which ye have {already} hold fast till I come.

The message has been the same through the years; Hold on! Stay true to the faith! Regardless of the hour and pressures, the Lord has always encouraged His own to hold on. During the dark days of persecution which saw so many persecuted unto death; during the dark days when many were forced, at the threat of death, to accept the dogma of the trinity; during the dark days when many were pressured to accept the watered down dogma of Lutheranism; Calvinism, etc., during these times of pressure from the permissive leaders, a time when compromise was the going thing, the warning is still the same:

HOLD ON!

Verse 26:

And he that overcometh, and keepeth my works unto the end, to him will I give power over the nations:

The promise is given to those who endure and live for the Lord in the face of adversity that someday they shall reign with Christ over this world. Better to suffer for a little while and reign with Him eternally, than to enjoy momentary glory and die eternally!

Verse 27:

And he shall rule them with a rod of iron; as the vessels of a potter shall they be broken to shivers: even as I received of my Father.

While opinions abound as to just what role the redeemed will play in that day when the Kingdom of Christ shall be established on this earth, and we shall reign with Christ over this world; one thing remains certain - we shall share in that glory!

Verse 28:

And I will give him the morning star.

In chapter twenty-two and verse 16 the Lord refers to Himself as the "bright and morning star." the "light" which Rome claims to shed to the world is darkness; the greatest darkness of all - spiritual darkness! To those who refuse to accept her dogma and instead obey the Lord and His Word, they are promised the true light.

It will be much better to embrace Jesus Christ, the true light, even in the darkest hour of tribulation; than to embrace the "light" of Rome and the beast.

Verse 29:

He that hath an ear, let him hear what the Spirit saith unto the churches.

All the churches the Lord encourages to have an ear for His voice. Those who wisely listen to the voice of the Lord will be those who will walk with Him in glory someday.

Many in the time of Thyatira listened to the voice of the Lord. Many today continue to listen to that VOICE.

COMPARISONS

The fourth parable of Matthew thirteen certainly becomes clearly applicable with this church at Thyatira. Both involve a woman. Both involve doctrine (leaven in Matthew, which Jesus told His disciples represented false doctrine.)

This seems to speak to us of that period when Rome began to hold full sway over the religious world. The inquisition would fit into this period. A time when in the name of the cross Rome sought to conquer and control the world under her religious system.

Jesus prophesied in Matthew 13:33 that a woman would someday *take leaven (*false doctrine*), and hide it in three measures of meal, till the whole was leavened*. This was the fourth mystery of Matthew thirteen. Thyatira is the fourth church of Revelation. In each of these passages there is a woman spoken of as the central character. When used in this sense in the scriptures, a woman is referred to in an evil, wicked manner - a false religious manner.

Rome taught and seduced the people into believing the pagan dogma of the trinity. She (Rome) took leaven (false doctrine) and hid it in three measures (trinity) of meal, till the whole world was affected.

The entire religious world has accepted, with very few exceptions, besides the true Church of Jesus Christ, the dogma of the trinity handed down to them from the church of Rome - who in turn borrowed it from paganism.

CHAPTER THREE

• SARDIS -IN DEATH THERE IS LIFE

Verse I:

And unto the angel of the church in Sardis write; These things saith he that hath the seven Spirits of God, and the seven stars; I know thy works, that thou hast a name that thou livest, and art dead.

Hath the seven... stars... While not trying to make a play on words, or, emphasizing something which should not be considered that important, it is of interest to notice that the Lord made a similar statement in His salutation to the church at Ephesus. With one difference; To Ephesus He said He was *holding the seven stars*. Here in Sardis He states that He *hath the seven stars.*

The church through the years has gone through that period when the clergy was made into a spiritual hierarchy. The church of Rome dressed her clergy in the robes of pomp and splendor - borrowing much of it from paganism. The clergy became the products of the church. They became hirelings of the system. Now instead of getting direction from the Spirit they were directed by the edicts of the church.

The Spirit was making itself known in the days of Sardis. John in his epistle states; 1John 2:27, *But the anointing which ye have received of him abideth in you, and ye need not that any man teach you: but as the same anointing teacheth you of all things, and is truth, and is no lie, and even as it hath taught you, ye shall abide in him.*

Taking Sardis as a representative church, we find that this warning is especially applicable. Sardis would represent that period in history beginning with the sixteenth century. The church has gone through the period in which it has been faced with great persecution at the hand of Rome. She has endured that dreadful period in which the Inquisition caused so many to be put to death rather than adopt the dogma of Rome.

We certainly believe that God has always had a church, that there never was a time when there was not a witness to truth in the earth. At the same time we must accept that this period must have been a very dark time for the people of the truth; the people of the Name.

This must have been the lowest ebb through which the church had gone.

God writes to remind this church it is He who hath - who possesses - the ministry. It is still God who calls and ordains men to preach His truth.

REFORMATION

Much has been written about the Reformation which rocked the religious world. On October 31, 1517, Martin Luther nailed his theses to the church door in Wittenberg, Germany, and thus that period called the Reformation began. It was no doubt commendable to Luther that he made such a decision, yet at the same time it must be pointed out that Luther, and others who followed his example, may have left the church of Rome, but they did so to only a degree. When confronted with the truth of Jesus' Name baptism, and the Apostolic message concerning the plan of salvation, they turned it down.

The churches which these men founded became formal, lifeless, religious institutions. They professed to have life when in reality they were dead. They were the Sardis church of the sixteenth and following centuries.

I KNOW THY WORKS... Activity does not always mean that God is pleased with us. A church could be very active and at the same time out of favor with God. It is great to be active in civil and social reform. It is great to be feeding the hungry and clothing the poor. It is great to have socials for the benefit of fellowship among the members of the church. It is great to have rock-a-thons; walk-a-thons, bazaars; rummage sales; fish fries, and you name it. We can have Youth Night; Ladies Night; Men's night; and Children's Night. We can have all kinds of meetings and activities which will fill our week, and more. But it is not activities of this nature which the Lord is looking for. When our play rooms are full and our prayer rooms are empty; when our organization is tops in the country, while our agonizing for souls is zero; when we are willing to go all out to make the church ball team; but are not willing to spend one hour in visitation; then surely the Lord says, I have not found thy works perfect before God.

It would seem from the reading of this letter that the Lord does not speak of some great evil in this church. But it would seem that it is more of a spirit of unconcern. A lazy spirit which was eating away at their spiritual life. They might have appeared active to those around them - but the eyes of the Lord probed deeper than their activities.

A NAME AND DEAD... They were alive with activities - but dead in the Spirit. This is the only church to which the Lord said, *"thou art dead!"*

It would seem that these words are conveyed to the church collectively. This is the condition of the church in general at this time. But even in the period in which these words are spoken against this church, there still remained some who refused to give in to the conditions which threatened their lives.

Verse 2:

Be watchful, and strengthen the things which remain, that are ready to die: for I have not found thy works perfect before God.

From this statement it would seem that there were those who, though surrounded with the spirit of Sardis, refused to give in to the pressures of the period. As long as it can be said of someone that they are still alive - although ready to die - there is still hope.

Verse 3:

Remember therefore how thou hast received and heard, and hold fast, and repent. If therefore thou shalt not watch, I will come on thee as a thief, and thou shalt not know what hour I will come upon thee.

As long as there is an opportunity to repent of one's sins there is still hope. The church has not reached that place where they cannot repent. Esau reached that place; a place of tears without feeling. A place of regret without help. A place of seeking without finding. A place of knocking when the door won't open. This is described in Hebrews 12:16,17. There is a point of no return. It would be a very foolish person - or church - who would play around the border.

William Milligan wrote of this church: "The world had been tolerated in Thyatira, the first of the last four churches; in Sardis, the second, it is more than tolerated. Sardis has substituted the outward for the inward. She has been proud of her external ordinances, and has thought more of them than living in the Spirit and walking in the Spirit. True piety has declined; and, as a natural consequence, sins of the flesh alluded to in the immediately following words of the epistle, have asserted their supremacy. More even than this, Sardis had a name that she lived while she was dead. She was renowned among men. The world looked and beheld with admiration what was to it the splendor of her worship; it listened, and heard with enthusiasm the music of her praise. And the church was pleased that it should be so. Not in humility, lowliness, and deeds of self-sacrificing love did she seek her "name," but in what the world would have been equally delighted with through the inspiring soul of it all had been folly or sin. A stronghold had been established by the world in Sardis."

The Lord's warning to this church that He would come unto her as a thief is not referring, it does not seem, to the rapture. Paul informs us; 1Thessalonians 5:4, *But ye, brethren, are not in darkness, that that day should overtake you as a thief.*

It probably is speaking of His coming to this church in judgment because of her condition.

Verse 4:

Thou hast a few names even in Sardis which have not defiled their garments; and they shall walk with me in white: for they are worthy.

We are told that the word Sardis means "a remnant," or "those who have escaped." Even in the time of apostasy there were those who refused to give in to the pressures which were exerted against them. There were those in Sardis who "escaped" into truth. Those who escaped from the encroachment of error which was swallowing up the church world.

The Lord uses the phrase even in Sardis, which seems to add significance to the fact that there were some who would not give in to the pressures of their day. Even in such a time, regardless of how dark it was, there were those who would not give up truth for tradition, or favor with men. Possibly we could use the phrase in our modem world conditions by saying there are those "even in Communist Cuba" who refuse communisms lies and live for God.

Borrowing some comments Mr Milligan: "These were to Sardis what "the rest" were to Thyatira. They were the "gleanings left in Israel, as the shaking of an olive tree, two or three berries in the top of the uppermost branches of a fruitful tree." They were the "new wine found in the cluster, and one saith, Destroy it not; for a blessing is in it." To them therefore great promises are given."

It is a great consolation to know that even in her darkest hour there have been those who have held true and faithful to truth without compromising. While it is true there is reference to only a few names, at least there are some! The promise which the Lord made to His church (Matthew 16:18), the gates of hell shall not prevail against it': continue to be true. Especially do we find this promise reassuring in this church period.

Verse 5:

He that overcometh, the same shall be clothed in white raiment; and I will not blot out his name out of the book of life, but I will confess his name before my Father, and before his angels.

As if to emphasize this promise, the Lord makes it twice; in verse four and verse five. The promise to those who overcome is that they will walk with Him in white. The white raiment would be in contrast to the darkness through which they have walked faithfully.

The garments of the "redeemed" are spoken of as being white (6:11; 7:9,14). The "wife" of Jesus Christ is spoken of as wearing garments which are of "fine linen, clean and white" (19:8). Of all the creatures upon this earth, man is the only one who does not have a natural covering. Sin stripped man of his garments of glory and praise. Consequently, he is the only shabbily dressed of all God's creatures. When we compare this to the promise that the Lord gives to the overcomer it adds significance to this promise. One day the overcomer will be the best dressed of God's creatures!

I WILL NOT BLOT OUT HIS NAME... Two things make this statement interesting; 1. Sardis is the only church to whom the Lord referred to the book of life. The tree of life was referred to in the letter to Ephesus to those who overcome; but only Sardis was given the promise of their name not being blotted out of this book of life before the Lord.

2. Since this church was the church which was spoken of as being dead, it is significant that reference is made to the book of Life. Life and death are the main themes of this letter to Sardis.

HE THAT OVERCOMETH... This phrase is employed in every

letter to the seven churches. In every period of life through which the church has found herself, she has had to have an overcoming spirit. Not all have been faced with the same problems and struggles, as is evident from these letters.

But all have had to overcome whatever obstacles confronted them.

We who live in America are not faced with the problems which many in the early era of the church faced. There are those in other countries which face much greater physical persecution then we do here in America. Yet it is also a time of overcoming to those who live in this twentieth century. The battle of those who live in America is probably more of a psychological battle than anything else. But it is a battle which many are losing! The spirit of the age is claiming a lot of victims today. No doubt if the Lord were to address a letter to His church in America He would include in that letter He that overcometh.

This church which lived in a time of spiritual death had in it those who continued to live while others were dying around them. Sardis stands out as an example to pattern after, in the sense of being determined to "live" when others are saying "die" all around us. It teaches that regardless of circumstances; regardless of pressures; regardless of who among us gives in to those pressures, we can make it through if we will only make up our minds to do so.

Joseph did not give in while in Egypt, a long way from family and home. Daniel did not give in to the pressures of Babylon though he never did get to return home. It is this kind of overcomer that the Lord is addressing in the church at Sardis. This kind of overcomer of the twentieth century will stand before Him some day in white and hear His, "Well done - Welcome home!"

Verse 6:

He that hath an ear, let him hear what the Spirit saith unto the churches.

Again, regardless of conditions or circumstances, we can have an ear to hear the voice of the Spirit. There has never been a time so dark, so cold, that the voice of the Lord has not spoken to His Church.

There has never been a century, nor decade, since Pentecost, that the Lord has not spoken to His Church.

A young man applied for a job with a certain company. Arriving at the place of interview, he was confronted with an office full of others who were there to be interviewed for the same job. There was a lot of talking and laughing in the crowded room, as people made acquaintance with one another and swapped stories. After a short while this young man arose and walked into the office. Some wondered why he had just walked into the office as no one had come out and invited him in. After a short while he reentered the room where the others were waiting to be interviewed with the news that he had gotten the job. The others, needless to say, were puzzled. Why was he chosen? How did he know to go into the office? Well the job was to fill the position of teletype operator. While he was sitting in the waiting room, a message was broadcast over the speaker system in morse code that the one who first heard the message and entered the office would get the job. The young man heard the message and understood it.

The others in the room were too busy visiting to listen to the message.

Someday soon a "voice" with a great message shall be conveyed to *all who have ears to hear what the Spirit saith unto the church,* which shall invite them home to be with the Lord. Only those who have "*ears to hear*" shall hear and understand the message.

"Living on one's reputation is a melancholy business. It is sad to see a threadbare merchant starving on the dwindling relics of his former future; to see the failing orator reproducing stale scraps of knowledge and rhetoric which once commanded applause; sad to listen to an old vocalist whose fame survives his voice; and saddest of all are those professors of religion who acquire no fresh strength and treasure, but who contrive to keep themselves in countenance by making the most of an ever attenuating reputation. We must not live in the opinion of others, but in our own rich and supporting consciousness; we must not live a fancied life in others' breath, but a real, true life in the purity and power of our own soul. It is not what we were, but what we are. How are things with us today? The true spiritual life is never merely retrospective. What am I now, and what my hope? Am I gaining victories, overtaking new work, attaining fresh graces, bringing forth fruit unto God?" (W L Watkinson)

Church of Brotherly Love

<u>Verse 7:</u>

And to the angel of the church in Philadelphia write; These things saith he that is holy, he that is true, he that hath the key of David, he that openeth, and no man shutteth; and shutteth, and no man openeth;

As mentioned previously, the Lord appears to each Church in his salutation in a character which is in keeping with the condition of that particular Church. This has been true with each Church thus far, so we should expect that it continue to be so with Philadelphia. We notice that in His salutation the Lord addresses Himself to this church in a manner which He has not used to any of the other churches.

None of the characteristics here mentioned are found in chapter one in the descriptions given of Him there. From this we can expect to find things quite different in Philadelphia from what we found in the other churches - and we do.

THE HOLY ONE... The first reference in the salutation from the Lord is *These things saith He that is holy.* This would no doubt speak of the condition of this church, as well as describe the One whose hand was upon this Church. Philadelphia was a church which walked in the will of God. It was a church of love, which its name implies.

The word "holy" speaks of separateness. While dwelling in the midst of such a busy area, the Church remained true to the Gospel of Jesus Christ and did not compromise these truths. The only way one can endure in Christ in any age is to remain separate from the world and its influences of evil and compromise.

Another term used is the word "True." Jesus Christ is the fountain of truth. Putting the two terms together, Holy and True, we have a combination which will succeed and triumph in any situation and any area.

Philadelphia was the Lydian city founded by Attalus II, Philadelphus (159-138 B.C.) The king was so named because of his devotion to his brother. The very name, "Philadelphia" implies that the spirit of brotherly love prevailed there. With so much love between one another in the church it is no wonder this church prospered.

Theologically long-lived, this admirable primitive Christian Church endured physically, spiritually, and by name, through more centuries than any of the other churches mentioned in the book of Revelation.

The key of David speaks of legal right or authority. Jesus Christ is our authority for promulgating the Gospel message to the world. This right has been granted to the Church. We have not only the responsibility to proclaim the Gospel - we have the right to proclaim it.

Verse 8:

I know thy works: behold, I have set before thee an open door, and no man can shut it: for thou hast a little strength, and hast kept my word, and hast not denied my name.

This Church that adhered to the Apostolic doctrine was specifically promised continuity by the Lord Jesus for not disowning His name. The spiritual endurance of the Philadelphian Church is further amplified by the fact that the physical city was in the geographical area that was often stricken with earth quakes. Yet in spite of this location, it survived.

A Christian witness, in spite of Moslem invasion and pressure, was maintained in Philadelphia through medieval and into modern times.

Cartographers and geographers have always associated the city of Philadelphia with Mount Tmolus. This famous mountain which always influenced western cities of Asia Minor, stood as a signpost to inland travelers. This main caravan route from Ephesus to the tablelands of northern Lydia meant that many different kinds of people were always going through this wonderland of trade and gold. All this had a tremendous impact on the economics of this city.

Not only was Philadelphia a center of trade, but extensive studies show that the rich soil there was great for vine-growing. Thus many excellent varieties of grapes grew around there.

Moreover, the big region around Philadelphia had and has extensive resources such as famous marble quarries, quarries of multi-colored stone for building, and the availability of multi-colored sand.

Besides being an important trade center, Philadelphia was also a center of communication. What a great place to be with the Gospel' With so many people in and out of Philadelphia, the Church thus had a great opportunity to preach to them, and they in turn went their separate ways to spread the Gospel even farther. In this we may see the "open door" which was set before the Church.

Verse 9:

Behold, I will make them of the synagogue of Satan, which say they are Jews, and are not, but do lie; behold, I will make them to come and worship before thy feet, and to know that I have loved thee.

The message to the church of Ephesus was that they could not bear them which are evil: and thou hast tried them which say they are apostles, and are not. In Ephesus there were false prophets. In Philadelphia there were false Jews.

The church of Smyrna was also bothered by those who professed to be Jews but were not. We commented on this matter in chapter two verse nine.

Verse 10:

Because thou hast kept the word of my patience, I also will keep thee from the hour of temptation, which shall come upon all the world, to try them that dwell upon the earth.

This profound promise has been taken to have reference to the time of the Great Tribulation. If the church of Philadelphia does also represent a certain period of time, or age, through which the Church passes, then this church would cover that period of time which takes it to the time of the tribulation.

The promise to the Church was that she would be kept "from" this terrible hour of trouble which is coming upon all the world. We have other promises, such as 1Thessalonians 5:7: *For God hath not appointed us to wrath, but to obtain salvation by our Lord Jesus Christ,* which promises the Church that she will not have to endure the time of tribulation as it does not apply to Her.

Verse 11:

Behold, I come quickly: hold that fast which thou hast, that no man take thy crown.

As with all the other letters, the Lord gives a warning to the church of Philadelphia as well. Jesus states the same warning of His quick return three times in the last chapter of Revelation. It is obviously not speaking about the Lord's return being in John's day. It is not speaking of the nearness of His return - but the quickness of His return. When he returns there will be no time for altar calls nor prayer meetings. We must make sure of our salvation lest we are found without an oil supply when the Bridegroom comes.

Verse 12:

Him that overcometh will I make a pillar in the temple of my God, and he shall go no more out: and I will write upon him the name of my God, and the name of the city of my God, {which is} new Jerusalem, which cometh down out of heaven from my God: and {I will write upon him} my new name.

The message to every church was "to him that overcometh." Regardless of the age, the same message is given to the church. Those who experience rapture will have overcome.

This church of Philadelphia is unique in that it does not receive one rebuke from the Lord. Instead, there are at least seven commendations from the Lord to this Church:

1. **"I know thy works."** The all-seeing eyes of the Lord record our every action. The actions found in the church were favorable.

2. **"An open door."** Opportunity to promulgate the Gospel message was given to the Church of Philadelphia in a greater measure than any previous church. This age would send out more missionaries and have the message spread more than any previous age.

3. **"A little strength**." This possibly could have reference to their humility.

4. **"Kept the Word."** What greater compliment could be given to any church than they had kept the Word of God?

5. **"Hast not denied my name**." The Church stands uniquely alone when it comes to the Name of Jesus Christ.

6. **Those who were of the synagogue of Satan** would have to bow before them in defeat. Victory belongs to the people of God.

7. **"I will keep thee."** The promise of being kept by the Lord speaks loudly of their faithfulness.

<u>Verse 13:</u>

He that hath an ear, let him hear what the Spirit saith unto the churches.

Again, regardless of the church age, the same warning is given to make sure we listen to, and take heed to, what the Spirit is saying to the Church.

THE LUKE-WARM CHURCH

<u>Verse 14:</u>

And unto the angel of the church of the Laodiceans write; these things saith the Amen, the faithful and true witness, the beginning of the creation of God;

This letter brings us to the last Church to which John writes, and to the last period through which the Church would endure. What is said about this Church could certainly be said about the age in which we are presently living.

As to just what the name Laodicea means, we have differing opinions. Some feel that because it is a compound word, it means "the rights of the people."

The word, we are informed, comes from two Greek words, "laos," which means people, and "dika" which means judgment. So, the name seems to mean "The church of the judgment of the people." However one may look at the meaning of the word, it remains that this is a period of time when the people are in control - or they think they are!

This is also pointed out, it would appear, in the salutation to this church. This letter is addressed to the church of THE Laodiceans. If we are to read it as it appears in the King James Version, then we see that no other Church is addressed in this manner.

The Church has reached the final stage of her history. This is the final mile. There will be no others to follow in the wake of Laodicea.

These things saith the Amen... This is a period in which Truth is becoming a rarity in many churches. While the true Church continues to proclaim the Word of God, she continues to be outnumbered by those who are satisfied with a social gospel.

The Lord addresses Himself to this church as the Amen. That is, the establisher of Truth, the faithful and true witness. The word "Amen" means "So be it." God speaks to this church as the Amen. A church which refuses to allow the will of God to be accomplished in her midst. In this salutation the Lord is addressing Himself to them in such a manner as to emphasize to them what they are not to Him!

Verse 15:

I know thy works, that thou art neither cold nor hot: I would thou wert cold or hot.

I know thy works... To no other church has these words been so revealing as to this church. While the Lord had made the same statement to all the churches, none is so revealing as to this church.

This church is neither hot nor cold. What is wrong here? This church is not a society of unbelievers or hypocrites. It is a church! Let us notice that God does not rebuke this church for unfaithfulness nor for allowing any false teachers in their midst. Nor does He condemn them for any heresy. It was not even a cold church! There was some Spirit there! But it was lukewarm.

Their worship was lukewarm. Their obedience was lukewarm. Their testimonies were lukewarm.

The question is raised, What caused this lukewarm-ness? I think we will find our answer when we get to verse twenty.

Verse 16:

So then because thou art lukewarm, and neither cold nor hot, I will spue thee out of my mouth.

Those who do not know God and who make no profession of knowing Him, could be labeled cold. Those who are active in the vineyard of the Lord, working, praying, worshiping, could be labeled Hot.

In between these two extremes lies the Laodiceans, lukewarm. They have enough religion to be called religious. Enough to be called a church. They are not guilty of any terrible sins. There is no mention of any "Doctrines of the Nicolaitanes," nor of any troubles from the "synagogue of Satan." There is not even any mention of any "Jezebel" bothering the people in this church.

Actually, this church would probably fit right in with todays society and churches.

Laodicea experienced no tribulation. There are no persecutors troubling Laodicea. Maybe that was one of the reasons they had grown lukewarm, there was not enough pressure being exerted against them.

If one had taken the time to examine this church, you would have probably found the most up-to-date machinery running this church. Services were carried out to near perfection. The choir, the soloist, the ushers, the minister, they all knew their role to fill and they filled it precisely.

While there was pomp and splendor, while there was order in all services, while they did sing the songs of Sion, and while the preacher did, at least on occasion, preach from the Bible, there was no fervor in what they were doing. There was religion without anointing. There was worship without excitement. There was preaching without anointing. It must be those of whom Paul spoke in 2Timothy 3:5:

Having a form of godliness, but denying the power thereof from such turn away. Jude also, in verse 12, spoke of those who were like, *clouds {they are} without water, carried about of winds; trees whose fruit withereth, without fruit, twice dead, plucked up by the roots.*

If Laodicea had been cold they would have probably wanted some heat to warm them up. But they were just warm enough to be comfortable.

Verse 17:

Because thou sayest, I am rich, and increased with goods, and have need of nothing; and knowest not that thou art wretched, and miserable, and poor, and blind, and naked:

C.W.M.Turner wrote: "About twenty-eight miles southeast of Philadelphia was the city of Laodicea situated in the midst of a rich farming community. Among its chief industries was the raising of a certain kind of black sheep with glossy wool from which garments were made almost like silk and which became famous throughout the Roman Empire. This industry brought great wealth to the city. There were also several other features that made Laodicea an important center, among which were large banking facilities, a noted school of physicians, and the tepid springs that were in the vicinity of the city and which are still in existence. These were luxurious for bathing but utterly unfit for drinking purposes. The "Collyrium," or "eye salve" was also made here which added materially to the prosperity of the city. All these things brought much trade and gave a prominence to the city which naturally induced a feeling of security and a spirit of independence was made manifest upon the rebuilding of the city after its destruction by the same earthquake which destroyed Philadelphia, at which time it was found that the help offered by the Roman government was not needed as they had wealth enough to rebuild the city without assistance from the government."

The self-sufficient spirit which prevailed in Laodicea is not unlike the spirit which prevails in our own day. Admiring the multi-million dollar structures erected today in the name of religion, with their steeples pointed heavenward, one can't help but conclude that this is certainly a financially blessed generation.

But what good is a cathedral if there is no Spirit in it? What good is unique architecture if the Lord is not moving through it? What good is overflowing offering baskets if the Lord is not being exalted and souls are not being reached with the Gospel?

And knowest not... What an indictment against this Church! It was said of the Antediluvians, Matthew 24:39, *And knew not until the flood came, and took them all away.*

What could be more frightening than thinking you are right when you are really wrong? The difference between the Antediluvians and the Laodiceans was the fact the Antediluvians did not claim to be right with God. They probably made light of Noah's work and messages. But the Laodiceans claimed to be people of God!

The term Lukewarm speaks of mixing Cold and Hot together. It would seem the Laodiceans were guilty of mixing the world with the church. It is alright to take the Church into the world. But it is never right to bring the world into the Church!

Thou art wretched... How is it possible for someone to be this miserable and not know it? How could someone be blind and not know it? You see this is the way the Lord saw this church. This is not the way they saw themselves.

Verse 18:

I counsel thee to buy of me gold tried in the fire, that thou mayest be rich; and white raiment, that thou mayest be clothed, and {that} the shame of thy nakedness do not appear; and anoint thine eyes with eyesalve, that thou mayest see.

Here we witness the mercies of God extended to this church. A church which is so out of step with Him and His will that He threatens to spew them out of His mouth!

While the Lord, in mercy, offers a remedy to them for their condition it is on condition that they "BUY" it. It is not going to given without them recognizing their need of it and their willingness to pay the price necessary to obtain it.

Buy of me gold... They thought they were rich. While they were in monetary things, they were paupers spiritually before God.

Buy of me white raiment... White raiment speaks of righteousness. While they had plenty of self-righteousness, they stood naked before God without His righteousness!

Buy of me eye salve... This was a near-sighted church. They could easily see their own possessions, but they could not see the needs of others.

Philip Mauro wrote: "Every bit of God's truth that is really ours, every bit of heavenly wisdom, instruction, and understanding that is ours, has cost us something; and if we are not willing to make some sacrifice of time, inclination, effort, to forego some indulgence, or some opportunity for earthly gain or enjoyment, then we have not yet learned the difference in value between tinsel and gold, between colored beads of glass and gems of the deepest mine."

Verse 19:

As many as I love, I rebuke and chasten: be zealous therefore, and repent.

The words which the Lord has spoken to this church, words which have been sharp and pointed, were words of a caring Father. If He did not love us He would let us go on our own selfish, self-centered ways without one word of warning to us.

While the condition of the church is despicable in His sight, even to the point that He states He will *Spue them out of His mouth*, still He offers them an opportunity to repent. Surely the Lord is merciful to usward and longsuffering with us.

Verse 20:

Behold, I stand at the door, and knock: if any man hear my voice, and open the door, I will come in to him, and will sup with him, and he with me.

Some would detach this verse from the letter to Laodicea and apply it generally to the church body as a whole. But it would seem that this is yet part of the letter to Laodicea. The letter is not concluded until we get through verse twenty-two.

We can conclude our Lord's position in this verse in at least two ways:

1. Because of the spiritual condition of this church he has been driven out of the church. He is no longer in the Church. Because of the worldliness, the Lord has been displaced by the people.

2. The Lord is just outside the door. He is standing at the door. In fact, He is knocking on the door for admittance into the church. The fact He is so near should be a consolation to the church.

G. Campbell Morgan wrote: "When Holman Hunt painted that wonderful picture of the thorn- crowned King outside the door knocking, he showed his picture to his dearest friend, in the studio before it was publicly exhibited. His friend looked at it, at the kingly figure of Christ, at the rough and rugged door, and at the clinging tendrils which had spread themselves over the door. Suddenly he said: 'Hunt, you have made a terrible mistake here.' 'What mistake have I made?' said the artist. 'Why, you have painted a door without a handle. "That is not a mistake,' replied Hunt. 'That door has no handle on the outside. It is inside."

Mr. Holman Hunt's picture was on display in a place at one time. In the front sat a man with his young son. They were silently observing the picture, when the little boy nudged his father and said, "Dad, why don't they let Him in?" The boy's father thought for a while and said, "I don't know, Jimmy. I expect they don't want Him to come in." Then after a silence the boy said, "It's not that. Everybody wants Him." And then, after a little more silence, he said, "I know why they don't let Him in. They live at the back of the house."

That little fellow may have had more wisdom in that answer than first meets the eye!

CONCLUSION

This story is left here without an ending. We are not told whether Laodicea opened the door or not. I would suspect that this generation is Laodicea. That part of the story has not been written yet. The call is now to the individual. If any man ... He is not calling the church as a whole here, He is speaking and inviting anyone who will hear His voice and open the door to Him. In doing so they will know the joys of His fellowship.

This can be known individually whether the entire local assembly enjoys this fellowship or not! In this dispensation the Lord deals with the individual, not a nation. As we are each responsible for our own individual response to the call of the Gospel, we cannot hide among our family or our tribe. Salvation is a personal matter. Wise will be the person who makes sure of his salvation.

CHAPTER FOUR

The Apostle John has been busy writing his letters to the seven Churches in Asia. The last letter has been drafted to the Church of the Laodiceans. The revelation, however, does not conclude with the message to this final church. God continues to show John, through the Spirit, things which captivates his attention.

Chapter four continues the Revelation. And what a revelation it is!

We are confronted with more symbols for which the Revelation is noted. These symbols speak to us wonderful truths which God reveals to His people through them.

After chapter four we will not be studying about the Church any more. The Church moves off the scene with the concluding remarks of chapter three. Possibly, here in chapter four we may have reference to representatives of the Church, but no direct reference to the Church. From now on we will have our mind directed toward events which will transpire on this earth as they deal especially with the people of Israel; the descendants of Abraham. It will not be until chapter nineteen that we will once again have the focus placed upon the Church.

Rapture chapter? Sounds exciting! Is this what this chapter is all about? While it is true the word does not appear in the holy writ, we are convinced that the teaching of such a glorious event is found there!

Whenever this glorious event does take place, the important thing that should concern all of us, is that we are ready for that event to take place!

THE BEGINNING OF THE END...

There is hardly a conversant person among us that does not agree that something drastic must happen in the near future. The feeling is not confined just to those who gather in churches and worship God either. The feeling of chaos and frustration is felt among those who walk the streets of our land as well.

To speak of pending chaos and trouble used to bring the label of Dooms-Day Prophet to those who propagated such a message. But today people are taking seriously the conditions which prevail in our nation and the world, which cry out that something has got to happen. We cannot continue down the same road we are presently traveling in the same manner we have been traveling it, without something happening which will bring about a great change. Whether one is speaking socially, politically, monetarily, or religiously, there seems to be a demand from every sector of our world that a change must take place.

There are those; Moonies, Hare Krishnas, Armstrongites and company, who would have us to believe that peace and love will flood the world through their own emissaries. That eventually good will overpower the bad, and crowd it out of this world.

On the other hand, there are those who would have us store up dried food-stuffs, enough to last us through that long period of trouble which is coming upon the world. Canned water, canned food, and plenty of guns and ammunition, is stored away by those who call themselves Survivalists. They are expecting to outlast the troubles which are coming. To crawl away in their hole in the ground and stay there until it is all over, then crawl back out and start all over again.

THE END OF THE WORLD...

The end is likewise presented in various views. It is according to who you are listening to as to how the world is going to come to an end. Some would have us to think that the Lord shall come back to this earth someday and annihilate every sinner that is still living and then set up His kingdom of peace on this earth. Others would have us to think that mankind will continue to stockpile his nuclear weapons until it reaches the point where someone starts pushing buttons, and the whole world will go up in one great nuclear holocaust. Completely obliterating every living thing on the earth. Leaving the planet wobbling, burned and cratered, through her destined orbits in the solar system.

This is just two of several theories about how it will all end eventually. When we dig into these theories - that is all they are, there is no solid scriptural foundation for these theories - and opinions of men. We come up with a lot of weird concoctions which are labeled "gospel." Only the Word of God will give us the right answers to our questions relative to this time of the end. Wise is the person who will take what they hear from the prognosticators of this world with a grain of salt, and look to the Word of God for the answers to our questions.

Verse 1:

After this I looked, and, behold, a door {was} opened in heaven: and the first voice which I heard {was} as it were of a trumpet talking with me; which said, Come up hither, and I will shew thee things which must be hereafter.

When the apostle John originally wrote this book of Revelation, he did so without dividing it into chapters and verses as we now find it in our Bibles. This division was made to the Bible in later years.

Verse one of chapter four was a continuation of verse twenty-two of the preceding chapter as far as John the Apostle was concerned. He did not see it as a break in his subject matter and the beginning of something different from what he had been writing about.

Notice first of all the term; AFTER THIS applies to what John had just finished writing. He had just written to the seven churches in Asia, which we have already studied about. In our study on the churches we sought to point out that these seven churches could represent periods through which the church has gone since Pentecost. While there were seven churches in Asia to whom John addressed his letters - there were actually more than seven - the messages seem to have a farther-reaching purpose than just being addressed to the seven local churches. They seem to have been representative churches representing certain periods of time since Pentecost. Note that the final church letter was addressed to the church of the Laodiceans. A church which was lukewarm, and the one who said she was rich and increased with goods, and had need of nothing. Laodicea certainly represents the age in which we presently find ourselves living, wouldn't you think? The last church of the age! If we do look at these churches in this manner, then the term AFTER THIS takes on added significance. For it would seem that John would then be saying; AFTER THE CHURCH HAS RUN HER COURSE. AFTER THE CHURCH HAS PASSED THROUGH THE AGES OF HER DESTINY...

Looking at this verse in this manner has prompted many to be of the opinion that this verse must be speaking of the rapture of the church. Looking at it in this light, let us consider some phrases which stand out in this verse:

A DOOR WAS OPENED... The opening of a door would signify either an exit out of some place, or an entrance into some place.

Both would be applicable to the church. We are waiting for an exit OUT of this world, as well as an ENTRANCE into His presence! So, regardless of how one may look at it, both would apply to the church.

IN HEAVEN... Before now our attention has been focused on the earth. The message of John has been directed to the Church on this earth. Now, suddenly, our attention shifts to heaven. And suddenly is a good way of describing how things will change for the Church at the time of the Rapture! One moment we will have our feet on this earth going about our various activities, and then, the next moment we will be caught up into the clouds to the meet the Lord in the air! WHAT A HOPE!

THE FIRST VOICE I HEARD WAS AS IT WERE A TRUMPET... John, as a representative of the Church, experiences in the Spirit that which the entire Church shall experience someday soon in reality.

Reading this statement makes one automatically think of the words of the apostle Paul in 1Thessalonians 4:16: *For the Lord Himself shall descend from heaven with a shout, with the voice of the arch-angel, and with the trump of God...*

Also his words in 1Corinthians 15:51,52: *Behold, I shew you a mystery; we shall not all sleep, but we shall all be changed, in a moment, in the twinkling of an eye, at the last trump...*

The sound which every child of God awaits is that of the Trump of God signaling His Church home to His side.

The use of the Trumpet to signal forth the Church to that meeting in the sky is not something new or different with the New Testament. We find in the Old Testament as God led Israel (the Church in the wilderness, Acts 7:38) through the wilderness, Trumpets were employed to call the people forward. In Numbers ten we find that Moses was directed to make two trumpets of silver. Silver being significant, as it spoke in typology of redemption. These trumpets were then used to call the people together for a special message from God. To call the elders together for a time of counselling. To call the men of war together in time of battle, as well as to call Israel forward in their wilderness march. Since Israel reached the land and subdued it, they have had no reason for sounding the trumpet to signal another march forward. Their marching days having ended. But the Church awaits that day when another trumpet blast will signal for Her to march forward into the heavens to meet the Lord.

WHICH SAID, COME UP HITHER... Again, this is the welcome call which every blood washed child of God awaits. While John heard these words spoken to him, one day we all shall hear that welcome sound in our own ears.

This was an invitation to John to come up to the Lord's side. We know from verse two that John, *in the Spirit*, was caught up. It was a spiritual experience to John. To those who hear that welcome sound in the near future it will not be a spiritual experience; IT WILL BE REALITY! Paul informs us that the Lord will then *change our vile body, that it may be fashioned like unto His glorious body* (Philippians 3:21).

THINGS WHICH MUST BE HEREAFTER... The last word and the first word of this verse are almost identical. They are in meaning: AFTER THIS -- HEREAFTER. The catching away of the Church will mark the end of a glorious history for the Church. A long and victorious history for the Church. Those blood-washed people! Those Jesus Name baptized people! Those Holy Spirit filled people!

These are those who have through the years been confronted with ever so many obstacles which have sought to prevent them from making it to their goal. Hell has fought against this people in its efforts to stop the progress of Her message. It is a battle-weary, battle-scarred, host of people who will at that time sweep up into the heavens to meet their blessed Lord in the sky. In that day they will come from the east, and from the west, from the north and from the south, to all meet together for a grand Hallelujah meeting in the sky. There will be martyrs there; from Stephen down to the last one who shall seal his testimony with his own life. There will be missionaries there who have jeopardized their health and life to carry this message to other lands and other peoples. There will be faithful saints who have been faithful to their local church and faithful to God through the years. All alike shall join together on that wonderful and glorious day of RAPTURE!

The term HEREAFTER speaks to us of events which will take place after the Church age. A time when the church has been removed from this earth, so these events can take place here. Events which the following chapters of Revelation deal with that will have far-reaching and earth-shaking results.

The catching away of the Church of Jesus Christ will mark the end of a glorious era and the beginning of another era for this earth. It is the dividing line between a great and glorious people, the church, and those who shall be faced with the horrible events which have never been faced by any other people since the time of Adam. On one side of that division are the radiantly happy people rejoicing with their Lord. On the other side will be those of this world who will be filled with fear and trouble because of those things which shall come upon them in that day of tribulation.

Verse 2:

And immediately I was in the spirit: and, behold, a throne was set in heaven, and {one} sat on the throne.

AND IMMEDIATELY I WAS IN THE SPIRIT... A very descriptive term to describe the suddenness of the Rapture. There will be no time for praying or making amends. Altar calls will be too late.

Paul, in describing the change which will take place in our body, spoke of the change occurring in "a moment, in the twinkling of an eye". It is almost impossible for us to fully grasp what this statement means in regards to time. Conversations will be cut off in the middle of a word. A good friend and brother had a good description of it when he said, "It will be "Halle" here and "lujah" there!"

I WAS IN THE SPIRIT... An expression which we have found John employing previous to this in describing his visions of Revelation. Through spiritual encounters John is moved from one point to another as he has revealed to him the events which will transpire in the last days.

John is now "taken" into heaven. While this was all done to John in the spirit, it signifies to us how it will actually take place one day when the Church is taken home in a moment. When we consider our space ships which have been traveling for years now seeking out the far-reaches of the universe, and which have not even come close to reaching a limit of travel in outer space, and to think we will be with the Lord in heaven in a moment of time, this gives one an idea of how the Lord is going to take His church home.

John's statement of I WAS IN THE SPIRIT, should also be taken seriously by each of us as well.

This is an indication of the condition in which we as well must be in if we expect to experience the catching away to be with the Lord.

BEHOLD, A THRONE... AND ONE SAT... In every instance in the Revelation where we have a reference to the throne in heaven it is always in the singular. There is never any reference to more than one throne! Even in Old Testament passages such as Isaiah 6, we have reference to only one throne and one sitting upon it.

Now it is true that the word "one" in this verse is in italics, which signifies that it was not in the original, the very next verse states "HE" in speaking of the one who is sitting on this throne. No indication whatsoever of more than one involved in this throne. Not only in this passage, but in every other passage which refers to the throne which will be seen in heaven, there is never a reference to more than One sitting on that throne. THAT ONE WHO IS SITTING ON THAT THRONE IS THE LORD JESUS CHRIST HIMSELF! Do we not find Jesus stating very clearly that the time would come when He would "SIT IN THE THRONE OF HIS GLORY" (Matthew 19:28)? John is witnessing that time of glory when the Lord Jesus shall reign on His throne. While the throne of which John speaks is in heaven, during the Kingdom age His throne will be established on this earth, but it will be the same One who will be sitting on that throne!

Verse 3:

And he that sat was to look upon like a jasper and a sardine stone: and {there was} a rainbow round about the throne, in sight like unto an emerald.

HE THAT SAT WAS TO LOOK UPON LIKE A JASPER AND A SARDINE STONE... We note in chapter twenty-one and verse eleven, that the JASPER stone is there spoken of as being CLEAR AS CRYSTAL. This could speak of the sinless beauty and perfect glory of our blessed Lord.

No flaw could be found about Him. He was without sin; neither was there any guile to be found about Him.

This CLEAR AS CRYSTAL Jasper stone is employed to refer to both the Lord Jesus Christ as well as the City of God which will be the home of the Church.

In fact, the term CRYSTAL is employed in referring to the THRONE upon which the Lord is sitting: The CITY which He is bringing down out of heaven for His Church; and the RIVER which flows out of the throne of God.

The other stone, SARDINE (or Sardius), is blood-red. What a picture of our Lord as referring both to His GLORY as well as to His SACRIFICE. The sinless Lamb whose blood was shed on Calvary to make Atonement for us.

Every redeemed Jew among that number who shall stand before this throne - and there will be many of them - will recognize the significance of these stones. They are the FIRST and LAST stones that were in the breastplate of the High Priest of Israel. (Exodus 28:17-20). He who is recognized by these two stones is the One who was also identified as the FIRST AND THE LAST, THE BEGINNING AND THE END.

Another thing to consider: The firstborn son of Israel was Reuben. Reuben means "BEHOLD A SON". The last son of Israel was Benjamin, which means "SON OF MY RIGHT HAND." Both names greatly significant of the One occupying this throne!

AND A RAINBOW ROUND ABOUT THE THRONE... This is no ordinary rainbow! An ordinary rainbow is composed of the seven primary colors of; Red, Orange, Yellow, Green, Blue, Indigo, and Violet. Notice, this rainbow is said to be LIKE UNTO AN EMERALD. The color of an emerald is sea green. The color GREEN in typology would speak to us of LIFE. The One who is occupying this throne is the giver of Life. It is IN HIM THAT WE LIVE, AND MOVE, AND HAVE OUR BEING (Acts 17:28).

The BOW reminds us of the covenant which God made with Noah after the flood (Genesis 8:20-22).

A bow which continues some four thousand-plus years later to be seen after storms reminding us that we are serving a Covenant keeping God who is faithful. Seeing this bow about the throne reminds us that the One sitting on this throne will keep His promise to His children.

Verse 4:

And round about the throne {were} four and twenty seats: and upon the seats I saw four and twenty elders sitting, clothed in white raiment; and they had on their heads crowns of gold.

FOUR AND TWENTY SEATS (THRONES)... The vision broadens to include a group of twenty-four sitting on thrones ROUND ABOUT THE THRONE.

The Greek word here translated SEATS is THRONES. It is translated SEATS in five places in the Revelation: 2:13; 4:4; 11:16; 13:2, and 16:10. In thirty-eight other places in the Revelation it is always translated THRONE. Why the translators chose to translate it SEATS in these five places we do not know. The Greek word for SEAT is a completely different word: "KATHEDRA."

Who are these FOUR AND TWENTY ELDERS? We run into differing views looking for the answer to this question. Let's examine the passage noting some things which can be of help in identifying them for us:

1. Note first of all, they are all crowned with crowns. We read of only the Lord Jesus wearing crowns; and His saints. There is nothing said in the Bible concerning angels wearing crowns. So, this would seem to eliminate them being angels.

2. The very term by which they are identified, ELDER, as well tells us these are not angels. Angels are never called elders.

3. Thrones are only associated with men and God. There are no references to angels sitting on thrones.

4. They are seen all wearing 'WHITE RAIMENT. Again, a term which does not apply to angels. We find the saints along with Jesus wearing white raiment, 6:11; 7:9; 19:8,14. The white speaks of righteousness, which the saints of God have been given through the cleansing blood of Jesus Christ.

From this it would seem that we could glean that what we have under consideration here are redeemed men who shall have the honor to sit with the Lord in some capacity of governing.

If they are representatives who appear before the throne of God for the redeemed, then it would stand to reason to assume that they represent BOTH Old and New Testament saints. We note in 5:9 that they join in singing the song of Redemption. So, they are redeemed men.

The tern "ELDER" is usually used in the Bible to refer to a representative head of a city, or a family, or a tribe or nation. Why the number 24? Numbers have a definite meaning to God in His Word. Possibly twenty-four would represent God's governing or Judging number. David, in 1Chronicles 24;1-19, made the 24 heads of the families of the priests to represent the entire priesthood. Possibly these 24 sitting on thrones represent both the Old and New Testament saints. We may also note that both Israel and the Church are represented in the New Jerusalem, 21:10-14.

Also, let us remember the promise which Jesus made to His Apostles in Matthew 19:28 concerning the time when He would sit on the throne of His glory, how they would be sitting on twelve thrones

JUDGING THE TWELVE TRIBES OF ISRAEL... Are twelve of these thrones we read about here in Revelation four occupied by twelve Apostles?

Verse 5:

And out of the throne proceeded lightnings and thunderings and voices: and {there were} seven lamps of fire burning before the throne, which are the seven Spirits of God.

OUT OF THE THRONE PROCEEDED... The LIGHTNINGS AND THUNDERINGS AND VOICES, must speak to us of the Judgments of God which He brings upon this world in this time of tribulation. Notice what is said in chapter 8 verse 5: *And the angel took the censer, and filled it with fire of the altar, and cast it into the earth: and there were voices, and thunderings, and lightnings, and an earthquake.*

We have the same expression employed when the seventh angel pours out the seventh bowl of Judgment upon the earth in 16:18.

The Judgments which will be brought upon this world during these dark days of tribulation will come from the throne room of God Himself1 and it is evident from what we read in chapter six that those who are on the receiving end of these judgments will be aware of where they are coming from (6:16,17).

This verse reminds us of when the Law was given from Sinai to the people of Israel, in Exodus 19: There, in verse sixteen, we note: *And it came to pass on the third day in the morning, that there were THUNDERS AND LIGHTNINGS... AND THE VOICE of the trumpet exceeding loud; so that all the people that was in the camp trembled.*

The Law of God was being given to His people. Which law would soon be broken and which would result in the Judgments of God being brought upon the offenders. The tribulation will be poured out upon the "offenders" of God's laws. The rebellion of men under the reign of the man of sin will be the ultimate defiance to the laws of God. Already we see this defiance through the efforts which are being put forth by the Humanist groups with their message that man is his own god and able to work out his own problems in his world. That he does not need a higher power than himself to save himself. This will be the message of the man of sin who will seek to promote himself and his message of hope to planet earth. The foolishness of man will fail miserably as the Lord thunders out His judgments upon the kingdom of the beast during this dark hour of tribulation.

SEVEN LAMPS OF FIRE BURNING... WHICH ARE THE SEVEN SPIRITS OF GOD... We have already touched on these seven spirits in our study from chapter one. One more thought though on these seven lamps, they remind us of the CANDLESTAND which stood in the Tabernacle in the wilderness in the holy place. The candlestand was the only light which the priest had to officiate before the Lord by during his services in the Tabernacle. The candlestand had seven branches which gave off the light for the holy place. Again, seven is the number which is associated with God and perfection or completeness. The divine light to guide men in his walk through this world comes from the throne room of God. To refuse that light is to accept darkness and to ultimately stumble through this world to a time and place of Judgment.

<u>Verse 6:</u>

And before the throne {there was} a sea of glass like unto crystal: and in the midst of the throne, and round about the throne, {were} four beasts full of eyes before and behind.

AND BEFORE THE THRONE THERE WAS A SEA OF GLASS LIKE UNTO CRYSTAL... We have referred to the Tabernacle in the wilderness already in our study. The comparisons are not accidental. As we have mentioned previously, the events which take place in the Revelation during the time of tribulation are certainly Jewish oriented.

Notice what we could "see" in this text in regards to the Tabernacle: The throne could correspond to the "MERCY SEAT AND ARK." The "FOUR LIVING CREATURES", could refer to the cherubims which "guarded" the mercy seat and Ark of God. We could compare the twenty four elders with the "PRIESTS" who officiated by course in the Tabernacle. And, as mentioned, the seven spirits with the "GOLDEN CANDLESTAND" which stood in the holy place of the Tabernacle. Later in our study we will see souls under the altar, which could certainly have reference to the "BRAZEN ALTAR" before the Tabernacle. And now, this "SEA OF GLASS" could have reference to the "BRAZEN LAVER" which stood between the altar of sacrifice and the Tabernacle. You recall that the laver was made from the "LOOKING GLASSES - MIRRORS" of the women of Israel.

Now the Tabernacle in the wilderness was to be erected according to the PATTERNS OF THINGS IN THE HEAVENS (Hebrews 9:23).

The priest would wash his hands (service) and his feet (conduct) in this laver before entering the Tabernacle. It spoke of cleansing. One purpose of tribulation will be to "cleanse" Israel (Zechariah 13:9). They will have sin purged from them as a nation. There are many among them now who do not worship God nor have their trust in Him. When tribulation has passed, Israel will stand cleansed before the throne of God.

We find an interesting point in chapter fifteen in regards to this sea. Notice here in chapter four we only have mention of the sea. In chapter fifteen it states it is "MINGLED WITH FIRE." Chapter fifteen reveals what the sea will look like AFTER Israel has been "washed" in this laver of cleansing.

IN THE MIDST OF THE THRONE... WERE FOUR BEASTS... The word for BEASTS is taken from the Greek word ZOON or ZOA. It could have been translated LIVING CREATURES, which would have given it a different view to our mind.

Just exactly what we have before us here, we are not for sure. We do note, however, that there is no mention of harps or crowns, or any other thing, associated with these creatures which would imply them to be in the same class as the elders on the twenty-four thrones.

They have something to do with the Throne of God and directing praise and attention to the One sitting on this throne. This we can readily determine by what we find them repeating continually. We could possibly call them guardians of the throne.

Verse 7

And the first beast was like a lion, and the second beast like a calf, and the third beast had a face as a man, and the fourth beast was like a flying eagle.

Note some Old Testament references: Ezekiel 1 :5, *Also out of the midst thereof came the likeness of four living creatures.* Also, we have from Isaiah 6:2,3: *Above it stood the seraphim... and one cried unto another, and said, Holy, Holy, Holy, is the Lord of Hosts.*

These as well remind us of the "CHERUBIM" which God placed at the entrance to the Garden of Eden to keep man from the Tree of Life.

In Ezekiel's description, we find he spoke of the cherubims having four faces; the front like that of a man, the right side like that of a lion, the left side that of an ox, and the back as an eagle. John here speaks to us as if these were each separate creatures. The first a lion, the second as a calf, the third had a face as a man, and the fourth beast was like a flying eagle.

Verse 8

And the four beasts had each of them six wings about him; and they were full of eyes within: and they rest not day and night, saying, Holy, holy, holy, Lord God Almighty, which was, and is, and is to come.

John's creatures had six wings. So, did those described by Isaiah, while Ezekiel's only had four. In Ezekiel, we find the creatures had wheels as well as wings. Possibly Ezekiel's vision had to do with their activity on this earth, while the vision of John was in heaven, the permanent home of the creatures.

Isaiah refers to his creatures as SERAPHIM. Ezekiel refers to his as LIVING CREATURES, the same as John. The one referred to in Genesis is called CHERUBIM. Evidently this is telling us there are different orders of these which are each adapted for their own service before God.

John speaks of them as being FULL OF EYES BEFORE AND BEHIND. In referring to their wings, John said THEY WERE FULL OF EYES WITHIN. This seems to emphasize to us that these are some type of guardians.

Another difference to be noted between the references in Isaiah, Ezekiel and here in Revelation, Isaiah's creatures were said to be ABOVE THE THRONE. Ezekiel's are said to SUPPORT THE THRONE, and John's were IN THE MIDST or AROUND THE THRONE.

They seem to be attendants or representatives of the throne of God, and not representatives of the Church. They summon forth the four horsemen in chapter six. And one of them hand over to the SEVEN ANGELS the seven vials (bowls) filled with the WRATH OF GOD, (15:7).

We have no reference to the creatures of Ezekiel saying anything specifically. Isaiah's are heard exclaiming HOLY, HOLY, HOLY unto the Lord. John speaks of these as well crying out, DAY AND NIGHT, HOLY, HOLY, HOLY, LORD GOD ALMIGHTY, WHICH WAS, AND IS, AND IS TO COME.

This should give us an indication as to what God thinks of praise. How much MORE we need to praise Him when we come to His house. If this is the continual employment of these creatures, that they continually, day and night, praise God, how much more should we be found praising Him!

Verse 9:

And when those beasts give glory and honour and thanks to him that sat on the throne, who liveth for ever and ever.

When these creatures exalted the Lord God in praise it overwhelmed the twenty-four elders on their thrones and they fell DOWN BEFORE HIM THAT SAT ON THE THRONE, AND WORSHIP HIM THAT LIVETH FOR EVER AND EVER. It is during this time that they CAST THEIR CROWNS BEFORE THE THRONE, SAYING, THOU ART WORTHY, 0 LORD, TO RECEIVE GLORY AND HONOUR AND POWER.

Thus, chapter four concludes with praise. If this chapter is a chapter of RAPTURE, then it certainly fits with all the expressions of praise that are found in it. For when the rapture of the Saints takes place, can you think of anything else that will be taking place by those redeemed from this earth than PRAISE!

Is this what John hears in chapter nineteen when he speaks about the VOICE OF MUCH PEOPLE IN HEAVEN, SAYING, ALLELUIA; SALVATION, AND GLORY, AND HONOUR, AND POWER,

UNTO THE LORD OUR GOD... ALLELUIA: FOR THE LORD GOD OMNIPOTENT REIGNETH.

It is in chapter nineteen that John witnesses the return of the redeemed from heaven following the Lord as He comes in Judgment upon the beast and his kingdom of evil. To say there will be a lot of praise and worship in heaven when the redeemed are caught up would be an understatement without a doubt!

In that myriad of voices who are exalting the One sitting on His throne, may our voice be found among them.

RAPTURE!

If what we have under consideration here in chapter four of Revelation is not the Rapture, then when does it take place in the Revelation?

There must be a time when the rapture would be noted in the Revelation, as there is so much attention given to the Church in chapters two and three. It is quite evident from these two chapters that attention is given to the Church here in the beginning of the Revelation.

The suggestion by some that the rapture is found in chapter fourteen, verses 14 through 20 will not hold up when closely considered. This is not a vision of the Rapture of the Church by John, but rather a vision of the battle of Armageddon. A time of judgment from God!

It is evident from the language which is employed in chapter nineteen that what John is witnessing in the voices which he hears from heaven, as well as the sight which he witnesses coming from heaven, that this must be the Redeemed ones. Among whom is the Church!

If John witnesses them coming from heaven following the Lord Jesus to the battle of Armageddon, then how and when did they get to heaven in the first place?

We know of no place in the Revelation, other than chapter four, to find a description of the rapture.

And the language which is employed in this chapter would certainly seem to be speaking to us about a rapture taking place.

The order of things in the Revelation would also seem to speak to us that this would be when the rapture would take place. Chapter One,

John is shown the vision of the glorified Christ. The One about whom the book is written, and whom the book reveals. It is the Revelation of Jesus Christ.

Chapter two and chapter three, the letters to the seven churches in Asia. This evidently being representative churches to whom John is told to write these letters, as there were evidently more than seven churches there.

And then, chapter four, a period following the Church age. The letters speaking of the conditions which exist in the Church then, as well as through the centuries since Pentecost.

Then chapter five, the book with seven seals which must be opened in order for the judgments to come upon the man of sin and the workers of iniquity. Such judgments which must take place to bring again Jesus Christ to reign upon this earth.

Then chapter six, the beginning of that period called tribulation which begins as the seals are opened one by one from the book.

There seems to be order in the Book, and chapter four fits that order regarding the catching away of the Church of Jesus Christ.

This will remove the hindering force which is present in the world today preventing the manifestation of the man of sin and the revealing of his plans to conquer mankind (2 Thessalonians 2:7,8).

The catching away of the Church will open the way for the man of sin and his cohorts to put into action his plans which will begin as outlined for us in chapter six of the Revelation with the riding forth of the white horse.

Verse 10:

The four and twenty elders fall down before him that sat on the throne, and worship him that liveth for ever and ever, and cast

their crowns before the throne, saying,

The redeemed worship the Redeemer. The twenty-four elders, if they represent the Old and New Testament believers are found doing what the people of God have always been doing, worshipping the Lord of Glory.

This action taken by the elders is repeated in chapter five verses eight and fourteen. They are worshipping the One who "liveth for ever and ever." The acknowledgment of the eternality of our Lord. As they pay homage to Christ, they acknowledge Him as being Lord of all.

Cast their crowns before the throne... When Jesus returns at the time of Armageddon, John describes Him as wearing "many crowns" (19:12). This signifies that He is Lord of lords and King of kings. By the elders casting their own crowns at the foot of the throne, and the One who occupies the throne, they acknowledge that He alone is worthy of being crowned.

The elders are not in possession of crowns by any right they possess. They are wearing crowns because of Christ, not by their own merits.

Verse 11:

Thou art worthy, O Lord, to receive glory and honour and power: for thou hast created all things, and for thy pleasure they are and were created.

All the redeemed among creation shall someday bring glory and praise and honor to the Lord Jesus Christ. What an exciting day of celebration that will be!

This verse points out the reason for creation to begin with, "for thy pleasure they are and were created." God wanted to share His glory and creation with mortals. Foolish are those who elect to ignore His invitation to join this vast throng who shall gather in that wonderful tomorrow to celebrate eternal victory and worship the Creator.

CHAPTER FIVE

Verse 1:

And I saw in the right hand of him that sat on the throne a book written within and on the backside, sealed with seven seals.

What a marvelous sight is unveiled before us in this interesting chapter.

And I saw in the right hand of Him that sat on the throne... As we noted in chapter four, the Lord sits high and lifted up on His throne with all the glorious colors of the rainbow about Him. The majesty of this sight must have been awesome to say the least.

While in chapter four John saw the Lord sitting on His throne before whom the four and twenty elders fell in worship; there was no mention at that time of anything in His hand. As chapter four depicts for us the rapture of the saints from the earth and their coming before the throne of glory; this chapter carries us beyond that moment of glory and praise. Now John sees that there is something in the hand of the One sitting on that throne. It is a book written within and on the backside, sealed with seven seals.

John becomes involved in one of the most fascinating mysteries of the Revelation. What he is witnessing in this chapter has far-reaching consequences.

Now we know that the earth and the entire cosmos is God's as Creator. This is evident from such passages as: *The earth {is} the Lord's, and the fulness thereof; the world, and they that dwell therein. For he hath founded it upon the seas, and established it upon the floods,* Psalm 24:1,2.

The land shall not be sold for ever: for the land {is} Mine, for ye {are} strangers and sojourners with Me. And in all the land of your possession ye shall grant a redemption for the land. If thy brother be waxen poor, and hath sold away {some} of his possession, and if any of his kin come to redeem it, then shall he redeem that which his brother sold, Leviticus 25:23-25.

If one of the Israelites lost their estate, then one of their near-kinsman could redeem his estate if possible. The problem which arose concerning the earth, however, was the fact that no mortal could ever hope to be able to redeem that which was lost in the garden of Eden.

What we find in the creation of man is the transfer to Adam dominion of the earth, for we read: *And God said, Let us make man in our image, after our likeness: and let them have dominion over the fish of the sea, and over the fowl of the air, and over the cattle, and over all the earth, and over every creeping thing that creepeth upon the earth,* Genesis 1:26.

But we know that the enemy entered the picture, and through his subtlety he deceived the first parents and brought about not only their fall from sinlessness and perfection, but also caused them to forfeit their dominion of the earth.

It is evident that this world is presently under the influence of Satan. His powerful force is seen everywhere. In fact, he is called *the god of this world* (2Corinthians 4:4).

As a lost estate of an Israelite could be redeemed by a near kinsman, then the earth as well had to be redeemed by a near kinsman. But no son of Adam could ever hope to qualify to be able to pay the price required to redeem this world. The only one who was able to do this was the Creator Himself. And yet, in order to redeem man and his world, He had to first take on manhood in order to be his near kinsman. And it would take more than mere money to pay the demanded price. The apostle Peter informs us: *Forasmuch as ye know that ye were not redeemed with corruptible things, {as} silver and gold, from your vain conversation {received} by tradition from your fathers; But with the precious blood of Christ, as of a lamb without blemish and without spot: Who verily was foreordained before the foundation of the world, but was manifest in these last times for you,* 1Peter 1:18-20.

- This is what Bethlehem was all about.
- This is what Calvary was all about.
- This is why Jesus came into the world.
- To redeem fallen man and to redeem the world.

Now, the question is, do we have anything in the scriptures to substantiate this teaching? Yes! In Jeremiah chapter thirty-two we find that Israel is about to go into Babylonian captivity. The prophet Jeremiah has been prophesying to Israel that this would happen. He has also been telling them that it will not be forever. They would return after the land has had time to enjoy her Sabbaths which Israel had been neglecting. In fact, it was while Daniel was studying the writings of Jeremiah that he realized that the time of Israel's captivity was almost up. He began to pray for the sins of his people Israel, and confess them before the Lord God. During this time of fasting and prayer, Daniel had a visit by an angel of the Lord who informed him that the seventy years which would signify Israel's return to their homeland, also signified something of much greater significance - It spoke of the seventy weeks of years which had also been pronounced upon the people of Israel which would only be fulfilled when their sins had been brought to an end, and everlasting righteousness - the millennium - had been brought to them.

During the time of Jeremiah's prophecy, the false prophets opposed him and encouraged the king and people to not listen to what Jeremiah was saying about the Babylonian captivity and the return to the land eventually. In this chapter, we find that the prophet is under house arrest. He is shut up in the court of the prison. During this incarceration, Jeremiah is told by the Lord that a cousin of his will come to him and offer him the right to redeem some land which was his right to do so as being near kinsman.

His cousin did come to Jeremiah while he was still in the court of the prison. *Buy my field, I pray thee, that {is} in Anathoth, which {is} in the country of Benjamin: for the right of inheritance {is} thine, and the redemption {is} thine; buy {it} for thyself. Then I knew that this {was} the word of the Lord*, Verse 8.

Jeremiah bought the property. He then took the evidence of the purchase and gave it to his trusted friend, Baruch. He told Baruch to take the evidence, that which was sealed according to the law and custom, and that which was open, and to bury it in a safe place.

The evidence was to be sealed and placed in a safe place, while the other copy which was not sealed normally would be on public display - like recording it on the books at the county seat. The public record would declare whose right it was to open the sealed evidence and claim ownership to the property.

In Jeremiah's case, it would seem there would be no safe place with the invading forces of Babylon coming to burn and destroy the city, so, the prophet had both the sealed and open copy buried in a safe place.

He was saying, by his actions, the time will come when Israel shall return to this land. When they do, I will take the sealed evidence of ownership to the land in Anathoth, and as it is my right to do so, I will open the seals which will declare that the property is rightfully mine.

In this the prophet was showing his confidence in Israel's return from Babylonian captivity. This seems to be the background for what is taking place here in chapter five of Revelation. The sealed book of ownership is in the hand of the One who is sitting on the throne. There is only one who can claim it - The Rightful Owner.

Verse 2:

And I saw a strong angel proclaiming with a loud voice, Who is worthy to open the book, and to loose the seals thereof?

The concern of finding the one whose right it was to open this book reaches into the heavens among the angelic host. For redemption involves heaven as well as the earth. Redemption will involve the whole of creation - heaven and earth.

The earth has been under the curse of the enemy long enough. There is a cry for one who is able to open the book, and thus show ownership to creation.

Verse 3:

And no man in heaven, nor in earth, neither under the earth, was able to open the book, neither to look thereon.

Search was made. Men were sought out. But there was no one who could be found worthy to take the book and open the seals. Paul also informed us - As it is written, *There is none righteous, no, not one: For all have sinned, and come short of the glory of God,* Romans 3:10,23.

• No son of Adam had ever been worthy of this right.

Verse 4:

And I wept much, because no man was found worthy to open and to read the book, neither to look thereon.

Because of what is at stake, there is great concern and alarm. If this is after the rapture; if this is a scene before the throne with the redeemed, raptured, saints looking on, then, there is no way the enemy of all righteousness can be driven from this earth - there is no way that the judgments of God's wrath can come upon the beast and his evil kingdom, until this book is opened. The opening of these seals will also produce the judgments of God upon the wickedness of Satan and his plans. Will redemption fail this close to reality? The awesomeness of this weighed so heavily upon John that he broke down and wept.

Verse 5:

And one of the elders saith unto me, Weep not: behold, the Lion of the tribe of Juda, the Root of David, hath prevailed to open the book, and to loose the seven seals thereof.

One of the elders? Is this one of the redeemed saints? Is this one of those who stand among that myriad of witnesses before the throne? Why wasn't it one of the angels? In all the other places, we find it is an angel which is showing John the things which happen during the tribulation.

Possibly it is one of the redeemed because one of the redeemed could relate to John and his feelings better. After all, one of the redeemed would better understand the significance of redemption. The angels have not been redeemed. Calvary was not for their redemption. It may have even been one of those who was brought forth from hades at the Lord's resurrection.

Notice that the elder identifies our Lord in three ways:

1. THE LION ...

The king of the beasts.

2. TRIBE OF JUDAH ...

The prophecy of the patriarch had long ago stated: *Judah {is} a lion's whelp: from the prey, my son, thou art gone up: he stooped down, he couched as a lion, and as an old lion; who shall rouse him up? The sceptre shall not depart from Judah, nor a lawgiver from between his feet, until Shiloh come; and unto him {shall} the gathering of the people {be},* Genesis 49:9,10.

3. ROOT OF DAVID ...

The promised seed of David had arrived. The One who was called the Son of David was here. The identity is certain. He is the promised seed of David had arrived. The One who was called the Son of David was here. The identity is certain. He is the one. The one the world had been waiting for thousands of years to come. Finally, the great day was here.

HATH PREVAILED... How did He prevail? He prevailed in the wilderness against the tempter's temptations. He prevailed through three years of ministry confronting every temptation known to the flesh. He prevailed against the demons which had so many to whom He ministered bound. He prevailed on Calvary in shedding His own blood which was the price of redemption for all mankind. He prevailed in hades when He conquered the one who had the power - or authority - over death. He prevailed when He took the keys of death and hades into His own possession. He prevailed!

The word "Prevailed" here, "nikao", is the same Greek word which we find spoken to all seven of the Churches of Asia, only we find there the word is translated "Overcometh."

- He who encouraged His church to overcome - overcame.

Verse 6:

And I beheld, and, Lo, in the midst of the throne and of the four beasts, and in the midst of the elders, stood a Lamb as it had been slain, having seven horns and seven eyes, which are the seven Spirits of God sent forth into all the earth.

Hearing the words of the elder brings a feeling of great relief to John. His tears cease their flowing. He turns to witness this lion who has come forward to take the book and open the seals. But instead of seeing a Lion, John sees a Lamb! At first one would think that a lion was needed for the task of throwing out the usurper of authority to this earth. At least that is the way we would reason it out.

But before redemption could come there had to be a Lamb slain. The shedding of blood had to take place. And it could not be the blood of some lion that would bring about redemption that was needed.

Before He could fill the position of conqueror over Satan and his forces, He first had to go to Calvary.

And as it was the Lamb who was slain on the cross, it is in this position that He is worthy of receiving the sealed book.

Having studied previously about the seven spirits which proceed from the throne of God, we note here that the Lamb - Jesus - possesses these seven spirits. They are seen in Him as seven horns and seven eyes. The Spirit which emanates from the throne and enters the life of every believer is the Spirit of Jesus Christ!

Verse 7:

And he came and took the book out of the right hand of him that sat upon the throne.

The moment had arrived! There must have been a holy quietness as this dramatic moment took place. The Lamb took the title book. It was His right to do so. He had come to claim that which had been kept in a secure place for millenniums. The time had finally arrived to lay claim on the possession.

We find that the prophet Daniel saw the vision the same as John: *I saw in the night visions, and, behold, {one} like the Son of man came with the clouds of heaven, and came to the Ancient of days, and they brought him near before him. And there was given him dominion, and glory, and a kingdom, that all people, nations, and languages, should serve him: his dominion {is} an everlasting dominion, which shall not pass away, and his kingdom {that} which shall not be destroyed,* Daniel 7: 13,14. Daniel saw this in a vision. He only saw certain aspects of it. He did not see the complete picture.

John, as he was there, saw it all. The dominion which Daniel speaks about which was given to this One whom he called the Son of man, is the dominion over this earth and creation. A dominion which will not be surrendered voluntarily. He must take it. That is what the opening of the seals will produce.

Verse 8:

And when he had taken the book, the four beasts and four {and} twenty elders fell down before the Lamb, having every one of them harps, and golden vials full of odours, which are the prayers of saints.

The prayers of the people of God do not go un-noticed. It may seem that they do at times. But somewhere - somehow - the Lord is preserving the prayers of the righteous. He who taught His own to pray - "Thy kingdom come" - now rejoices to witness their joy over the answer to this prayer which has been prayed by the righteous down through the centuries.

It is of interest that John notes they fall down *"before the Lamb"*. While some have attempted to show by this chapter that the Lamb is the second person in the Godhead taking the book from the first person, the Father, in the Godhead, this is not the way it is at all.

The vision is to reveal the One who alone is worthy of opening the seven-sealed book. He is worthy, not because He is God - but because He has been to Calvary. Because He was the Lamb which taketh away the sins of the world.

For one to say there are two persons in this passage is to stretch their imagination somewhat. And yet, at the same time it would not be an intelligent statement to state that He was taking the book out of His own hand. That would be like saying He was His own father. We are more intelligent than to say that.

What we do witness here is Jesus as Son. Jesus as Lamb. God produced a body which He called the Son of God. The flesh was the Son of God. It was that flesh which was the Lamb of God. It was that flesh which went to Calvary and paid the price of redemption for all of us.

John is here witnessing that sacrifice - as the Lamb - laying claim on that which He has rightfully paid for through His own sacrifice on Calvary.

Verse 9:

And they sung a new song, saying, Thou art worthy to take the book, and to open the seals thereof: for thou wast slain, and hast redeemed us to God by thy blood out of every kindred, and tongue, and people, and nation;

Job (38:7), spoke of how *the morning stars (angels) sang together*, and all the sons of God shouted for joy when the creation was made. But here is a song like had never been sung before! No one has ever heard nor sung this song - whether in heaven or on this earth.

They have harps - millions of them! - as they sing praises and thanksgiving to the Lamb who has redeemed them.

Now, the twenty-four elders who may be representatives of the entire body of the saved, are singing, but it is evident that from what is said here that it is more than just the twenty-four elders singing this song - "hast redeemed us to God by thy blood out of every kindred, and tongue, and people, and nation". Here is a song of praise which resounds all over heaven. The redeemed are singing!!!

Now some of today's religious would not feel at ease singing this song. Because they do not sing it in their services on the earth. Examine their hymnals and you will find that they have removed the songs about the blood out of them. They wouldn't feel comfortable singing this song, as the redeemed praise the Lamb for shedding His blood to redeem them. Of course, I would doubt that those who refuse to sing about the blood now will have much to worry about being faced with having to sing it then! If you can't sing about the blood now - you won't sing about it then!

Verse 10:

And hast made us unto our God kings and priests: and we shall reign on the earth.

We find that some three times the Revelation states that the saints are made kings and priests (1:6, 5:10, 20:6). Just exactly what this implies we will have to wait to find out, but somehow during that time of the Kingdom Age when Jesus shall reign as King of kings and Lord of lords, we shall reign with Him over this earth. How and in what capacity, we do not know for sure. We can, however, state that there is a glorious future which awaits those who will make up their mind now to live for God.

Verse 11:

And I beheld, and I heard the voice of many angels round about the throne and the beasts and the elders: and the number of them was ten thousand times ten thousand, and thousands of thousands;

John hears in the background - and all around - the singing of the redeemed. The happy voices of an innumerable host of angels as they join in this time of praise and thanksgiving.

It is beyond our finite mind to fully grasp just what kind of sound this will be when the host of the redeemed - which no doubt will number into the millions - is joined by the innumerable host of angels.

No earthly choir has ever assembled to come anywhere near that sound. In fact, all the choirs of the earth, if they gathered together could not compare with that heavenly choir which will be singing in that day.

The term ten thousand is taken from the Greek word "murias", which means an innumerable number. A number which cannot be counted for number. The same word is found in Hebrews 12:22, where there we find it translated - innumerable. There is no way we could count that number of angels which are before the Lord.

Verse 12:

Saying with a loud voice, Worthy is the Lamb that was slain to receive power, and riches, and wisdom, and strength, honour, and glory, and blessing.

This is the second doxology in the Revelation. The first one (4:11) was for the Lord's work of creation. This one is for His work of redemption.

Note there are seven attributes spoken of here directed to the Lord Jesus. Consider some other scriptures which are parallel passages, employing the same Greek work as are found here in this seven-fold praise:

POWER – *"DUNAMIS"*… as the sun shineth in his strength (Revelation 1: 16). RICHES – *"PLOUTOS"*… But my God shall supply all your needs according to His riches in glory by Christ Jesus (Ephesians 4:19)

WISDOM – *"SOPHIA"*… For the wisdom of this world is foolishness with God (1Corinthians 3:19).

STRENGTH – *"ISKUS"*… And thou shalt love the Lord thy God ... with all thy strength (Mark 12:30).

HONOUR – *"TIMEE"* ... crowned with glory and honour (Hebrews 2:9).

GLORY – *"DOXA"* ... to whom be praise and dominion for ever (1Peter 4:11).

BLESSING – *"EULOGIA"* ... the fulness of the blessing of the gospel of Christ (Romans 15:29).

Verse 13:

And every creature which is in heaven, and on the earth, and under the earth, and such as are in the sea, and all that are in them, heard I saying, Blessing, and honour, and glory, and power *{be} unto him that sitteth upon the throne, and unto the Lamb for ever and ever.*

Redemption for this world will involve more than just that number which John sees around the throne. The curse of bondage brought about due to the fall of man in the garden involved more than just Adam and his sons. The curse touches all of creation. Paul spoke of *how the whole creation groaneth and travaileth in pain together until now .... waiting for the adoption, to wit, the redemption of our body*, (Romans 8:22,23).

Is the animal creation concerned about redemption? You better believe they are. Listen to the words of the Psalmist: *Praise the Lord from the earth .... beasts, and all cattle; creeping things, and flying fowl* (148:7-10).

The effect of the curse touched the animal world as it did the human family. When redemption is brought about for this world this curse will be lifted and the wolf and the lamb shall feed together (Isaiah 65:25).

Peace shall permeate the entire of God's creation when the King reigns.

Verse 14:

And the four beasts said, Amen. And the four {and} twenty elders fell down and worshipped him that liveth for ever and ever.

The whole assemblage, upon concluding their song of praise, falls down in worship to the one of whom they were singing.

While John describes for us what happens in two or three verses, or so, we cannot begin to fully grasp just what it will be like when this actually takes place.

One thing is for certain: It will be a great time of praise and worship. A time when the heavens will ring with the sounds of the redeemed praising their Redeemer. It is little wonder that the Lord takes His redeemed off this earth for this time of rejoicing. Such singing and worship would no doubt cause tidal waves - maybe even cause buildings to fall down - or whatever!!!!

• THIS WILL BE A REDEEMED HOST WITH REDEEMED BODIES ...

CHAPTER SIX

THE WEEK IS HERE!

When we say the WEEK, just what does this have reference to anyway? What week? Why the term week? Are you talking about seven days?

Well, the week is that last week of the Times of the Gentiles which the Bible speaks about. It is the last seven years of the four hundred and ninety that Daniel was told would come upon his people Israel.

Right at the beginning of the chapter we are confronted with some interesting characters; Four horses with riders riding forth across the land. Who are these riders? What are they doing?

The last week, or seven years, prior to the Lord's return to this earth will be filled with a lot of activity. In fact, with the tremendous increase of activity in our own day it would seem that the world is gearing up for those last seven years.

The majority of the book of Revelation is taken up with the account of what takes place during those last seven years before the Lord returns to this earth. The first three chapters of Revelation cover a period of about two thousand years, while the following sixteen chapters are dealing primarily with only even years!!!

This emphasizes to us the importance which the Lord placed upon these closing seven years.

Chapter six begins the week. Chapters four and five are like a pause between the rapture and the beginning of the week, before the action actually begins. When it does begin, though, it will not end until the Lord comes and brings an end to the activities of the beast and all those who will be involved in the battle of Armageddon.

THE WEEK BEGINS ...

Chapter five has ended. The singing fades away. The One who alone is worthy to claim the earth as His own, and who alone is worthy therefore to loosen the seven-sealed book has been identified.

In this seven-sealed book is the record of events which will reveal the events which will come upon the earth during this time of the end. Events which will bring about the expulsion of those who have usurped authority of this earth.

All eyes must be on the Lamb as he takes the book to begin opening the seven seals. The opening of the first seal will begin the most momentous events which this earth has ever experienced. No period of man's history can compare with the following seven years which are about to begin as the first seal is opened. When this week of seven years has finished the earth's, rightful King will be revealed and He will come in great power and glory to reign upon this earth. Those who have usurped ownership of this earth shall be destroyed and truth shall triumph!

For at least six millenniums the earth has been in the sway and under the influence of this enemy of God and His will for His creation. His influence is evident by the condition in which we find the world and her inhabitants living in at this time. Sin is openly accepted. Immoral lifestyles have become classified as "sexual preference." Humanist theories have taught man that he should believe in himself. That he does not need a higher power. A Supreme Being, to direct his life.

Little by little the moral fiber of the world has eroded through the years, until, at last, to be moral is to be a misfit in this society. To rebuke sin and debauchery is to be labeled a "Religious fanatic."

But the tide is about to turn. The day of sin is just about to end. The Seal of Judgment that will begin the final week of man's day is just about to open.

THE SEVENTY WEEKS

It was Daniel who received the vision of the Seventy Weeks. He read about it through the studying of the writings of the prophet Jeremiah, while he was in Babylonian captivity. Daniel understood that Israel would only spend seventy years in Babylonian captivity. That after seventy years, during which time the land would enjoy her Sabbaths, Israel would be permitted to return to her land and to rebuild their cities. Realizing this period was about up, Daniel began to pray and fast for the nation of Israel.

During this period of confession to God and consecration, Daniel received a heavenly visitor who came to inform him that the seventy years which he had been praying about and studying, had another, and far more significant, meaning. So, Daniel was told about the seventy weeks of years which had been pronounced upon his people Israel. We find all of this in chapter nine of the book of Daniel, beginning with verse twenty-four.

Now the expression "seventy weeks" literally means seventy sevens of years. If the angel of the Lord had meant actual days, it would have no doubt been expressed as it is in chapter ten and verse three.

It is of interest to notice that God has ever dealt with His people Israel in periods of time which, it would appear, could be divided into periods of four hundred and ninety years each:

- 1. The call of Abraham to the settling of the Land of Promise, approximately 490 years.

- 2. The time of the Judges to the first king of Israel, approximately 490 years.

- 3. From the time of the first king of Israel, Saul, to the dispersion to Babylonian captivity, approximately 490 years.

- 4. Now Daniel's vision of 490 years which will involve the remainder of his people's history to the time of their Messiah's return to this earth to establish His kingdom among them.

This vision given to Daniel of the "seventy weeks" is one of the most important recorded in the Word of God! It sets the date of the first coming of Jesus Christ, and gives the length of the reign of the antichrist.

When the angel Gabriel came to Daniel, he informed Daniel that while his people would be restored to their homeland at the end of the seventy years, which he had been studying about in the writings of Jeremiah, the prophecy would also involve a much longer period of time. Gabriel also told Daniel that the longer period would be for four hundred and ninety years! Or, seventy weeks. Gabriel also told Daniel the reason for these seventy weeks, or 490 years which his people would endure. In fact, he gave him six reasons!

In everything God has done with His creation there has been purpose and there has been order. This is no exception. The things which Daniel is told about to happen to his people is for a purpose.

Let us consider the reason for these 490 years that Israel must go through before they will have their Messiah reigning over them.

• 1. TO FINISH THE TRANSGRESSION.

Israel was in bondage right then because of her transgression against God. In a short while they would enjoy a few years of respite. During this time, they would return to their homeland and rebuild their city and their Temple. They would suffer more trouble. In a little over five hundred more years their Messiah would come whom they would reject and this would result in them being driven out into an even longer period of dispersion than the one they were ending in the days of Daniel.

The height of their transgression against God must have been when they cried in judgment hall CRUCIFY HIM! CRUCIFY HIM! They continue to abide in their transgressions till this day. It will only be when their Messiah does return to this earth to bring victory and deliverance to them that they will at long last acknowledge Him as Messiah, and the long period of transgressions will at last come to an end. That is the purpose of this last seven year period - to bring about this glorious end!

• 2. TO MAKE AN END OF SINS.

Sin is a "missing of the mark." Israel has missed the mark many times in their past history. She is out of fellowship with God at the present due to the fact that she did not recognize Jesus as their Messiah.

The fire of tribulation which Israel will endure in this time of the end will be for the purpose of purifying them. (Zechariah 13:9). In this we see the love and mercy which God has for his people Israel.

Though Israel has sinned against the Lord time and again through the years, He will yet lay His hand upon them to bring about their salvation. It will take the fires of tribulation to purify Israel from their sins.

• 3. TO MAKE RECONCILIATION FOR INIQUITY.

Reconciliation for sins was made on Calvary when Jesus shed His blood for sin. But Israel, as a nation, has not appropriated this blessing upon themselves. Because of this they continue with their sin upon their record. Notice Ezekiel 36:24-30, where the prophet speaks of the time when the Lord shall bring about a cleansing to His people Israel.

When the seven year period of tribulation is completed Israel will once again be reconciled to their God. Remember Jesus told them they would not see Him again until they would say: Blessed is He that cometh in the Name of the Lord. Having rejected Jesus, they refused their opportunity to be reconciled to their God.

• 4. TO BRING IN EVERLASTING RIGHTEOUSNESS.

There have been momentary periods when Israel has enjoyed sweet fellowship with their God. Times when they walked in the will of God and enjoyed His bountiful blessings upon their life. But it has been many years since that time! Israel for many years now has been without a king, without a prophet, without the glory of the Lord upon them. They are anything but RIGHT with God at this time.

But when the clouds of tribulation have all cleared away, when the King comes to reign on this earth and over His people Israel, this will begin a period of EVERLASTING RIGHTEOUSNESS. Never again will Israel be dispersed. Never again will they be without the fellowship of their God. Never again will they be without their King.

• 5. TO SEAL UP THE VISION AND PROPHECY

These events which the angel is informing Daniel about will bring a complete end to the prophecies and visions relative to the people of Israel. When they at last have all been fulfilled, then Israel shall rejoice in complete peace and victory with their Messiah.

Much of the Bible is taken up with prophecies concerning this people. Most of the book of Revelation is prophecies concerning this people. The last seven year period will see the fulfillment of final prophecies concerning this people.

• 6. TO ANOINT THE MOST HOLY.

The prophet Ezekiel speaks to us about a beautiful temple which will be built in the Middle East. It is not the temple which the man of sin enters - but the Temple which Israel shall worship in during the time of the Kingdom Age. This prophecy probably has reference to the anointing of the most holy place of this temple.

While some seem to be of the opinion that this has reference to the anointing of the Lord Jesus when He returns to this earth, it does not appear that this is what the prophecy is speaking about. The term "MOST HOLY" is never found employed in the Bible referring to a person! It refers to a place!

The temple will be built when Israel has at last been brought through their purging fires of tribulation. When they at last are cleansed from their sins and transgressions and are thus ready for such a temple. They are not in a spiritual condition now to worship God as long as they are out of favor and fellowship with Him. The fires of tribulation will take care of that problem.

THREE PERIODS...

Now it does not take much of an imagination to see that the angel of the Lord separated this period of 490 years into three separate periods of time.

FIRST - The seven sevens, or forty-nine years. During this time Israel would return to their home- land and rebuild their temple.

SECOND - This period would involve sixty-two weeks, or 434 years. This would take Israel to the time when their Messiah would be cut off. This speaks of Calvary and the crucifixion of Jesus Christ.

THIRD - This is the period which is yet to be fulfilled. Seven years remains of the seventy weeks. This has prompted the term "Daniel's Seventieth Week." There has been a long parenthesis between the sixty-ninth and seventieth week. During this time the Lord has been taking out of the Gentiles a "people for His name."

So, as we approach this final week of man's day: the last years of the TIMES OF THE GENTILES, we find excitement in the air! So much is going to happen in these final seven years that it is over-whelming just to consider its significance.

But the first seal is just about to open to begin this final week of unrivaled events which shall come upon this earth.

THE SEALS ARE OPENED...

<u>Verse 1:</u>

And I saw when the Lamb opened one of the seals, and I heard, as it were the noise of thunder, one of the four beasts saying, Come and see.

AND I SAW... This is a very familiar term employed by John throughout the book of Revelation.

John is a witness to the events which unfold before him prophetically. He was chosen by God to be the eyewitness of these last days exciting events.

It is the Lamb Himself who begins to open the seven-sealed book. He is the one whose right it is to pronounce the time for the judgments to come upon the world and thus bring about the deliverance of the earth out of the hands of the usurpers and into His own hands.

There must necessarily be a purging of the people of Israel to bring about their salvation and deliverance. And there must necessarily be a final showdown, as it were, between the forces of good and evil. Man, in his evil plans must be made to realize that it is God who rules in the heavens and who is in control of this planet as well. Those who have, and will, openly oppose God and righteousness, will in that day be made to realize that God is not only a real force, but also will not tolerate the ungodly ways of mankind.

AND I HEARD, AS IT WERE, THE NOISE OF THUNDER... It is important that we notice this statement by John. As the Lamb prepares to open the first seal John hears a noise that sounded to him like thunder. A descriptive term for the coming storm which is about to be unleashed upon this world of evil. The storm mankind is about to experience will be such as has never been known by any previous generation of the sons of Adam!

COME AND SEE... This is the statement made by one of the living creatures. Some feel that in the original the statement was only "COME." That the creature is not talking to John, but rather to the horseman to come forth. Yet in every instance, except when the second seal is opened, we hear John responding by stating, *And I saw... And I beheld...* And I looked. John is being invited, it would seem, to behold the panoramic view which is being unfolded before him of the events which will take place in the last of the times of the Gentiles.

What John may at first have considered a terrible circumstance in which to find himself, banned to this desolate Island called Patmos, all for preaching the Gospel, he soon realized that it was all for the will and purpose of God to be fulfilled in his life.

If John had not been faithful to proclaim the Word of God, and thus to bring the wrath of the people upon him, and to be ultimately banned to this island, then he would not have received from the Lord these wonderful visions which he recorded in the Revelation.

In this we are reminded that regardless of how the outward circumstances may look in our life, if we are walking in the will of the Lord, there is a purpose for everything which happens in our life.

It may not at first seem too bright, but if we are faithful the Lord will bring us through to great victories.

Those responsible for banning John to this island probably felt that by doing so they would get him out of commission. What they were really doing was getting John into a position and condition to where he could witness the things which God showed him in the Revelation.

THE WHITE HORSE AND RIDER...

Verse 2:

And I saw, and behold a white horse: and he that sat on him had a bow; and a crown was given unto him: and he went forth conquering, and to conquer.

Now, here is where we get into different opinions as to just who this first horse rider is. Some contend that this is Jesus riding forth bringing forth the judgments upon this earth. But this does not seem to be right to us. Jesus is the one who is opening the seals. Would He be opening the seals and carrying out what the seals reveal as well?

At least one commentator was of the opinion that this is the Church riding forth to bring judgment to the earth. That as saints are seen wearing white in chapter nineteen, and they are involved in the judgment of the earth, they are the ones depicted here riding forth on the white horse. Again, we must disagree with this opinion. The main reason we would disagree is the fact that the Church is not here during this period of time. She has been raptured BEFORE this period begins. The Church is not involved in the tribulation until the time of Armageddon when she returns with the Lord to bring victory to His people Israel, and destruction to the empire of the beast.

It is our opinion that this must be the man of sin. The anti-christ, who is riding forth. He is beginning his conquest in search of world power.

It would appear that what John is describing is that of an individual. He is given a crown. There is a bow in his hand.

It will be the purpose of the man of sin when he appears on the scene to come forth conquering as this rider is shown doing.

Now, the troubles which follow with the succeeding three horses are indicative of that which follows one who is ambitious in his plans to conquer. There will be trouble which will be left in the wake of the man of sin.

When the man of sin comes, he shall come with flatteries and false promises as the Bible informs us in such places as Daniel 7:8, 24-26.

Another thing one should consider is the fact that unless this is the man of sin, when is he revealed in the Revelation? If he is not revealed here, then we do not find him revealed until we get to the middle of the week in chapter thirteen. This would not be harmony with other prophecies relative to his coming. He shall confirm the covenant with Israel for one week (Daniel 9:27), and it would be necessary that this take place at the beginning of the week.

Some have made a play on the fact that while he is mentioned having a bow in his hand, there is no mention of any arrows. They take this to mean that he is appearing in a peaceful manner. While this may be true, at the same time we would enquire, what does a man have a bow for if he does not plan to use it? To those who get in his way he will employ whatever force is necessary to get what he wants!

Somehow this man shall be elevated to a high position of authority and power. How he attains this position we are not told. We do have some hints, I suppose we should call them, in such statements as; ... *come in peaceably and obtain the kingdom by flatteries*, (Daniel 11:21). In fact, DECEIT, FLATTERIES, PEACEABLE, are words which we find Daniel employing to mark the coming of the antichrist.

When he attains this position of power, it will be one of the greatest deceptions the world has known since the woman ate the forbidden fruit in the Garden.

Because of the trouble which besets the world today, we find a generation who is ripe for such a man to enter the scene. We feel the only reason he has not made his entrance as of yet is because the Church is still here. Mercy is still extended. The signs of the end time are all around us. We know of no prophecy which needs to be fulfilled before the Lord could come back for His Church!

SOME COMPARISONS...

The similarities of Matthew twenty-four and Revelation six are so great that they are worthy of our consideration at this point. Jesus is answering the three-fold question put to Him by His Apostles: ... *when shall these things be? and what {shall be} the sign of thy coming, and of the end of the world?* Matthew 24:3.

The very first sign Jesus spoke of was: *Take heed that no man deceive you,* Verse 4. This man riding on this white horse, coming forth to dazzle the world with his brilliance is the great deceiver. He shall deceive Israel into accepting his confirmation of their covenant. He shall deceive the world into thinking that he has the answers to the problems which beset the world.

The next sign which Jesus gave was: *And ye shall hear of wars and rumours of wars: see that ye be not troubled,* Verse 6.

A comparison of this warning with what the second horse and rider brings to the scene reveals that it is speaking of the same thing.

The third sign Jesus gave was: *...and there shall be famines...* Verse 7.

Again, we see the third horse and rider brings such a famine to the world that the rider is seen carrying a pair of "balances" in his hand.

The fourth sign Jesus gave was: *... pestilence ...* Verse 7.

This is the fourth horse and rider which is the pale horse of death and hell.

The fifth sign Jesus gives: *...there shall be earthquakes in divers places...* Verse 7.

This speaks of the opening of the sixth seal in Revelation six which brings about the great earthquake upon the earth.

Now, one could go into greater detail in comparing these passages, but suffice it to say that the evidence seems strong enough to conclude that Jesus was warning those who would be spiritually alert of the days of trouble which will soon come upon His people Israel in the last dreadful and dark days of tribulation.

The increase in these conditions in our generation, should be a warning to all of us that the day of the Lord's return for His church must be near at hand. No other generation has witnessed the widespread, and great increase, as well as simultaneous occurrences, of these signs which Jesus spoke about in Matthew twenty-four.

Jesus warned all of us in Luke 21:28, *And when these things begin to come to pass, then look up, and lift up your heads; for your redemption draweth nigh.*

• IT MUST BE LOOKING UP TIME!

THE SECOND SEAL IS OPENED:

Verses 3, 4:

And when he had opened the second seal, I heard the second beast say, Come and see. And there went out another horse {that was} red: and {power} was given to him that sat thereon to take peace from the earth, and that they should kill one another: and there was given unto him a great sword.

The opening of the second seal produces the riding forth of the second horse and rider. This horse is RED. He was given power to take peace from the earth, and that they should kill one another: and there was given unto him a great sword.

This statement seems to allude to the fact that there had been peace previous to this on the earth. The first horse and rider brought peace to the troubled world. What kind of peace, and how that peace came about, we are not told. But, there is one thing which does seem obvious - the peace was short-lived!

There can be no lasting peace on this earth, regardless of who is president or leader of world forces, until the Prince of Peace comes and brings peace. What peace man may be able to bring about through treaties, or threat, will not last. It is destined, according to the Word of God, to not last long!

While the man of sin is shown as being a man of peace on the first horse, there is really war and hatred in his heart. His words may be smooth as butter, as the Old Testament writer put it, but war is in his heart. This horse and rider is beginning to show the true colors of the man of sin and his kingdom of evil.

The ultimate goal of the man of sin will be world dominance. To gain that position, he will bring about a patched-up, make-believe, peace. A peace which the world will fall for. In fact, John informs us that the world will be found later to wonder after the beast. (13:3).

The desperation of the hour will bring men to their knees. They will in turn become willing to surrender their freedom and lives to the one who promises them peace. A peace which he not only cannot produce, but which he does not really intend to produce!

THE THIRD SEAL...

Verse 5:

And when he had opened the third seal, I heard the third beast say, Come and see. And I beheld, and lo a black horse; and he that sat on him had a pair of balances in his hand.

Each horse rider is seen carrying some kind of weapon in his hand. The first is shown with a bow. The second one has a great sword in his hand. The third one at first notice may not appear to be a weapon, but upon closer examination, one realizes that he probably has the most deadly of all the weapons thus far!

Verse 6:

And I heard a voice in the midst of the four beasts say, A measure of wheat for a penny, and three measures of barley for a penny; and {see} thou hurt not the oil and the wine.

He is shown with a pair of balances in his hand. He controls the power of commerce. It has been stated by different people that he who controls the economy of a nation also controls the nation! This weapon is more deadly inasmuch as people will have to either bow to the demands of this rider or suffer the awful consequences of starvation and deprivation.

When the world computer, which we are told is located in the European Economic Communities country of Belgium, begins to function in its completed state: That is when the other nations of the Western World Nations are completely connected and functional, then the plan spoken of by John in Revelation thirteen becomes an awesome possibility. And when one considers that the man who is able to control the computer could also possibly control the economy system of the Western World, then it certainly becomes evident that it can become a reality.

World conditions are getting to such a place that all of this is becoming more of a possibility with each passing month.

There are several who strongly feel that the monetary conditions which exist in the Western World today is not the result of happenstance. That it is being planned and brought about by those who control the currency systems of the Western Nations.

114

This horse and rider seems to be speaking to us of that time when men will be compelled to accept the system which will be offered by the beast.

THE FOURTH SEAL ...

Verse 7:

And when he had opened the fourth seal, I heard the voice of the fourth beast say, Come and see.

Verse 8:

And I looked, and behold a pale horse: and his name that sat on him was Death, and Hell followed with him. And power was given unto them over the fourth part of the earth, to kill with sword, and with hunger, and with death, and with the beasts of the earth.

The opening of the fourth seal reveals to John a pale horse (corpse-like color) riding forth on the scene. Following this pale horse was hades. There is no mention of another horse and rider which is hades. It would seem that hades is the result of what this horse and rider brings to the world. The pale horse is bringing death to mankind.

It is of interest to note that the Greek word translated PALE here is "chloros." It is the same word which is employed to note the color of grass in Mark 6:39. That, of course, is green. Green in typology speaks of life. Yet this rider is called death. How significant! What the man of sin promises to mankind is just the opposite of what he actually brings to them.

Another interesting note here concerning the death which this rider brings to mankind; It is said that *power was given unto them over the fourth part of the earth, to kill with sword, and with hunger, and with death, and with the beasts of the earth.*

This seems to emphasize the tremendous amount of life which will be lost during this period of time. Many will evidently refuse to accept the beast and his policies, knowing that to do so will result in their sealing their doom eternally.

The very fact that many will refuse to submit to the demands of the beast will no doubt merely enrage him that much more and bring about more bloodshed. Defeat and refusal are two words which he will not be able to tolerate.

The word translated here, "BEASTS", is from the Greek word "theerion." The word which is used to describe the four BEASTS before the throne, and who announce these four horses and their riders, is NOT the same Greek word! The Greek word for these four creatures is "zoon." The Greek word "theerion" means a wild, or dangerous, or venomous beast. It is used at least thirty-eight times in the Revelation, and in every place it is used it is used as a symbol for an ungodly, wicked leader!

So, these beasts of the earth could be speaking about those who share the spotlight with the man of sin and do his dirty work for him. It is for sure the man of sin will be surrounded with a lot of henchmen who will carry out his commands. They will have no feelings for the life of others. They will probably be, like the man of sin himself, possessed by the devil himself!

The horrors which this world will know during that time are beyond our mind to fully comprehend at this point in time. Those who are not a part of the Body of Christ and who are left behind when the rapture takes place, will face these horrible conditions which John is writing to us about here as the seals are opened.

When it speaks of a fourth of the world being killed by the fourth horse and his rider, this reveals to us the horrors of that hour which the world will know. If we are to consider the fourth part of the world population, then we are to consider well over one billion people!! Even if we are only to consider one fourth of those nations which are involved with the Beast and his reign - that is, the Western nations - we are still faced with an astronomical figure of death and mayhem which will cover the land in that dark hour!

We have read and shuddered at the record of deaths which have been brought about by the communist leaders such as Stalin of Russia, and Mao of China. Men who had no feelings for the life of others.

Without blinking an eye they could issue orders which would result in the deaths of millions. But how does their record compare with that one which is to come?!

THE FIFTH SEAL ...

<u>Verse 9:</u>

And when he had opened the fifth seal, I saw under the altar the souls of them that were slain for the word of God, and for the testimony which they held:

The opening of the fifth seal presents to John an entirely different scene than what he had been thus far witnessing. He sees an altar, and under the altar, the souls of men who have been put to death for their testimony.

The altar is a familiar sight to John. It is the brazen altar of sacrifice which stood before the Temple and upon which the sacrifices of the people were offered. But who are these under the altar?

It is evident that these are NOT Church saints who have died in times past. For they have been resurrected when the Lord took His church out of this world. And, besides, they are under the altar which has a Jewish connotation. This would not apply to the Church. Nor would we consider the prayers which John hears coming from these martyrs as being prayed by Church saints. Saints would not pray this type of prayer.

THEIR PRAYER

Verse 10:

And they cried with a loud voice, saying, How long, 0 Lord, holy and true, dost thou not judge and avenge our blood on them that dwell on the earth?

Who are they? Consider that once the church has been raptured there will no doubt be many people who will open their Bible's once again to consider what has taken place all around them. Realizing that they have been left behind, they will no doubt begin to consider what, if anything, they can do to avoid an eternal damnation. The only answer for many will be for them to sacrifice their own life in refusing to surrender to the beast and his policies. There is no doubt that many will do just that and will give their life rather than be lost eternally in the lake of fire.

Consider that at the beginning of the tribulation all the true believers have been raptured. When the tribulation begins, there are no true believers in the strict sense of the word. That is Church saints.

Members of the Body of Christ. There will, however, be plenty of people who were church members who will be here at the beginning of the tribulation. People who have been exposed to the Word of God even though they did not obey it to the degree of being born into the family of God.

Something must happen here during the first few months, or years, of the tribulation period which results in many being convinced of their need to refuse the demands of the beast. Could it have something to do with the 144,000 which are sealed in chapter seven? (See our chapter on them.)

Also, remember, that for three and one-half years of the tribulation the Lord will have His two witnesses preaching against the beast and his plans. Can we imagine what influence these two witnesses will have upon the people!

Consider as well all the Apostolic Churches which will stand as mute reminders of the truth which once echoed from them! What kind of influence will these silent witnesses have upon the people during this terrible time!

There will no doubt be many contributing factors which will all work together to bring about the saving of many during this dark period.

These have withstood the beast and his message which has resulted in them feeling the sting of the beast's wrath which has resulted in their death. They chose death over living during the reign of the beast, and then spending an eternity in the Lake of Fire.

It would seem evident from their prayers that these are not Church saints. We live in the dispensation of mercy. In a time when our Master told us to love our enemies. As they cry for the Lord to avenge their blood, it reminds us of the imprecatory prayers to be found in such places as Psalm 35:55: 59: and 94.

Verse 11:

And white robes were given unto everyone of them; and it was said unto them, that they should rest yet for a little season, until their fellow servants also and their brethren, that should be killed as they {were}, should be fulfilled.

White robes were given to them. (How do they give white robes to souls?) While we may not be able to fully understand nor explain this statement, it certainly informs us that the Lord considered their life to be righteous and just enough to be clothed in white robes, which speaks of righteousness.

Then they are told that they must wait yet for a little season, until their fellow servants also and their brethren, that should be killed as they were, should be fulfilled. So, there are others who shall suffer the same fate during this dark period of seven years.

Possibly John is shown these at the beginning of the week to give us the proper perspective concerning those who will die during this week. They are evidently among the first who suffer martyrdom during the week. There will be others, probably many others, who will as well give their life rather than submit to the demands put upon them by the beast and his system of evil.

These are among that number which we will find later when we get to chapter twenty who shall be called forth at the end of the tribulation to reign with Christ and the redeemed during the millennium.

The terrible price which they paid may seem so cruel at this point in the tribulation, but the end result will be glorious. After all, it is the end results which are the most important. So, what if we miss out on a few things in this life because of our decision to live for God, we will not miss these things while we are walking down the street of gold in that beautiful City of God!

THE SIXTH SEAL...

<u>Verse 12:</u>

And I beheld when he had opened the sixth seal, and, lo, there was a great earthquake; and the sun became black as sackcloth of hair, and the moon became as blood;

And I beheld... Again, John speaks as an eyewitness of the events which are taking place. He does not explain how he sees these things. Whether he sees them in his mind, or whether, somehow, he is shown them appearing in vision form before him, possibly in the heavens. However, John is seeing these things, he is recording them just as he sees them.

What he sees at the loosening of the sixth seal is a very frightening scene.

There was a great earthquake... By John making mention of the earthquake occurring makes us to realize that this is no ordinary earthquake. (If there is such a thing!) This earthquake, however, must be greater than any previous one that has shook this earth before. It seems to be a herald of things to come.

Up until now we have been reading about what man is doing during the tribulation. The four horsemen who have been riding forth bringing with them their problems for humanity. The souls seen under the altar, which is a result of what man has done.

When we get to the sixth seal, however, we find that it is God who is bringing these events upon the earth because of what man is doing!

This begins that period of time when mankind - rebellious mankind - will witness the wrath of God upon them.

Mr. Dake, in his book, Revelation Expounded, stated: "There are to be four great earthquakes during Daniel's Seventieth Week."

These four great earthquakes, each brought about by the wrath of God, are seen:

• 1. Here with the sixth seal being opened.

• 2. When the seventh seal is loosened, 8:5.

• 3. When the seventh trumpet sounds, 11:9.

• 4. When the two witnesses ascend, 11:13.

When Jesus Christ was crucified the sun refused to shine, the sky got dark. There was an earthquake. All of these heavenly phenomena showing God's displeasure with what was being done by sinful man. During this time of the wrath of God upon man during the tribulation, we will once again see that God is showing His displeasure at what sinful man is doing on this earth.

The dark days of tribulation are marked at their beginning and their ending with heavenly phenomenon.

The sun becoming black as sackcloth of hair, and the moon becoming as blood are events which we are to take as actually occurring. When this period begins, there is no doubt left in the minds of men as to why it is happening. They know that it is the wrath of God!

The man of sin may attempt to explain it away as to some atmospheric problem, but the man on the street will know that it is God who is showing His displeasure at what is taking place on this earth. We are not to suppose that because of what is happening here with the sun and moon, that this means they cease to function. That is, we are not being informed that the sun and moon will cease to function when this seal is opened. It is evident from the further study of the Revelation, that this is not the case at all. In fact, when we get to chapter sixteen and the pouring out of the vials of wrath, we will find that the sun at that time becomes so hot as to scorch men!

This is one of the many cosmic events which will be brought upon mankind during these dark days.

- There will be others to follow!

Verse 13:

And the stars of heaven fell unto the earth, even as a fig tree casteth her untimely figs, when she is shaken of a mighty wind.

The stars of heaven fell unto the earth... Again, it would not be possible to take this statement to mean actual stars falling to this earth. We know from science that stars are, in many cases at least, much larger than the earth. There would be no way that the stars could fall upon this earth.

This reference to stars is taken from the Greek word "aster," which has reference to any luminous body. What John evidently saw was a great rain of meteorites as they rained down upon the earth.

Heaven is putting on a vivid display before the eyes of all mankind. It is as if heaven is saying to the inhabitants of earth that it is not pleased with the affairs of men. And it is evident from the reaction of those dwelling on this earth at that time they are aware of this fact!

Verse 14:

And the heaven departed as a scroll when it is rolled together; and every mountain and island were moved out of their places.

And the heaven departed as a scroll... This is more of the heavenly manifestation of God's displeasure of mankind. Again, we are not to think that it is at this time that 2Peter 3:10 is fulfilled. Heaven does not pass away at this time. Continuing our study in the Revelation will reveal this. But something awesome is happening in the heavens and witnessed upon this earth by those who are living here at that time. Something which brings a terrible fear to all those dwelling on this earth at that time.

God is witnessing to mankind that heaven is disturbed by the actions of man.

and every mountain and island were moved out of their place... The effect of the earthquake and the cosmic disturbances are witnessed upon the mountains and islands. They are seen by John trembling and moving about by the terrible shaking which the earth is undergoing by the earthquake of God's judgment upon this earth.

Keep in mind that this is the beginning of the judgments of God's wrath upon this earth. This is merely the sixth seal being opened. There are seven trumpets to sound forth after this. There are three woes to come upon the earth after this. There are seven bowls to be poured out yet, after this! This is the beginning of that very dark period of time when God moves upon the affairs of mankind which are displeasing to Him.

• What a terrible day to be living on this earth!

• What a wonderful day to be living with the Lord at that time in the heavens!

Verse 15:

And the kings of the earth, and the great men, and the rich men, and the chief captains, and the mighty men, and every bondman, and every free man, hid themselves in the dens and in the rocks of the mountains;

And the kings of the earth, and the great men, and the rich men ... People from all walks of life have their attention riveted on the display of awesome power which the heavens are presenting, as well as the earth which is shaking beneath their feet.

Men who had in the previous months helped to persecute, and to slay, those who dared resist the beast and his plans, are now staring into the judgments of the wrath of the God whom they represented.

They may have laughed at those puny people who fell beneath their hands, but they are not laughing now at their God!

Verse 16:

And said to the mountains and rocks, Fall on us, and hide us from the face of him that sitteth on the throne, and from the wrath of the Lamb:

People everywhere will be seeking shelter from the rain of the meteorites; from the tumbling of the buildings affected by the earthquakes; from the great tidal waves created from the islands moving out of their place by the earthquake. They who have refused the ROCK OF AGES are now seeking refuge in the caves and mountains of the earth. Any place that appears to be a place of safety from the troubles which are falling all around them.

... and from the wrath of the Lamb... Those who have embraced the atheistic and humanistic views that there is no God and man is his own god, are deserting these views enmass.

Those who denied the existence of God are now trying to find some place to hide from Him. They acknowledge Him in their cries! *Hide us from the face of Him that sitteth on the throne!*

John does not inform us that the mountains and rocks do fall on them to hide them from His face. We know there is no hiding place from the Lord Jesus Christ!

But what a paradox we find in the phrase, *the wrath of the Lamb...* We think of the term LAMB as applying to the gentleness and love; to the kindness and humbleness, of the character of Jesus Christ. It is difficult for us to vision the wrath of the Lamb! We associate the Lamb with submission to Calvary and death. We associate the Lamb with a meek spirit.

What we have here is anything but meekness! What we have here is an angry God. We have Jesus making another whip, this time, not to drive money changers from His temple, but to teach sinful men a lesson which they will remember eternally!

Is this the time that the prophet was speaking about when he wrote; For the day of the Lord of hosts shall be upon everyone that is proud and lofty .... *And they shall go into the holes of the rocks, and into the caves of the earth, for fear of the LORD, and for the glory of His majesty, when He ariseth to shake terribly the earth,* (Isaiah 2:12,19).

One would think that such a display of horror which is here displayed by the people, would bring them to their knees for mercy. One would think that there would be a great change of heart and attitude toward God and His power. But such is not the case! As we venture further into the Revelation, we will find that things seem to settle down a little, for a while at least, and men returning to their former ways.

Instead of finding them praying and seeking God, we find them later cursing God. Possibly they are told what they are witnessing was a freak cosmic storm which passed away. There will be, no doubt, some explanation for it from the beast and his cohorts. And evidently a lot of people must have believed them. The ways of man are foolish!

Verse 17:

For the great day of his wrath is come; and who shall be able to stand?

This is the day of the wrath of God upon evil mankind. Man, who has rejected the message of salvation which has been given through the years by His ministry and Church. Man has rejected the mercies which He has extended to them in their lifetime.

Who will be able to stand in this day? To those against whom God's judgment is meted out, there will be no place whatsoever that they will be able to hide from His judgment of wrath. They have refused the hiding place in the Rock of Ages. Now, they will experience facing these judgments of wrath without mercy - and without a hiding place.

CHAPTER SEVEN

• **A PAUSE IN THE ACTION ...**

Verse 1:

And after these things I saw four angels standing on the four corners of the earth, holding the four winds of the earth, that the wind should not blow on the earth, nor on the sea, nor on any tree.

AND AFTER THESE THINGS... We find John employing the term "After" quite a few times in the book of Revelation. While chapter seven has been thought of as being a parenthetical chapter, at the same time it would appear from this statement at the beginning of the chapter that it is a continuation of what John had just been describing to us in the previous chapter. It does, however, involve the opening of the sixth and seventh seal. So, it is possible we could take John's term here, After these things, as a term denoting an insertion here to inform us that God will not be without a witness during the dark times of chaos which will hang over the earth at that time like a blanket.

The angels of verse one are posed ready to unleash the judgments of God in their proper order.

John has just described for us the awful results of the opening of the first six seals. The sixth one being of such intensity that the heavens are affected by its power. There seems to be a terrible storm which shakes the entire cosmos. It causes people to cry for safety. Even crying for mountains and rocks to fall on them to hide them from the face of "*Him that sitteth on the throne.*"

Now, John is speaking to us of four mighty angels who are holding the winds back from blowing upon the earth. First there is a terrible tempest sweeping across the earth, and now there is a terrible calm.

The events which John is describing for us in the book of Revelation will be anything but a Sunday School picnic! First a great gale of terrible wind which will wreak havoc on the earth; and then an awesome stillness which will reach down into the soul of man!

The SEAL.

Verse 2:

And I saw another angel ascending from the east, having the seal of the living God: and he cried with a loud voice to the four angels, to whom it was given to hurt the earth and the sea,

This chapter presents to us an interesting study - among the many to be found in the book of Revelation. There are various opinions to be found among Bible scholars as to just what this chapter is all about.

Verse 3:

Saying, Hurt not the earth, neither the sea, nor the trees, till we have sealed the servants of our God in their foreheads.

John hears a mighty angel cry out to the four angels who are holding the four winds of the earth, to withhold their judgments until after he has sealed the "*servants of our God in their foreheads.*"

What is this seal which is placed in the foreheads of these tribes? Also, why the seal? If what is recorded for us in chapter fourteen has any bearing on our question, then it would seem that they will have the Name of Jesus inscribed on their foreheads (note 14:1).

If this is the case, then what a testimony! Here are 144,000 Jews; 12,000 from each tribe who are witnessing throughout the world with the name of Jesus on their forehead! Jesus, the one whom their forefathers rejected and had crucified!

Why are they sealed? Well, this has presented different opinions as well. Who is not familiar with the claim made by the Jehovah Witnesses that the 144,000 are those who will be saved from the earth.

Of course, this is not the only area in which they are so far off-base with their dogma!

Now, we find when we continue our study of the book of Revelation, that the time will come when the beast will issue a demand that all receive a mark in their right hand or forehead which will identify them with his system. Could this be, at least in part, in opposition to this group of 144,000 who have the name of their God in their forehead!

THE TWELVE TRIBES ....

Verses 4-8:

And I heard the number of them which were sealed: {and there were} sealed an hundred {and} forty {and} four thousand of all the tribes of the children of Israel. Of the tribe of Juda {were} sealed twelve thousand. Of the tribe of Reuben {were} sealed twelve thousand. Of the tribe of Gad {were} sealed twelve thousand. Of the tribe of Aser {were} sealed twelve thousand. Of the tribe of Nepthalim {were} sealed twelve thousand. Of the tribe of Manasses {were} sealed twelve thousand. Of the tribe of Simeon {were} sealed twelve thousand. Of the tribe of Levi {were} sealed twelve thousand. Of the tribe of Issachar {were} sealed twelve thousand. Of the tribe of Zabulon {were} sealed twelve thousand. Of the tribe of Joseph {were} sealed twelve thousand. Of the tribe of Benjamin {were} sealed twelve thousand.

In noting the tribes whose names are mentioned here, one by one, as they are sealed, it becomes obvious that the listing here is different from what we find elsewhere when we have all the tribes listed together. This is not unusual, as we do find that in other places where the tribes are listed together there is a different arrangement of their names.

We note here that Levi is included in the list. We know that Levi was the tribe of priests, but they were not given any of the inheritance in the land as they were the tribe chosen by the Lord to be the priests for the people. While they were given cities to dwell in, they were not allotted any of the land like the other tribes were.

We note also that Dan is conspicuously absent from this listing. Along with Ephraim. Now Joseph is evidently listed instead of Ephraim. As Joseph was one of the original sons of Jacob, while Ephraim was the son of Joseph. This, in turn, means that Levi must be occupying Dan's place in the listing.

In some manner or other the Lord always has twelve listed together, even though when we count the two sons of Ephraim (as they are sometimes counted with the twelve) we come up with thirteen tribes. Why Dan is absent in the listing here has produced different opinions. We personally feel that he is absent simply because there are none among his number at this time who are worthy to be included in that listing. I know we could refer back to Old Testament scriptures which speak to us of the sins of Dan as being the first tribe to fall into idolatry (Judges 18:30,31). But when it comes to sin, we could find where ALL the tribes were guilty before God.

Scripture will not bear out the theory that Dan is missing because there are none of his descendants living at this time. When we consider other passages in which we find the tribes listed together we will also find Dan among their number. Such as when the land will be divided among the tribes during the time of the Kingdom Age, or Millennium (Ezekiel 48).

So, suffice it to say that God chose not to include Dan nor Ephraim in that listing of those who were sealed for a special purpose during the time of the tribulation because it is His choice to make as an All-Wise God.

Now, if these are sealed to be witnesses to the world during the first half of the week, what an impact that will be to the world during this dark time. Couple this with the Two Witnesses who are witnesses as well, and you will have a powerful witness to the world during this period of time. Is this why we then have the reference to the number which John could not number in the following verses of this chapter? It would seem with such a powerful force witnessing through the world the effects have got to be awesome!

There are those who feel that the 144,000 are sealed for the purpose of being witnesses during this period of the first half of the week. They are sealed, some feel to preserve them through the trumpet judgments which are getting ready to be unleashed upon the earth.

John hears a mighty angel cry out to the four angels who are holding the four winds of the earth, to withhold their judgments until after he has sealed the "servants of our God in their foreheads."

There are those who feel that the 144,000 are sealed for the purpose of being witnesses during this period of the first half of the week. They are sealed, some feel to preserve them through the trumpet judgments which are getting ready to be unleashed upon the earth.

You recall that Jesus had said, in that chapter which deals with last day events previous to His return to this earth (Matthew 24.) that, *This gospel of the kingdom shall be preached in all the world/or a witness unto all nations; and then shall the end come.*

Later when the fifth trumpet is sounding forth, there was a command given to the angel who opened the bottomless pit to permit the locusts to come upon the earth, that they should not hurt those who have the seal of God in their foreheads. This is evidently a reference to this 144,000.

ANOTHER GROUP....

Verse 9:

After this I beheld, and, lo, a great multitude, which no man could number, of all nations, and kindreds, and people, and tongues, stood before the throne, and before the Lamb, clothed with white robes, and palms in their hands;

We step right out of our study about the 144,000 and are immediately confronted with another group which presents to us an interesting study.

Again, John employs the term **AFTER THIS.** After witnessing the sealing of this host of 144,000 for a special purpose ordained by the Lord, John then sees another number, which he said, "No man could number."

Who is this great host of people? Where do they come from?

Well, first permit us to say who they ARE NOT! They are not the church! Why some want to classify them as the church we do not rightly know. But from other passages we know these are not the church who have been raptured before now and are with the Lord somewhere in the heavens.

Nor are these the Jews who are saved during the tribulation. John informs us that these are people out of, "all nations, and kindreds, and people, and tongues." So, they are from many nations, not just the Jewish nation.

Nor is this the group which John has been just telling us about. There John tells us plainly that they are 144,000 in number. These, however, are without number there are so many of them.

Verses 10-12:

And cried with a loud voice, saying, Salvation to our God which sitteth upon the throne, and unto the Lamb. And all the angels stood round about the throne, and {about} the elders and the four beasts, and fell before the throne on their faces, and worshipped God, Saying, Amen: Blessing, and glory, and wisdom, and thanksgiving, thanksgiving, and honour, and power, and might, *{be} unto our God for ever and ever. Amen.*

WHO ARE THEY???

Verses 13,14:

And one of the elders answered, saying unto me, What are these which are arrayed in white robes? and whence came they? And I said unto him, Sir, thou knowest. And he said to me, These are they which came out of great tribulation, and have washed their robes, and made them white in the blood of the Lamb.

One of the elders standing near asked John the same question. John replied, *Sir, thou knowest.* The reply of the elder gives us our answer as to who they are; *These are they which came out of great tribulation, and have washed their robes, and made them white in the blood of the Lamb.*

Contrary to the opinion of some there will be many who will be saved during the dark days of the tribulation. God has never had a period of time in which men could not be saved if they would only obey His word and will. The tribulation period will be no different in this respect.

Now we are aware of the false conception by some that if I don't make it in the rapture I can just wait and give my head during the tribulation which will assure me of salvation. Well, to such a supposition our response is, If you do not have the will to live for God now, it is not likely that you will have the will to give your head in that hour! In fact, if you have the opportunity to live for God now and you refuse to, it is not likely that you will even be given the chance to give your head and be saved in that day!

Those who have been exposed to the truth and refused it had better not be making any plans of being in that number which John is describing for us here in this chapter. Paul informs us of those who, as he states in 2Thessalonians 2:10-12: *And with all deceivableness of unrighteousness in them that perish; because they received not the love of the truth, that they might be saved. And for this cause God shall send them strong delusion, that they should believe a lie: That they all might be damned who believed not the truth, but had pleasure in unrighteousness.*

AN EXPLANATION ...

There are multitudes of people in this world who have not been exposed to this glorious truth like we have. There is no telling how many people there are in foreign countries who have not yet been taught the truth. Plus, look at all those in our own country who have not been reached yet with truth.

As mentioned previously, God has never permitted man to live on this planet in any period of time in which there was not a plan of deliverance offered to him. Man may not have always accepted it as a whole, such as the Antediluvians, but it was there for them.

A careful examination of this multitude as described for us by John may help us to understand who they are.

a). If, as we have previously studied, the twenty-four elders of chapter four are representatives of the saved church, or raptured ones, then notice that the Bible states that they are sitting before the throne. At the same time notice that John says this multitude is standing before the throne.

b). Also, this group has palms in their hands. This reminds us of that group which waved palms and spread their garments before the Lord when He entered Jerusalem. Palms are symbols of servants. When we look at the Elders of chapter four we notice that they have harps and golden vials.

c). John is informed that this group which could not be numbered came out of great tribulation. This statement could not be made of the church, even if the church were to go through this time of tribulation, because hundreds of thousands of church saints have died long before this time of tribulation. So, it could not be said of the Church that they came out of great tribulation.

Another point: If John was witnessing the Church, would he not have recognized them as such? It would seem from verses 13 and 14 that John did not know who they were!

d). It is conspicuous that no mention is made of any crowns being on the heads of these saved ones. We know from chapter four that crowns are on the heads of the representatives there.

Verse 15:

Therefore are they before the throne of God, and serve him day and night in his temple: and he that sitteth on the throne shall among them.

e). John is informed that this group before the throne will serve him day and night. The Church at home with Jesus will not be servants. One's wife is not a servant of her husband, but, rather, a sharer of his blessings.

f). Another phrase worthy of our consideration is where John is informed that this group had washed their robes and made them white in the blood of the Lamb. They are evidently saved because of what they did. Their refusal to accept the Beast and his empire, and their acceptance of the message proclaimed to them. As a child of God, we are not saved because of what we did - but rather because of what he did!

Verse 16:

They shall hunger no more, neither thirst any more; neither shall the sun light on them, nor any heat.

g). John is informed that this group will hunger no more. This possibly has a reference to the suffering which they endured during the dark days of the tribulation in which the only way many could purchase anything was only if you had the mark of the Beast.

Verse 17:

For the Lamb which is in the midst of the throne shall feed them, and shall lead them unto living fountains of waters: and God shall wipe away all tears from their eyes.

When we speak of eternal salvation though, we come to a different understanding of the term. Yet, again, we find that people are saved differently. We are not saved in the same manner that Abraham or a Daniel were saved. Yet we know they are just as saved as we are saved. Look at Elijah, he was saved in a whirlwind and chariot! Look at Enoch, he was saved by walking into heaven! Now they both went to heaven. They are somewhere with the Lord right now. If that is not being saved I don't understand the meaning of the word!

Now, when the church is taken off this earth to be with the Lord in the heavens, the message of the church will, I presume, go with the Church. If there will be no more Church on this earth once it has been removed, then it would stand to reason that there would be no more need of the message which the church preached as well. The message of the church is to get people in the church and ultimately saved.

If one could not get into the church once the church is taken out of this world, then it would not seem that this message would be proclaimed any more once the church is gone.

HOW ARE THEY SAVED?

As to just what will be required of this group whom John sees standing before the throne of God, we will just have to wait until that day to find out.

We do know, however, that there will be many who will be saved during those dark days of tribulation.

This should give us a wonderful feeling. Knowing that the Beast who shall attempt to conquer the world for himself, will have those who will refuse to bend to his demands fills us with a good feeling.

The Hebrews who in Daniel three refused to bow to the image of the king of Babylon, Nebuchadnezzar, has some company in that area in these who will refuse in that dark day of Nebuchadnezzar's anti-type.

Truth has always triumphed through the ages. God has always had a people in every age of man.

This period will be no exception. When the world is facing her darkest hour: When sin is unleashed upon this earth like it has never been, as the Church is removed which has acted as a buffer-zone for so long: When the Beast rises to his pinnacle of power and demands that all, small and great, rich and poor, receive his mark, it is great to know that there will still be those who will refuse to give in to the pressures of the hour.

They shall rise in a glorious hour of great victory to stand before the throne of the Lamb and join others who have through the ages stood for God and His will for their life.

THERE IS ONLY ONE CHURCH!

Because we love this truth so much we are tempted to over-react when we hear anyone speak of people being saved. We know that in order to be saved now one must repent, be baptized in the Name of Jesus Christ, and be filled with the Holy Ghost. That is a settled fact which the Bible is very plain about. And we have supposed that once the church is removed from this earth there will be no further opportunity for anyone to get baptized or receive the Holy Ghost. We have supposed that when the Church leaves, so leaves the Spirit of God. In this we are somewhat selfish it would seem to me. Who gave us a monopoly on the plan of salvation? Who informed us that no one could be saved unless they come to our church and heard it at our mouth?

When we speak of this number who is saved during these dark days of tribulation, let us not think for a moment that we are referring to a group of people who "luck" into salvation. That is not the case at all! From what John hears about this group, *They shall hunger no more, neither thirst any more...* it would seem this gives us an indication of what they have been through. Possibly some of them are those seen under the altar in chapter six. They have, no doubt, suffered during these dark days because of their stand for the right and their refusal to bend to the demands of the Beast and his edicts.

Like weary pilgrims who have weathered the long and harsh journey, they are seen receiving the refreshing comforts of their heavenly Father. Never again will they have to endure what they have just come through.

WHAT DO THEY OBEY?

What message did they obey? Those who embrace this glorious message of the Apostles know how to appreciate the truth. It cost our Lord, and His apostles their life that we could now possess this truth.

Consequently, we seek to guard it dearly. Because of this feeling which we have for the truth, we want to know what others do to be saved. If I had to be baptized in the Name of Jesus Christ to be saved, did these in this passage must be also? If I had to receive the Holy Ghost, what about these in this great number, did they receive the Holy Ghost?

Now we could debate this issue for a long time and still not come to a conclusion which would convince all of us. What the Lord requires of those who are saved after the church is gone from this earth is something which the Lord determines - not I!

When we study the subject of salvation, we find that salvation is something God brings to one's life.

Salvation is deliverance from something. Noah knew salvation because he was delivered from the flood. Lot knew salvation because he was delivered from Sodom and the fire which destroyed it.

Jonah knew salvation when he was delivered from the belly of the whale.

The gathering which will take place someday in the heavens with our Lord and all those who have been saved by His mercies through the years will be a sight that will be overwhelming and awe-inspiring, no doubt.

In the face of the enemy there is a message of truth and hope proclaimed. A message which is embraced by multitudes from every nation and kindred and tongue. Enduring the hardships of the age they at last come forth victorious over the enemy. Standing then before the throne and the Lamb they rightly rejoice. And we shall rejoice with them for their victory!

- WHAT A DAY AWAITS THE FAITHFUL!

SOME THOUGHTS

This chapter has been called a parenthetical chapter. The events which transpire in this chapter it would seem, do not occur at this point in the Revelation chronologically. That is to say, between the events of chapter six and chapter eight. This is not the only place in the Revelation where we find John writing of events which do not actually occur at the place where they are recorded in the book.

You recall those seen under the altar in chapter six were told that they should wait until, their fellow-servants also and their brethren, that should be killed as they were, should be fulfilled. It stands to reason that at least some of those in that great number in this chapter would include this group who have been martyred for their testimony.

This is like a pause in the action of Revelation while John is introduced to some very important people who play an important role in the events which transpire in the time of the Tribulation. Those who are chosen as special witnesses for this period; and those who endure the terrible hardships of this period of time.

Notice that the first group - the 144,000 - are chosen by God. They are selected by the Lord and a seal is placed upon them to identify them to the world as to who they are. They had nothing to do with choosing themselves, evidently. That is, they did not aspire to this position. They did not work toward this end. This is not to say they had not dedicated their life to the will of God, they had. This was the reason they were chosen.

The second group, however, stand before the throne because of their decision to be in this group. It was their choice to stand for God and righteousness during this period of time. They washed their robes. They refused the beast and his empire of evil. They refused to bow to the pressures exerted against them. They gave their life rather than give in to the pressures (at least many of them probably did!).

These two groups stand out in the book of Revelation to emphasize to us the mercies of God; the will of God; the eternal purpose of God. God will have mercy on those who will dare stand for Him, regardless of the age. God will have a people regardless of the age. He always has, and He always will.

To be honored to be in the number which makes up the Body of Christ is an honor which is not to be taken lightly. To know the Lord in the fullness of salvation; to be in that number which hears the trump of God sound and calls us from this earth will be glory beyond description in this life. No one else - no other group - shall know the joys which shall be known by the RAPTURED ONES!

But God does not restrict His salvation to the Church Rapture. It extends beyond that period. It is wonderful to know that during that period called tribulation, during the time when the beast shall reign with his wicked ways, God will have a people who will refuse to bow to him.

CHAPTER EIGHT

Verse 1:

And when he had opened the seventh seal, there was silence in heaven about the space of half an hour.

• AND WHEN HE HAD OPENED THE SEVENTH SEAL:

Chapter seven has broken the sequence of the seven seals. There is a pause in the action as our attention is directed to those who are saved during this dark period of seven long years. Now, after the pause, our attention is once again on the seals. The HE who is doing the opening is the same as mentioned in verse one of chapter six, THE LAMB.

The seventh seal.

Once more we meet with the numeral seven in the book of Revelation. This seven has great meaning. Seven being a number which speaks of completion as well as perfection, this seven brings us to the last seal, at whose opening interesting and awesome things begin to happen.

The first thing to catch our attention at the opening of this seal is that we are told there is SILENCE IN HEAVEN ABOUT THE SPACE OF HALF AN HOUR. There are differing views as to just what this silence is all about. Why thirty minutes of silence? Does the thirty minutes mean thirty minutes as we know thirty minutes, or is it too symbolic?

There is an interesting occasion when Paul was faced by the howling mob in Jerusalem and threatened with his life, being taken into security by the chief captain, he asked if he could speak to the crowd, and when he was given permission to do so; we have in Acts 22:2, the following: (*And when they heard that he spake in the Hebrew tongue to them, they kept the more silence: and he saith,*). There it was the silence of surprise to be able to listen to what he was about to say.

Here it may be a moment of surprise as well as the Lord begins to unfold to the world what is getting to take place.

Some have taken the reference to the seven years which is called "one week" in symbolic language; and as one year in Bible language was 360 days in length; this would make the thirty minutes equal to about seven and one-half days! Looking at it this way does bring up some interesting thoughts to our attention. Remember that God waited for seven days after shutting Noah in the ark before He caused the rain to come upon the earth. It seemed to be a period of mercy waiting as God gave mankind one last chance to consider their ways.

This must be an awesome attention-grabbing silence as quietness settles all over heaven. And may we notice that it does say this silence is in heaven!

The opening of this seventh and last seal will bring upon this earth the Judgments of God's wrath. It is the Judgment upon sin which has been building for six thousand years. It is a judgment upon the beast and his kingdom of darkness which has openly opposed God.

This silence is like the lull before the storm. And the storm which is about to burst forth has never been witnessed previously!

Habakkuk 2:20: *But the Lord {is} in his holy temple: let all the earth keep silence before him.*

Here the prophet seems to be saying the same thing as recorded in Revelation eight. The Lord is preparing to come forth in Judgment upon wicked men, and the command is to have a time of silence as heaven prepares.

There is another prophet which joins in this manner of speech regarding the preparation of the Lord for a time of battle; Zephaniah 1:7, *Hold thy peace at the presence of the Lord God: for the day of the Lord {is} at hand.*

The expression *Hold thy peace* has the same meaning as that employed by Habakkuk for Keep silence.

And also, Zechariah 2:13, *Be silent, 0 all flesh, before the Lord: for he is raised up out of his holy habitation.*

Again, the reference is to that of the Lord coming forth in Judgment upon sin. So, the silence at the opening of the seventh seal seems to be the quietness before the storm. The events which are about to transpire now are given more emphasis by the apostle as he takes more space to describe these events than was taken for the previous six seals.

Verse 2:

And I saw the seven angels which stood before God; and to them were given seven trumpets.

Are these the same which are referred to in chapter one as the "*Seven Spirits before His throne?*"

Whether they are or not, it is evident that these are special servants of God who are connected with His throne. It is to them that are given the seven trumpets which are to sound forth the Judgments of God.

We are informed that in the Apocryphal book of Enoch there is reference to these seven angels as Archangels whose names are: URIEL, RAPHAEL, RAGUEL, MICHAEL, SARAKIEL, GABRIEL, and PHANUEL. Whatever their names may be, it is evident they are very special angels, anointed for a special work, before the throne of God.

The use of trumpets to sound forth messages are familiar with the story of Israel. Israel could readily identify with the use of trumpets; we note in the book of Numbers that Moses was instructed there to have two trumpets made of silver. Silver speaking of redemption in typology is significant. The trumpets were to be used for different purposes:

• 1. Signal the people to presence of God, Exodus 19:16,19.

• 2. To regulate the marching's of the tribes through the wilderness, Numbers 10:2,5,6.

• 3. To call the people together for an assembly before God, Numbers 10:2,3,7.

• 4. To announce a feast, Leviticus 23:23-25.

• 5. To sound an alarm against an enemy, Nehemiah 4:18,20.

• 6. To herald the anointing of a new king, 1Kings 1:34-41.

• 7. To gather the people for a religious service, Nehemiah 12:35-41.

Regardless of what significance one may place on the sounding forth of the trumpets in times past, we know that they are about to play a very important role in the events which will transpire in the time of the Tribulation.

Trumpets are related to the announcements of royalty: 1Kings 1:34.

Trumpets are also associated with the manifestation of the terrible majesty and power of God: Exodus 19:16.

Trumpets connect with the overthrow of the ungodly: Joshua 6:13-16.

Trumpets also proclaimed the laying of the foundation of God's Temple: Ezra 3:10.

Seiss commented: "The Apocalypse is not a poem in Jewish dress, but the Jewish ceremonies were an earthly poem of the Apocalypse."

Before the angels sound forth with their trumpets though, John describes something else which takes place that attracts our attention:

Verse 3:

And another angel came and stood at the altar, having a golden censer; and there was given unto him much incense, that he should offer {it} with the prayers of all saints upon the golden altar which was before the throne.

This angel has a golden censer with "MUCH INCENSE," which he is to offer with the "PRAYERS OF ALL SAINTS." The altar which is referred to here is the Golden Altar of Incense. In the Tabernacle it was representative of the prayers of the saints.

Some argue that this angel is JESUS standing in His office of High Priest. Augustine, Bede, to mention two familiar names: That Christ in His human character and priestly office, may be called *another Angel*, as the high priest on the day of atonement is called *an angel* with reference to his ministrations, believes that Christ is called in chapters 10:1; 14:17; 18:1; 20:1.

In verse eight of chapter five we note that the four creatures and the twenty-four elders, all have vials which are full of odors, which are the prayers of saints.

So, it would seem from these verses alone that our prayers are not sent up in vain. The Lord knows when His children pray. If the psalmist could speak about having his tears put in a bottle, then surely we can accept that our prayers are as well kept by the Lord in some manner. Let us recall that it was said of Cornelius that his prayers had *come up for a memorial before God*, (Acts 10:4).

Verse 4:

And the smoke of the incense, {which came} with the prayers of the saints, ascended up before God out of the angel's hand.

It would be impossible for us to know the accumulative amount which fills these vials from the prayers of millions of people of God through the ages! Jesus taught us that we should pray for those who despitefully use us and to love our enemies. The Lord has assured us that vengeance belongs to Him. But think of those who have boasted through the years about persecuting the children of God! Especially in this day of tribulation it will seem that the man of sin will have the upper hand in matters. It seems that the man of sin and his cohorts are winning. Well, they may win a few battles, but it will be those who refuse to give in to the pressures exerted against them by the man of sin who will win the war! It will be the children of God who will come out victors in the end. God has not forgotten nor overlooked the troubles which His people have gone through down through the ages of time.

Verse 5:

And the angel took the censer, and filled it with fire of the altar, and cast {it} into the earth: and there were voices, and thunderings, and lightnings, and an earthquake.

The Altar, let us remember, is the Golden Altar of incense which in the Tabernacle represented the prayers of the people of God. Through the many years of trouble which Israel endured throughout the Old Testament era, as well as since the first century, they prayed for vengeance upon their enemies. We can find many of the imprecatory prayers in the Psalms, such as Psalm 68. Now, Judgment is going to come to their enemies. This will be their greatest enemy of all who will oppose them during the tribulation.

What took place when the angel poured out his censer upon the earth, is identical with what happens when the seventh trumpet sounds, and the seventh vial is poured out; (11:19; 16:18). The Judgments of God begin to be poured out upon wicked man and his evil plans.

<u>**Verses 6,7:**</u>

And the seven angels which had the seven trumpets prepared themselves to sound. The first angel sounded, and there followed hail and fire mingled with blood, and they were cast upon the earth: and the third part of trees was burnt up, and all green grass was burnt up.

The Trumpet Judgments are often compared with the plagues which were brought upon Egypt by Jehovah. This first Trumpet Judgment compares with the seventh plague upon Egypt.

We know that many things in the Revelation are symbols, representative of something, or someone else. At the same time, many of the things which we find recorded by John are very real and very literal. There are those who would spiritualize everything in the Revelation. These Trumpet Judgments become such things which some choose to spiritualize. However, if the plagues upon Egypt were real - and who among us would argue they were not! - then why should we suppose that these Trumpet Judgments are not real as well.

AND THE THIRD PART OF TREES WERE BURNT UP... Consider something for thought:

As the tribulation progresses and the Judgments of God continue, you will note that the results also grow in intensity:

- 6:8, One-fourth of earth die.
- 8:7, One-third of vegetation dies.
- 8:9, One-third of sea dies.
- 8:12, One-third of day darkened,
- 9:18, One-third of men killed.

The troubles which befall planet earth and its inhabitants do not wear away with time, they grow worse!

<u>**Verse 8:**</u>

And the second angel sounded, and as it were a great mountain burning with fire was cast into the sea: and the third part of the became blood;

The second Trumpet Judgment corresponds with the First Plague upon Egypt, as the waters are greatly affected.

There are those who feel that what John saw here, and what he describes in his own understanding, is possibly a great meteor hurling into the Sea. Then there are also those who feel that John was describing a nuclear explosion.

Whatever we are reading about here, it has astounding results! As it plunges into the Sea, a third of the ships in the Sea are destroyed, along with one-third of the Sea creatures. The Mediterranean, of which John is here speaking, is a very busy place by ships from the nations who are keeping a close eye on the events which are taking place in the Middle East, as it continues to be a cauldron of stirring trouble with no lasting peace in sight.

With the stockpiling of nuclear warheads by the super powers of the world; by the fact that any nation of super power status will be involved in the events which will be transpiring in the Middle East at this time, it is not without support to suppose that there will be some nuclear explosions during these dark days. The man of sin and his co-horts seek to gain control of not only the Middle East, but also there are others who are seeking control of the Middle East as well. In particular, we speak of the Russian Bloc countries and powers.

Whether a nuclear blast, or a huge meteor from space, the results are shocking.

Verse 10:

And the third angel sounded, and there fell a great star from heaven, burning as it were a lamp, and it fell upon the third part of the rivers, and upon the fountains of waters;

Again, John witnesses what may have been a meteor falling out of the sky. This one falls into the rivers which feed the Sea, and the lakes. By John speaking of how it affected a third of the rivers and a third of the lakes, it would lead us to consider that this is no mere meteor falling in one place into the earth. One meteor falling to the earth would affect only that place where it fell, but this Judgment affects a large area of rivers and fountains of waters.

• AND THE NAME OF THE STAR IS CALLED WORMWOOD.

Verse 11:

And the name of the star is called Wormwood: and the third part of the waters became wormwood; and many men died of the waters, because they were made bitter.

Wormwood is a perennial herb which is very bitter. It is used to manufacture absinthe. There is, however, another interesting thing about wormwood for our consideration: We are informed that in the Russian language according to the Ukrainian Dictionary, the word for wormwood is Chernobyl! This is the place where the nuclear accident occurred in 1986 which affected thousands of people living in that area. Chernobyl is a bitter wild herb which is used as a tonic in some parts of Russia.

With so many nuclear warheads available to world powers, it is possible that when push comes to shove, someone will resort to them to try to gain the upper hand. If this is what takes place during this dark time of tribulation, the result will be devastating to those living there.

MANY MEN DIED OF THE WATERS... Up until now there had been no direct reference to people dying. Now, however, many people die. If men do resort to the use of some nuclear devises, many thousands could conceivably die!

<u>Verse 12:</u>

And the fourth angel sounded, and the third part of the sun was smitten, and the third part of the moon, and the third part of the stars; so as the third part of them was darkened, and the day shone not for a third part of it, and the night likewise.

This Trumpet corresponds with the ninth plague upon Egypt as darkness covered the land of Egypt.

Much has already happened during this chapter as the Trumpet Judgments have been sounding forth. With all the effects, which they have had on the earth, we can assume that the scientist's, along with those aligned with the man of sin, have been busy trying to explain what has happened to the earth's ecological system. They will never attribute it to the Judgment of God, of course. They will have some explanation as to why such startling things have occurred.

Third part... We do not understand clearly Just what this statement means. Now we, of course, understand what one-third of something is, but we do not fully understand how the lights in the heavens will be affected so that they do not shine for one-third of the time.

Now, it is evident whatever happens it is not forever. How long the lights are affected this way we are not told. But we do find upon turning to chapter sixteen that at a later time, when the fourth angel pours out his bowl Judgment upon the earth, that the sun will increase in intensity its heat which shines upon the earth. (16:8,9) This may be used by the enemy to his advantage as well, when the sun returns to its normal rate of shining.

The word "smitten" is found only here in the New Testament. Just exactly what the term means we are at a loss. Somehow the angel of the Lord, at the direction of the Lord, will SMITE the sun, moon and stars, which will result in their loss of light for one-third of the time.

We can imagine that when this happens, it will greatly affect the temperature of the earth. If it continues for several weeks or months, it is likely to have drastic effect upon the earth's climate.

This could all result in some violent reactions in the atmosphere, producing storms of great magnitude. Let us remember the words of Jesus in Luke 21:25,26: *And there shall be signs in the sun, and in the moon, and in the stars; and upon the earth distress of nations, with perplexity; the sea and the waves roaring; men's hearts failing*

them for fear, and for looking after those things which are coming on the earth: for the powers of heaven shall be shaken.

Verse 13:

And I beheld, and heard an angel flying through the midst of heaven, saying with a loud voice, Woe, woe, woe, to the inhabiters of the earth by reason of the other voices of the trumpet of the three angels, which are yet to sound!

John reminds us again that he is a witness of these events which he is describing for us: **I BEHELD**.

What a sight it must have been to this aged apostle!

The events which have already taken place have no doubt shaken the earth terribly. Those who are living here at that time must be greatly disturbed at the terrible phenomenon which has taken place.

Now there seems to be a pause in the action, as another angel flying through the air declares with solemn warning that there are yet more dreadful things in store for those who live on this earth.

One wonders if there will be an actual angel at this time during the tribulation which will be seen by many as it flies through the air with its message of gloom and doom! If they do witness such a sight, how frightening this would be!

The angel sounds forth his message **WITH A LOUD VOICE**. There is no doubt those living on this earth will be able to hear the booming voice of this messenger of doom.

The angel sounds forth, **WOE, WOE, WOE**, three times. There are three more trumpets which must sound forth their Judgments yet.

What the reaction will be of those who are living on the earth during this time would be a matter of speculation on our part. We may suppose what we would do in such circumstances, but even that would be speculative. It is one thing to say what we would do in certain situations, and quite another thing to be actually faced with them! Whatever their reaction, it is evident that God means business in what is taking place at this time. Men have rejected God. They have made mockery out of His Word.

The man of sin in particular, has challenged God, and denied his existence, claiming that he himself is God. It is upon such hard, ungodly men, that the Judgments of God will fall in that day.

Wise will be the person who will hide himself away in the Rock of Ages right now, so that he can be safe from the storm which is right now brewing.

Chapter Six began the week which is to end the **TIMES OF THE GENTILES.** It describes for us the events which will transpire as the "Man of Sin" makes his way to the top of his pinnacle of power.

Chapter Seven speaks to us about those who will be saved during this week of tribulation. There are no descriptions given in chapter seven of any events which take place during this week. There are no activities in this chapter, just a reference to those saved.

Chapter Eight presents to us the continuation of the Tribulation. But it also presents to us something else: Here it is God in operation. It is God bringing His judgments upon wicked mankind during this period of time. While in chapter six the man of sin may seem to be in control, it is evident here that God is in control.

This chapter begins the Trumpet Judgments which do not conclude until we get to chapter eleven.

The question is often raised as to how far reaching the Tribulation will be? Will the entire world be involved in the Tribulation? Or will it only be those countries that are associated with the Man of Sin?

While this question may be open for personal conjecture, it will be an awesome time for whoever is involved!

Considering these events which will transpire during this dark period makes one feel that much more thankful that he is a child of God and safe in the everlasting arms of mercy!

CHAPTER NINE

• THE PLOT THICKENS ...

As we draw deeper into the Tribulation period, things become more awesome to consider. The chapter under consideration certainly bears this out.

It is difficult for us who live in the United States, free from conditions as described in these chapters, to fathom that such conditions will one day exist. This has tempted some to brush off the events described by John as actually taking place. Some would have us to think the book of Revelation is all history. That it has been fulfilled in history with the many wars and troubles among the Middle Eastern nations. But this argument we refuse to accept!

There are too many things which are happening in our own day to let us know they are leading up to those events which are getting ready to be unleashed upon this world. In the political world; In the scientific world; In the religious world. In whatever direction one chooses to explore, he will find signs which are informing us that Revelation chapters six through nineteen are just about to begin happening!

Chapter eight began the sounding of the Trumpet Judgments from God. The events which were described in that chapter were enough to cause one to sit up and take notice. But, chapter nine continues the Trumpet Judgments, as well as the beginning of the three woes which were pronounced upon mankind.

Chapter eight described four Trumpet Judgments. Chapter nine will only describe two! This also informs us that as the Revelation continues, the intensity grows as well.

Wise will be the person who has made their calling and election sure with God...

We may think of these judgments as being wrath from God against ungodly men, which in one sense they are. But, on the other hand, we may also witness the mercies of God through all of this. God has sealed one hundred and forty-four thousand, who must be witnessing to the people about the Beast and his policies. We have had an angel flying through the air crying out the "WOES" which are coming on the earth. Along with the many thousands who had been exposed to the Word of God prior to the rapture, but did not go up in the rapture, who will know what is going on and will refuse to join the system of the Beast. All of these will be witnesses against the Beast and his system of evil. This would bound to have a tremendous effect on the people. In this we see the mercy of God.

All of these troubles which are coming on the world, are they not things that should cause men to wake up and cry out to God for mercy and repent of their wicked ways?

So, it does not appear that all is judgment without mercy. That all is wrath with no love mixed with it. There is plenty of mercy and love manifested to humanity; it is just that humanity, as a whole, elects to ignore mercy and continue their ungodly rebellious lifestyles.

Verse 1:

And the fifth angel sounded, and I saw a star fall from heaven unto the earth: and to him was given the key of the bottomless pit.

The sounding of the fourth Trumpet and the Fifth Trumpet has been interrupted only by the voice of the angel flying through the air with his message of warning to the inhabitants on earth; Woe, woe, woe.

It is of interest to point out here as we begin our study of this chapter, that the terrible catastrophes which have fallen thus far have been directly affecting the earth. That is, the trees, the grass, the water, etc. Man has been affected by what has taken place thus far only indirectly.

THINGS ARE ABOUT TO CHANGE!

With the destruction of trees, grass, etc. those involved with the beast have probably explained the problems away as some ecological, atmospheric, problem. The waters which were affected have probably been treated by now, somehow. The sun which was affected for one third of each day - as well as the moon at night - has, probably by now returned to its normal light, and men have returned to their ways of the past; ignoring these as warnings from God; continuing their ungodly and sinful ways; refusing to repent of their wickedness.

The first woe is about to come upon this earth which will get the attention of everybody who is involved!!!

... and I saw a star fall from heaven unto the earth: and to him was

given the key of the bottomless pit. This statement presents to us a very interesting, and thought-provoking, matter. When we studied in chapter eight about the star which fell from heaven (v 10), we pointed out then that possibly what John was witnessing was a meteor, because of the effect it had on the waters.

Now, however, John speaks of this star with a personal pronoun. Not only does he speak of him as "him," but also, we are informed that someone gave to this star "the key to the bottomless pit." It would seem this could only be speaking of some intelligent being, as such language could not apply to a meteor, nor to a literal star.

There are differing views as to just who this star could be. Several feels that this is referring to Satan himself. We do have such passages as:

Isaiah 14:12, *How art thou fallen from heaven, 0 Lucifer, son of the morning!*

Luke 10:18, *And He (Jesus) said unto them, I beheld Satan as lightning fall from heaven.*

2Corinthians 11:14, *And no marvel; for Satan himself is transformed into an angel of light.*

To strengthen their argument, we are informed that the passage should read; *"and I saw a star fallen from heaven."* That it is speaking of something which has already taken place. We do know that Satan has "fallen" from his position of authority in heaven.

We know from such passages as Revelation 1:18, that Jesus Christ is in possession of the keys to the underworld. Would He trust them to one who has through the millenniums sought to destroy all that God has stood for? Would He trust the keys to the one who tempted Him in the wilderness, tried to get Him killed during His ministry, and has tried to get everybody to deny Him since? Would He trust the keys to the underworld; the place of demon forces, to one whose entire purpose is to thwart the plans of God in this earth?

While there is no way one can be certain as to the identity of this star from heaven, it would seem that it would NOT be Satan himself. It is quite possible that it is the same angel we witness in chapter twenty who at that time binds Satan in this same "bottomless pit."

The word *bottomless pit*, is literally *"the pit of the abyss."* The word abyss comes to us from a root word which means "without depth." So, the term "*bottomless*" is a proper interpretation.

The fact that this "*star*" has come down to this earth to open this abyss lets us know that the way into this abyss must be on this earth. As to just where this entrance may be, or how one might enter this abyss would be speculation on our part. The fact there is a key to this abyss seems to imply an entrance of some sort. Reading of this pit in chapter twenty we note there is mention of a key there as well, and the angel unlocked this place and shut the devil up in this place and set a seal upon the entrance (1-3).

The fact that it is bottomless presents an interesting puzzle to us. How can any pit be without a bottom? Could it be that this abyss is in the center of the earth, with no bottom? Going in any direction would result in facing a ceiling, as a ceiling would be in any direction.

In Luke sixteen we read the story of the rich man and Lazarus. After they both died, they went to the abodes of the dead; saved and lost. This place had at least two compartments to it; one place where Lazarus was - the place of the saved. The other place where the rich man was - the place of the lost. Between the two places was a great separation which the Bible called a great "gulf." Some have suggested that the abyss mentioned here - and elsewhere - could be yet another compartment of "hades."

Reference to this "bottomless pit" is found some seven times in the Revelation; 9:1, 2, 11; 11:7; 17: 8; 20:1,3.

FALLEN ANGELS...

Satan in the beginning was a very special creature of God. It would seem from Isaiah 14:12 that he was known as "*Lucifer, son of the morning.*" This title possibly refers to Satan as "Day Star." From Ezekiel 28:12-14, we have an interesting description of a character that must be none other than Satan himself. What we read about him there presents a very interesting picture of this angel of the Lord who chose to rebel against God and His authority. Because of his pride he formed a rebellion against God.

A rebellion which resulted in him being thrown out of heaven, as well as many of the other angels who joined in his rebellion, since that day it has been the determination of Satan to destroy the plans of

God. This effort had it's beginning in the garden with the first couple. And this effort has continued for some six thousand years now.

There are a lot of things we do not know nor understand about the spirit world. Just who - or what - are the demons which abound in our world today? Where did they come from? What happened to all the angels which fell with Satan? If they are not free to move about, why is Satan? Are these fallen angels the demons which torment people? Are these demons dis-embodied spirits from a pre-Adamic race seeking bodies to dwell in?

THE ANGELS...

The angels were created by God. Hebrews 12:22 refers to their "innumerable" number. A term which means there is a great host of them. We have the same term in Revelation seven referring to those who have come out of the Great Tribulation (7:9). It does not mean they cannot be numbered, but that their number is great. God knows how many He created in the beginning.

There is no scripture that implies that God created more, nor that He continues to create more, angels. Their creation was a one-time event, evidently. Satan was one of those created angels.

The angels, like the human creation, have ranks of position. We have studied about those whose position of responsibility was around the throne of God (4:6; 8:2). We have reference in the Bible to the archangel Michael. They seem to have special appointment to either certain people, or certain areas, of this world. Michael is referred to as the great prince which standeth for the children of thy people.

It was Gabriel who was sent to Mary to announce to her the birth of the Savior, Jesus Christ. This seems to connect him to redemption and the Church.

The angels are involved in the affairs of the Church today. Hebrews 1:14 informs us that they are Ministering spirits, sent forth to minister for them who shall be heirs of salvation. Again, in Hebrews 12:22, where the writer is speaking about the Church, he refers to the innumerable company of angels, which attend the Church.

The apostle Peter, speaking about the Holy Ghost given to the Church, states that the angels "desire to look into" this experience (1Peter 1:12). They are very involved and concerned about the affairs of mankind.

Paul, in writing to the Corinthian Church, in dealing with the issue of hair, states that the woman should have long, uncut, hair - which is given to her for a covering, and which she needs to pray and worship God - because of the angels.

It is evident from Daniel 10:12-21, that the angels are very much involved in what is going on in this world. Daniel had been praying and fasting for three weeks when he had a very special vision (vs 5-9). After the vision an angel appears to Daniel to speak to him about the things of which he had been fasting and praying. He informs Daniel (v. 12) that his prayers had been heard from the very first day but that he had been hindered in getting to Daniel until then (v. 13). The hindrance the angel referred to was what he called the prince of the kingdom of Persia. It was only after Michael came and helped him that he was able to leave and come to Daniel.

It is evident from what is said here by the angel that there is a spirit world which is just as real as this physical world in which we live. The reference to the prince of the kingdom of Persia, is not a reference to some human prince!

THE ANGELS WHICH FELL

• The Other Angels!

Just as there is a great network of angels who are working for the Lord, there is also another network who are working for the Devil. We speak of his angels as his ministering spirits which abound in this world doing his will.

Not only are there demonic forces active in our world, but there are also those who permit the devil to use them to promote his cause. Note what Paul stated in 2Corinthians 11:13,14: *And no marvel; for Satan himself is transformed into an angel of light. Therefore it is no great thing if his ministers also be transformed as the ministers of righteousness,' whose end shall be according to their works.*

Paul had called these "ministers" of Satan, false apostles, deceitful workers, in verse 13, who, he said were, transforming themselves into the apostles of Christ.

Those who use the church and religion for their own selfish end would fit into this category. It may seem difficult to conceive that anyone would stoop so low as to use the work of God as a pretense to receive recognition and position and wealth in this world - but there are those who do!

From what we may glean from the Word of God the devil has a highly organized system which operates at his bidding.

We may glean some interesting information about these demons of evil and wickedness from such passages as:

Mark 5:3, ... *and no man could bind him, no, not with chains.*

Here we note that demons can manifest supernatural strength.

Mark 5:5, *And always, night and day, he was in the mountains, and in the tombs, crying, and cutting himself with stones.* The demons can inflict harm to those whom they dwell in. Or, at least, cause those they indwell to harm themselves.

Mark 5:12, *And all the devils (demons) besought Him, saying, Send us into the swine, that we may enter into them.*

Demons need a body to dwell in.

Mark 5:9, *And He asked him, What is thy name? And he answered, saying, My name is Legion: for we are many.*

From this verse, we may note two things; a) More than just one demon can possess a body - or dwell in a body. b) By the fact the Lord asked the demon what his name was would imply that they are identifiable.

Mark 7:25, *For a certain woman, whose young daughter had an unclean spirit, heard of him, and came and fell at His feet.*

The demon which lived in this young girl was an unclean spirit.

Mark 9:17-25. Here was a father who brought his son to Jesus who was demon possessed. From this story, we glean the effects which demons can have on those they dwell in. Note what is says the demons caused this young man to do: ... *teareth him: and he foameth, and gnasheth with his teeth, and pineth away.*

And verse 20: *And they brought him unto Him: and when he saw Him, straightway the spirit tare him; and he fell on the ground, and wallowed foaming.*

We do not feel that the scriptures teach us that the Devil can take our life, but we do feel that the scriptures teach that he will bring bodily harm to those who permit him to dwell in them. And while he may not be able to take your life (Life came from God and only God can take it back!), he is behind the depression; the guilt; the frustration, which drives people sometimes to destroy their own life.

Also, verse 25: *Jesus called the demon(s) who dwelt in this young man, thou foul spirit ... thou dumb and deaf spirit.*

Luke 13:11,16; *And, behold, there was a woman which had a spirit of infirmity eighteen years ... Ought not this woman, being a daughter of Abraham, whom Satan hath bound.*

It was Satan who had caused this woman to be in the condition she was in. The weakness and curvature of her body had been brought about by Satan.

Acts 16:16, *And it came to pass, as we went to prayer, a certain woman with a spirit of divination.*

This ability to foretell or predict the future did not come from God. **IT CAME FROM THE DEVIL!**

So, from these passages, as well as many others, we can glean somewhat about the activity that is going on in the spirit world of Satan. His emissaries of wickedness and evil are very active in our world today just as they have been from the beginning. As we study the book of Revelation it would seem that their activity will increase as the end draws nearer.

In fact, Paul seems to be saying that when he wrote in 1Timothy 4:1-3; *Now the Spirit speaketh expressly, that in the latter times (the last days) some shall depart from the faith giving heed to seducing spirits, and doctrines of devils (demons), forbidding to marry, and commanding to abstain from meats.*

In Matthew 12:43-45, Jesus gave an interesting lesson on unclean spirits. He told how that when the unclean spirit leaves the body he has been dwelling in, he goes elsewhere seeking some other body to dwell in. Having found no other body, he attracts other spirits that are more wicked than he is, and they all come back and enter that man to make his condition a lot worse than previously. So, from this we may understand that demons attract demons.

WE ARE NOT HELPLESS!!!
WE HAVE THE POWER!!!!

We are not left to fend for ourselves against these forces of evil. The Holy Spirit filled child of God has authority resident within him to overcome and defeat the emissaries of Satan.

Jesus said He would give His apostles *...power against unclean spirits...* That same power is resident in the life of every child of God.

When Satan comes with his enticements to commit evil, we do not have to give in to him nor listen to his suggestions, regardless of how they sound. James gives us some instructions as to what to do when confronted by the enemy; Submit yourselves to God. Resist the devil, and he will flee from you. (4:7).

Notice, James said; RESIST THE DEVIL... But before he instructed us to resist, he first said; SUBMIT... TO GOD. If we have not first submitted our life to God in obedience to His will for our life, then chances are Satan is not going to pay any attention to our attempt to resist him.

The apostle Peter instructs us to; *Be sober, be vigilant; because your adversary the devil, as a roaring lion, walketh about, seeking whom he may devour: Whom resist stedfast in the faith, knowing that the same afflictions are accomplished in your brethren that are in the world.* 1Peter 5:8,9.

1John 4:4, *Ye are of God, little children, and have overcome them: because greater is He that is in you, than he that is in the world.* Romans 8:37, *Nay, in all these things we are more than conquerors through Him that loved us.*

THE FIRST WOE COMES!

As the angel - or star - opens this bottomless pit we read of the first woe which comes upon mankind:

Verse 2:

And he opened the bottomless pit; and there arose a smoke out of the pit, as the smoke of a great furnace; and the sun and the air were darkened by reason of the smoke of the pit.

Today when volcanos erupt, they spew forth terribly black smoke and ashes which cover objects in their path.

Possibly the entrance to this bottomless pit lies in a volcano. Where ever it may be, when the "star" opens the door to it, smoke boils out that is so thick and so vast in amount that it darkens the sun.

When the smoke came down around Mount Sinai in Exodus nineteen, the people trembled at the sight. Now, this was a manifestation of God's presence with them. What will be the reaction of people on this earth when the dark, boiling, clouds of smoke come rolling out of this bottomless Pit during the tribulation?

The mention of the sun being darkened by the smoke seems to imply that the sun is now back to its normal light after being darkened for a third of the time by the fourth trumpet.

Verse 3:

And there came out of the smoke locusts upon the earth: and unto them was given power, as the scorpions of the earth have power.

LOCUSTS... Hell, the bottomless pit, hardly seems a likely place for a breeding ground for locusts!

When we get the description of them in verse 7 through 10, it is evident that what John is witnessing is no mere ordinary locust as was familiar to those who lived in the Middle East.

When John saw these creatures, their appearance to him was that of locusts, swarming forth from the billowing black smoke boiling forth out of the pit.

As with other areas of the Revelation, we have differing views as to what is under consideration here in regards to these swarming locusts. One writer stated: "Briefly then, the various symbols here presented to our view all point, and in no uncertain way, to that marvel of history, the empire founded by the false, prophet, Mohammed, an empire of vast dimensions that was established and extended through an unprecedented combination of stupendous military forces and mighty spiritual energies ... For Islam is a mystery of the darkest character... In other words, the facts of Islamism agree exactly with the meaning of the symbols shown in these visions." (Mauro)

There came out of the smoke locusts... John was witnessing all that was taking place on the earth during the tribulation period from his vantage point in the heavenlies. What he witnesses coming out of the abyss appears to him like great swarms of locusts. They darkened the sky like hordes of locusts. They came forth out of the earth like locusts. It is evident from reading what they do that these are not ordinary locusts. It is of interest to note that the first time we come upon the mentioning of smoke in the Bible is in Genesis where it speaks of the destruction of Sodom and Gomorrah. There, as it is here in the Revelation, it has to do with judgment upon wicked men. Smoke speaks to us of darkness, and darkness speaks to us of sinful men and their wicked ways which are committed in the secrecy of darkness.

WHO ARE THEY?

Verse 4:

And it was commanded them that they should not hurt the grass of the earth, neither any green thing, neither any tree; but only those men which have not the seal of God in their foreheads.

If we dare to consider that these locusts are actually literal locusts, then this would be a strange command given to them.

When the eighth plague fell upon Egypt it resulted in the land being invaded by locusts; *...and they did eat every herb of the land, and all the fruit of the trees...* (Exodus 10:15).

Here, however, these locusts are commanded not to touch the vegetation at all. This being the natural appetite of locusts, it becomes a strange command and presents to us the question as to whether these are really locusts or not?

First of all, how do you give commandments to locusts? You can only give commands to something - or someone - who has the intelligence to receive the command and carry it out.

This seems to emphasize that much more that what we are considering here is something more than a swarm of locusts flying through the air.

While we know that locusts can certainly be a nuisance to mankind, we could hardly think of them as being a physical enemy to man.

Only those men which have not the seal of God... The command to these "locusts" is to hurt only those who do not have the seal of God in their foreheads. We know of only one group of people who have the seal of God in their foreheads, that is the 144,000 of chapter seven.

This seems to add emphasis to the important role which this 144,000 play in the Revelation events.

If they have been chosen to be messengers against the Beast and his wicked empire during this time, how revealing this will be when these creatures seek out only men who do not have the mark of God on their foreheads as the 144,000 have. Like the days in Egypt when darkness covered Egypt, but there was light in the camps of Israel. God made a distinction between those who were His and those who were not. That distinction is also evident here as well.

Now, while no mention is made here about those others who have refused the mark of the Beast, and refused to go along with his wicked reign, it would stand to reason that they would not be affected by these creatures as well.

Now, let us consider for a moment just what, or who, are these "locusts" who come out of this abyss and are given the command to not hurt the vegetation but only men; and only men who do not have a mark on their forehead!

First of all, they are commanded to not eat any of the vegetation; which is the natural food of locusts.

Second; How can such a command be given to locusts?

Third; How could locusts, not only hear such a command, but also search out only men who do not have a mark on their forehead?

Fourth; From verse eleven we find they have a king over them. Proverbs 30:27 plainly informs us that locusts do not have a king over them!

Fifth; The description of these creatures in verses 7- 9 certainly infers they are not locusts per se.

Sixth; They come out of the abyss and the smoke which no ordinary locust could survive.

Seventh; By the fact they torment men, and men seek to flee from them, seems to point out that these creatures are indestructible.

Now, let us also consider that this must be literally taking place as well. These locusts are not just nightmares brought upon ungodly men during the tribulation.

Everything that is said about them is literal. The smoke; the abyss; the trees and grass; the men they are to torment; the fact they are given an intelligent command, etc.

While there may be differences of opinion as to just what or who these creatures are, who are in number so great and so fearsome that John describes them as great swarms of locusts, it remains that these are evidently not ordinary locusts.

It is quite possible that what we have under consideration here are demonic spirits who have been held in bondage for this very moment. Are these the angels which *sinned, that were 'delivered. ... into chains of darkness, to be reserved unto judgment* (2Peter 2:4). These are the angels who joined forces with Lucifer in his rebellion against God, who when Lucifer fell, they were placed in chains and kept in darkness for an appointed time. We have usually interpreted Peter's words to speak of "judgment" as referring to the White Throne judgment. But what is tribulation but the judgment of God upon wicked men!

When we examine what Jude has to say about this matter we note that he presents it in an interesting and thought provoking manner; And the angels which kept not their first estate, but left their own habitation, he hath reserved in everlasting chains under darkness unto the judgment of the great day.

Jude's reference to the great day has reference to the Day of the Lord. We find several references to this period of time in the Old Testament prophets. It has reference to the time when the judgments of God will fall upon mankind. This would include the Tribulation period as well!

The fact they have a "king" over them implies that they must be intelligent beings. Whether they are fallen angels, or demonic spirits, they come forth to bring judgment upon wicked men.

What a scene unfolds before us as these creatures swarm out of the abyss and go searching - they don't have to look very far - for those who do not have the seal of God on their forehead. The distinction is no doubt obvious to those who feel the sting of torment which is inflicted upon them.

Verse 5:

And to them it was given that they should not kill them, but that they should be tormented five months: and their torment {was} as the torment of a scorpion, when he striketh a man.

If these are the fallen angels, they must be frustrated by the fact; a) They can only strike those who do not have the mark of God on their foreheads, therefore they cannot bring any harm to the people of God, the very ones they would no doubt like to harm. b) They do not have the power to bring death to people; which they would probably like to do as well.

These locusts are permitted to go forth across the land seeking out those who do not have the seal of God on their forehead, whom they will torment for five months. They are given the command that they should not kill them. For five long months, these creatures from the deep strike out at those who do not have the seal on their forehead.

This could create hatred - as well as jealousy - against those who have the seal on their forehead and thus escape this horrible torment. Like Israel of old who were protected from the plagues which tormented Egypt, those who have been sealed by God during the tribulation will likewise be preserved from this invasion from the abyss.

The sting of the scorpion is a very painful thing.

WHEN MEN CAN'T DIE!

Verse 6:

And in those days shall men seek death, and shall not find it; and shall desire to die, and death shall flee from them.

The torment of the creatures from the abyss is so painful that men seek death as a means of escape from them.

We do not fully understand the meaning of this verse concerning men seeking to die and not being able to. Death is a very common thing today. There is someone committing suicide every day of the year. But for some reason men are not able to die during this five-month period when these creatures are tormenting them.

We do know that it is God who is the author of life, and if He so wills that one should not die, they will not.

Death would be an easy escape from these creatures. The purpose of them being permitted to come upon the earth is to torment men - not kill them.

While this may seem like such cruel and unusual treatment permitted by God upon mankind, let us keep in mind that these men are those who have rejected the message of the Church; they have joined the system of the Beast.

Another thing, could this be an act of mercy on God's part to try to get men to repent of their wickedness? We find from verse twenty-one that even though such horrible things happen to them, they still do not repent!

<u>Verses 7-9:</u>

And the shapes of the locusts {were} like unto horses prepared unto battle; and on their heads {were} as it were crowns like gold, and their faces {were} as the faces of men. And they had hair as the hair of women, and their teeth were as {the teeth} of lions. And they had breastplates, as it were breastplates of iron; and the sound of their wings {was} as the sound of chariots of many horses running to battle.

The description here given by John has prompted a lot of views as to just what is being described. When one first examines these verses, we get the impression of some weird and frightening creatures coming forth out of the abyss.

On closer examination, though one finds some interesting information. Vincent states; "The likeness of a locust to a horse, especially to a horse equipped with armor, is so striking that the insect is named in German 'Heupferd hay-horse,' and in Italian 'cavaletta little horse.'"

Olivier, a French writer states, "It is difficult to express the effect produced on us by the sight of the whole atmosphere filled on all sides to a great height by an innumerable quantity of these insects, whose flight was slow and uniform, and whose noise resembled that of rain."

Some have suggested that these are special creatures which have been created by God for this purpose. We do not believe this is the case however. God is not the creator of such wicked creatures. We had rather think that all that God has created was good and beautiful. If these creatures are the fallen angels who followed Lucifer in his rebellion against God, then they got into this condition because of what they did, not what God did! If these are demonic spirits, then they are involved in the work of Satan - not God.

PROPHECY OF JOEL ...

We do find some interesting statements in the prophecy of Joel, who prophesied of this day and the troubles which would be found during this period of tribulation: ...*let all the inhabitants of the land tremble: for the day of the LORD cometh... A day of darkness and of gloominess, a day of clouds and of thick darkness, as the morning spread upon the mountains: a great people and a strong; there hath not been ever the like, neither shall be any more after it, even to the years of many generations. A fire devoureth before them; and behind them a flame burneth: the land is as the garden of Eden before them, and behind them a desolate wilderness; yea, and nothing shall escape them. The appearance of them is as the appearance of horses; and as horsemen, so shall they run. Like the noise of chariots on the tops of mountains shall they leap, like the noise of a flame of fire that devoureth the stubble, as a strong people set in battle array. Before their face the people shall be much pained: all faces shall gather blackness. They shall run like mighty men; they shall climb the wall like men of war; and they shall march everyone on his ways, and they shall not break their ranks: They shall run to and fro in the city; they shall run upon the wall, they shall climb up upon the houses; they shall enter in at the windows like a thief The earth shall quake before them; the heavens shall tremble: the sun and the moon shall be dark, and the stars shall withdraw their shining,* 2:1-10.

The words of Joel are so similar to those of John in the book of Revelation that it would seem they are referring to the same thing. The words of Joel depict for us a picture of an invasion against which there is no defense. These creatures run upon the wall, they climb up upon the houses, and they enter in at the windows like a thief. There is not only no escaping from them, and no place to hide from them, neither can one choose death to escape their torment!

DESTROYED

<u>Verse 11:</u>

And they had a king over them, {which is} the angel of the bottomless pit, whose name in the Hebrew tongue {is} Abaddon, but in the Greek tongue hath {his} name Apollyon.

This presents to us more evidence of the organization in the domain of darkness. Satan is the head of this underworld kingdom of darkness and wickedness. Under Satan are those who hold positions of authority.

The king who is mentioned here that is over these creatures of the abyss is not Satan. This is the angel of the bottomless Pit.

The name of this king, given here in both Hebrew and Greek, means destroyer.

There is no mention made as to what happens to these creatures after this five-month period is ended. It is possible they are once again herded back to the abyss. If they are creatures such as angels that have fallen, then they are eternal beings and cannot die. If this is the case, then they would have to either be placed back in the abyss, or, if demonic spirits, enter the bodies of men on the earth.

ANOTHER WOE ON ITS WAY

Verse 12:

One woe is past; {and}, behold, there come two woes more hereafter.

The first "woe" has taken up five months. Five months of terrible torment to those who do not have the seal of God on their forehead, as they are stung by these locust-like creatures from the abyss.

Possibly this is the same angel we read about in 8:13, who warned of the coming three woes, who is now making the announcement that only the first one has passed, there remains two more!

THE SIXTH TRUMPET SOUNDS

Verse 13:

And the sixth angel sounded, and I heard a voice from the four horns of the golden altar which is before God,

We studied about this "golden altar" in our previous chapter. This is the altar of incense which stood before the entrance into the "Holy of holies" in the Tabernacle and Temple. It speaks of prayer and worship.

I heard a voice... This voice, like so many others in the Revelation, remains unidentified. John makes no mention as to wondering whose voice it is. Of course, he could possibly know the source of the voice without identifying who it is doing the speaking. But the indication is that he merely hears the voice without knowing the source.

The four horns of the golden altar speak in typology of power. The altar symbolizing the prayers of the people; the horns symbolizing the power of those prayers.

The number four points out that the altar was square, not round, nor octagon, or many sided. The number four also represented the four sides of the Tabernacle on which Israel camped. Each side was represented by the horns.

The first time we came upon an altar in our study of Revelation was in chapter six, where we found the souls of those who had been slain for the Word of God, and for the testimony which they held. You recall their prayers for vengeance upon those who had slain them. That vengeance is now being meted out with the trumpet judgments and woes which are coming upon wicked mankind.

Verse 14:

Saying to the sixth angel which had the trumpet, Loose the four angels which are bound in the great river Euphrates.

This verse presents some interesting questions; a) Who are these four angels? b) Why are they bound? c) How long have they been bound? d) How could they be bound in the Euphrates River?

It is the angel with the sixth trumpet that has the authority to loosen these bound angels.

By the fact that these angels are bound seems to indicate clearly that they are not good angels, but evil angels. Angels which took part in the rebellion with Lucifer, who are now bound in this great river. We have mention of the Euphrates in one other place in the Revelation, and that is when the sixth angel of the vials pours out his vial in 16:12.

Euphrates was one of the Rivers which branched off from the river which ran out of Eden (Genesis 2:14). It has been suggested that possibly the original Euphrates was destroyed or displaced by the tremendous upheaval produced by the great deluge in Noah's day. And that a new River was produced by the geological changes made by the deluge, with the caverns of the old Euphrates remaining intact underground, and this could be where these angels are presently bound.

The record does say these angels are bound in the great river Euphrates. We do not understand how four angels could be bound in the flowing waters of this river. But there are many other things our finite mind does not comprehend! How, and where, these angels are bound, it is evident that they are bound by God's decree. And if God decrees a thing must be - it will be!

Euphrates has an interesting history. As mentioned, the Euphrates was connected to the site of the first parents' home; Eden. Possibly somewhere near the river the first murder was committed. After the flood Nimrod built the city Babylon on the Euphrates. It was the site of the first rebellion against God after the deluge (Genesis 11). It was at Babylon that Nimrod helped to found the Chaldean mystical system of religion. A religion which was based on a trinity of persons who were deified; Nimrod, his son Belus, and Semiramus, his mother/wife. This was the origin of the trinity which was later adopted by the Church of Rome and introduced under the guise of religion as the Father, Son and Holy Spirit.

The River Euphrates was the North and East border given to Abraham for the Land of Promise. It is of interest to note that this boundary has never been enjoyed by Israel. The farthest east they have ever possessed was just east of the Jordan River when the two and half tribes decided to live there when the rest of Israel went into the land to the west of Jordan (Numbers chapter 32). The time will come when Israel will stretch out her borders to include the territory east of Jordan and north of their present borders, all the way to the Euphrates!

Verse 15:

And the four angels were loosed, which were prepared for an hour, and a day, and a month, and a year, for to slay the third part of men.

We have no indication as to how these angels had been bound, nor how long they had been bound. The term: an hour and a day, and a month, and a year, has produced differing opinions as to just what is meant by this time period. The two primary opinions being: a) There is a set time on God's time schedule when these angels will be loosed. Not a minute before nor a minute later. b) As the first "woe" lasted five months, this "Woe" will last a little over thirteen months.

I quote Vincent, the Greek scholar: "For an hour and a day and a month and a year. This rendering is wrong, since it conveys the idea that the four periods mentioned are to be combined as representing the length of the preparation or of the continuance of the plague. But it is to be noted that neither the article nor the preposition are repeated before day and month and year. The meaning is that the angels are prepared unto the hour appointed by God, and that this hour shall fall in its appointed day and month and year."

Everything is on schedule with God! Nothing is behind nor ahead of schedule! It is great to know that we serve a God who operates thus.

To Slay The Third Part Of Men... We do not know for sure how to interpret this statement. If this is speaking about the Nations under the Man of Sin, the amount would be one thing; If it is speaking about all the Western nations, we would have yet another figure. And, if it is speaking about the entire world, we would have still another figure.

We do recall that during the opening of the fourth seal (6:8), *one-fourth of mankind were killed.*

If we were to take the population of the world, which is approximately seven billion, and use this figure as a basis for these verses, we would have about 2,300,000,000 slain with the fourth seal opening. This would leave approximately four and one-half billion on earth. Now, with this judgment resulting in the death of one-third, this would mean approximately 2,300,000,000 more would be killed!

Regardless of how one may look at these figures, the results are catastrophic!

- **200,000,000!**

Verse 16:

And the number of the army of the horsemen {were} two hundred thousand thousand: and I heard the number of them.

What a tremendous horde that is unleashed upon this world by these four evil angels which are loosed from Euphrates! 200,000,000! No such army has ever been assembled on any battlefield of the world! There has been the supposition that this is Red China. That only China could put this many men on the battlefield today. We do know that the river Euphrates will be dried up (16:12), so that the kings of the east - which could include China - may have a way prepared for them to invade Israel. But if we are going to contend that this number refers to actual horses and actual men riding them into battle, then we must back up to the fifth trumpet and the first woe, and declare that these locusts were actual locusts as well? It would seem evident from the description that follows that this is no army that belongs to the world of mankind.

Possibly each of the four evil angels have fifty million of these under their command. If the fifth trumpet judgment produced a terrible woe upon mankind, this one produces an even greater woe!

Verse 17:

And thus I saw the horses in the vision, and them that sat on them, having breastplates of fire, and of jacinth, and brimstone: and the heads of the horses {were} as the heads of lions; and out of their mouths issued fire and smoke and brimstone.

The word *vision* that is employed here is translated in 4:3, as *sight*. In fact, these are the only places the word is employed in the Revelation. What John saw was not merely a dream or vision, it was a horrible sight of what was about to come upon the world!

Such a description of evil forces has never been witnessed nor described previous to this. This has prompted a lot of explanation as to what this "means." Some have explained it as having reference to battles already taken place in history.

It is evident that what we have described here is not a description of any army of men gathered for battle. No mere horse could be described in this manner. It seems hardly likely that any battle will be fought in this age of technological warfare on horses!

The reference to the fire and smoke has prompted some to think it has reference to tanks or jet planes. First of all, where would any nation get this many to bring on the battlefield?

It is interesting to note the many references to the numeral three that is employed in the Word of God. Notice here we have a reference to the breastplates of the horses as being of; jacinth, and brimstone, and fire.

Also, the method which is employed by these creatures to kill one-third of mankind, is fire and smoke and brimstone.

- And they kill one-third of mankind.

Demonic forces are becoming more prevalent in our world today. As far-out as it may seem there are thousands who actually worship Satan! With the increased use of drugs and narcotics there is also an increase in demonic forces which are closely related to the drug world.

Dope, drugs, etc. affect the mind, and it is the mind which the Devil attacks. It is through the mind that he seeks to control a person.

As the time of the end approaches the influence of demons will increase. Satan unleashes his forces of evil against mankind in an attempt to destroy them, and bring them to Hell!

It would seem from what we have noted here in this chapter, with the evil forces coming out of the abyss, and now with these forces coming from the river Euphrates under the command of four bound angels, that God permits Satan to release these demonic forces upon the world.

The colors associated with these horses is interesting;

• Fire would be fiery RED.

• Hyacinth would be the color of the flower, DARK BLUE.

• Brimstone would be light YELLOW.

Verse 18:

By these three was the third part of men killed, by the fire, and by the smoke, and by the brimstone, which issued out of their mouths.

Either one of these substances would result in death. Fire would certainly kill men. Smoke would suffocate men. Brimstone would poison men. To die by anyone of these means would be horrible deaths. In fact, these are probably the three most horrifying deaths one could die!

Fire - To burn to death would result in a horrible death!

Smoke - To suffocate from smoke is a horrible death! Many of those who die in fires die from the smoke, not the flames.

Brimstone - Sulphurous gases strangle and poison to death. Another horrible death!

This is belching forth from the mouths of these demonic creatures. Men have written about dragons with fire belching out of their mouth; well, many will witness something more horrifying in appearance than a dragon which will blow forth death to those they come in contact with.

We can certainly imagine that mankind will attempt to fight back against these invading creatures. It is quite possible that some of them may even be killed - who knows? If they are able to kill some of these creatures, then what happens to the demonic spirit(s) which controlled them? Do they then roam about seeking human bodies to invade?

Also, we are confronted with the question we had with the locusts, what happens to these creatures when their time of invasion is finished?

Also, let us note that it is not the horsemen who do the killing - as is normally done when horses are employed in a battle - it is the horses themselves!

Verse 19:

For their power is in their mouth, and in their tails: for their tails {were} like unto serpents, and had heads, and with them they do hurt.

The creatures take on yet a weirder appearance as John refers to the fact that they have tails like no ordinary horse has. These horse-like creatures have tails that are in appearance as serpents. While the locust creatures stung like scorpions with their tails, these creatures bite with fangs like serpents.

It would seem from the statement and with them they do hurt, that, like the locusts' sting, the serpents bite is not meant to kill but to torment. So, there will be death by their mouth with the fire, smoke and brimstone; and if any escape death from this, there will be the serpent like bite which will send poison into the bloodstream which will hurt.

Verse 20:

And the rest of the men which were not killed by these plagues yet repented not of the works of their hands, that they should not worship devils, and idols of gold, and silver, and brass, and stone, and of wood: which neither can see, nor hear, nor walk:

We are given an interesting clue as to who these creatures will attack by the statement made in this verse; *yet repented not of the works of their hands...* From this statement, it seems evident that these demonic creatures have their attention drawn against those who are followers of the Beast and his system of evil.

Like Israel in the time of Egyptian bondage, those who refuse the mark and system of the Beast will be singled out and exempted from this plague of creatures from the River Euphrates.

Note also that this invasion of demonic creatures from the Euphrates is referred to as "these plagues". Plagues are brought upon mankind - like those upon Egypt - by the Lord Himself. It is evident that this is a judgment from God. It is not a quirk of nature.

If the 144,000 have been witnesses against the Beast and his empire of wickedness; If there have been thousands who have refused the Beast and his mark; If the two witnesses have been witnessing during this period of time, then think of the influence these witnesses have had on people. It is quite possible that many thousands have been convinced not to accept the mark nor join the system of the Beast. And if all of these are exempted from these creatures, how this must infuriate the Beast and his followers!

It would seem that those who are followers of the Beast have reached the point now to where they have given themselves over to the worship of devils (demons). Satan has unleashed his forces of evil against mankind which has resulted in many thousands becoming Satan worshippers. We have but a fore view of what will happen during the tribulation with the many who are Satan worshippers now. If we have the several thousand who worship Satan now, what will it be like when the Church has been removed and the restraining force lifted for the entrance of the Beast and his kingdom of darkness!

Associated with Satan worship is also idolatry, seen in the words of this verse that men are worshipping idols of gold, etc.

Before we wonder how it is that modern man with his great intellect could stoop to worshipping idols, stop and consider these "intellects" have been idolaters for years! Anyone who would try to sell the idea that man evolved from inanimate substance into his condition today, must be considered an idolater! These great "intellects" would have us think that the universe all started with some inanimate beginning. They would have Genesis 1:1 read; "In the beginning, hydrogen...."

Thus in their denial of the creation story as recorded in Genesis they become idolaters. They continue this theory to its extremity during the tribulation by giving themselves over to the Beast and his wicked plans.

NEITHER REPENTED THEY

Verse 21:

Neither repented they of their murders, nor of their sorceries, nor of their fornication, nor of their thefts.

It would no doubt be safe to say that no other age of people has witnessed what the people of the tribulation will experience. The troubles which we have studied about in the past few chapters are very frightening, to say the least. Being faced with such horrifying plagues from God, it would appear that men would fall on their face in repentance. As a whole, they do just the opposite! Why? How could people face such things, knowing they are from God (6:15-17), and not repent? Possibly the following will give us some help;

Ephesians 4:17-19; *This I say therefore, and testify in the Lord, that ye henceforth walk not as other Gentiles walk, in the vanity of their mind, Having the understanding darkened, being alienated from the life of God through the ignorance that is in them, because of the blindness of their heart: Who being past feeling have given themselves over unto lasciviousness, to work all uncleanness with greediness.*

2Thessalonians 2:10-12; *And with all deceivableness of unrighteousness in them that perish; because they received not the love of the truth, that they might be saved. And for this cause God shall send them strong delusion, that they should believe a lie: That they all might be damned who believed not the truth, but had pleasure in unrighteousness.*

When men have hardened their heart to truth, they become susceptible to believing anything! That is what has happened to the people spoken of here by John, no doubt!

Their murders... Remember when the second seal was opened and the red horse rode forth, it was said at that time; *power was given to him that sat thereon to take peace from the earth, and that they should kill one another.* With the entrance of the Beast and his system of wickedness, the gates are opened for all kinds of provocations.

The murders which they are mainly held guilty of before God are no doubt the people who have refused to join the system of the Beast which has resulted in many of them being killed (6:9-11). Those who have died for their testimony, and refusal to join the system of the Beast and take his mark, will be avenged shortly.

Nor sorceries... Usually when we find the word "sorcery" we usually think of witchcraft and wizards. God gave warning to Israel in the Old Testament against going after these practices (Leviticus 19:31; 20:6; Deuteronomy 18:9-13). When we get to the New Testament, however, we find the subject is dealt with in another light.

The word which is employed here in Revelation 9:21, is from the Greek word "pharmakeia." (Pharmah-Kiyah). The word transliterated into English is the word that it is more familiar to us "Pharmacy."

When we look at the meaning of this word we find that it means; "enchantment with drugs."

So, John is here giving us a description of the conditions of men during the dark days of the tribulation. They are so carried away with their drugs that they refuse to repent of their sinful ways. Also, notice the words which are associated with this addiction; fornication, murders, and thefts. Such things that we also find associated with those who are obsessed with this horrible habit today.

The propaganda which is given by the Devil to those who become hooked on this habit of the drug world, is far from the reality which shall come upon all those who fall prey to his temptations.

More and more people are becoming dependent upon drugs and their influences. Many feel they could not live if it were not for their drugs which help them get through the day. The sad picture is that many become so controlled by their dependence on these drugs that they will do anything to get their desires satisfied. Sell their bodies; rob, steal, and kill!

There is another place in the Revelation which speaks of the doom of those who have forsaken God for the things of the world. Chapter eighteen describes the fall of the city of wickedness. After speaking of the many things which will happen to the city and those things which will cease to be found there, the Lord concludes with another reference to this subject; *"for by thy sorceries were all nations deceived."* (18:23). Again, we have the same word, "Pharmakeia." We could read this verse thus; "by their enchantment with drugs were all the nations deceived." So, we find the effect drugs will have upon those of that day - as well as the way in which God looks at the matter.

Another place where we find reference to the subject is 21:8. In the midst of the listing of all those who will not enter heaven - including all liars - we have the word *"sorcerers."* Now this word is from the Greek word "Pharmakeus", which is pronounced; Pharrna-kois. The meaning of this word is different from the previous references. This word means "An enchanter with Drugs." Or, "One who prepares and uses magical remedies." This would have reference to the "pusher" of drugs. Those. who sell drugs for profit to those who have become hooked on their habit.

From this passage, we can readily see the terrible doom which awaits those who are found guilty of pushing drugs. They are of that crowd who are only interested in their greedy gain derived from this habit which they are pushing, and which destroys so many lives.

In 22:15 we have the words; *"For without are dogs, and sorcerers."* Now this is the same word which is found in 21:8, but many feel that the reference here refers also to those who use drugs offered by the pusher and not just the pusher.

Both alike are kept out of that beautiful city. (It would not be a beautiful city for very long if they were permitted to enter) Everywhere we find this vice being permitted the lowest of humanity may be found. Men stoop to the lowest degree in their lust and determination to satisfy the lust and desire which bums in their heart. Note that those who use and push drugs are classified after "dogs ... " This is their rightful place in society, as well as in the eyes of God. Those who would push drugs on innocent children to get them hooked so they in tum may be forced to buy more drugs from them are certainly in the right company to be classified with dogs!

We find that Paul also employs the word in his epistle to Galatia, 5:20; *"Idolatry, witchcraft."* The word *"witchcraft"* is the same word, "Pharmakeia."

Paul lets us know that, those who are guilty of such practices, Shall not inherit the Kingdom of God. While this has been found in our Bible ever since the Holy Spirit inspired holy men to write these words, they have surely never been needed as they are being needed today in our society. Young people - as well as Moms and Dads - need to read, and re-read, these passages today, as it is the youth who are falling prey to this terrible habit. The ultimate doom is death! It is easier to never take that first marijuana cigarette; that first pill; that first snort of coke.

Their fornication... The conditions which exist today will continue - only getting worse! The sexual revolution which has changed our society into a do-as-you-please generation is evident during the tribulation. Our society has been bombarded through the media that promiscuity and illicit sexual practices are accepted today. Hollywood has portrayed to our generation that marriage is not only not necessary, but something to be made light of. The television has piped its filth of sexual promiscuity into the home in our generation. Included are also the many publications which offer their version of the loose immoral lifestyles which are accepted by today's society.

The Gays have come out of their closets and publicly proclaimed their preferred lifestyle. While this is bad enough in our society, we could live with those who choose to live such an immoral manner of lifestyle, (we live with drunkards, and liars - which are no worse!), but when they invade the class rooms of our public schools and seek to influence our children into thinking that this is a normal lifestyle; that it is up to them if they decide to live this way, then this is too much!

The homosexual community has not only invaded the rest of society with their immoral and ungodly type of lifestyle, now society is being invaded with the disease from the homosexual community as well: AIDS! This frightening disease is invading the rest of society through blood transfusions; through other means of transmitting this horrible disease.

This word carries the idea of fornication in the wide range of meaning. It involves all illicit sexual activity, as well as spiritual fornication. While the world, in general, stands condemned for its illicit sexual practices, it is also guilty before God of spiritual fornication. Especially during this time of tribulation when the false prophet has erected an image to the beast and commanded that all should worship this image. The wholesale surrender to this demand will amount to fornication. Instead of worshipping God, the Creator of all things, man chooses to worship an invention of man's own hands.

When men's remedies are accepted, instead of God's commands; when men bow to an image made by sinful man, instead of falling prostrate before the throne of God, there can be but one consequence = judgment!

We read of the judgments visited upon the Antediluvian world, as well as Sodom and Gomorrah, for their wicked and ungodly lifestyles; the people of the tribulation period will likewise be visited for their sins. In fact, someone has said that if this generation was not judged for their wickedness, then Sodom and the Antediluvian world would have to be apologized to. Well, it is for certain that Sodom will not be apologized to! This generation will be judged for their sins and wickedness!

NOR THEIR THEFTS... What would this include? In what way are these being labeled thieves? What have they been guilty of stealing?

Would this include Virtue? Honesty? Youth? Purity?

How many parents are "stealing" from their children the privilege to be exposed to the Word of God that will save them from hell, by refusing to bring them up in Church and in a godly home atmosphere?

How many have stolen from our youth through the introduction into the drug and dope world? How many have stolen from our youth through their introduction, forcefully or otherwise, into the pornography world?

The conditions which exist at this time are at their lowest ebb as far as godliness is concerned. The Church has been removed from the earth. The only church which is left are those who deny the blood of Jesus Christ; the power of the Spirit; the Name of Jesus Christ, etc. Those Spirit-filled, Blood-washed, Jesus' Name baptized, people have all left this earth to be with the Lord in the heavens. Since Pentecost they have been the only people who have stood between this ungodly world and judgments from God. The Church has been the means of holding back - to some degree, at least - the deluge of ungodliness from this world through the message She has preached and the life She has lived.

In this ungodly condition man stands guilty before God. A holy God shall judge unholy man with a holy judgment!

CHAPTER TEN

• THE ANGEL WITH THE LITTLE BOOK

Verse 1:

And I saw another mighty angel come down from heaven, clothed with a cloud: and a rainbow {was} upon his head, and his face {was} as it were the sun, and his feet as pillars of fire:

It is impossible for us to fully fathom the condition which the world is in at this point in time. No war has ever brought upon the world those things which have prevailed on this earth during the sounding forth of the first six trumpet judgments from God!

The world has been devastated by the events which have transpired. The rivers and oceans of waters have been greatly affected. The forests and grasses of the fields have been greatly affected. Mankind, with the coming invasion of the demonic creatures out of the abyss, and then from the Euphrates River, have been left shaken beyond description.

John has been in heaven witnessing these events from that vantage point. Now he must be back on the earth as this opening statement of this chapter seems to indicate.

This chapter, like chapter seven, which took place between the sixth and seventh seal, has been referred to as another parenthetical chapter. These events taking place between the sixth and seventh trumpet judgments.

Mighty angel... We have references to angels dozens of times in the Revelation. In fact, someone said they are mentioned more than sixty times in the Revelation!

Like the "*another angel*" of chapter eight (v. 3), we are confronted with differing views as to who this "mighty" angel is. The camp is divided by the commentators. On one side, we have those who contend the angel is Jesus Christ Himself. On the other side, we have those who contend he is just another of the many angels mentioned in the Revelation.

The argument of those who contend this must be Jesus Christ Himself, refers to the fact that this angel is mentioned as having a "*rainbow about his head... and clothed with a cloud, his face as it were the sun, and his feet as pillars of fire."* And by the fact that he places his feet, one on the sea and the other on the earth, shows that he is declaring ownership. Reference is made to the description given by John in chapter one, as he witnessed the glorified Lord. When comparing the vision of chapter one with the description here of this angel, we can note some similarities.

On the other side of this matter are those lined up who strongly feel this is NOT Jesus Christ. First of all, the term "mighty angel" does not necessarily mean a reference to Jesus. We have the same word in 5:2, where there it is translated "strong angel." It is evident there that it is NOT Jesus Christ, as He is presented later as the "Lion of the tribe of Judah", and the "Lamb."

Another thing to point out that seems to confirm that this is the Lord Jesus Christ Himself, is that He has a book in His hand. Is it the book we read about in chapter five that He took from the hand of the Ancient of Days? Again, by placing His foot on land and sea, is He not declaring ownership, and the book in His hand is the one which he has opened to bring these events upon man during this time of tribulation?

As for the description of glory which accompanies this angel, we note in 18:1, *And after these things I saw another angel come down from heaven, having great power; and the earth was lightened with his glory.* Here is yet another angel which John witnesses coming down from heaven, and this one manifests such glory that the earth is lightened by the glory. Yet there does not seem to be any who want to say this is Jesus Christ. And let us recall that even Moses, after he had been in the presence of God for some time, had his face to shine with such glory that he had to put a veil on his face so he could speak to Israel, as the glory which shone from his face was too much for Israel to look upon. So, God has anointed both angels and men with His glory on special occasions.

The reference to a rainbow was upon his head could have symbolic significance. As this is a book of symbols and signs, this could be yet another one of those signs. The "rainbow" reminds us of Genesis and Noah and the promise which God made to Noah and mankind concerning the great deluge which had just destroyed the inhabitants of earth. The bow was to be a reminder of the promise which God made that day that this would never happen again. Could this sign not to be a reference to the fact that God will keep His promises! At this juncture of time, it would seem that God has forsaken His creation. Look at the world!

Look at the havoc all around! Look at the death and dying! Look at the expressions on the faces of those who have looked at the creatures ravaging the earth with their terror. Who could look at all this and still conclude that God was anywhere around, or concerned about the earth! Well, God is very much around, and He is very much concerned about what is going on in this world. And the conditions of havoc which are brought upon the world are not the results of a God who hates His own creation; but the results of that creation who has rebelled against his Creator and rejected His Word. The only consequence to such an attitude is judgment! That is what is taking place during the tribulation. And the angel with the rainbow *"upon his head"* seems to be saying, I know what is going on! I have not forgotten my promise! It will all be alright in the end!

Verse 2:

And he had in his hand a little book open: and he set his right foot upon the sea, and {his} left {foot} on the earth,

The Revelation is a book of books. We witnessed the great concern over the seven-sealed book of chapter five. Now here is one in the hand of the angel who comes down from heaven to the earth. In chapter twenty we note the Book of Life as well as the books which the dead are to be judged out of.

So, we have some very interesting and very important books mentioned in Revelation. Most seem to agree that this book is the same book which is mentioned in chapter five. There, in chapter five, it was sealed with seven seals. These seals have been opened now, and the book appears in the hand of the angel opened.

It may be so that this book is the same book as in chapter five which Jesus took, as He was the only one worthy to take the book and to loosen the seals; but there are some interesting points worthy of our consideration:

First of all: the Greek word for book as spoken about in chapter five is "biblion." (bib-lee'-on) The Greek word for the little book mentioned here is "bibliaridion." (bib-lee-ar-id'-ee-on) It is a diminutive of "biblion." We could say it today, Book and Booklet.

So, it does not seem to refer to the same book.

Also, if the book of chapter five is the title deed to the earth which had been usurped by Satan as many contend, and contained the judgments which would bring about the restoration back to the

rightful owner; then how could it be referred to as a little book?

Something which is of such great importance, and having such far-reaching significance, could hardly be labeled a little book, it would seem.

And, if Jesus alone was worthy to take the book and loose the seals, would He then give it to an angel to bring to this earth?

And, if this is the same book, would it then be given to a man to eat?

WHAT IS IT THEN?

First let us notice that it is said the book is open. This signifies a revealing. It is not something which is hidden. Unlike the book of chapter five which was sealed, and which could only be opened by someone who could be found worthy, this book has been opened to reveal its contents.

John was told to go to the angel and take the book out of his hand and eat the book. This is a gesture which we find elsewhere in the Bible which speaks of man receiving the Word of God. For instance; Jeremiah 15:16, *Thy words were found, and I did eat them; and thy word was unto me the joy and rejoicing of mine heart: for I am called by thy name, 0 Lord God of hosts.*

Ezekiel 3:1-3, *Moreover he said unto me, Son of man, eat that thou findest; eat this roll, and go speak unto the house of Israel. So I opened my mouth, and he caused me to eat that roll. And he said unto me, Son of man, cause thy belly to eat, and fill thy bowels with this roll that I give thee. Then did I eat {it}; and it was in my mouth as honey for sweetness.*

In both of these examples the purpose for eating the "book," or "roll" as it is called in Ezekiel, was to enable the prophet to speak the word of the Lord to the people. And as soon as John eats the book, he is then told that he "must prophesy again."

HE SET HIS RIGHT FOOT UPON THE SEA... LEFT FOOT ON THE EARTH... If we continue with the thought that the book of Revelation contains a lot of signs and symbols, then we would look at this statement as symbolic as well.

First of all, consider the awesomeness of this sight which John witnesses. Imagine an angel so huge as to be able to place one foot on the sea and the other on the land! If we are to consider this angel as being some kind of gigantic personage, then what about when John comes and takes the book out of his hand in verse ten?!

At least one commentator felt that the reference to the sea was a reference to the nations, while the reference to the earth was a reference to Israel. We do know that it is Israel and the nations who have our attention in this book.

When we get to chapter thirteen, we will find that the Beast comes out of the Sea. Which is, evidently, a reference to the masses of humanity. In other words, he will come from among men.

Also, in that chapter we find that his cohort, the false prophet, comes out of the earth! By his very title, false prophet, this denotes that he is a religious man.

So, we have a world political system man who rises to the top as the Man of sin; and we have a religious man who joins his team and helps to bring about the system which will demand that all mankind be numbered and marked.

However, one may choose to look at this, it would appear that the Lord is saying, I have my foot on both the world and my people Israel; I have my foot on the political system of mankind, and the religious systems of mankind.

The placing of the foot signified ownership. It also signified defeat and victory over a foe.

Before this period under consideration in the Revelation has expired, not only will the people of God know that the Lord He is God, but the whole of creation will know that He is God!

Verse 3:

And cried with a loud voice, as {when} a lion roareth: and when he had cried, seven thunders uttered their voices.

We do not know what the angel cried out as a roaring lion, unless we find it in verse six. Did the angel say anything? Or was his voice a roar of claim to what was rightly the Lord's? The lion has been used for both a reference to the Lord Jesus as well as to the Adversary,

Satan. Satan is referred to in 1Peter 5:8, *as a roaring lion, walketh about, seeking whom he may devour.*

Our Lord Jesus is also referred to as *the Lion of the tribe of Juda* in Revelation 5:5. While Satan may be considered the king of this world; our Lord is King of kings and Lord of lords! And one day even Satan himself shall bow in obeisance to our Lord.

seven thunders uttered their voices... Once again, we come upon the numeral seven in our study of this interesting book.

Since when did thunder have a voice?

Vincent says: "The Jews were accustomed to speak of thunder as the 'seven voices.'"

There is an interesting Psalm which depicts for us the seven voices of the Lord:

Psalm 29:

• v. 3, *The voice of the LORD is upon the waters ...*

• v. 4, *The voice of the LORD is powerful...*

• v.4, *The voice of the LORD is full of majesty ...*

• v.5, *The voice of the LORD breaketh the cedars ...*

• v.7, *The voice of the LORD divideth the flames of fire ...*

• v.8, *The voice of the LORD shaketh the wilderness ...*

• v.9, *The voice of the LORD maketh the hinds to calve ...*

It is also in this Psalm, verse three, that we read: *The God of glory thundereth.*

As to who - or what - these seven thunders are we are not told. It is left, at this time, to our speculation.

Verse 4:

And when the seven thunders had uttered their voices, I was about to write: and I heard a voice from heaven saying unto me, Seal up those things which the seven thunders uttered, and write them not.

Just what these "*Seven Thunders*" said will remain a mystery until we know even as we are known. Whatever it was they said, it must have had something to do with the events which were about to transpire at this point in the tribulation. Something which, evidently,

God did not want told before it came to pass.

Now you recall that John had been told *Seal not the sayings of the prophecy of this book.* (22:10).

The book of Revelation was to be an open book because it dealt with the events which would transpire during the last days of the "Times of the Gentiles" prior to the return of Jesus Christ to this earth. So, the book; the message of the book, is to be open: but the particular statements made here by the seven thunders are not to be made openly known to all.

- This is the only place in the book of Revelation where we have the command to "seal up" something.

When we consider the book of Daniel, which is so closely connected to Revelation, we find an interesting passage relative to this one. In fact, it may have reference to the same thing! This is in chapter twelve. Daniel had just been told about how there would be a time of trouble for the people of Daniel (Jews). Daniel is then told to shut up the words, and *seal the book, even to the time of the end.* (12:4).

This prompted Daniel to inquire (verse 6), How long shall it be to the end of these wonders? Then in verse seven we have the interesting comparison to what John witnessed in our chapter under study; *And I heard the man clothed in linen, which was upon the waters of the river, when he held up his right hand and his left hand to heaven, and sware by him that liveth for ever that it shall be for a time, times, and an half.*

In Bible prophecy, the term "time" has reference to one year. This would seem evident from such passages as Daniel 4:16 and 7:25, and also Revelation 12:14 and 13:5. So, by the mention of *time, times, and an half*, we conclude the reference is to three and one-half years.

We are reaching that point in our study of Revelation in which the Middle of the Week is reached, and the final three and one-half years are about to begin. It is this final three and one-half years that have that period of time which becomes the darkest days of all during the tribulation. The Beast will issue his edict to take his mark - or else! It is during these three and one-half years that the Man of sin becomes identified as the Beast!

Believe it or not, there are those who would have us to think they know what these seven thunders uttered. We are informed that the

Seventh-Day Adventist's have presumed to declare what they said.

Someone has said they are the seven crusades. And there are others who have suggested what they said.

How is it that men so far removed from the event can suggest what was said, when John who heard what was said, was not permitted to write it down? There is no one among us who can know what they said. The time will come when it will be revealed if it had to do with the events which would transpire during the rest of tribulation week.

DELAY NO LONGER!

Verses 5, 6:

And the angel which I saw stand upon the sea and upon the earth lifted up his hand to heaven, And sware by him that liveth for ever and ever, who created heaven, and the things that therein are, and the earth, and the things that therein are, and the sea, and the things which are therein, that there should be time no longer:

It would seem from this statement that this further shows that this angel is not the Lord Jesus Christ. If this were the Lord Jesus, why would He be lifting His hand toward heaven to swear by the One in heaven?

We note in Hebrews 6:13, *For when God made promise to Abraham, because He could swear by no greater, He sware by Himself.*

In lifting his hand toward heaven and swearing to the One who liveth for ever and ever, we can identify the One to whom he is swearing by such statements as:

1:8, *I am Alpha and Omega, the beginning and the ending, saith the Lord, which is, and which was, and which is to come, the Almighty.*

1:18, *I am he that liveth, and was dead, and, behold, 1 am alive for evermore ...*

1Timothy 6:16, *Who only hath immortality ...*

He is further identified by the statement: *who created heaven...* We note from such passages as:

4:11, *Thou art worthy, 0 Lord, to receive glory and honour and power: for thou hast created all things, and for thy pleasure they are and were created.*

Colossians 1:16, For by Him were all things created, that are in *heaven, and that are in earth...*

John 1:3, *All things were made by Him; and without Him was not any thing made that was made.*

The One who is sitting on the throne in heaven at this time is Jesus Christ. This is evident from what John writes in chapter four. It is to this One - Jesus Christ - that the angel lifts his hand and swears. that there should be time no longer... "Time" is from the Greek word "kronos" which means either time or delay. It is evident from the fact that the tribulation continues, as we noted from Daniel 12:6, for time, times, and an half, or three and one-half years. The statement is not that time, per se, is stopping; but that there would be no delay to fulfillment of the eternal plan of God regarding the tribulation and those things ordained of God. So, to better understand the statement, we should read; "*that there should be delay no longer.*"

When we consider the longsufferings of our Lord toward man through the years, (2Peter 3:9); when we consider how long God has been dealing with Adam's sons; when we consider that it is the will of God to dwell among His people and reign over them on this earth as King of kings and Lord of lords; then we can better understand and appreciate this statement by the angel.

LET THERE BE DELAY NO LONGER!

LET THE KINGDOM ARRIVE TO PLANET EARTH!

LET THE FULFILLMENT OF GOD'S DIVINE PLAN FOR MAN AND CREATION COME TO IT'S GLORIOUS CONCLUSION!

Just think, only about three and one-half more years till the Lord returns to this earth with His redeemed and establishes on this earth His kingdom. It is this that Daniel makes reference to in his interpretation of Nebuchadnezzar's dream (Daniel 2:44,45).

THE MYSTERY OF GOD

Verse 7:

But in the days of the voice of the seventh angel, when he shall begin to sound, the mystery of God should be finished, as he hathdeclared to his servants the prophets.

We should take verses five through seven together in order to get the entire sentence. When we do this, we can better understand this verse in connection with the preceding statement about delay being no longer. The sounding forth of the seventh trumpet marks the last trumpet judgment, and also introduces the vial judgments which are the concluding judgments prior to the return of Jesus Christ to this earth.

Possibly we could read the statement: "Let there be delay no longer; but let the seventh angel begin to sound forth his trumpet, marking the conclusion of tribulation and return of Jesus Christ!"

When the seventh angel sounds - and he will not sound his trumpet until we get to chapter eleven and after the second WOE is past - then the mystery of God is to be finished. Just what is this mystery of God?

First, let us consider the term finished. This word is from the Greek term "teleo." The meaning of the word speaks of that which has reached its end. And, also interesting, this word is found in other places in the Revelation; 11:7; 15:1,8; 17:17; 20:3,5,7. Something which has been declared by the prophets is about to come to the desired conclusion.

Mr Dake, in his book Revelation Expounded, makes four points of interest concerning this mystery:

• 1. It is to be finished during the days of the seventh trumpet.

• 2. It is glad tidings.

• 3. It has been proclaimed by the prophets since the world began.

• 4. It has been delayed throughout the ages.

Mr Dake felt that this could only refer to Satan being cast out of heaven.

• 1. It will take place during the sounding of the seventh trumpet.

• 2. Satan being cast out would certainly be good news to all of heaven.

• 3. The casting out of Satan has been proclaimed by the prophets from the earliest of times.

• 4. It is the one event which has been delayed through the centuries.

When Satan is cast out of heaven in chapter twelve, this will certainly be a glorious time of victory to all of heaven, as well as mark the quickly approaching conclusion of the tribulation and return of Jesus Christ.

There are several mysteries mentioned in the Word of God.

One interesting reference to the *mystery of Christ* is found in Paul's epistle to Ephesus, (3:3-9).

The mystery of which Paul speaks concerns the Church being established on this earth which would include both Jew and Gentile. People who through the many centuries since Abraham stepped on the scene and the Jewish nation had its beginning, did not fellowship one another. In fact, the Gentile nations were considered as heathen, and dogs, to the Jewish mind. That these two people would be brought together into one common bond is something which, though it was referred to by allusion and prophetic reference in the Old Testament, did not seem could ever be a reality. When the Lord returns, and establishes His kingdom on this earth, there will be a glorious and beautiful blending together of these people who will share in this kingdom.

There are other things which one could consider a mystery which could also apply to this statement, it would seem. Why has a holy God permitted sin to thrive among His creation? Why have the righteous suffered through the centuries? Why did God choose Israel as His elect on the earth? Why did God permit Satan to have free course to operate on this earth?

All of these things will be answered with the conclusion of the tribulation.

To realize that all of these things will find their glorious conclusion at the appearing of Jesus Christ, and John hears the reference to the conclusion of these things must have stirred within his heart a great anticipation for this to become a reality.

Although this glorious end is something which is certain to happen, it would not be for a while yet.

Those in chapter six under the altar were told they had to wait; those who are suffering under the man of sin at this time, will also have to wait for a while longer. God will not appear with His kingdom until it is time. God works by a time schedule. He will not be late, nor will He be early.

Verse 8:

And the voice which I heard from heaven spake unto me again, and said, Go {and} take the little book which is open in the hand of the angel which standeth upon the sea and upon the earth.

There is no way for us to know how long the angel stood with a foot on the sea and the other on the land with this book open in his hand, but he is still standing there, and John hears the command to go to him and take the book from his hand!

This may seem like a presumptuous action to take, but when the Lord speaks, we should be ready to obey regardless of how against the "grain" it may appear to be to us.

SWEET & BITTER

<u>Verse 9:</u>

And I went unto the angel, and said unto him, Give me the little book. And he said unto me, Take {it}, and eat it up; and it shall make thy belly bitter, but it shall be in thy mouth sweet as honey.

This statement by John in asking the angel to give him the book, seems to also tell us that this angel is not the Lord Jesus Christ. For one thing it would seem that the Lord is the One who is talking to John out of heaven. Secondly, it does not seem likely that John would be telling the Lord to give him the book.

As mentioned previously, John is told to "eat the book." While this may seem like a strange thing to demand of the Apostle, as noted before, this is not something new.

At the first reception of the Word of God, it many times brings a wonderful feeling of great joy and excitement to our life. The initial commitment brings a wonderful feeling of relief to our mind. The time comes though, when the responsibility of obeying the commands of His Word may cut against the flesh. The "old man" will have to be continually kept under the control of the Spirit. At times this may taste "bitter" to the flesh. But to those who permit the Word of God to be the guide for their life they will be blessed greatly.

<u>Verse 10:</u>

And I took the little book out of the angel's hand, and ate it up; and it was in my mouth sweet as honey: and as soon as I had eaten it, my belly was bitter.

We cannot be as a "picky" child who only wants to eat certain things. Usually, those things are not what his mother prepares for the meal! If the flesh could have his way we would only want to hear and receive those things which would make us feel good all the time. We would be like the people in the times of the prophet, who would declare *"speak unto us smooth things. "*

The command, however, is to eat it all. Those things which go against the "grain" are usually those things which we need the most. If we will permit the Word of God to direct our life, not only will we be blessed of the Lord, but our life will be richer for it as well.

Verse 11:

And he said unto me, Thou must prophesy again before many peoples, and nations, and tongues, and kings.

We are informed that the Greek word "epi" which is here translated "before" could also be translated - and possibly should be in this case - "Of."

John, of course, was a prisoner on a barren island called Patmos. He had no way to preach to nations and people and kings. Except it be through the pen! In this manner John, would certainly speak to *many nations, people, tongues and kings.*

But looking at the word as meaning "of', we see that John was not through at this point in writing the book of Revelation. There remained many other things which he must write about. These things would involve "peoples, nations, tongues and kings.

John thus becomes the means whereby God outlined the future that reaches down to the end of this century - and beyond! The things of which John would write would involve people of all walks of life, and most particularly the people of Israel.

So, don't put your pen away John, the Lord seems to be saying, there remains much to be written.

CHAPTER ELEVEN

If we could, for the moment, ignore the chapter divisions - as John originally wrote the Revelation - we would see that this is a continuation of what was transpiring in chapter ten. John has received the book from the hand of the angel, having eaten it, and hearing the message that he must prophesy again, etc., he is then given a reed to measure the temple of God. It is evidently the same angel who has given him the reed to measure with.

This chapter takes us back under the Old Testament structure of events. We have under consideration in this chapter several things which are evidently Jewish oriented, which informs us that God is moving among His people Israel at this time.

By the mention of the many things Jewish, it is evident that the Church is not on the earth at this time in the Revelation.

Verse 1:

And there was given me a reed like unto a rod: and the angel stood, saying, Rise, and measure the temple of God, and the altar, and them that worship therein.

And there was given me a reed like unto a rod... The reference to the "reed" and the "rod" carry a two-fold thought. One is that not only was John to measure the temple, etc., but also reference to the rod seems to indicate judgment, or the ruling whereby God will rule Israel. Reference had been made (2:27) how that the rod spoke of ruling. Also, we have reference to the rod as a means of chastisement and punishment (Psalm 2:9; 23:4).

and the angel stood, saying, Rise, and measure the temple of God... We have had no direct reference to the temple of God being on earth at this time. In fact, the only two places where there is reference to a temple before now in the Revelation is in regards to a promise which is given to the church and those who overcome (3:12); and to those of the great multitude who had come through the great tribulation (7:15).

Now this cannot be the temple of Herod, as this temple has long since been destroyed by Titus, the Roman general and his invading forces when they overthrew Jerusalem in 70 A.D. This was some twenty or more years before John hears these words.

Now, either Israel has built a temple by this time, or, this cannot be a literal temple. It could be of symbolic significance.

This cannot be the temple which is spoken of by the prophet Ezekiel either (42:), as it will evidently be built in Shiloh.

Paul in his epistle to the Thessalonians (2Thessalonians 2:4) spoke of a temple into which the man of sin would enter and declare himself God. This could evidently be the temple which John is told to measure. It is a temple which was to be built at a later time in Jerusalem.

If this is speaking of a temple which is yet to be built in the city of Jerusalem, then it is possible that even the man of sin himself will assist in bringing about the erection of this temple. This would be especially so if the temple is to be erected on the old temple site where the Moslem Mosque of Omar now resides.

The term measure would seem to carry with it more meaning than just determining the dimensions of a building. This seems to be further emphasized by the fact that there are no dimensions even given!

It would seem that this command to John seems to be saying that the time has come for the complete and eternal separation to God of all those things which are His, from association and contact with that which is not His. It is the measuring of ownership! It is to mark off that which belongs to God. The man of sin has made his claims, God decrees that which is His!

and the altar... This would evidently be a reference again to the golden altar, as the brazen altar was not directly connected to the temple. Again, the golden altar speaks of worship; of prayer; or fellowship with God through our daily communion With Him. Only the people of God have this privilege to know fellowship and communion with God. While the man of sin declares that he is God, and the false prophet decrees that all must worship him, God is saying, True worship belongs to Me! The true worshipper will worship Him and Him alone!

and them that worship therein... Even those who are worshippers of God are measured off as His.

Those who have committed their life to the Lord belong to Him. He lays claim on them. Your worship is important to God. He delights in the worship of His people.

With our attention being drawn to the temple and those who worship therein, along with the altar, we are reminded of the Jewishness of the Revelation. The people of Israel are the primary subjects of the major portion of the Revelation. Especially Chapters six to nineteen.

<u>Verse 2:</u>

But the court which is without the temple leave out, and measure it not; for it is given unto the Gentiles: and the holy city shall they tread under foot forty {and} two months.

The court of the temple was not off-limits to the Gentiles, only the temple area. This statement to John not only reminds us of this, but it also informs us that God is concerned right now for His people Israel. It is His people Israel that judgment - measuring - will come through the Great Tribulation. A judgment which will result in many of them acknowledging Him as Messiah and turn their heart to the Lord. The time will come when the Gentile nations will be judged, but right now it is Israel who will be judged through the fires of tribulation.

This also brings to our attention an interesting prophecy made by our Lord during His ministry found in Luke 21:24, *And they shall fall by the edge of the sword, and shall be led away captive into all nations: and Jerusalem shall be trodden down of the Gentiles, until the times of the Gentiles be fulfilled.*

When Israel re-took their beloved city completely in the June 1967 war, there were several who got excited that this prophecy was being fulfilled. While Israel did indeed regain her beloved city - and would relocate her capital there - she still exists with the most holy place of Jerusalem occupied by the Mosque of Omar, the Dome of the Rock.

Also, during the tribulation period Gentile powers will again be a dominate force in the city. In fact, the prophet Zechariah informs us (chapter 14) that the city will once again fall into the hands of the Gentiles. But it will only be for a short while as the Lord will then come to bring deliverance to His people in that time.

The *times of the Gentiles* is an expression which speaks of the period of time in which Gentile influence and domination would be felt in the land of Israel and over the people Israel. It had its beginning with Nebuchadnezzar overthrowing Jerusalem and taking Israel captive in

Babylon. Daniel spoke of Babylon as being the first of a succession of Gentile powers who would influence, harass, and rule over Israel.

This Gentile domination will continue until the Lord Himself comes in great power and glory at the time of Armageddon. He will bring judgment to His people Israel and will bring to an end the rule of the Beast and the Gentile's lordship over Israel once and for all time.

There are two expressions that we should not get confused: *times of the Gentiles*, and *fullness of the Gentiles*. Paul in Romans 11:25 spoke of the *fullness of the Gentiles*. These do not refer to the same thing! The *times* of the Gentiles has to do with Israel and her being dominated and influenced by Gentile powers. The *fullness* of the Gentiles has to do with the Church. God, at the rejection by Israel of Jesus Christ, declared that He would take out of the Gentiles a people for His name. The term *fullness* speaks of complete. A filling up. When the time which has been allotted to the Church age by God has ran its course, He will call His Church away. When the last one has been added to that number which brings about the fullness, then the Lord will call His Church away.

and the holy city shall they tread under foot forty and two months... The expressions: *forty and two months, time, times, and half a time, thousand two hundred and threescore days*, all have reference to the same period of time. They are synonymous terms. They are all speaking of three and one-half years.

This statement also affirms that the times of the Gentiles did not end with the taking of Jerusalem in 1967. The times of the Gentiles will continue until the Lord comes (the Stone cut out of the mountain without hands), smites the image upon his feet (that is in his completed form and condition.)

Now the Jews reckoned their year with 12 months of thirty days each usually. They would add an extra month every so often to bring their calendar into line with the seasons. So, the Jewish prophetic year would have 360 days in it.

The word "ethnos", which is here translated "Gentiles", is employed some 23 times in the Revelation. In every other place, it is translated "nations."

Verse two speaks of "*forty two months*." Verse three speaks of "*a thousand two hundred and three-score days*." Chapter 12, verse 6, says "a thousand two hundred and threescore days." And verse 14 states "a time, and times, and half a time." Daniel uses the phrase "midst of the week" (9:27). All of these terms are referring to the same period of time: the last half of the week. Or, three and one-half years.

So, God is saying to John, the Gentiles have forty-two more months; three and one half more years, to trod down - or control - the city of Jerusalem. At which time the Lord Jesus shall come with His Church to bring judgment to this world and especially to the people of Abraham's seed.

Jude said Enoch spoke prophetically of that great event like this: *Behold, the Lord cometh with ten thousands of His saints. To execute judgment upon all, and to convince all that are ungodly among them of all their ungodly deeds which they have ungodly committed, and of all their hard speeches which ungodly sinners have spoken against him* (Jude 14,15).

At that time there will be great rejoicing among the people of Israel. Until then, though, times are going to get very dark indeed, as the last half of the Great tribulation sets in!

Verse 3:

And I will give {power} unto my two witnesses, and they shall prophesy a thousand two hundred {and} threescore days, clothed in sackcloth.

We enter into an area of much interest and differing views as to just who these two characters that pop up on the scene are. We do not have a formal introduction to either one of them. Our subject had been the measuring of the temple, etc., then abruptly we are introduced to two men who are called "*my two witnesses.*"

Those who attempt to dogmatically assert who these two witnesses are will find they are faced with a lot of differing viewpoints. There are differing opinions as to who they are. The majority of opinions, however, seem to come down to three major views; Moses and Elijah; Enoch and Elijah; Symbolic. In looking at the arguments put forth by each, and examining their points which they employ to "prove" their argument, we conclude that the last view should be excluded altogether. It is evident from what is said about these two witnesses that they are not symbolic, but, rather, two men who will preach one day for three and one-half years.

In reading the views of the various commentaries on this subject, we found that they were pretty well equally divided; that is, there were several voices in each group claiming they were right in their assumption. Let's consider their arguments:

Symbolic... The number two, like other numbers in this book, has a symbolic meaning. Two is the number of Divine sufficiency in testimony. The two witnesses they are ideal persons; and they have the characteristics of Moses and Elijah, who were pattern witnesses. The two witnesses might well symbolize the witnessing remnant of Judah as a whole. It is possible that the 144,000 are the two witnesses.

Enoch and Elijah... Those who feel these are two actual persons all agree that one of the two must be Elijah. The prophet Malachi seems to make this clear when he declared in his closing remarks - which were also the closing remarks of the Old Testament prophecy: *Behold, I will send you Elijah the prophet before the coming of the great and dreadful day of the LORD.*

Some have taken the comments made concerning John the Baptist that he was the fulfillment of this prophecy (Matthew 11:14; 17:10-13; John 1:19-23). John the Baptist, though, was not Elijah. He came in the spirit of Elijah, and some of his characteristics were very similar to that of Elijah; but, John himself stated when he was asked if he was Elijah; "And he answered, No" (John 1:21). One of the important things which Malachi stated Elijah would do when he came was to appear before the coming of the great and dreadful day of the LORD. This day speaks of the time when God's judgment of wrath is poured out upon this earth, which, of course, does not fit the time when John witnessed before the Lord Jesus came to be baptized of him in Jordan. Another thing, Jesus said when Elijah came, he would restore all things. This, of course, did not occur when John came.

One argument that Enoch is the other witness is that he has never died and therefore he must return to the earth to die. This is why, some argue, that the Lord took him to heaven before he died so that in the time of the end he may return as His witness and then die. Both Elijah and Enoch being the only two people who did not die. Hebrews 9:27 is referred to to support the idea that it must be these two who are coming back to die; ... *it is appointed unto men once to die* ... But this verse speaks of an APPOINTMENT! not an ultimate thing. There will be many thousands of saints who will not see death as they will just be changed at the coming of the Lord for His Church. Everybody does not have to die! Paul very clearly points this out in 1Corinthians 15:51.

Some of the Apocryphal writings refer to Enoch as being the other witness. According to the tradition of the Arabs, he wrought miracles before the flood. It is interesting to note in the question to John by the Pharisees they asked, *If thou be not that Christ, nor Elias, neither that prophet...* THAT PROPHET?? Some feel this statement has reference to Enoch. But if they meant Enoch, who was familiar to all of them, why didn't they say so? A similar reference was made concerning Jesus Christ (Matthew 16:14).

 The Gospel of Nicodemus has the following statement: I am Enoch who pleased God, and was translated by him. And this is Elijah the Tishbite. We are also to live to the end of the age: but then we are about to be sent by God to resist Antichrist, and be slain by him, and to rise after three days, and to be caught up in the clouds to meet the Lord.

One argument was that this must be Enoch and Elijah, the only ones who have not died, who will return to die, or Jesus would not be the firstfruits of the eternal state. But the firstfruits which Paul makes reference to is concerning the resurrection of Jesus as the firstfruits of them that slept. Jesus became the firstfruits of those who come forth from the grave victorious over death, hell and the grave. If one never dies there would be no need of getting victory over death and the grave! Both Enoch and Elijah were translated into heaven. Obviously, they had to be glorified in order to do that. If that is the case, they can't die! The raptured living saints will not get victory over the grave by going to it! They will never be in it!!

Another thing to consider regarding Enoch, he was a Gentile, and these two witnesses will evidently be ministering to the Jewish nation against the Beast and his empire of evil.

Elijah and Moses... Someone said: I can only identify them by their works. If they are not Moses and Elijah, they sure are stealing Moses' and Elijah's thunder!

The miracles which are performed by the two witnesses certainly correlates with the miracles performed by Moses and Elijah; stopping the rain; turning water to blood, are the two miracles which are mentioned. We do know that Moses had power during his life to perform these miracles, but we do NOT know from the scriptures that Enoch did.

One said it was sheer nonsense to say that Moses was the other witness, as this would make him living three times and dying twice. To this reasoning, we would reason; Did not Lazarus; the widow of Nain's son, the daughter of Jairus, and others, also die twice?

The vision which is seen by John is also seen by the prophet Zechariah, 4:11-14. As the LORD said, *These are the two olive trees, and the two candlesticks standing before God of the earth.* The two who are referred to in Zechariah are evidently the priest and the governor of the land, which would have been Joshua and Zerubbabel. These two had been anointed of the Lord to rebuild and restore the city of Jerusalem, after the Babylonian captivity. They were types of the two witnesses who will come to proclaim the end to the "Babylonian" power and the time to "rebuild" Jerusalem for the time of the Kingdom will be at hand.

Another argument that this could be Moses is the fact that Moses was seen along with Elijah on the Mount of Transfiguration with Jesus Christ. Also, there were two witnesses seen in shining garments at the resurrection tomb (Luke 24:4). There are also two witnesses at the Mount of ascension dressed in white apparel (Acts 1:10). Could these have been the same two who were seen on the Mount of Transfiguration?

So, our conclusion? Like many other interesting matters in the Revelation and prophecy, it would not be wise of us to be dogmatic as to who they are. While it would appear that the evidence points strongly toward it being Elijah and Moses, this is another area of knowledge we will not possess until the event actually takes place. When it does take place, I want to be witnessing it - if we do at all - from heaven's viewpoint, not from the earth! Another thing to consider; God has raised up men before to fulfill His will, can't He do it again?

I WILL GIVE... THEY SHALL PROPHECY... These two statements made concerning the witnesses seem to indicate that John is being told their witnessing is in the future. That is, in the chronological order of the Revelation, it would seem that they have not come on the scene up to this point in time. If this is the case, then it would seem to be saying that their prophecy will be taking place during the last half of the week and not the first half.

Some feel that they will witness during the first half, and the Beast when he comes to his full power will then have them killed as he enters the temple and proclaims that he is God.

But the expressions such as used in this verse; *"a thousand two hundred and threescore days."* As well as the term *"Time, times, and a half',* and *"forty-two months",* are terms which seem to always refer to the last half of the week.

Now, lest we think that the time element would prevent them from witnessing during the last half of the week, we could assume that they are witnessing according to the Jewish reckoning of time; whose years are 360 days long. But, at the same time, they are witnessing during the Times of the Gentiles, who reckons time as 365 days to the year!

CLOTHED IN SACKCLOTH... Sackcloth was an emblem that was recognized by all Israel of national mourning. The troubles which Israel are enduring through this dark period of time called Tribulation are because of their sins and rejection of their Messiah. It is a time of mourning for all Israel.

Verse 4:

These are the two olive trees, and the two candlesticks standing before the God of the earth.

The vision of Zechariah which refers to the candlesticks and Olive trees is in chapter four. Note the reference is to these as they are "standing" before the Lord. It is true that Zechariah's vision had immediate reference to Zerubbabel and Joshua, but like so many other prophecies, it must have had farther reaching significance as well. This is evident from the reference made here in Revelation to the same two. One of the characteristics of Elijah is his comment when he is first introduced to us: *As the LORD of Israel liveth, before whom I stand,* (1Kings 17:1).

They are standing before the Lord as soldiers at attention waiting for their orders to march forward.

When they receive those orders, it will be to speak out against the most wicked government that has ever existed on this earth. Their witnessing will result in many being converted, without a doubt, but it will also result in their own death on the altar of sacrifice!

In the prophecy of Zechariah concerning the two Olive Trees (4:3,11-14), they are closely related to the golden Candlestick with its seven lamps. In fact, from verse twelve, the indication is that the oil which flowed into the candlestick to feed the lamps, flowed from the two Olive Branches.

When asked by the prophet as to who they were, the Lord replies, *These are the two anointed ones, that stand by the Lord of the whole earth.*

Now the two anointed one's in the days of Zechariah were evidently Zerubbabel, the Governor of the land, and Joshua, the High Priest. They were among that group who had returned from Babylonian captivity to the land of Promise, to re-build Jerusalem and re-establish the worship of Jehovah among the remnant who had returned to the land. It was said of Zerubbabel; The hands of Zerubbabel have laid the foundation of this house; his hands shall also finish it (4:9). The two "Witnesses" in the days of the remnant returned from Babylonian captivity had the responsibility it would seem to rally the people to rebuild and to restore the Temple and worship in Jerusalem once again.

The two Witnesses of Revelation will no doubt be proclaiming to the remnant of Israel in that day that it is time to return to the Lord with all their heart. It is time to re-build the Temple and welcome the King back home! The Kingdom is soon to arrive! Let us prepare for it! But there is something which stands in the way of the Kingdom of Christ being established on this earth during this time: The Beast and his empire of evil! So, the two Witnesses will probably be witnessing against the Beast and his system of evil and warning the people to refuse to join his system.

Verse 5:

And if any man will hurt them, fire proceedeth out of their mouth, and devoureth their enemies: and if any man will hurt them, he must in this manner be killed.

The Lord had said to Zerubabbel that it would not be by power nor by might that he would conquer in his battle; but it would be *by my Spirit*, the Lord informed him. The Spirit of God will likewise be with these two Witnesses in a very unique manner.

They will be preaching against the Beast and his system of evil. This, naturally, will result in the Beast and all his cohorts hating them. But with all modem technology at their disposal, the Beast will still be unable to do anything about these Two Witnesses, at least not for three and one-half years! Like Elijah of old, when the enemy sought to bring harm to him, he called fire down from heaven which devoured his enemies! Those who attempt to bring harm to these two Witnesses will likewise feel the sting of judgment against them.

The statement *fire proceedeth out of their mouth*, is another symbolic statement in the Revelation. It speaks of power to inflict their enemies with judgment by speaking the word against them. A similar statement is made concerning our Lord when He returns to bring judgment to this earth at the time of Armageddon (19:15). This further emphasizes to all that the Witnesses are unique messengers with a special anointing from God Himself upon them. What tremendous affect this must have on the people they are witnessing to! Only the spiritually blind among Israel and those to whom they witness, would cause them to not recognize that these two men are messengers direct from God. The wise among Israel and the people will stir themselves to refuse the Beast and his system which demands that they take his mark.

When the Lord does return to judge His people Israel, and the world, they will stand without excuse. They will have had two unique Witnesses who have stood before them for three and one-half years warning them against accepting the line which the Beast is giving.

This verse lets us know that the Witnesses will have a mission to fulfill for God and nothing will stop them from fulfilling that mission!

If any man will hurt them... These two Witnesses have been appointed by the Lord to witness for three and one-half years. Nothing, nor no one, will prevent them from fulfilling this obligation. It is evident from verse seven that men are not able to kill them because they have been appointed a certain period of time to witness, and God will not permit anything to happen to them until this period of time has expired. They are beyond purchase, and they are invincible to destruction by their enemies.

We can only imagine the tremendous effect this will have on all involved with these Witnesses. To the Beast who will hate them and attempt to stop their message, there will be frustration without a doubt. To the Jew, to whom their message is primarily directed, there surely must be a tremendous awe to witness the power which is manifested through these two men. The Jew would have to trace back in his history a long time to find a prophet that could be likened to those who are witnessing in their streets at this time!

Verse 6:

These have power to shut heaven, that it rain not in the days of their prophecy: and have power over waters to turn them to blood, and to smite the earth with all plagues, as often as they will.

These have power... indicates that the power lies in both of the witnesses! It does not appear that one has the power to do certain things, while the other one has power to do other things. They both are given the power to bring judgments upon the world during their ministry.

That it rain not in the days of their prophecy... Is this indicating that there will be no rain on this earth for three and one-half years? If this is the case, then the length of this terrible drought will be the same as that during the days of Elijah! (James 5:17) Imagine - if you can! the terrible drought which will grip the country if it does not rain for three and one-half years! The devastation which will cover the land during this time will be shocking to those who must endure these terrible times.

And have power over waters to turn them to blood... One of the reasons that some contend these two men are Moses and Elijah is because of these two references to what they do during their ministry. But let us notice, this is speaking of what takes place during the two Witnesses ministry during the tribulation - not what happened hundreds of years before! These events are what takes place during the Tribulation, it is not a reference to past judgments wrought by these men.

We do know that Moses and Elijah, during their lifetime, did these two very things. Two miraculous things which were brought about because of the sins of the people.

Moses, a representative of the Law, brought the judgments of plagues against Pharaoh and Egypt. Elijah, a representative of the prophets, brought the judgments of drought during the days of Ahab, the king of Israel who permitted his wife Jezebel to bring Baal worship into the land.

And to smite the earth with all plagues, as often as they will... The terrible things which happen during the sounding forth of the trumpet judgments were spoken of as plagues (9:20). If this is an indication of what these two men can bring upon the world, then imagine what horrible conditions will prevail during this dark time!

We are not informed as to what these plagues may be which these Witnesses are able to bring upon the world, but they must be horrifying to say the least!

The plagues which Moses brought upon the land involved only the land of Pharaoh - Egypt. The drought which occurred during the ministry of Elijah, as far as we know, primarily involved the land of Israel - and possibly some surrounding territory. But the plagues of judgment which these men bring upon the world during their ministry is spoken of as to "*smite the earth.*" It would seem to imply that their judgments will have much farther reaching results.

Verse 7:

And when they shall have finished their testimony, the beast that ascendeth out of the bottomless pit shall make war against them, and shall overcome them, and kill them.

Do these two unique men know just how long their ministry is to last? Do they know they have been sent to this earth to witness to the elect of God for three and one-half years only? We do not have any scriptural answer to these questions, but it would be our assumption that they do know.

While their ministry only lasts for three and one-half years; the same length as our Lord's while upon this earth, what a tremendous influence they will have upon all people! Again, we are not informed as to who nor how many they influence to reject the Beast and his system, but it would seem evident from the power which is to be manifested through them that they will have a tremendous effect on many people.

We are not informed as to the range of their ministry either. Do they travel over the world? Do they minister only in Jerusalem? With the technological advancements which have been made in our modern world, it would seem likely that they and their message will be broadcast via satellite to a world-wide audience.

The fact they will be witnessing for three and one-half years is another proof of the mercies of an all-loving God. These two Witnesses; the 144,000 sealed from among the twelve tribes of Israel, along with the angel flying through the air with his message of warning, are all messengers of mercy sent from God to warn people about the Beast and his system of evil!

The Beast... out of the... pit shall overcome them, and kill them... This is our first reference in our study of the Revelation to the Beast by this name. We will have more about him when we get to chapter thirteen where there he will be introduced in great detail to us. By the reference to the man of sin as the Beast also seems to indicate this is the last of the week.

The term *make war with them* seems to be out of character with the fact that there are only "two" witnesses. How do you make war with two men?

Because of the tremendous power which has been demonstrated by these two Witnesses, the Beast will employ all the power at his disposal to bring about the death of these two men who are causing so much trouble for him and his plans.

And shall overcome them... When the Beast is able to bring death to these Two Witnesses - something that no one had been able to do before now, though many have tried - does this make him to think that he is winning the battle? Does this give him a sense of false security? It will appear to be a victory for the Beast. He may win this battle - or at least appear to win it - but he will not win the war!

It would appear from the statement made in verse five that many had attempted to kill these men before now, but they had all failed in their endeavors. In fact, not only had they failed, but they themselves had been killed while attempting to bring harm to the Witnesses! It is possible that armies were sent against them, but to no avail! They were immortal until their time was up that they had been commissioned to witness on the earth.

This brings into sharper focus the character that is here called the Beast. What men and armies and weapons could not do, the Beast is able to accomplish. More will be said about him when we get to chapter thirteen, but suffice it to say at this juncture, he is more than just a mere man!

Kill them... The fact the Witnesses are killed indicates they are not angels. They are two mortals, who, for a while, are given such power that they cannot be killed.

The fact that the Beast kills them further indicates his brutal, affection-less, attitude toward any who stand in his way as he aspires for the power to conquer and control the world.

<u>**Verse 8:**</u>

And their dead bodies {shall lie} in the street of the great city, which spiritually is called Sodom and Egypt, where also our Lord was crucified.

Their dead bodies... For three and one-half years these two men had been invincible against all those who had attempted to bring harm against them. Now the Beast will accomplish what others were not able to accomplish to this point - kill them!

The statement "bodies" seems to add emphasis to the attitude the people have concerning these great men who had come with their message from God for them. They are merely two bodies which lie exposed to the eyes of all who pass by.

The great city... This seems to indicate the growth which Jerusalem would experience. This growth is becoming quite evident in our day. Israel has now moved her capital to Jerusalem, which increased its importance, not only to the Jews, but also to the entire world.

Spiritually called Sodom and Egypt... If it were not for the last statement in this verse, we would be hard pressed to determine just where this city is located. There are a lot of large cities in our world today which could fit the description of being like Sodom and Egypt!

Sodom reminds us of wicked immorality. Egypt reminds us of bondage. From this statement, it would appear that Jerusalem becomes a wicked center of immorality and rejection of God, which binds the souls of men under a regime of Beast-like servitude.

Conditions are such in this capital city of all Jewry that invites the Man of Sin to enter their temple and declare to them - and the world - that he is god! We can only speculate as to the conditions which would permit such an occurrence.

While we may be prone to think of Israel as being a spiritual nation because of her heritage, in reality she is not! The thousands who have come home to the land of their fathers, are nothing like the fathers who once walked this country by faith. While there is a remnant among the world of Jewry who are seeking Jehovah and a spiritual revival for Israel, the people as a whole are far from revival.

This city which has had such an interesting history will continue to catch the spotlight of the world even in this time of great trouble. The history of Jerusalem dates far back into the Old Testament story.

Its name means "Peace." It has known very little peace, however, through the years. And the history of the Jews, as well as the "Times of the Gentiles," will find their end in this city. To the Jew it will be the long anticipated end they have been praying for when Messiah would come and bring peace to them and their country. To the Gentile lords who have been seeking power and control of the world, they will meet their "waterloo" at the battle of Armageddon.

There are several references to Jerusalem in the Old Testament regarding her being compared to Sodom and Egypt; Isaiah 1:9,10; Ezekiel 16:46,53; 23:3,8,19,27.

Our Lord was crucified there, and now His two witnesses die there. In between - as well as before our Lord's crucifixion - there have been many others who have died in this place.

Jesus, as He ministered through the streets of that city, met with a lot of opposition. He wept over the city (Luke 19:41-44), because of their rejection of Him, and because of what was coming upon them because of that rejection.

Jesus said: *Nevertheless I must walk to day, and to morrow, and the {day} following: for it cannot be that a prophet perish out of Jerusalem.* (Luke 13:33).

In Matthew 23:37,38 Jesus states: *0 Jerusalem, Jerusalem, {thou} that killest the prophets, and stonest them which are sent unto thee, how often would I have gathered thy children together, even as a hen gathereth her chickens under {her} wings, and ye would not!*

Behold, your house is left unto you desolate.

Verse 9:

And they of the people and kindreds and tongues and nations shall see their dead bodies three days and an half, and shall not suffer their dead bodies to be put in graves.

In the commentaries which we have read that were written prior to the advent of the television, and the satellite systems, this statement was not elaborated on to any great detail. The only way possible that "nations" of people could "see" the dead bodies of these two witnesses would be through the television medium. Now, with the advent of the satellite system, it has become an even greater possibility.

Now, because of the satellites which orbit our planet, every nation can view the same thing at the same time! We are living in that period of time when the Word of God is being fulfilled down to the minute detail!

And shall not suffer their dead bodies to be put in graves... This, if nothing else, emphasizes to us the spiritual condition of the people during this time. Even though the mob was wild and mad with their crazy ideas of having our Lord crucified, they at least permitted His body to be removed from the cross for burial.

Suffer... The Greek word signifies "to permit." So, it would appear that there were some who wanted to give these two unique men a proper burial but were forbidden the privilege. There is a purpose behind their twisted logic of permitting their bodies to lie in the street of their city.

Verse 10:

And they that dwell upon the earth shall rejoice over them, and make merry, and shall send gifts one to another; because these two prophets tormented them that dwelt on the earth.

First, notice that the scene takes in the entire earth! The rejoicing and merry-making is not confined just to the city where the bodies are left in the street. It has spread through the earth.

What a statement! It is like a holiday! It is like Christmas time throughout the world! It is as if some horrible enemy has been vanquished at last! The depravity of man sinks to a new low! Only the spiritually blind, and spiritually bankrupt soul could make such merriment at such a time.

While no mention is made concerning those who have taken heed to the message of the Witnesses, and who have not joined in with this mob, they are not doubt staying clear of this mob lest they wind up beside those two lying in the street.

Because these two prophets tormented them that dwelt on the earth ... How did these two witnesses torment these people? Again, note that it stated: *"on the earth."* This seems to indicate that the messages of the two witnesses was not confined just to the city of Jerusalem. Their message must have been directed to ALL the earth.

It is strange that these two messengers who were sent by God, and who brought a message from God to deliver to the people of this planet, are considered as tormenters because of their message! This is saying, in essence, that the message of God torments! And the rejoicing is not just over the death of these two men who have been preaching to them for three and one-half years, but it is also because the voice of God has been stopped from the mouth of these two men. It is as if the people are rejoicing that the Beast has killed God! For these two men certainly proclaimed that they were speaking for the Lord, and if they were killed, then, in essence, the God who sent them lies dead with them.

It may seem far-out to a sane and sensible mind that anybody could think this way, but the world has plenty of people in it right now who would shout at the news that God is dead.

Paul asked the Galatians, Galatians 4:6: *Am I therefore become your enemy, because I tell you the truth?*

That which tormented the people was the truth which the witnesses were proclaiming. To the soul who does not want to live for God, conviction - the Word of God - the testimony of a child of God, torments.

This has ever been the nature of mankind since the fall in the garden. That which we need, we don't like. Paul spoke of this conflict of the flesh in Romans 7:15: *For that which I do I allow not: for what I would, that do I not; but what I hate, that do I.*

The flesh is ever in conflict with the spirit. The Adamic nature seeks to control the spirit and bring it into subjection to the lusts and desires which burn in the heart of the fleshly man. Those who have given themselves over to the gratification of the fleshly man, will rebel against anyone, or anything, which speaks out against his chosen lifestyle.

Those who have chosen to follow the Beast, and to accept his system, along with his mark, will become mad at the message of these witnesses. They will attempt to stop their mouth, without success. Only the Beast is able to kill them. When that happens, the people rejoice at the sight.

Verse 11:

And after three days and an half the Spirit of life from God entered into them, and they stood upon their feet; and great fear fell upon them which saw them.

The partying stops! The TV cameras have probably been focused on their bodies since they were dropped in the street three days before. Multiplied millions have gawked at the sight of these two bodies lying in the street of Jerusalem. The cameras have probably panned the crowd which gathered around the street, partying and making merriment at the death of these great men.

Probably someone close to the men caught a movement from one of them as the spirit of life stirred anew in them. His cry of alarm will ripple through the mob, and down the street. The cameras linked to the satellite broadcasting the event around the world, will catch it as well. Programs will be interrupted with the news bulletin that will shock, not only those near the scene, but around the world as well.

They had witnessed for three and a half years; now they have been dead for three and a half days. Then life enters back into their body. When the resurrection takes place, the change will be very quickly. Paul spoke of it happening in *"the twinkling of an eye."* But the resurrection of these two men seems to be very elaborate. First there is the stir of life - then they stand up on their feet.

Like the great celebration in the time of Belshazzar, the banqueting will stop suddenly! Like a slap in the face, that which they have been rejoicing over is suddenly taken away from them.

Great fear fell upon them... This could also be translated "exceeding terror." What people are witnessing shakes them down to the core. In all probability, there will be many who will die of heart failure - if the Lord allows it - at the sight which takes place right before their eyes.

This great fear is not to be taken in the sense that repentance is soon to come from them. It is not a godly fear which worketh repentance. It is a fear that frightens!

Again, there is no mention made concerning those who are not party to what has been going on. The many who have taken heed to the message of the witnesses. The focus is on those who have opposed them and their message. We can only suppose that at the news of the witnesses coming forth to life, great joy will fill their heart, and fill them also with a great hope.

Verse 12:

And they heard a great voice from heaven saying unto them, Come up hither. And they ascended up to heaven in a cloud; and their enemies beheld them.

We are not given the comments - if any - that come among the two witnesses as all of this is taking place. Were there some closing remarks after life has entered into them again? As they stared into the cameras that were sending their pictures around the world, did they also deliver a message to the world?

As the two witnesses stand on their feet, there is a thundering voice from heaven which speaks to the witnesses, inviting them to come up to heaven.

Did others hear the voice? or did just the two witnesses hear it? The statement *"a great voice,"* may imply that others heard it as well. If they did, this would without doubt add great significance to what is unfolding before their eyes.

By the fact there is no mention here of any mass repentance and turning to God by the people seems to imply that the people, as a whole, are so far into the system of the Beast that they are beyond redemption. If they have already taken his mark at this time, then there is no hope for them regardless of what takes place before their eyes!

Come up hither... These are the same words which John heard - 4:1.

And they ascended up to heaven in a cloud ... This is what was said about the ascension of Jesus Christ. That a cloud caught him out their sight.

This is resurrection! This is another segment of the First Resurrection. First was the resurrection of Jesus Christ, the "firstfruits" from among the dead. Later, there was the rapture of the Church. Now we have the resurrection of these two witnesses. Still later there will be the resurrection of the tribulation saints. This will complete the first resurrection (Revelation 20:1-5).

And their enemies beheld them... They who had mocked them. They who had been partying for the past three days because their enemy was dead. Now they witness their "enemy" slip away from their grasp into the everlasting arms of Jesus Christ.

Beheld... This is from the Greek word "theoreo." The word is a strong word which implies a "transfixed stare." It is without doubt that the people will be staring, with mouths gaped open, and eyes bugged out, at the sight of these two men being lifted off the ground and into the heavens. There will probably be some more who will fall over in a faint as this takes place!

This is a preview of what is going to happen just a little later. The Beast has gloated, and the people have rejoiced, at the thought that the enemy has been put to death. But, wait a minute! The enemy is not dead to stay! And the Beast, who has been making his boasts how he will conquer even God Himself, is shaken. While he may rally the people and yet shake his fist at God, the ultimate end has already been spelled out. The Beast may seem to win a few battles during this dark period called Tribulation, but the war is not over until we get to chapter nineteen, and there it is evident who wins!

Verse 13:

And the same hour was there a great earthquake, and the tenth part of the city fell, and in the earthquake were slain of men seven thousand: and the remnant were affrighted, and gave glory to the God of heaven.

The city, again, is Jerusalem. As if to put a punctuation mark at the end of what has just taken place, God sends an earthquake through the city just as soon as His witnesses are removed from it.

It is of interest to note that during the ministry of Elijah, there were 7,000 who were preserved by the Lord who had never bowed the knee to Baal. Here there are 7,000 killed in a judgment from God for bowing the knee to "Baal," - the anti-christ.

the remnant were affrighted, and gave glory to the God of heaven... This is the first reference to men giving glory to God when a judgment of His wrath has fallen. Up till now men have refused to repent, or to give any honor to God.

The reference to this being the remnant would probably have reference to the remnant among Israel, instead of the remainder of people living in Jerusalem. It will be the remnant who will be saved during the tribulation. And to see the judgments of God fall upon those who have been bringing so much trouble upon them would surely prompt them to rejoice and give glory to God.

Verse 14:

The second woe is past; {and}, behold, the third woe cometh quickly.

The fulfillment of the second woe, and the introduction of the third woe, is the same as that given after the first woe was past - 9:12.

We were told, when first introduced to the "woes" which were coming on the earth, that there would be three of them, and they would come in conjunction with the remaining three trumpet judgments, (8:13).

Because of this fact, it does not appear that the second woe concludes with the earthquake in Jerusalem and the rapture of the Witnesses. The second woe occurred during the sixth trumpet judgment.

The reason we have it mentioned here is because we are about to hear the seventh trumpet judgment sound forth, which would introduce the third woe! The third and final woe will be the greatest of the three, for it will involve Satan being cast down to the earth (12:12).

Verse 15:

And the seventh angel sounded; and there were great voices in heaven, saying, The kingdoms of this world are become {the kingdoms} of our Lord, and of his Christ; and he shall reign for ever and ever.

Some have mistakenly supposed that Paul's reference in 1Corinthians 15:52 to the last trump has reference to this trumpet.

Such is not the case though. Paul is speaking about the resurrection and rapture of the living. He uses the expression last trump possibly because there will be a trumpet blast for the dead and one for the living. Note how the passage reads:

Behold, I shew you a mystery; We shall not all sleep, but we shall all be changed, In a moment, in the twinkling of an eye, at the last trump: for the trumpet shall sound, and the dead shall be raised incorruptible, and we shall be changed.

Possibly also the reference to a last trump in regarding the rapture has reference to the fact it is the conclusion of the Church age.

The seventh trumpet judgment here has reference to a judgment from God, and evidently occurs about the middle of the week.

After giving the narrative of the Two Witnesses, and of their death, and resurrection and ascension into heaven, the apostle returns to the sequence of the trumpet judgments.

There is reason to believe that the events covered by the sounding of the seventh trumpet last throughout the remaining three and one-half years of the tribulation. One reason for this supposition are the words John hears in 10:7: *But in the days of the voice of the seventh angel, when he shall begin to sound, the mystery of God should be finished.*

Also, from the words in our verse under consideration here; *The kingdoms of this world are become the kingdoms of our Lord ...*

When all has come to its pre-determined end, our Lord Jesus shall be found reigning as King of kings, and Lord of lords!

Great voices in heaven... John hears this wonderful exclamation coming from many voices from heaven. He also makes reference to many voices coming from heaven in chapter nineteen. The voices must surely be the redeemed who were raptured some three and one-half years before.

We are not to suppose that the Lord takes over the kingdoms of the earth at this time! This statement is made in anticipation of the event. The seventh, and final, trumpet judgment, when finished will bring our Lord back to this earth for a glorious reign as King of the earth.

The motive behind the actions taken by the Beast and his cohorts is usurpship of the earth. To control the world! This was predicted long ago in a Psalm; The kings of the earth set themselves, and the rulers take counsel together, against the LORD, and against His anointed, saying, Let us break their bands asunder, and cast away their cords from us, (2:2,3).

This prophecy was recognized by the early church as well- Acts 4:23-26.

So, knowing that delay will be no more; that the sounding forth of the seventh trumpet will bring to a conclusion the Tribulation - and the return of Jesus Christ - the shout from heaven in anticipation of this fact!

The kingdoms of men have been short-lived. The Beast will reign, at the best, only seven years. How long shall our Lord reign?

And He shall reign for ever and ever... Or, as it is said in the Greek; To the ages of the ages. Daniel, in speaking of that kingdom said: *The God of heaven shall set up a kingdom, which shall never be destroyed. and it shall stand forever*, (2:44).

Again, we are not to think that the Lord comes at this juncture of the tribulation, but this is spoken in anticipation of that glorious event which the seventh trumpet will bring the world to when finished.

Verse 16:

And the four and twenty elders, which sat before God on their seats, fell upon their faces, and worshipped God,

When we studied the fourth chapter was the last time we saw these twenty-four elders on their thrones. There we concluded they must be representatives of the redeemed. So, we find them at the beginning of the tribulation as they are found sitting on their thrones in the presence of God. Now they are seen in the middle of the tribulation in anticipation of the conclusion of the tribulation when the King shall return to this earth, and they with Him. We shall meet them again at tribulations end when that glorious day arrives when the King returns to claim the thrones of the world!

It is of interest to note that the last time we saw them in 5:14, just prior to the opening of the seals and tribulation, they were on their faces before the throne of God. Here again they are prostrate before Him.

Verse 17:

Saying, We give thee thanks, 0 Lord God Almighty, which art, and wast, and art to come; because thou hast taken to thee thy great power, and hast reigned.

The One on the throne before whom they fall down in worship, is the Lord Jesus Christ. This is evident from such passages as; Matthew 19:28; Revelation 3:21; 4:1-8.

The expression Lord God Almighty, is Adoni-Elohim-Shaddai.

• **Jesus Christ is our Adoni** - Our Lord, our Master, and Ruler of our life.

• **Jesus Christ is Elohim** - our God, the only God of our life, who has created in us a new creation.

• **Jesus Christ is Shaddai** - the Almighty who lives and reigns on the throne of our heart.

The expression *which art, and wast, and art to come*, is the same expression which is made by the Lord Jesus in 1:8; I am Alpha and Omega, the beginning and the ending, saith the Lord, which is, and which was, and which is to come, the Almighty.

Because thou hast taken to thee thy great power... The kingdoms of this world are not freely and willingly given over to Jesus Christ as rightful King. Can you imagine the reaction if Jesus were to come and ask Russia to give the reins of government to Him? Or, what if He were to ask the United States for control of the government? This authority is not willingly surrendered. Power has an intoxicating effect upon men. In fact, when the Lord does come to reign on this earth, He will have to wrest this power from men as they will oppose the Lord! This is what Armageddon will be all about.

and hast reigned... Again, it is evident from what follows in the book of Revelation this is not taking place at this time. This is spoken in anticipation of that event. Someone has said the term could be translated shown thy self as king. By what has taken place, and what is taking place, it is evident that Jesus Christ is rightful King, and He is showing that right and power by what is taking place during the tribulation.

The seventh trumpet judgment results in Satan being cast out of heaven, which would certainly be a show of who is Master!

Verse 18:

And the nations were angry, and thy wrath is come, and the time of the dead, that they should be judged, and that thou shouldest give reward unto thy servants the prophets, and to the saints, and them that fear thy name, small and great; and shouldest destroy them which destroy the earth.

And the nations were angry... This expression again reminds us of Psalm two, where it speaks of; Why do the heathen rage, and the people imagine a vain thing?

There are some unanswered questions concerning the nations and their alignment in the last days.

While we may speak of a one-world government, at the same time the scriptures seem to indicate that all nations will not fall in line behind the Beast. We have not convinced ourselves just what role the United States will play in all of these events. It would seem, as a whole, the nations have given their allegiance over to the Beast, who has promised so much. The nations in doing so, have passed the point of no return. Joining forces with the Beast means they join him in his opposition to God. and thy wrath is come ... This is the reason for tribulation - or one of the reasons - to bring about a surrender and defeat of man and his lofty rebellious ways against God and His authority.

From the very beginning of the tribulation, when the sixth seal was opened, it was evident that what was taking place was the wrath of God; For the great day of His wrath is come; and who shall be able to stand? (6:17).

and the time of the dead... Many thousands have already been raised from their graves and death at the rapture. Many others will join them at tribulations end when the Lord Jesus shall come and bring them forth who have died during the dark days of tribulation.

This could also have reference to the dead among the unrighteous, for they shall come forth at the Great White Throne to be judged and condemned to the Lake of fire.

Whatever dead is in reference here, it is already set. The judgment is pre-determined. The culmination of the judgment will bring about the vindication of the righteous of the ages!

that they should be judged... None shall escape judgment! ALL will be judged. The judgment of the Church at the Lord's coming. The judgment of the tribulation saints at His coming to the earth. The judgment of all the dead at the Great White Throne.

and that thou shouldest give reward unto thy servants the prophets, and to thy saints, and them that fear thy name, small and great... How many hundreds of thousands have been true and faithful for years, who shall be shining as stars in that wonderful day! There are times when the struggles of life; the oppositions against the flesh; the pressures about you, when the flesh does not feel like going one step farther; But then we think of that day! IT WILL BE WORTH IT ALL!

Jesus told His Apostles (Matthew 19:28) that when He sat on His throne of glory, they too would sit on thrones judging the twelve tribes of Israel. We have references throughout the Word of God concerning the rewards which will be granted to those who live for God in this life. Paul spoke of crowns which will be given to certain people. Peter spoke of a special crown for those who were faithful shepherds. Whatever the reward may be, it will be worth it all just to make it to that City and to look on the face of the One who made it all possible for each of us to be saved!

Now the *"time of the dead"* in reference to the lost who are dead - and will die later - their resurrection is over a thousand years away; but it is certain!

and shouldest destroy them which destroy the earth... This is an interesting statement! God created the earth as a beautiful place. When man was placed on this earth it was beautiful. Man was given the responsibility to have dominion over this earth, to care for it. In fact, this could be referred to as the first commandment given to man by God. This dominion and care has since resulted in chaos and corruption!

The prophet Isaiah stated: *The earth also is defiled under the inhabitants thereof,* (24:5).

The results of man's habitation of planet earth is war-scarred countries; de-forested land; a threatened ozone layer; polluted waters; polluted air, etc.

Besides what man has done to the planet, consider what man has done to each other! After all we are all just a part of the earth - having been created from the dust! One of the greatest areas of corruption lies in the many millions of lives that are depraved, degraded, and destroyed because of sin.

The word which is employed here - destroy - is also the word - corrupt. How evident this is in society at large today! When Bibles and prayer has been banned from public schools, while homosexuals and evolutionists have been given the green light to teach their own thing. When some sixty-plus million unborn babies have been slaughtered since 1973, while men scream because some baby seals are killed. The system is all mixed up. The system is not working for the honest, God-fearing citizenry as a whole! The child of God whose heart is stirred at the sight of an abortion clinic; at the sight of our young people being destroyed by alcohol and drugs; at the sight of the ungodly having their way in society while the godly are punished, will not have long to wait for the tables to be completely reversed.

- Victory day is coming! And coming soon!

Mr Morris, in his book, The Revelation Record, stated: "Seven great events are thus anticipated by the elders as they worship on their faces before Christ, the Almighty Lord:

• 1. He has displayed His mighty power over all creation;

• 2. He has demonstrated Himself to be King of all kings;

• 3. He has observed the implacable anger of all nations against Himself;

• 4. He has manifested His righteous wrath against all living in rebellion;

• 5. He has prepared the final judgment for all the unsaved dead;

• 6. He has provided a gracious reward for all who believe and obey Him;

• 7. He has ordained eternal destruction for all who have corrupted the earth."

Verse 19:

And the temple of God was opened in heaven, and there was seen in his temple the ark of his testament: and there were lightnings, and voices, and thunderings, and an earthquake, and great hail.

We have had references made by John to the "throne" in heaven; to the "altar" in heaven, but this is John's first reference to the "Temple" in heaven.

That there is a temple in heaven is confirmed by such passages as Isaiah 6, where the prophet got a glimpse of it himself. The writer of Hebrews states that the earthly tabernacle which Moses pitched in the wilderness was patterned after the true tabernacle, *which the Lord pitched, and not man,* (8:2).

Also, when our Lord died and resurrected, He took His blood into the Holy of Holies in heaven to sprinkle His blood on the mercy seat in that temple which is in heaven, thus purchasing eternal redemption for each of us! (Hebrews 9:12)

A reference to the temple being opened seems to imply that once again the prayers and worship of the people of Abraham is accepted by heaven. This emphasizes the Jewishness of this time period on the earth, as a reference to a temple does not apply to the Church. When we enter that City of God there will be no temple there. The temple with its various attachments of altar, laver, etc. does not speak of the Church but of Israel. As attention is focused on Israel at this time, this seems to emphasize that the time of their deliverance is near at hand! It won't be long now till He comes to bring everlasting deliverance to the people whom He called the apple of His eye!

The ark of His testament... Much speculation has abounded in the last few years concerning the Ark of God. There have been many claims concerning this sacred of all vessels of Israel as to where the original Ark is located. One of the Apocryphal books (11 Maccabees) claims that in the time of Jeremiah when Nebuchadnezzar was preparing to invade Jerusalem, Jeremiah took the Ark and hid it from him. That it was later taken secretly into Ethiopia.

Much speculation continues to abound concerning the Ark of God. What record we have left us in the Old Testament concerning the invasion of Nebuchadnezzar and his forces, there is no mention made concerning the Ark of God being taken into Babylon. The record in 2Kings, 2Chronicles and Jeremiah, mention some of the holy vessels but there is no mention made of the Ark.

When we consider the importance of the Ark to Israel, as well as to God, we are prone to feel strongly that the Ark was NOT taken into captivity with the people!

While we have no scriptural proof as to just what happened to the Ark, when we consider the history and events which surround the Ark, we have difficulty in accepting that God permitted the heathen hands to possess it.

Is it not possible that what John is witnessing here is the same Ark!

The Lord gave instructions to Moses when in the wilderness with Israel to erect a Tabernacle in the wilderness. This was to be the meeting place with God for Israel. The first instructions pertained to the Ark of God (Exodus 25:10). The Ark of God was to reside in the inner most area of the Tabernacle, in a room called the Holy of Holies. Specific instructions are given as to the dimensions, etc. The Ark was to be overlaid with gold. It was a very expensive item in the Tabernacle.

Only the priest's, sons of Kohath, were permitted to carry the Ark. They could carry it then only after it was carefully covered.

Only the High priest could enter into the Holy of Holies on one day a year.

When the Ark was stolen by the Philistines many years later, the power of God which was present with the Ark as it was placed in the room with the god of the Philistines, witnesses to the glory which was attached to it.

When the people of Beth-shemesh sought to examine the Ark after it was sent back by the Philistines, 50,070 were slain for touching it! (1Samuel 6:19).

Later, when David is king and he attempts to bring the Ark to Jerusalem, Uzzah touches the Ark because the oxen who are pulling it on a cart stumble and he is afraid the Ark will fall, and Uzzah is slain!

So, with the history which surrounds this Ark, and the fact that no mention is made of it when the forces of Babylon invaded Jerusalem and took the holy vessels out of the temple, (2Kings 25:13-20; 2Chronicles 36:), and the fact that there is no mention made of it years later when the remnant return and rebuild the Temple, there must have been some provision made by God to take care of this sacred vessel of all Jewry.

If God could take two men - Enoch and Elijah - to heaven without them dying; If Jesus Christ ascended bodily into heaven, and if we expect at the trumpet sound to ascend into His presence, then why should it be a thing so difficult to accept that God could - or would - take the Ark to heaven!

According to Revelation 22:2 the tree of life will be found in the new paradise of God. Do you think the first tree of life was destroyed by the deluge? Do you think there would be two trees of life?

Is it not possible that both the Tree of Life and the Ark of God were removed from this earth by the Lord before the flood could reach the Tree of Life, and before the hands of the heathen could reach the Ark of God?

7th Seal: *There were voices, and thunderings, and lightnings, and an earthquake...*

7th Trumpet: *There were lightnings, and voices, and thunderings, and an earthquake, and great hail...*

7th Vial: *There were voices, and thunders, and lightnings; and there was a great earthquake ...*

The similarity is so close in all three that this has caused some to think that what occurs when the seventh seal is opened includes the 7 Trumpet judgments and the 7 Vial judgments.

It would seem more likely that they are three separate events which occur during the tribulation. The 7th seal occurring at the first part of the tribulation; the 7th trumpet during the middle part, and the 7th vial at the conclusion of the tribulation.

Thus, we come to the end of this very eventful chapter. And as we do so we prepare to enter another chapter which also presents a most fascinating study!

CHAPTER TWELVE

- *And there appeared a great sign in heaven: a woman clothed with the sun...*

- THE WOMAN

- THE DRAGON

- THE MANCHILD

- THE ARCHANGEL

- THE REMNANT

The great battle in the heavens...

There are those who feel that verse nineteen of the preceding chapter actually goes with this chapter.

John had witnessed the temple in heaven being opened in verse nineteen, and there he saw the Ark of God, along with the attending demonstration of God's power and glory. Now there appears a wonderful as well as interesting sign before John.

Now chapter eleven presented to us some interesting opinions as to who the Two Witnesses are. As we noticed in our study, there are differing views as to their identity. Well, when we get to this chapter we really come upon an intriguing and interesting study, which when we go to the commentators we find a great variety of opinions as to which is involved in this chapter. This chapter presents five different subjects:

- 1). The sun-clothed woman.

- 2). The dragon.

- 3). The Man child.

- 4). Michael the archangel.

- 5). The remnant of the woman.

Now we have no problem with the dragon - we know he is Satan from what is said in verse nine. We have no problem with Michael the archangel, we have been introduced to him before.

Our problem lies with the identity of the Woman, the Man child, and the Remnant of the woman.

But primarily with the Woman and the Man child. If we can identify the Woman, then we can identify her remnant.

COMMENTARIES...

We examined eleven different commentaries on this subject and found a wide variety of opinions as, to who the Woman and the Man child are:

Matthew Henry: "The Woman is the Church. The Man child is Christian religion."

Adam Clarke: "The Woman is the Church. The Man child is the dynasty of Christian emperors beginning with Constantine."

Pulpit Commentary: "The Woman is the company of believers earthly and heavenly."

Philip Mauro: "The Woman is the Israel of God; all saints. The Man child is Jesus."

Dr. Ironside: "The Woman is Israel. The Man child is Jesus and the church."

Dr. Scott: "The Woman is the church. The Man child is Jesus."

F J Dake: "The Woman is Israel. The Man child is the 144,000."

J McKeever: "The Woman is the church. The Man child is the overcomers."

Dr. Turner: "The Woman is all the people of God from the time Of Seth. The Man child is the church."

Henry Morris: "The Woman is all the redeemed. The Man child is Christ and the redeemed."

LaHaye, Larkin, McGee, Malqo: all agree that the Woman is Israel. The Man child is Jesus Christ.

If we are going to decide by majority vote, then obviously the last mentioned are in the majority:

The Woman is Israel, and the Man child is Jesus Christ.

Now there are other opinions that possibly should be at least mentioned here. The Roman Catholic church expositors wanted the world to think that the Woman was Mary. Mary, as you know, has been highly exalted by the Catholic Church, even to the point that they have exalted her to the throne of heaven.

Mary Baker Patterson Glover Eddy presented the thought that the woman was a highly symbolic picture of HERSELF! And the Man child represented that which she brought - Christian Science; and the dragon was "mortal mind," endeavoring to destroy her new religion!

Dr McGee said in his comments, "Several female founders of cults have not been able to resist the temptation of seeing themselves pictured in this woman. Joanna Southcott said that she was the woman in Revelation 12, and in October 1814 she would have the man child. This event never took place, yet her followers numbered up to 200,000 in the last century. A female preacher in California, who became famous or infamous - however you care to express it - toyed with the idea that she might be the woman mentioned in this chapter."

Verse 1:

And there appeared a great wonder in heaven; a woman clothed with the sun, and the moon under her feet, and upon her head a crown of twelve stars:

First, the word "wonder" could be better understood if it was read "sign." 'There appeared a great sign in heaven. "This is from the Greek word "semeion." Translating the word as sign lets us know that what is written in this chapter is symbolic and not literal. By employing this word to introduce us to what follows adds significance to the study. The Lord did not want us to think that what is described here was literal. While many of the things described in the Revelation are literally taking place, by the opening statement that this is a great sign, we are informed that what is taking place is symbolic in nature.

Also, let us point out that this sign is seen in heaven. So, the scene unfolds before John's eyes as he gazes into the heavens, not as he looked upon this earth. What he had just been describing for us about the two witnesses did take place on this earth. Then John's attention is drawn to heaven by the sound of the voices rejoicing that the Kingdom of God was coming, and the Temple was opened revealing more glories to John. With his eyes still fixed on this awe-inspiring scene, John then witnesses what he describes for us in this chapter.

Let us examine to some extent the arguments which are put forth by some of the commentators as to their views and reasons for their views concerning the characters spoken about in this chapter. James McKeefer: "An interpretation which I lean toward is that the woman is the church, and the man child represents the overcomers. It is possible, then, that the birth of the man child could be referring to a transformation experience wherein God will give us a special power that we will need to go through the remainder of the tribulation."

Adam Clarke: "That the woman here represents the true Church of Christ most commentators are agreed. In other parts of the Apocalypse, the pure Church of Christ is evidently portrayed by a woman. The Christian Church, when her full time came, obtained a deliverer (the man child), who, during the Divine providence, was destined - To rule all nations. The heathen Roman empire ... The man child mentioned in this verse is the dynasty of Christian emperors, beginning with Constantine's public acknowledgement of his belief in the divinity of the Christian religion... A succession of Christian emperors was raised up to the Church; for the Roman throne, as Bishop Newton observes, is here called the throne of God, because there is no power but of God."

Pulpit Commentary: "The woman is undoubtedly the Church of God; not necessarily limited to the Christian Church, but the whole company of all who acknowledge God, including the heavenly beings in existence before the creation, as well as creation itself. "And she brought forth..." This reference and Psalm 2:9 leave no doubt as to the identification of the man-child. It is Christ who is intended."

C M Turner: "By a careful comparison of the scriptures to which we have called attention, with the statement that is made in verses 10,11 concerning a company of people which are designated as "Our brethren," we gather that this symbol of the "woman and her seed" is a pictorial representation of the people of God from the time of Seth - when men first began "to call themselves by the name of the Lord," to the second coming of Jesus Christ. "The man-child referred to in verses 3, 4, 5 represents the overcoming saints of this dispensation of Grace who will be ready to be caught up to meet the Lord in the air in fulfillment of 1Thessalonians 4:13-17."

Henry Morris: "The woman, therefore, includes Israel (the faithful remnant in Israel, that is) but must go beyond Israel, back to the beginning, the woman thus represents the whole body of the believers. As the true Israel was symbolized as the wife of Jehovah and the true church as the bride of Christ, so the great woman must represent all true believers, beginning with Eve herself. (Man child) That the primary fulfillment of this promise relates to Jesus Christ is clear from the reference here to Psalm 2:7-9. As noted before, however, this promise applies also in a secondary sense to all who genuinely believe on Him and are therefore included along those who conquer with Him. Even as the woman in the great sign-vision applies ultimately to all the people of God before the birth of Christ, especially not only in Christ Himself, but in all who would believe on His saving name and who, therefore, are in Christ."

J Dake: "The woman is a symbol and we must deal with her as a symbol and clearly differentiate between her and the thing she symbolizes. This woman symbolizes, we firmly believe, National Israel. Israel is the only company of people in Scripture that is spoken of as a married woman.

"The Bible recognizes only three classes of people in the world today; the Church, the Jews, and the Gentiles, 1Corinthians 10:32. At the time this woman travails, in the middle of the week, the church will have been removed from the earth leaving only the last two classes.

"If the sun, moon, and twelve stars mean anything they can only symbolize the same as was seen in the dream of Joseph in Genesis 37:9-11, namely, the twelve tribal heads and their parents. Here the whole twelve tribes are seen in national restoration, in the symbol of the woman.

"We believe the man child symbolizes the 144,000 Jews who are the "firstfruits" to God from Israel.

"It has been conclusively proved that the woman represents Israel. Since this is true, it follows that Israel cannot bring forth a company of Gentiles.

"The man-child represents a company of living saints only, for the woman will travail and bring forth the complete man-child in the middle of the week.

"How could the dragon kill the man-child if it were composed of dead, or even resurrected people? This proves that the man-child represents a company of living people only, who will be still in natural bodies with the possibility of being killed.

"The time of the rapture of the 144,000 shows them to be represented by the man-child. If the 144,000 are seen on earth up to the middle of the week, and in heaven immediately after the seventh trumpet which blows in the middle of the week, then they are sure to be raptured as the man-child in the middle of the week. We have seen that the Old Testament and the Church saints will be caught up to heaven before the Seventieth Week and that they will be with God in heaven, represented by the elders. We have also seen that the tribulation saints will be martyred principally after the rapture of the man-child, but not caught up until about the end of the week. The only other place for the insertion of the rapture of the 144,000 is in Revelation 11:12. Therefore, the man-child must be the 144,000 who will be caught up under the seventh trumpet, for, immediately after this trumpet they will be seen in heaven before God, Revelation 14:1-5."

It is evident from what is described for us here in this chapter that what is taking place is symbolic. No woman - nor child - could literally fit the descriptions which are given here in this chapter.

A woman... While there is a reference made of the Church - the redeemed - in chapter nineteen (verse 7) as being the wife of the Lamb; there is no other reference to the Church as being a "woman."

While the church is symbolically referred to as being female in gender, the thought behind this statement in this passage seems to imply a married woman, for this woman is pregnant and about to bring forth her child. So, we rule out the idea that the woman here is the church.

Clothed with the sun, and the moon under her feet, and upon her head a crown of twelve stars... Symbolically connected with this woman are these symbols. Such a symbolic statement automatically brings our attention to the dream of Joseph and the family of Israel to whom the dream applied. The dream, evidently, referred to Israel and his wife, and the sons of Israel, who, along with Joseph, would be twelve in number.

As the book of Revelation during this time is dealing with Israel, it seems that this must have reference to the nation Israel. She will face the darkest time of her history during this tribulation, but deliverance will come to her through the One Whom She delivered to this world.

The majority of commentators agree that this must be Israel. Israel certainly was referred to in the Old Testament as the wife of Jehovah, to which the term woman could apply.

The remainder of events which transpire that involve the woman as well apply to the people of Israel, as we shall see in our study of this chapter.

Verse 2:

And she being with child cried, travailing in birth, and pained to be delivered.

No other nation of people has suffered as much for so long as the people of Israel. During their many dark days of persecution and suffering, their prayers of agony have ascended, as they pray for the Messiah to come and deliver them from their many afflictions.

While it is true that they have brought troubles upon themselves in many instances because of their rebellion against God, but this does not do away with the fact that they are God's elect. God made a covenant with their father Abraham, which covenant God will fulfill, even though it will take the tribulation to bring Abraham's descendants into a condition for fulfillment of this covenant.

The prophet Isaiah stated:

66:7 = *Before she travailed, she brought forth; before her pain came, she was delivered of a man child.*

66:8 = *Who hath heard such a thing? who hath seen such things? Shall the earth be made to bring forth in one day? (or shall a nation be born at once? for as soon as Zion travailed, she brought forth her children.*

It would appear from the context that the prophet is speaking of events which would transpire many years removed from the time of his prophecy. A time which reaches down to the end of this age.

Verse 3:

And there appeared another wonder in heaven; and behold a great red dragon, having seven heads and ten horns, and seven crowns upon his heads.

John is confronted with another sign in heaven. This time it is a "dragon-like" creature. Again, we would point out that the characters portrayed in this chapter indicate that what we are considering are "signs" and not actual persons or things. Even if we were to consider some pre-human creature that may have roamed this earth, it would not be found in heaven!

We have no great problem deciding just who is depicted here as a great red dragon; that is evident from reading verse nine: it is Satan!

The word *dragon* is employed some thirteen times, and only in the book of Revelation do we find this reference in the New Testament. It depicts Satan in his role as a *"murderer from the beginning,"* (John 8;44). It depicts Satan as the relentless persecutor of the people of God.

Satan is here called great because of the tremendous influence he has had on the human race since the very beginning of our sojourn on the earth. The Word of God speaks of him as *the Prince of the powers of the air*, and *Prince of this world*, (Ephesians 6:12; John 12:31; 14:30; 16:11).

This is the first time we come upon the dragon in the book of Revelation. In the following chapter, we will see his association with the Beast, the man of sin. When that time comes, the man of sin will be indwelt by the dragon - Satan - or his emissary. That is why we have this study here in preparation of the time when the dragon would be cast out of heaven and will then enter the man of sin.

GREAT... Because of the tremendous influence which Satan has had on the powers of this world. And because of the power he will continue to manifest until the time of his judgment.

RED... Because of the countless numbers of lives he has destroyed in his mad rage against the creation of God. He is "bloodied" with the blood of the people of God!

DRAGON... Because he is ferocious and without feelings toward those whom he destroys. The one who at one time was referred to as Lucifer, Son of the morning, is now referred to as a Dragon, because of the change in his character, He now represents all that is dark; all that is evil; all that is bad.

HAVING SEVEN HEADS... Here we have the number seven associated with Satan. That number which speaks of perfection and completeness. It is here associated with Satan no doubt because he is here depicted in his final stage. He will be putting on his final effort to bring about the destruction of mankind, and the defeat of God and His kingdom.

The seven heads also speak to us of empires, governments, that in the Word of God are considered to be world empires. We note this in chapter thirteen and chapter seventeen. These seven heads are associated with the man of sin as well as representing seven empires that have existed in time and who have been enemies of the people of God, Israel. More will be said about them when we get to the next chapter, and especially when we get to chapter seventeen.

SEVEN CROWNS UPON HIS HEADS... Crowns speak to us of authority and power. They speak to us of reigning. We know that it is God who permits men to rise to positions of power (Daniel 5:22).

It is God who ordains the power of authority (Romans 13:1). Yet at the same time we know that Satan corrupts world leaders and influences leaders to govern contrary to the will of God. This is evident from the stories in the Old Testament concerning the kings which ruled Israel. Though God ordained the lineage of David to be kings over His people Israel, many of these kings permitted Satan to influence them in walking contrary to the will of God.

So here we note that Satan is wearing crowns, as he is the one who is in control, or reigning, in many instances.

It is sad to note that many countries have started out as moral and godly nations, only to resort to ungodly practices later. Our own nation is certainly a good example of this. A nation which was founded on godly principles, and by men who believed in moral standards for the home and the nation. The United States is a long way off center from what she was two hundred years ago! While Satan may be wearing these crowns, showing that he is the one who reigns over the nations of the world, the time will come when the rightful King will come, and Satan will lose his crowns!

Verse 4:

And his tail drew the third part of the stars of heaven, and did cast them to the earth: and the dragon stood before the woman which was ready to be delivered, for to devour her child as soon as it was born.

His tail drew... We have the description of Lucifer's fall from his lofty position in the Kingdom of God given to us in Isaiah 14:12-15.

We do not have, however, any statement in the Word of God as to when this took place. It evidently took place prior to man being created and placed on this earth, as Satan appears in the garden shortly after creation.

Not only has Satan fallen because of his jealousy over the position which God holds in heaven, but his jealousy continues to cause the battle between good and evil; between heaven and hell. The term "tail" could possibly have reference to his influence. That which follows him. Lucifer was so influential that many of the other angels fell into the same snare. His "tail" (influence) pulled their allegiance away from God and to him. Consequently, they will share in the same judgment (2Peter 2:4; Jude 6).

The third part... Satan's influence was very effective. We have no way of knowing for certainty the number of angels which were created, but there must have been many millions - or billions. Lucifer spread his influence till it touched many millions of his fellow angels.

The stars of heaven... It is assumed by most everyone that this has reference to the angels. We have already had references to stars in our study of Revelation, which, evidently, was speaking of angels.

It is evident that we are not to take this statement literally. Just as the other things which we have been studying about in this chapter, John is witnessing a great "sign" which is taking place. We know from what science informs us that literal stars would be much larger than the earth, so we are not to consider this reference as being literal stars.

And did cast them to the earth... Somehow - and this is open to discussion to many - these fallen angels are involved in the work which is going on on this earth under the control of Satan. They abide in a kingdom of darkness.

Now something should be inserted here regarding the influence which Satan has in this world. While it is true that he influenced one-third of the angels to follow him in his rebellion; that would leave two-thirds who did not follow him! So, we could deduce, that for everyone angel Satan has on his side, the Lord has two on His side. So, the child of God has two-to-one odds favor on his side! We are not on the losing side! We are on the winning side! Even the odds tell us that!

This statement about Satan's influence over the third of the angels, and their being cast down to the earth, does not seem to be taking place at this time in history. That is, what is spoken about in this verse is not evidently taking place at this particular time historically in the Revelation. John is speaking of what the Dragon did. This is the one who drug one-third of the stars with him in his fall. Their fall, evidently, is not taking place in the middle of the tribulation week.

And the dragon stood before the woman... for to devour her child... The rebellion which Satan started in the heavens was continued on this earth. Satan brought his jealous spirit with him to this earth.

There are a lot of things which remain cloudy regarding the pre-Adamic condition of this world and the world of angels and God during that time. Many strongly feel that the description of this world given in Genesis 1:2; *And the earth was without form, and void; and darkness was upon the face of the deep. And the Spirit of God moved upon the face of the waters.* is not a description of the original creation. (Note Isaiah 45:18). Regardless of the condition of this earth prior to man's arrival here, it was not long after man did arrive that Satan was here as well. From the very first Satan has tried to destroy everything good and everything that God has created. Since winning the battle with Adam in the garden, Satan has won a lot of more battles Many have fallen prey to his snares since the garden. While many battles have been won - the war is not over yet!

At the beginning the promise of a coming Deliverer was that it would be the "seed" of the woman. There was no indication as to when nor what woman would be involved. Consequently, Satan has been working with every family and every child that has ever been born into this world. He started his attack with the first son born to Adam and Eve, and his attack continues to this day. In later years, the promise of Messiah was narrowed to that of Abraham's seed. Consequently, the attack of Satan against the people of Abraham was stepped up.

When the announcement was made to the lowly virgin in Nazareth that she was the maiden chosen of the Lord to bring into this world the Messiah, Satan set the wheels into motion against Him. While we have no recorded words of what he may have done during the nine months Mary waited for His birth, it is likely that Satan was active then as well. It was not long after His birth that he put it in the mind of Herod that his throne was in jeopardy, and he had the children of Bethlehem killed.

We likewise do not have much information regarding our Lord's years of infancy to the age of thirty when He began His public ministry. But once He publicly announces Himself, Satan begins his attack.

First it was against the Lord directly. When this failed to accomplish victory for him, he causes others to attack Jesus. During our Lord's three-plus years of ministry Satan is busy trying to destroy Him.

With all of his efforts he fails! Crucifixion and the grave were not victories for Satan - but victories for Christ and all those who know Him as Savior!

Satan has always been an enemy waiting to destroy the work and the people of God. While he has been able to destroy many - there are many others who are beyond price. There are plenty of Shadrach's who refuse to bend or bow to the demand to worship anyone or anything other than the Lord God!

Verse 5:

And she brought forth a man child, who was to rule all nations with a rod of iron: and her child was caught up unto God, and {to} his throne.

The term "man child" is a peculiarly interesting one. The word from which we have "man" taken is the same Greek word which is also translated "male" (Galatians 3:28). Vincent stated: "The object is to emphasize, not the sex, but the peculiar qualities of masculinity - power and vigor."

Man child... To think that God would come to this earth in the form of a babe astounds the mind.

The greatest manifestation of love the world has ever known was when God robed Himself in flesh and walked among His creation for thirty-three plus years.

Every step He took was upon ground that He Himself had made.

Every cup of water He put to His lips was formed by droplets that He had brought into being. And every heart to which He gently spoke was alive with the breath of His life. The God who made us had now come to walk among us. To look us in the face - to take us by the hand - to wipe our weeping eyes - to tell us of the Father and His love.

That the child is Jesus Christ seems to be the only answer which will properly fit the descriptions which are here given to us. Romans 9:4,5: *Who are Israelites ... whom as concerning the flesh Christ came.*

Galatians 4:4,5: *But when the fulness of the time was come, God sent forth his Son, made of a woman, made under the law, To redeem them that were under the law, that we might receive the adoption of sons.*

Galatians 3:16: *Now to Abraham and his seed were the promises made, He saith not, And to seeds, as of many,' but as of one, And to thy seed, which is Christ.*

Again, the woman seems to be Israel; and the child which Israel has given to the world seems to have been Jesus Christ.

Who was to rule all nations with a rod of iron... We have but to consider Psalm 2:9, as well as Revelation 19:15, to realize this must be referring to Jesus Christ; *Thou shalt break them with a rod of iron; thou shalt dash them in pieces like a potter's vessel.*

And out of his mouth goeth a sharp sword, that with it he should smite the nations: and he shall rule them with a rod of iron: *and he treadeth the winepress of the fierceness and wrath of Almighty God.*

Both above passages have direct reference to Jesus Christ, and both refer to the rod of iron which He will wield in ruling - "shepherding" - the nations at the time of His return to this earth.

and her child was caught up unto God, and to His throne... The ascension of Jesus Christ was witnessed by many of His followers from Mount Olivet. The enemy did not accomplish his desire in destroying either Jesus Christ nor His message. His attempts through the years since have as well failed to destroy the work which Christ established upon this earth, the promise given by Jesus Christ; The gates of hell shall not prevail against it (Church) is certainly still in effect.

Jesus Christ is evidently not on this earth during these days of tribulation. In fact, He is the one who is opening the seals and bringing about the tribulation events.

Another thing we should keep in mind in our study of the book of Revelation is the fact that it is the revealing of Jesus Christ (1:1). Jesus Christ is being revealed through this book, and through the events which take place during this time period. When the tribulation has expired the Lord Jesus Christ will be highly exalted and lifted up as King of kings, and Lord of lords. All will acknowledge Him as such in that day.

Verse 6:

And the woman fled into the wilderness, where she hath a place prepared of God, that they should feed her there a thousand two hundred {and} threescore days.

This passage brings to mind the words of Jesus in the chapter in Matthew where we find Him mentioning the tribulation by name:

Matthew 24:15-21: *When ye therefore shall see the abomination of desolation, spoken of by Daniel the prophet, stand in the holy place, (whoso readeth, let him understand:) Then let them which be in Judaea flee into the mountains: Let him which is on the housetop not come down to take anything out of his house: Neither let him which is in the field return back to take his clothes. And woe unto them that are with child, and to them that give suck in those days! But pray ye that your flight be not in the winter, neither on the sabbath day: For then shall be great tribulation, such as was not since the beginning of the world to this time, no, nor ever shall be.*

It would appear that what we have had up to this point has been the historical aspect of the battle which Satan has waged against the work of God on this earth. Leading up to the time of the ascension of Jesus Christ. Verse six then takes us to the time period in the tribulation in which the people of Israel are under tremendous fire from the Beast and his system of darkness. That between verse five and six we have the church age. And as the book of Revelation is primarily a Jewish book, the attention is given to the events which will transpire around this people during this period of time.

Into the wilderness... There are different opinions as to just what is meant by this statement. Some feel that Daniel eleven is speaking about a battle which will take place during the middle of the tribulation week, which will result in many nations being caught in the conflict except Edom, Moab and Ammon. This is what is presently called Jordan territory. That the people of Israel will flee to this place for refuge during the last part of the week.

We are not for sure what the term that they should feed them has reference to. Who the they are in this statement is an unanswered question in this story.

A thousand two hundred and threescore days... The same expression we found in chapter eleven in reference to the ministry of the two witnesses. It refers, evidently, to the last three and one-half years of the tribulation. Or, to the actual Great Tribulation, when the Beast will turn his power and hatred against anyone - especially the Jews - who oppose his system. So, the nation of Israel will survive this another holocaust. It will be a very trying time as well as a very dark time, but there will be those who will survive because God will provide for them a means of preservation through this period. Remember Jesus had said in Matthew 24:13: *But he that shall endure unto the end, the same shall be saved.* We do know that God took care of ancient Israel for forty years during their wilderness wanderings.

If He did it then, He can do it again! We may not be able to locate the site geographically - but God knows where it is and how He will care for those upon whom His hand will be laid the second time. Some feel the place the woman flees to is the ancient city called Petra. The famous rock city that is hewn out of the mountains. It was the almost impregnable capital of the Edomites.

Verse 7:

And there was war in heaven: Michael and his angels fought against the dragon; and the dragon fought and his angels,

That there would be war in heaven presents to us an interesting as well as strange statement of fact. The scriptures teach us that Satan to this point has access to heaven. We have but to consider Job to realize this. Satan has been identified as the Prince of the power of the air, (Ephesians 2:2). Paul, in speaking of the warfare of the child of God, states that we are fighting against Principalities. against the rulers of the darkness of this world, against spiritual wickedness in high (heavenly) places. (Ephesians 6:12). His access to heaven has come to an end. The fulfillment of all things is swiftly coming to a close.

Why has Satan had access to heaven through the years? God will have a tried people. A proven people. Satan's access to accuse the people of God has been a part of that process. Also, Satan as an angel had access to the heavenlies before his fall. He had the ability to go and come in the vast kingdom of God. This ability was not taken away from him when he fell. So, as an angel - though fallen - he still may soar into the heavenlies. But this privilege is about to come to an end.

This is another reason - no doubt - that the heavens will pass away (2Peter 3:10). Satan has defiled that holy place with his presence, and God will have a house cleaning and will remove all things which have contaminated His heaven and earth. He starts by kicking out the one who has contaminated things the most - Satan!

Michael and his angels fought... Michael is called "the archangel" in Jude verse nine. Michael is the only angel who is called an archangel. As mentioned in a previous study, the Jewish legends tell us there are seven archangels. We do not have mention of this number nor their identity in the Word of God.

Some feel there must be other archangels because of Daniel 10:13, where we note; *Michael, one of the chief princes...* If he is one of the chief princes, there must be others.

It seems that Michael is usually found related somehow to the people of Israel. Another angel which is mentioned by name in the Bible is Gabriel. Gabriel was the one chosen to announce the birth of the Messiah to Mary. In this we have him related to the redemption plan and thus the Church.

His angels... This statement seems to imply that the angels are organized into ranks under the command of certain leaders among them such as Michael.

Michael had confronted the Devil before this, as we find described for us in Jude, verse nine. On that occasion, it involved the body of Moses, this time, however, it is not for argument. It is for a battle which involves heaven.

And the dragon fought and his angels... The angels who joined Lucifer in his fall from heaven is under his control and they join in the battle against Michael and the angels of God.

What kind of battle could this be? What kind of weapons will be employed?

That this will be a real battle there seems to be no one who expresses any doubt. We have read of the many activities of angels throughout the Word of God. We have read of the angel wrestling with Jacob; we have read of the two angels taking Lot and his family by the hand and leading them out of the city. We have read of the angels visiting Abraham. We have read of the angel who visited the enemy Assyrian camp and killing 185,000 in one night. So, the angels are very active in the affairs of men on this earth.

After Jesus resurrected, He invited His disciples to touch Him to see that He was more than just a spirit. Although he possessed a glorified body which could appear, and disappear, at will, He still could be touched and felt. We are informed in chapter twenty of Revelation that an angel will take Satan and bind him in the bottomless pit under a chain. So, from this we can see that Satan can be touched as well.

Although spiritual beings possess unique qualities which we mortals do not possess - at least not yet - they still possess bodies with some sort of material substance that can be felt; wrestled with; bound; tempted, etc.

Verse 8:

And prevailed not; neither was their place found any more in heaven.

God being sovereign could have destroyed Satan from the very beginning when Satan first opposed His dominion. Or, he could have destroyed Satan at this time with the mere expression of His will. But instead, He permitted this battle to take place in the heavens between the forces of good and the forces of evil.

That is the way it has been from the beginning. God could have kept a "hedge" around his people through the years and prevented Satan from getting to any of them. But God's way is the way of testing. He will have a proven people.

And prevailed not... We have no way of knowing how long this battle was waged in the heavens. Did it last for months, or was it over in a few minutes? Why did the forces of darkness under the command of Satan even fight against Michael and his host in the first place? Did they really think they could win in a battle against Michael and the angels of heaven?

This is the final result of the powers of darkness. While they have waged a warfare through the years against the people of God, the ultimate end will be victory for those who stand for the Lord.

Neither was their place found any more in heaven... In their rebellion against God and His kingdom they lost their position in glory. At the same time, they retained the right to heaven, being able to go and come at will. Now, after this final battle, this right is as well taken from these emissaries of darkness. Never again will they enter into the heavenlies. Never again will they know the feeling of soaring into the heavens as the other angels of God.

It is a terrible loss to not be able to attain to something that could be within your reach if the price was paid. We all have an invitation to heaven. Many will never know the joys of accepting that invitation and enjoying the raptures of that city. But these have been there! They have enjoyed in the some distant past the joys of that celestial place. They had their place in that Kingdom long, long ago.

Now, through their own decision to follow Satan, they have forfeited that right and that privilege. Their place is forever abandoned. Their names for ever removed from that heavenly place. What a loss! What a terrible tragedy!

<u>**Verse 9:**</u>

And the great dragon was cast out, that old serpent, called the Devil, and Satan, which deceiveth the whole world: he was cast out into the earth, and his angels were cast out with him.

"Appropriately enough, this is the very middle verse of the Book of Revelation, and the event it describes marks again the middle of the tribulation period." (Morris)

Dragon... Serpent... Devil... Satan... It is interesting that the names and titles of this enemy of all righteousness is so emphasized. There can be no doubt as to who the Lord is talking about here!

Dr. McGee writes: "Old Serpent takes us back to the Garden of Eden. Our Lord said, "*he was a murderer from the beginning.*"

The words *old* and *beginning* are akin, according to Vincent.

Devil is a name which comes from the Greek diabolos, meaning slanderer or accuser. He is so labeled in verse ten, the accuser of the brethren. That is the reason that believers need an advocate.

"Satan means Adversary. He is the awful adversary of everyone of God's children."

The enemy who came in many disguises to deceive and bring confusion into the life of millions of people is here depicted by names appropriate to fit the character who bore them.

Which deceiveth the whole world... What a sad indictment against the entire world! Regardless of the position in life, people have been deceived. This deception reaches from the highest pinnacle of power to the lowest station in life. From the Garden of Eden to the thatched roof hut; from the king to the pauper, all alike have been deceived by this great master deceiver and liar.

Someone wrote: "Satan is to be dreaded as a lion; More to be dreaded as a Serpent; And most to be dreaded as an angel."

"Educated and ignorant, king and pauper, male and female, Jew and Gentile, strong and weak, young and old, black and white - all are deceived by him. All the world's high-sounding philosophies, conceived ever so brilliantly by profound thinkers - whether pragmatism, idealism, gnosticism, determinism, hedonism, materialism, transdentalism, existentialism, deism, or any of the countless others, and regardless of the eminence of the geniuses with whose names they are associated - Aristotelianism, Platonism, Hegelianism, Marxism, Maoism, Confusianism, Buddhism, Kantianism, Freudianism - all are man-originated, man-centered, and man-honoring, rather than God originated, God-centered, and God-honoring. They are all merely varieties of humanism, rather than theism, exalting man rather than God and thus helping to carry out Satan's attempt to dethrone God." (Morris)

Wordsworth said: "The deceits by which Satan cheated the world in oracles, sorcery, soothsaying, magic, and other frauds, are here specially noticed. These were put to flight by the Power of Christ and of the Holy Ghost, in the preaching of the gospel by the apostles and others in the first ages of Christianity. Our Lord Himself, speaking of the consequence of the preaching of the seventy disciples, reveals the spiritual struggle and the victory: I was beholding Satan as lightning fall from heaven (Luke 10:17,18).

And he was cast out into the earth... his angels... with him... This is a two-fold rebuke and humiliation to Satan. First of all: His place in heaven is forfeited. Never again will he be privileged entrance into that holy place. Secondly: He is cast down to this earth where he will have to confine himself and his activities. The high and lofty one who was going to exalt his throne above the stars of God, suddenly finds himself degraded to this lowly earth! Then, eventually, he will be degraded even lower when he is confined for one thousand years in the bottomless pit. Then, into the lake of fire for ever and ever.

Not only is the future of Satan one of continual degrading, but all those who choose to follow his example and influence will find themselves on that same down-ward road. It is all downhill for those who join forces with Satan and his associates.

The final downward slide will be at the great White Throne judgment when all whose name is not found in the book of life hear their awful doom to depart into the lake of fire.

His angels were cast out with him... Those who choose to follow in the steps of Satan will suffer the same judgment! Whether angel or men, only the foolish would elect to follow this evil one.

Does this statement mean that the fallen angels also had access to heaven? If the fallen angels had access into heaven, then what is the meaning of the words found in 2Peter and Jude: ... *delivered them into chains of darkness... he hath reserved in everlasting chains under darkness.*

It is probable that the reference here to the angels of Satan is a reference to those who minister unto him. His messengers of evil. If the angels who fell into his snare in the beginning have all been placed under arrest in chains awaiting the judgment, then this would not likely have reference to them. Unless the chains are spiritual in nature. These are the demonic spirits which do the bidding of Satan in his kingdom of evil and darkness.

Verse 10:

And I heard a loud voice saying in heaven, Now is come salvation, and strength, and the kingdom of our God, and the power of his

Christ: for the accuser of our brethren is cast down, which accused them before our God day and night.

For some six thousand years of man's history on this earth, Satan has had access into the heavens, where he has continually accused the people of God. Possibly heaven will reveal in that day the conversations which went on between Satan and God during that time. We do have the record of two such conversations in the book of Job (1:6-12; 2:1-6). If these are an indication of other conversations, then it would appear that Satan has but one goal in mind; to destroy everyone who stands for God in opposition to him.

Now is come... The casting out of Satan marks the end of his influence in heaven. What were the reactions of the angels of God when Satan would make his way to the throne? God who had promised ultimate victory has kept His word. It has been a long time in coming - but it is here at last!

Salvation...

Salvation - or deliverance - has at last come. As long as Satan is loose and going to and fro, there will not be complete deliverance. His being cast out of heaven indicates ultimate victory and deliverance. The time of the end of all things is at hand. Never again will the angels of heaven, nor the inhabitants of this earth, have to face the temptations hurled at them by Satan and his host of evil.

And strength...

The casting out of Satan has shown who is the stronger of the two powers. Satan and his angels have fallen in defeat before the angels of the Lord.

And the kingdom of our God... This statement lets us know that the kingdom has not been established yet. The kingdom for which Christ told His disciples to pray will now come to this earth. The kingdom which had been made up of those who were born again was a spiritual kingdom, which shall now join with the Lord very soon to return to this earth to establish His kingdom upon this earth. A physical, literal kingdom, for the inhabitants of earth. Before there can be a kingdom of peace established on this earth, the one who destroys peace must first be gotten out of the way.

The power of His Christ... Jesus Christ will come to reign as King of kings and Lord of lords. Jesus had promised His apostles that if they would follow Him, in the time of the regeneration they would sit on twelve thrones as well, judging the twelve tribes of Israel.

For the accuser of our brethren... This would indicate that the one who is proclaiming this from heaven is one of the redeemed! This would also indicate that the raptured must be aware of what is taking place on this earth during the tribulation. If they are not aware of what is taking place on earth in detail, at least they are very much aware of the fact Satan has been expelled from heaven. Throughout the Revelation we have reason to think that the raptured saints are involved in what is going on.

Which accused them... Note that this expression is in the past tense! He had accused them - but no more! His days of accusing the saints of God before His throne are over with forever.

Realizing that ultimate victory will come to the people of God gives one a great feeling of hope and consolation.

This statement of Satan's work is not found anywhere else in the New Testament.

Verse 11:

And they overcame him by the blood of the Lamb, and by the word of their testimony; and they loved not their lives unto the death.

To each one of the seven churches Jesus had said: *He that overcometh...* The word given to those who are confronted with the tribulation was, *But he that shall endure unto the end...* Ultimate victory is held out to those who will endure. To those who will overcome. Those who stand with victory in their possession on that day will have come through their own valleys and trials and temptations. They have each travelled their own personal path to that city. While each life may be uniquely different, they will all have one thing in common - They are all overcomers!

By the blood of the Lamb... Some through the water - some through the fire - but all through the blood! Those who feel offended at the use of the term "blood" would feel out of place in that crowd! There is no other means of reaching that city and that place of victory, but through the blood. It is because of the blood that we know salvation. We will not stand there because of our own merits of accomplishments. It will be because of His blood.

And by the word of their testimony... The greatest testimony anyone will ever give will be the life they live before others. As the saying goes; "What you are makes so much noise I can't hear what you say."

While it is true that our life is a silent yet forceful witness to others, at the same time we are admonished to Sanctify the Lord God in your hearts: *and be ready always to give an answer to every man that asketh you a reason of the hope that is in you with meekness and fear,* (1Peter 3:15).

Jesus said: But ye shall receive power, after that the Holy Ghost is come upon you: and ye shall be witnesses unto me (Acts 1:8).

It is not enough just to live right. We must tell it to others as we go through life. By putting into words the feelings we have in our heart we are able to convince others of the reality of living for God.

And they loved not their lives unto the death... Some feel this reference is speaking about those on this earth during this time. That they, because of the great persecution they are facing, must have a great love of God. Love that surpasses the love even of their own life. This may well be the case, but we know the same love must be possessed by all who would live for God. Paul spoke of the love which he had for the Lord when he states; *For I am ready not to be bound only, but also to die at Jerusalem for the name of the Lord Jesus,* (Acts 21:13).

The tremendous pressures which will be placed on people during the tribulation will force people to make a decision as to whether to take a stand for Christ or accept the mark of the Beast. If they accept the mark, they will doom their life eternally. If they refuse to accept the mark, they will place their life in jeopardy and could very well be martyred. Eternally speaking, the latter would be the wisest choice!

Verse 12:

Therefore rejoice, {ye} heavens, and ye that dwell in them. Woe to the inhabiters of the earth and of the sea! for the devil is come down unto you, having great wrath, because he knoweth that he hath but a short time.

What a tremendous contrast is found in this statement! On one side, there is encouragement for rejoicing by those in heaven. On the other side, there is a woe pronounced to those who live on this earth at this time. While it may not have always been this obvious, the contrast has always been there between Satan and God. Between heaven's glory and Satan's woes.

The redeemed have been in heaven with the Lord for some three-plus years at this time. We suppose they have been witnesses of this great battle which has taken place between Michael and his angels, and Satan and his angels. All of these redeemed have had their own personal struggles and wars with Satan during their sojourn on this earth. Many interesting stories could be told by this host of redeemed who have fought the good fight of faith and overcame the enemy during their lifetime on this earth. To now see this enemy cast out of heaven, down to the earth, calls for rejoicing over his defeat.

Woe to the inhabitants of the earth... Satan has lost the battle in the heavens. He, along with his angels, have been driven out never to return to this place. We do not know if they continued during the intervening years since the original fall, seeking to influence other angels to follow them, if they did, this influence is removed for ever by their removal from heaven. They now focus their entire attention on this earth. Is it any wonder that when we open the following chapter we are introduced to the man of sin as the Beast! For Satan shall at this time enter this man and possess him!

Because he knoweth that he hath but a short time... The time which Satan has left for his dirty work on this earth is three and one-half years! Knowing that his time is this short, he musters all his forces for an invasion of this earth like it has never witnessed to this time. A dark cloud is about to descend over this earth, wrapping it in darkness and chaos. The next three and one-half years will be the darkest; the bloodiest; the most horrible years that this earth has ever faced. No previous period of history - regardless of how dark it may have seemed - will compare with this period of time.

Rallying all his forces Satan will make one final effort to defeat the purpose and plan of God. It will all be in vain! While he will conquer many lives during this period, the ultimate victory belongs to Christ and those who choose to follow His will for their lives'.

Woe to the inhabiters of the earth... and the sea... This is the third woe which was announced would come upon the earth. As mentioned in our previous study, the woes increased in intensity, this one being the worst yet! No woe could be greater than having Satan and all his forces of evil coming down on you with great wrath, having just lost face in a battle with the angels of God.

Just what is meant by and of the sea, is not clear. We do know that previous judgments have fallen on the sea, as in chapter eight. We also know that the sea is busily occupied by the many ships of the super-power nations, both on top and underneath the waters. So, regardless of where men may dwell, the effects of Satan and his wickedness will be felt.

Having great wrath... The enemy has always been mad. He has been mad at the workings of God on this earth. He has been mad at anyone and everyone who dared resist his many temptations which he continually brings against mankind. He is mad at anyone who would refuse to surrender to the Beast and his mark. But he has been made even madder by the fact he has lost this great battle in the heavens, and now has been cast out of heaven down to this earth.

The horrible consequence of his wrath will be the manifestation of the Beast, in whom Satan will himself dwell. The Beast will be the personification of Satan in human form on this earth.

Verse 13:

And when the dragon saw that he was cast unto the earth, he persecuted the woman which brought forth the man {child}.

There has always, since the days of the Jewish nation, been those who have sought to eradicate them and their memory from this earth. Throughout their long history there are records which show the attempts brought against them to destroy them as a people.

Hitler is but one of the latest attempts among many to try to destroy this people.

When the dragon - Satan - is cast down to this earth, he directs his fury against one people in particular: Israel. The descendants of Abraham. While there will be many who are not Jews that will refuse the Beast and his mark (7:9-17), it will be the nation of Israel who will face the greatest fire of his wrath, because of what they represent; the message of One God. The God whom Satan is opposed to, and whom Satan wants to bring down from His throne.

Probably upon being cast down to this earth, Satan will then enter the man of sin, influenced him to break the covenant which he had previously confirmed with Israel, some three and one-half years before. He will influence him to enter the Jewish sacred place and declare himself to be god and demand their worship of him as such. To which Satan knows the Jewish mind will rebel against such a suggestion.

Israel will thus enter into a period of time which will be the fires of Zechariah 13:9. *A time of trouble such as they have never faced before* (Daniel 12:1) in their long history as a people. Only the coming again of Jesus Christ will prevent their total annihilation from this earth by the forces of the Beast.

But that is just exactly what will happen in the darkest hour of Israel. The One whom their fathers had crucified nineteen hundred plus years before will return to deliver His people in a great victory!

Verse 14:

And to the woman were given two wings of a great eagle, that she might fly into the wilderness, into her place, where she is nourished for a time, and times, and half a time, from the face of the serpent.

Wings of a great eagle... It is interesting to note that when Israel escaped from Egyptian bondage there was reference made concerning that escape as "eagles' wings;" Exodus 19:4: *Ye have seen what I did unto the Egyptians, and how I bare you on eagles' wings, and brought you unto myself.* The eagles' wings could speak of a speedy deliverance. When the dragon is cast out of heaven down to this earth, he will probably move swiftly, knowing that his time is short. Changes will probably take place quickly and drastically, as Satan enters the man of sin.

As the chapter is evidently filled with symbols, the reference to "*eagles wings*" is no doubt symbolic as well. During the returning of the outcasts of the Jews to their homeland in the past few years since their re-independence as a nation, there have been groups who have been brought in by plane who had never flown before. An allusion was made by one of these groups to the Old Testament prophecies which referred to eagles' wings as being these planes which brought them home. God, they felt, was fulfilling His promise to them.

She might fly into the wilderness... We would not think that the reference to eagles' wings would refer to planes due to the size of the land which Israel occupies. That is, if the reference to the wilderness refers to a wilderness in their own land. With modem technology in warfare, planes would be vulnerable to rockets and missiles which the enemy will no doubt have in their possession. Now, if she is going someplace other than her own present-day land area, then the symbol having reference to planes could certainly apply.

Let us remember the words of Jesus at this time, when He spoke of the events which will transpire prior to His return to this earth:

When ye therefore shall see the abomination of desolation, spoken of by Daniel the prophet, stand in the holy place, (whoso readeth, let him understand:) (The beast declaring that he is god, 2Thessalonians 2:4). *Then let them which be in Judaea flee into the mountains: Let him which is on the housetop not come down to take anything out of his house: Neither let him which is in the field return back to take his clothes. And woe unto them that are with child, and to them that give suck in those days! But pray ye that your flight be not in the winter, neither on the sabbath day: For then shall be great tribulation, such as was not since the beginning of the world to this time, no, nor ever shall be,* (Matthew 24:15-21).

Jesus emphasized when this flight was to take place; At the time of the abomination of desolation standing in the holy place. He emphasized the speed and urgency of their escape; Don't go back into the house.

The Beast will enter the temple of God in the middle of the week, declaring himself to be god, and demanding the people to worship him. This will be right after the dragon is cast out of heaven to the earth. His fury will then be turned against the people of Abraham. It is this time, no doubt, that is in consideration in this passage in Revelation.

We know that when Israel escaped from Egyptian bondage the deliverance was not by planes, although there is reference to their deliverance as being with eagles' wings. We do know, however, that their deliverance was brought about through the help of angels protecting them and keeping the enemy from them. If this happened thirty-five hundred years ago - it can happen again! There is no doubt in our mind that God will have special angels watching over and helping His people Israel during this difficult time. There have been several reports alluding to angels being present during Israel's wars since her independence.

Into her place... This is an interesting statement! While Israel may not know at the present where this place is, God does! He not only knows where it is, He has had it prepared for them for this specific time!

Where she is nourished... God who took care of their forefathers for forty years during their wilderness wanderings, will once again take care of His people miraculously. How and by what means they will be nourished is left to our speculation at this point. We do know, however, that the God who fed millions each day with manna for forty years; the God who commanded a raven to feed His prophet; the God who multiplied oil in the cruse and meal in the barrel; the God who multiplied fish and loaves in His hands to take care of thousands one day, can well take care of this group of Jews who will escape from under the clutches of the man of sin and his cohorts in this dark time of tribulation.

Why does God allow a group of Jews to escape into this place of security, while others are dying at the hand of the Beast? First of all, God is sovereign. We may not understand what He does nor why He does certain things. Someday, possibly, we will have an understanding to all such questions that come to our mind now. Secondly, by the very fact that a group of people elude the snares of the man of sin, and are able to live right under his nose without him being able to destroy them, will be a tremendous insult to the Beast. It will be a tremendous testimony to the greatness of God. While the Beast makes his boasts of being the greatest and most powerful man on earth, there will be a group of Jews living nearby whom he is unable to destroy! What an insult to his ego!

For a time, and times, and a half time... The same expression which we have considered in our studies before (like 11:2,3; 12:6), only expressed there as *"forty-two months;" "a thousand two hundred and threescore days."* They all three seem to have reference to the same period of time; the last three and one-half years of the tribulation.

Usually when we think of Israel and the time of Jacob's trouble; the tribulation, we think of them as going through seven years of horrible times and very dark and trying times. While this is certainly true, and the Bible makes this clear that they will; at the same time, it is evident that here is a group who during the middle of that seven year period are rescued from the storm and kept in a place of security for the remainder of this time. So, it would seem from this passage that many of the Jews will escape death and the snares of the Beast by making it to this place of refuge.

From the serpent... The preceding verse refers to the enemy as the dragon who was persecuting the woman (Israel). The name here switches to serpent. It is repeated in the next verse, then reverts back to dragon in the two concluding verses. We do not know why the names are interchanged in this passage.

It is evident from verse nine that we are considering the same character, whether he be called dragon, serpent, or Satan. As mentioned previously, the term serpent reminds us of the garden of Eden and his appearance there in a cunning, deceitful manner. No doubt Satan will employ his many tactics to try to bring about the destruction of this people who are a thorn in his side.

Verse 15:

And the serpent cast out of his mouth water as a flood after the woman, that he might cause her to be carried away of the flood.

The term flood when employed symbolically in the Bible speaks of various kinds of troubles and problems which beset the people of God. For example: Psalm 69:15, *Let not the waterflood overflow me, neither let the deep swallow me up, and let not the pit shut her mouth upon me.* Isaiah 59;19, *So shall they fear the name of the Lord from the west, and his glory from the rising of the sun. When the enemy shall come in like a flood, the Spirit of the Lord shall lift up a standard against him.*

It is highly possible, speaking in terms of today's highly modern techniques of warfare, that the enemy will fire missiles, or some type of artillery after the fleeing Jews.

Just exactly what the term means is open for our speculation at this point. We do know, however, that this is the only place the expression is found in the New Testament. So, it is peculiar to this verse and to this occasion.

Interpreting the statement in symbolic language, as we have the rest of the chapter, we conclude that it is no doubt a reference to some form of weaponry which is employed by the Beast in an effort to destroy those escaping from his grasp. Note another example of this type of terminology regarding the enemies of God's people in an effort to bring destruction to them; Jeremiah 46:8, *Egypt riseth up like a flood, and his waters are moved like the rivers; and he saith, I will go up, and will cover the earth; I will destroy the city and the inhabitants thereof*

Regardless of what it may be which the enemy will employ in his attempt to destroy Israel, his efforts will be in vain, as the following verse states:

Verse 16:

And the earth helped the woman, and the earth opened her mouth, and swallowed up the flood which the dragon cast out of his mouth.

Much of what is said in this passage takes us back to the Old Testament time of types and shadows. Again, we are reminded of the Egyptians and their efforts to retain Israel as slaves in bondage. At the Red Sea, we find this statement being made; *Thou stretchest out thy right hand, the earth swallowed them. This is in reference to the Red Sea swallowing up Pharaoh's forces who tried to pursue Israel across the bed of the Sea.*

Another thought that should not be overlooked here is the fact that the term earth in the Revelation is employed symbolically to speak of the wicked. So, it is not beyond reason to consider that God will employ the people of the world to aid His people in their efforts to get away from the Beast. Let us recall that Jesus taught His disciples that they should make friends of the unrighteous (Luke 16:9).

There is a statement made by Dr Seiss in his commentary on Revelation that is of interest: "It is the region and time of miracle when this drinking up of the river which the Dragon sends against the woman occurs. It is the region and time when there is to be a renewal of wonders, "like as it was to Israel in the day that he came up out of the land of Egypt" (Isaiah 11:15,16), It is the region and time of great earthquakes and disturbances in the economy of nature. (Zechariah 14:4; Luke 21:25,26; Revelation 11:13,19.) And there is reason to think that it is by some great and sudden rending of the earth that these pursuing hosts are arrested in their course, if not enmasse buried up in convulsion. At least, the object of their bloody expedition is thwarted. They fail to reach the Woman in her place of refuge. The very ground yawns to stop them in their hellish madness."

Paul states in Romans 8:31, *What shall we then say to these things? If God be for us, who can be against us?* If the Lord be on our side no enemy shall overtake us, to bring to naught His divine will for our life. John declares in 1John 4:4, *Ye are of God, little children, and have overcome them: because greater is he that is in you, than he that is in the world.* For God to employ nature to assist His people would not be anything new nor different. He has been doing that for millenniums!

If we are considering the ground opening up in an earthquake or something of that nature, and swallowing up the pursuing enemy forces, what a slap in the face to the one who ordered them pursued! After all the Beast has just declared that he is god! and if he is god, how can it be that even nature would work against him!

Now, as we considered in the previous verse, if this flood that has been sent against the fleeing Jews are weapons, then something happens to their weapons and they fall harmless in the sands of the wilderness.

Verse 17:

And the dragon was wroth with the woman, and went to make war with the remnant of her seed, which keep the commandments of God, and have the testimony of Jesus Christ.

Having been insulted before his people, the enemy seeks to avenge his pride.

Our study in this chapter has emphasized that this passage is highly symbolic. This is evident from the descriptions given to us of the characters involved. That being the case, we should also consider this woman fleeing as being symbolic as well. While in the forepart of our study on this subject we noted that the woman seems to refer to Israel. When we get here to the woman fleeing, we should define what is meant by the Woman representing Israel. It is evident from the reference to the remnant here, that the woman cannot be isolated to one particular group or person. Are we to consider that the Woman speaks of the nation? And the leaders of that nation would represent that nation? Do we have those leaders here who are escaping into the wilderness, away from the Beast? We do know from what information we have received that there are security measures which have been taken to secure the safety of our leaders, the President and others in commanding positions, in times of all-out war. Such a place of security has already been established in the mountains of Virginia. Is this the leaders of the nation escaping, and when this happens the Beast, out of his fury, then turns his attention on all the other Jews that may be found? The term remnant could not only speak of a few in number, but also the "remainder."

The Jew being hunted down is nothing new to their history. They have experienced this on other occasions when their enemies sought to exterminate them. The pogroms will once again be instituted, as the Beast issues his edict that all Jews are to be killed. It will be a very dark and bloody time for Israel!

The term *remnant* is always employed in the scriptures in reference to Israel. The Church never has the reference "remnant" employed for Her. The Church will not be saved piece-meal. There will not be a remnant of the Church saved; THE WHOLE CHURCH WILL BE SAVED!

Unable to get those who have escaped, the Beast seeks to vent his wrath against those who remain in the area, and where ever he has authority.

This will be the last great anti-Semitic effort which will engulf the world. There have been many times in their long history that the Jews have faced annihilation, only to come forth stronger than before. Like the Church, their destiny is sealed by God. Nothing, nor no one, can prevent the ultimate victory which will come to both the Church and the descendants of Abraham.

Which keep the commandments of God... Those who have refused to observe the commandments of God have probably already succumbed to the influence of the Beast. Only those who are spiritual among the people will see the dangers in what the Beast offers, and refuse his offers.

Again, Israel as a nation are not spiritual. Although they have a rich spiritual heritage, the nation as a whole is not spiritual. It is the few among them who are spiritual, and who will refuse to go along with the Beast regardless of the promises he makes.

And have the testimony of Jesus Christ... This is a very interesting statement! One of the main reasons that the Jew is enduring this dark period of time in their history is due to their rejection of Jesus Christ as Messiah. They have contended since that first century that He was not their Messiah. This was one of the reasons their fathers had Him crucified; because He claimed to be Messiah, and they considered that blasphemy, and thus punishable by death.

Something - or someone - has reached this group called remnant and convinced them that Jesus Christ is indeed their Messiah! Has it been the hundred and forty-four thousand? Or the two witnesses?

Now because of their commitment to the One whom their fathers had crucified, their life is placed in jeopardy! The result of this pressure against this remnant will be them becoming even that much more dedicated to this one called Jesus Christ!

CHAPTER THIRTEEN

• One of the most fascinating chapters in the book of Revelation!

It is from this point that the Great Tribulation begins. This chapter marks the beginning of the last half of the week.

The man we were introduced to in chapter six riding on his white horse, is now presented to us as a Beast out of the sea!

He now has a cohort who joins him that John saw come up out of the earth. He is called the False Prophet. They are both influenced - if not possessed - by Satan himself.

The Beast has been making his moves to gain control of the empire that he is now head of. With Satan being cast out of heaven, and now entering this man of sin, he is given that power and authority that he has been aspiring for.

The darkest hour in the history of the Jews - and even of the world - is about to engulf this world.

The forces of hell are unleashed to bring down every nation and power on the earth - and most particularly the Jews - the descendants of Abraham.

While it is now only three and one-half more years before the Lord returns to this earth in power and vengeance, it will be the longest three and one-half years - they will seem to be the longest, no doubt, to those who must endure them - in man's history.

There have been seven chapters devoted to the first half of the week (counting the parenthetical chapters), and there will be seven chapters describing the remaining half of the week.

Our study in this interesting book grows more interesting as we travel deeper into this book! This chapter becomes a very fascinating one regarding the events which shall transpire during these seven years just prior to the return of Jesus Christ to this earth.

Revelation thirteen is a continuation of what we have just studied in the previous chapter. The war in heaven, the dragon being cast out to the earth. Then, the dragon having lost the war in heaven, and being unable to destroy the "woman," is furious and determines to bring his wrath upon the inhabitants of this earth. Particularly the Jews. To do this, Satan indwells a man of prominent position whom he can control and use in his attempt to bring down the will of God on earth in His chosen people, Israel.

We have reached the middle point in the last week (seven years) of the "Times of the Gentiles" prior to the return of Jesus Christ to the earth. Or, as it is termed, His second advent. Having studied about some interesting characters in chapter twelve, we now come upon two more interesting characters in this chapter: The man of sin, and his cohort, the False Prophet.

Verse 1:

And I stood upon the sand of the sea, and saw a beast rise up out of the sea, having seven heads and ten horns, and upon his horns ten crowns, and upon his heads the name of blasphemy.

Some feel that this verse should begin *And he stood...* That the reference is to Satan, not John.

That Satan, having been cast down to the earth now stands before the masses of humanity and calls forth a despicable character which he can use to further his evil work on the earth. It would seem, however, that this is no doubt a reference to John, not Satan. John is the one who has been describing the events which have been taking place, and John is the one who continues to do so after chapter thirteen. So, we feel the reference is to John, not Satan.

SAND OF THE SEA... The sea in Revelation no doubt has reference to the great Mediterranean Sea. Yet, like so many other expressions employed in the Revelation, the reference to a sea could also have a symbolic significance. In this instance the reference evidently is to the masses of humanity. The "beast" is to come from among the masses of humanity.

A BEAST... Considering the study of Revelation in its entirety, we feel that this is the same one whom we were introduced to in chapter six. At that time, he was riding on a white horse, and appeared to be a man of peaceful intentions. Now, in the middle of the week, his true colors come through, especially now that the dragon - Satan - has been cast down to the earth. His approach from now on will not be in a peaceful manner.

The study of the beast is an interesting - as well as controversial - study. Like many other things in the Revelation, there are many differing views concerning the beast; as to who he is; where he will come from, etc.

It is in the book of Daniel where we find so many references to beasts. The term "beast" is employed to speak of their methods of gaining power in the world. A beast mangles and devours and destroys.

The man of sin will fit into this category. What unfolds from this point on fits a beastly character.

Without feelings, the Beast will bring havoc to all who withstand his demands, and who stand in his way of gaining world control. It is no wonder that this period is referred to as the darkest hour the world has ever known!

There are several titles that are given to the beast/man of sin in the Bible. To mention a few of them we refer to the book of Clarence Larken:

"The Assyrian" - Isaiah 10:5,6; 30:27-33 "King of Babylon" - Isaiah 14:4 "Lucifer" - Isaiah 14:12

"The Little Horn" - Daniel 7:8; 8:9-12 "A king of fierce countenance" - Daniel 8:23 "The Prince that shall come" - Daniel 9:26 "The wilful king" - Daniel 11:36

"The man of sin" - 2Thessalonians 2:3-8 "Son of perdition" - 2Thessalonians 2:3-8 "That wicked" - 2Thessalonians 2:3-8 'Antichrist" - 1John 2:18 "The beast" - Revelation 13:1 ,2.

Many feel that he was the one Jesus was having reference to when He said; I am come in my Father's name, and ye receive me not; if another shall come in his own name, him ye will receive, (John 5:43).

HORNS... The horns of the beast speak to us of power.

CROWNS... Diadems. These speak to us badges or recognition of dominion.

He possesses power and great authority.

FOUR INTERESTING SYMBOLS

There are four symbols in this chapter which catch our attention:

- • 1}. The Dragon
- • 2}. The Sea

- 3}. The Beast out of the sea
- 4}. The Beast out of the earth.

We know who the dragon is by our study of the previous chapter, and him being identified for us there in verse nine as Satan.

In referring to chapter 17:1,15, we find there that the angel informed John that the "many waters" is a reference to Peoples, and multitudes, and nations, and tongues. So, the "Sea" in this passage must as well refer to many peoples.

The "Beast" captures our attention because there is so much said about him in the Revelation. And because there are so many references made about him in the Old Testament prophecies - as well as the New Testament. Some thirty-two times the symbol of the beast is referred to here in the Revelation.

While what is said here concerning the beast does not seem to be speaking of a person - what person could be described in such a horrible manner? - at the same time it would seem that from the many personal pronouns and references made concerning him, we should also consider him as a person! When we consider the same beast in 17:8, it is evident that more than just a person is involved here. When we consider the seven heads and ten horns, and we consider what is said about him in 17:3, it would seem that more than a person is involved in the beast. We conclude that Politically speaking the beast represents a system: an empire of evil. Personally, speaking the beast represents a man, a person of evil intentions.

The beast speaks of a person, as well as a nation, or kingdom of power. Just as Nebuchadnezzar was Babylon; Darius was Persia; Alexander was Greece; David was Israel, etc., that is they represented the nation they governed, even so the beast is the empire - or power - of wickedness which is here referred to as a beast. A beast with seven heads and ten horns.

This Beast is, by common consent, identical with "that Wicked," of which Paul wrote to the Thessalonians; but that monster instrument of Satan is called "that man of sin." This Beast is also clearly identifiable with the wilful king of Daniel; but that king is in every resect treated as an individual person, the same as Cyrus, Darius, Xerxes, or Alexander.

He is repeatedly described as "the Beast that cometh up out of the abyss." The "abyss" cannot mean less than the under-world, the world of lost spirits. The receptacle and abode of demons, otherwise called "hell." Ordinary men do not come from such a place. One who hails from that place must be either a dead man brought up again from the dead, or some evil spirit which takes possession of a living man.

The reference to the seven heads and ten horns of the beast is explained in chapter seventeen. We will wait until we get to that chapter before we elaborate on what these seven heads and ten horns are speaking about.

Verse 2:

And the beast which I saw was like unto a leopard, and his feet

were as {the feet} of a bear, and his mouth as the mouth of a lion: and the dragon gave him his power, and his seat, and great authority.

In Daniel chapter seven, we find Daniel witnessing four great beasts came out of the sea, diverse one from another. (Vs. 3) As Daniel describes them one by one, the characteristics of each beast can be noted in this one beast which John witnesses coming out of the Sea! Daniel's beasts were four separate Beast's: Lion, Bear, Leopard, Dreadful. The beast that John saw had all four of these characteristics; Like a leopard; feet as a bear; mouth as a lion; dragon giving him his power.

Dr Scofield, in his foot notes, as well as many other commentaries, feel that these four beasts are to be compared with the image of Nebuchadnezzar's dream which consisted of four materials. The image and four materials had reference to the four empires which were to come upon the world and over Israel, down to the time of the end. While the comparisons do make sense, at the same time there are others who feel that the four beasts of Daniel seven are speaking of nations which will come into power in the last days. One reason is for the statement found in verse seventeen; "These great beasts, which are four, are four kings, which shall arise out of the earth." Note, Daniel is told they shall arise out of the earth. At the time Daniel saw this vision and heard these words, Babylon had already been overthrown!

We are considering a person, and we are considering a political power structure as well. A system which will rise in the last days and seek to gain control of the world; economically; politically, and religiously. This system will seem to be working too! Only the coming again of Jesus Christ, who will bring victory to the oppressed, will prevent the man of sin and his cohorts from accomplishing their goals!

Henry Morris has this to say about these beasts: "Thus it seems probable that the four beasts of Daniel 7 represent four great kingdoms (or, possibly, confederations), one each from the north, south, east, and west, like the four winds striving over the sea. The beast of the west (the lion with eagle's wings) might, for example, represent the British lion with the American eagle, or the western alliance in general. The second is a great devouring bear, which could well be the Russian colossus and her communist satellites. The third is a four--headed, four-winged leopard, possibly symbolizing a future alliance. Revelation 16: 12 prophecies the coming of "the kings of the east" and Daniel 11:44 speaks of troublesome "tidings out of the east". The leopard is the widest ranging of the great carnivores and is yellow with black spots. The fourth beast, evidently unidentifiable in terms of animals known to Daniel, was "dreadful and terrible, and strong exceedingly," eventually dominating the other three beasts. It would then, presumably, as the "south wind," represent the Mediterranean nations themselves, occupying roughly the territory of the old Roman empire, both north and south of the Mediterranean Sea. It was "diverse from all the beasts that were before it literally, "confronting it" and soon would conquer and assimilate the others, at least to a degree."

If we choose to look at these beasts in this manner, then it would appear that when John sees them, at this juncture in the Revelation, or, time of tribulation, the fourth beast has reached his pinnacle of power, and in so doing has, in some manner, conquered - or controls - the other nations involved in this period. That would be the reason we see him as a mixture of the other beasts.

The dragon gave him his power... seat..., and great authority... The obsession to conquer and control has lived in the hearts of men through the ages since the time of Nimrod, in the days of the Genesis story. As the world grew larger in number and in conquered land area, the dream of conquering the world became a larger dream. Through the centuries there have been those who have risen aspiring for this power in their own hands. In our own generation, we have witnessed such men as Hitler, who made such aspirations known, and who attempted to make his dreams become reality.

With the world being so far-flung today the idea of one man controlling the entire world's populace seems too far-fetched to ever become reality. At the same time, however, when we consider the economic systems the world is gradually - but surely - adopting, which involves that mind-boggling invention called the "computer," it becomes more of a possibility! More and more we are all being brought into a system which requires computer recognition to purchase major items, or to do business in our world. Once the system functions fully it would not be an impossible thing to see how that one could be cut off from the system by the removal of their number from the computer system, or, a mark of some sort placed within the computer beside their number informing all that this person is to be rejected. More about the computer later.

Before any man, regardless of how intelligent; how bombastic; how ingenious, he may be, will ever reach such a pinnacle of power he will have to be helped to that position by some greater power and influence than his own. Satan, in his grand scheme to control and to destroy every life that he possibly can, will see the opportunity of doing just that through the life of this man whom the Bible calls here "the Beast." Whoever this man may be he will be influenced, if not possessed, by Satan himself! Before Judas betrayed the Lord, it was said of him: Then entered Satan into Judas surnamed Iscariot (Luke 22:3).

That such a character can come to the forefront and dominate so many lives, may seem somewhat far- fetched at this point, but the time will come when such a thing will take place. In fact, it is evident from the troubles which beset the world's nations right now that something is going to take place in the near future which will be an attempt to correct these problems. Nations are reeling from economic problems, not only here in the United States, but in many other nations as well. Many of the third world nations are being buried under a red sea of debt that they cannot repay. There is political instability in many nations in our world today. With these problems, the world is getting in the right condition to welcome the coming "messiah" who will promise so much. When they say, "peace and safety", then look out! the apostle Paul warned us.

While history has left us the records of such men as Nebuchadnezzar; Alexander the Great; the Caesar's; Napoleon; Hitler, etc., none of them will compare with this one which is to come on the scene in that day.

The prophet Daniel spoke about this man in his book. He saw him as a horrible beast in chapter seven, or at least, this is a description of the government he will head. Daniel also calls him the *little horn.*

What Daniel witnessed concerning the four beasts was that they were consecutive powers, beginning with Babylon; then to Medeo-Persia; then to Greece; then to Rome. What John is describing is the culmination of what these four powers represented. While the four powers described by Daniel each continued for several years; the beast that John is describing will have but three and one-half years to reign.

The Beast is an individual administration, embodied in one particular man. Though he is held up by ten kings – or governments – they unite in making him – the Beast – the one sole head of their system in the last days.

Paul spoke of him in his epistle to the Thessalonians (2:3-12), as the son of perdition, the man of sin, and the lawless one.

He will be a man of great influence and power over the people of the world in the last days. While there have been many stories which have been told, and re-told in the past several years, no one at this juncture of life knows who he is. In fact, Paul lets us know that he will not be revealed until the hindering force which is presently in the world is removed. While it may satisfy one's curiosity to find out the identity of this one who is to come, I for one would not want to stay around just to find out who he is!

Mr Seiss in his lectures on the Apocalypse, states: "This man of sin will be an exceedingly attractive, fascinating, and bewitching personage. He draws upon himself the intensest admiration and homage of the world. John beheld, and all the world wondered after the beast. Mankind are represented as so struck, captivated, and entranced by the contemplation of his wonderful qualities and powers, that they even render willing homage to the one who could give them so glorious a leader, and join in honoring and glorifying him as a very god of wisdom, power, daring, and ability. They can conceive of none like him and celebrate his praise as the Invincible.

The adoring cry is: 'Who is like the beast?' And who is able to war with him? It cannot be otherwise than that this man is supreme in whatever is admirable to the taste, judgment, and imagination of the world."

One of the titles that he is known by is that of "Antichrist." John makes this reference to those who deny that Jesus Christ is come in the flesh in 1John 4:3. He will be opposed to all that Christ is and all He stands for. In fact, he will blaspheme God, and overcome the saints, killing many of them during his tenure as the Beast. Let us notice some contrasts between Jesus Christ and the antichrist. The antichrist will oppose not only the people of God during the tribulation, but will, at Armageddon, oppose Christ Himself. And as he will claim to be the answer - the Messiah - to the world, it is interesting to notice the contrasts between the real and the false:

• Jesus Christ came from above; John 6:38: Antichrist is from the pit; Revelation 11:7; 17:8.

• Jesus Christ came in His Father's name; John 5:43: Antichrist will come in his own name; John 5:43.

• Jesus Christ humbled Himself; Philippians 2:8: Antichrist exalts himself; 2 Thessalonians 2:4.

• Jesus Christ was despised of men; Isaiah 53:3; Luke 23:18: Antichrist will be admired by men; Revelation 13:3,4.

• Jesus Christ did His Father's will; John 6:38: Antichrist will do his own will; Daniel 11:36.

• Jesus Christ came to save; Luke 19;10: Antichrist comes to destroy; Daniel 8:24.

• Jesus Christ is the good Shepherd; John 10:4-15: Antichrist is the idol (false) shepherd.

Zechariah 11:16.

• Jesus Christ is the true vine; John 15:1: Antichrist is the vine of the earth; Revelation 14:18.

• Jesus Christ is the truth; John 14:6: Antichrist is the lie; 2Thessalonians 2:11.

• Jesus Christ is the holy One; Mark 1:24: Antichrist is the lawless one; 2Thessalonians 2:8.

- Jesus Christ is the Son of God; Luke 1:35: Antichrist is the son of perdition; 2 Thessalonians 2:3.

- Jesus Christ is the mystery of godliness; 1Timothy 3:16: Antichrist is the mystery of iniquity; 2Thessalonians 2:7.

While some may wonder how people could possibly be influenced to follow someone like this, the same could be asked about those who followed Hitler! Those who followed Jim Jones! Those who follow some guru from India! Men when in desperate straits become gullible to swallow a lie when it is dressed in such a manner that it sounds like the truth.

Verse 3:

And I saw one of his heads as it were wounded to death; and his deadly wound was healed: and all the world wondered after the beast.

This is an interesting verse which has produced various opinions as to how it should be interpreted.

Mr LaHaye stated: "As already seen, Antichrist will die and be resurrected,"

Mr Turner stated: "A better interpretation of this statement with reference... in harmony with the context, is that this king will be a lineal descendent of the line of Syrian kings referred to in verses 6-20, and that he is none other than Antiochus Theos Epiphanes raised from the dead... "

Several other commentators are of the opinion that the Beast will be killed during some war during the tribulation, and will later be raised from the dead, thus propelling him to the top.

Just what does this verse state? I saw one of *his heads as it were wounded to death.* Notice first John did not state that the Beast was wounded to death, but one of his heads! The Beast has seven heads, the seven heads, according to 17:10, are representative of seven kings, or leaders of nations.

Five of these kings had died by the time John is writing the Revelation. One was then in power, and one was yet to come to power. The Beast (v.11) continues this succession of kings who rise to power in the world - especially against Israel. He is the eighth, and of the seven; that is, he is a continuation of the power represented by these seven previous kings. Now, one of these heads received a death-like blow. Are we to consider that a person - a king - received a death blow? Or do we consider that it is his kingdom, of which he is the representative head, that received the death blow?

John in chapter seventeen, verse 10, informs us that: And there are seven kings: five are fallen, and one is, and the other is not yet come; and when he cometh, he must continue a short space.

So, from this statement we may conclude that during the time of John the sixth king was living. That is, the sixth kingdom was in power at that time. We know from history that the kingdom which was in power in the time of John was Rome. The Caesar's, in their succession to the throne, represented the sixth kingdom or king. Taking this into consideration, we have but to count back over five kings (kingdoms) which involved the people of Israel to identify the preceding kings or kingdoms. Going backwards we find; Greece; Medo/Persia; Babylon; Assyria; Egypt. We may turn to Daniel chapters seven and eight and find the identity of the last three. Then we may turn to such passages as Isaiah 52:4 and find the identity of the other two; Assyria and Egypt.

Dr Scofield, in his comments stated: "Fragments of the ancient Roman empire have never ceased to exist as separate kingdoms. It was the imperial form of government which ceased; the one head wounded to death. What we have prophetically in Revelation 13:3 is the restoration of the imperial form as such, though over a federated empire of ten kingdoms; the "head" is "healed" i.e. restored; there is an emperor again - the Beast,"

Others strongly feel that it will be the man of sin, the Beast, who will be killed and resurrected to life. We share one more opinion. This one by Dr McGee: "Satan has no power to raise the dead. He is not a life giver; but he is a devil, a destroyer, and a death-dealer. The Roman Empire is to be revitalized and made to cohere in a miraculous manner under the world dictator, the Beast - yet verse 3 seems to demand a more adequate explanation than this. I believe that the Beast is a man who will exhibit a counterfeit and imitation resurrection. This will be the great delusion, the big lie of the Great Tribulation period. His stroke of death was healed shows the blasphemous imitation of the death and resurrection of Christ. The challenge will be, "What has Christ done that Antichrist has not done?" The faithful will say, "Christ rose from the dead." Their boast will be, "So did Antichrist!" The Roman Empire will spring back into existence under the cruel hand of a man who faked a resurrection; and a gullible world that rejected Christ is finally taken in by this forgery,"

When we consider verse twelve, we are prone to accept the arguments that it is the beast that is "killed." Yet, at the same time, we have difficulty in accepting any resurrection of a wicked person prior to the Great White Throne judgment! And we certainly have trouble accepting any resurrection performed by Satan!

Paul in his passage on this man, 2Thessalonians 2:8-12, has something interesting to say that possibly explains what is taking place here: *And then shall that Wicked be revealed, whom the Lord shall consume with the spirit of his mouth, and shall destroy with the brightness of his coming: {Even him}, whose coming is after the working of Satan with all power and signs and lying wonders, And with all deceivableness of unrighteousness in them that perish; because they received not the love of the truth, that they might be saved. And for this cause God shall send them strong delusion, that they should believe a lie: That they all might be damned who believed not the truth, but had pleasure in unrighteousness.*

John informs us in 17:8: *The beast that thou sawest was, and is not; and shall ascend out of the bottomless pit, and go into perdition.*

By this statement it implies that the "Beast," is represented as a person. The system of evil, which the term "beast" speaks, will originate in hell, and will not be cast into the lake of fire. It will be an individual who will be cast into perdition.

Paul wrote in 2Thessalonians 2:9, 10: *Even him, whose coming is after the working of Satan with all power and signs and lying wonders, And with all deceivableness of unrighteousness in them that perish.*

Whatever takes place here the result is all the world wondered after the beast. Something took place which resulted in the world being awed by the results. There is no doubt that Satan will pull out all stops in his last-ditch efforts to sway the masses to follow him and his super star, the Beast – the man of sin.

Verse 4:

And they worshipped the dragon which gave power unto the beast: and they worshipped the beast, saying, Who {is} like unto the beast? who is able to make war with him?

Whatever takes place; a fake resurrection, or something which deceived the people into thinking that what had taken place was nothing short of miraculous; results in the world worshiping the dragon.

If it seems far-fetched to think that people will actually worship Satan, all one needs do is consider what is going on in our world right now in Satan worship! With each passing year, it appears the influence of Satan worship - following the occult; delving into the spirit world of Satanism with the rock music; drugs; etc., - grows with more interest among the world's youth. Satan has a tremendous following right now of people who have willingly given their life over to him. When the Church has been lifted from this planet, and the seals of tribulation begin to open and unloose the deluge of judgment which is coming upon this world during that time when Satan is cast out of heaven during the middle of the week; Satanic influences and powers will be more prevalent than ever before on this earth. The powers of hell with all its demonic force will unleash itself upon planet earth. The mock resurrection (or whatever it is), will be the crowning touch for Satan. He has been wanting the worship of men since the beginning. That was one of his main tactics against Jesus Christ. His temptation for Christ to fall down and worship him and the promise that the kingdoms of this world would then be His. Jesus, of course, refused his temptation and offer, rebuking him. Well, now Satan has someone who is willing to sell his soul to Satan for this power. When the world witnesses the demonstration of this "miracle" they too will worship Satan. Satan will become intoxicated by their worship!

They worshipped the Beast... They make a god out of this man who promises so much, and who demonstrates such awesome power. The souls of men have become so degraded because they have rejected the message of the Church. That is why they are in tribulation! They have rejected the warnings of the 144,000 sealed from the tribes of Israel. They have rejected the two Witnesses.

This statement they should be considered considering what all is taking place during this time. It would not appear that we should consider that this statement should be taken to mean that every living soul on this planet during this time will worship the dragon or the Beast! But *they* who are followers of the Beast - and they are numerous - will, upon witnessing this wonder, fall down in worship to their hero.

Who is able to make war with him... It is as if there is a sigh of relief that at last, we have someone who will protect us from nuclear holocaust. At last we have someone that will keep us safe from wars.

The fear which grips many hearts is that of nuclear warfare.

Verse 5:

And there was given unto him a mouth speaking great things and blasphemies; and power was given unto him to continue forty {and} two months.

I quote from Mr Morris: "The mouth of the beast, like the roaring of a lion (v 2), began to roar great things. The dragon, who gave him his authority, also now gives him great pronouncements to make to the world. Counterfeiting God's divinely impaired prophets of old, he makes satanically-inspired proclamations and predictions, filled with blasphemies against the true God and His Christ, foretelling their imminent destruction and the freedom of mankind from all restraints or righteousness and fear of judgment."

By the Beast making such a statement lets us know that he has become a puppet in the hands of Satan. He is now manipulated by Satan himself. While he makes his boasts of being so great and so powerful, he is nothing more than an instrument of evil in the hands of Satan. He is not his own man. He belongs to Satan.

Those who are following him are likewise tools in the hand of Satan. While they may brag about their liberty and freedom which they enjoy, they are at the same time slaves to a master who will ultimately bring them down to the greatest bondage of all - Hell! With his blasphemies, he makes against God, he no doubt boasts that he will bring God down from His throne. Why would God permit such blasphemous statements against Him? Why would He permit such atrocities to be committed? God is permitting man to run his course. The decision to follow the Beast or to follow the Lord is a decision which is left up to man. The decision of the man of sin to surrender his life and will to Satan was his to make as well. Judgment will not fall upon him until the time has come for it. Judgment will not fall upon those who follow the Beast either, until it is time. BUT JUDGMENT WILL COME!

And power was given unto him to continue for forty and two months... Again, we have the expression, forty-two months. As we mentioned previously in our study, this statement seems to always refer to the last half of the week. That is, the last three and one-half years of the tribulation.

Satan, when he was cast out of heaven, knew that his time was short.

Knowing this he enters this man to bring about the destruction of as many lives as he possibly can in the short period of time he has left.

Three and one-half years! What a short period of time to sell one's soul for! While it is likely that the man of sin does not realize that he only has three and one-half years to enjoy his power, this is a very short period of time to sell out to Satan just to enjoy this power.

We have no way of knowing at this time who will have any knowledge of the Word of God relative to these prophecies. The Jews have refused to accept the New Testament writings as being from God. If this refusal continues in the tribulation, they will likely accept what is being said here about this period. At the same time, there would probably be plenty of people who were exposed to the Word of God and these prophecies, who will realize the period involved. Possibly this will give a lot of people the courage to endure this dark time.

Verse 6:

And he opened his mouth in blasphemy against God, to blaspheme his name, and his tabernacle, and them that dwell in heaven.

The law had decreed in Leviticus 24:16: *He that blasphemeth the name of the Lord, he shall surely be put to death.*

As if in open defiance of the Word of God, the Beast raises his voice in a blasphemous statement against God and what He stands for. Not content to just blaspheme God, he blasphemes His name. In seeking to exalt his own name he attacks the Name above all names!

Jesus Christ received His name by inheritance (Hebrews 1:4). The man of sin has received his name through brute and wicked force.

Jesus Christ has a name which is adored by millions; the man of sin has a name which causes men to shudder. Having a name which is despised causes the beast to seek to cover up his short comings by making loud and brash boasts, and attacks against the name which is opposed to and greater than his own.

And his tabernacle, and them that dwell in heaven... This statement is not only interesting, but it also seems to reveal that the beast is aware of the rapture which has taken place. He knows there is a God who reigns from the heavens. He is aware there are people who have escaped his hands and are safely in the presence of the Lord.

It is not completely clear as to just how this phrase should be understood. That is, what does the reference to the "tabernacle" mean? Where is the tabernacle? Is it the one he entered when he made his claim to being God? Or is it in heaven?

Many feel the word "and" should not be inserted before them. That the phrase should read; "and his tabernacle, them that dwell in heaven." The word dwell means to tabernacle. The terms could be employed interchangeably.

George Ricker Berry translates this statement thus: "... to blaspheme his name, and his tabernacle, and those who tabernacle in the heaven,"

Vincent stated: "The literal sense would be - to blaspheme the name and Tabernacle which dwell in heaven."

We know Satan has just been cast out of heaven, and no doubt he influences the beast to turn his wrathful statements toward heaven because of this. Like the unruly boy who has been expelled from school for his behavior, he sticks his tongue out at the teacher - from a safe distance, of course!

Them that dwell in heaven... Those who have been raptured and are now enjoying the blessings of heavenly joy, are safe in the arms of Jesus Christ. They are completely out of the reach of the beast.

They are on the victor's side and will soon return to this earth for a show of that ultimate victory over the beast as well as Satan. They who are in heaven at this time are not only out of reach of the beast, but they have also gotten complete victory over Satan. They are those who have lived victorious lives on this earth and are now enjoying the rewards of their labors.

Whether or not those who are in heaven at this time realize what all is going on down here on this earth during this period is a matter of conjecture as well as debate. Having received our glorified bodies; and having been taken into heaven, would lead us to think that the saints will know what is taking place down here. Also, when we consider the references in the Revelation to those who seem to be part of the redeemed who are somehow involved in John's account, it would seem the church will be aware of the activities going on during this time.

Verse 7:

And it was given unto him to make war with the saints, and to overcome them: and power was given him over all kindreds, and tongues, and nations.

The beast - that is what he is now that Satan has entered and taken possession of him - turns his wrath toward the one group of people who determinedly resist him - the saints. There is nothing he can do about those who are dwelling in heaven, but there is a lot he can and will do about those who resist his plans on this earth.

Daniel also makes mention of this war which he will bring against the people who resist him: *I beheld, and the same horn made war with the saints, and prevailed against them,* (7:21). The *horn* which Daniel is referring to is the *little horn* of the fourth beast which rose from among the ten horns of the beast. This is a reference to the man of sin - the Beast of Revelation thirteen.

The beast in his rage will bring bitter judgment against all who stand in his way of world Dominance. Those who will bring his greatest wrath upon them will be those who acknowledge Jesus Christ as Lord. This he will not be able to stand; especially after he himself has declared that he is god!

Some have a little problem with this reference to the *saints* in this verse, and at the same time understanding the rapture taking the church out some three-plus years before this. But the term *saints* here has reference to those people who are doing their best in these difficult times to live for God.

Their only hope for deliverance and escape from hell is to refuse the mark and suffer the wrath of the Beast. And evidently many will choose to do this.

Evidently during the first three and one-half years of the tribulation period there have been a lot of people who have been proclaiming the Word of God. There has no doubt risen a great host of people who are studying their Bible's like they never studied them before. We do not know for sure just who all will be witnessing to the people at this time, but many will realize the time that they are living in and will turn to God with all their heart. It is against this people that the Beast will direct his attacks.

There have been many who have died already, and many more will die before this week is over. We saw some of these martyrs in chapter six. We will see all of them in chapter twenty.

While Daniel spoke of this same conflict, he goes on to say something which we do not find in John's writings in Revelation. Note the following verse of Daniel 7:22: *Until the Ancient of days came, and judgment was given to the saints of the most High; and the time came that the saints possessed the kingdom.*

So, it will be a very dark time, but deliverance will ultimately come to those who will be faithful.

Remember, Jesus in speaking of this time stated: *But he that shall endure unto the end, the same shall be saved.*

And to overcome them... Let us look at this statement in the light of what takes place during this period of tribulation. Let us put the word "overcome" here in its proper perspective. We usually associate the term to mean to conquer, to subdue, to bring under control. Yet, we could also use the word regarding the crucifixion of Jesus Christ. The world overcame Him and crucified Him. But did they conquer Him? Did they bring Him under their control? The obvious answer is NO! The same will hold true here as well. There will be many who will die. There will be many who will suffer persecution at the hand of the beast and his cohorts. At the same time, however, they will not surrender their devotion and allegiance from God to the Beast.

And power was given him over all kindreds... tongues... nations... Again, let us notice that we are informed that what the beast acquires in his wicked pursuit of control of power, is given to him. Where does this power come from? This we are told in verse two: *and the dragon gave him his power...*

If we were to take this verse literally, without referring to any other passage of scripture in the Word of God, we would think that the entire world falls under the control of this man at this time. That is not the case though. The term *all* does not always mean all in the strictest sense of the word.

Everybody will not, nor will every nation, submit to the beast and his demands. This will be one of the reasons for Armageddon! It will be a final showdown for control of the world. The ultimate outcome which is already given to us in the Word of God!

Now, clarifying this statement does not mean that we are implying the beast will not affect the entire world with his policies. He certainly will, without a doubt!

Verse 8:

And all that dwell upon the earth shall worship him whose names are not written in the book of life of the Lamb slain from the foundation of the world.

We were informed in verse four that *they worshipped the dragon... and they worshipped the beast.*

Here we are informed as to who *they* are. Again, we have the word *all* to consider in the same manner as we did in the previous verse. It is evident, again, from other passages that the entire world per se will not worship the beast.

One movement which is gaining momentum in our day is that of "humanism." Humanism teaches that man controls his own destiny Man is his own god. Worship the creature and not the Creator, is the message of humanism. What we are witnessing here in this verse is the apex of this dogma, it has reached the point that men are worshipping men. Such philosophy will end in a great and bitter disappointment to all who embrace such hopes.

Book of life of the Lamb... Reference to the *Book of life* is only found in the book of Revelation, and once in the book of Philippians (4:3). There are references to the book, like in Exodus 32:32, but the primary references to the book by name is found in the Revelation.

This is an interesting verse and statement. Quoting from George Ricker Berry's Greek-English New Testament, he translates it; "And shall do homage to it all who dwell on the earth whom have not been written the name from (the) founding of (the) world in the book of life of the Lamb slain."

One question surrounding the subject of the *Book of life* if we are written in it when we are saved, then what about the children?

While the mode of salvation at this time may be debatable, the important thing is that they have made that commitment and have their name in the Book of life of the Lamb. For those who are faced with the demands of the Beast, there will be no alternative left to them but to recant, to accept the mark of the beast, and go to inevitable perdition with him: or be driven away into the mountains, the wilderness, the dens and caves of the earth, or any place to hide in safety.

Slain from the foundation of the world... This as well is an interesting phrase; we know that Jesus died on Calvary somewhere around 30 AD. So, it is not possible that He was slain before the world was ever created! But, in the mind and will of God He was! Before there was a world; before there were any humans on this planet, God had a plan which included Calvary! Calvary, and the Church, were not accidents!

We could look at this phrase by emphasizing that Jesus was slain *from* the foundation. Calvary's sacrifice included both the Old and New Testament of believers. The shed blood of Jesus Christ was not just for the church. It was to take care of the sins of the Old Testament believers as well. Every sacrifice of the Old Testament was looking forward toward Calvary! So, from the foundation of the world to the last sinner whose sins are remitted because of Calvary, His blood was shed for man-kinds sins.

Verse 9:

If any man have an ear, let him hear.

We noted a phrase like this that was given to all the seven churches in Asia by John in his letters to them. There is, however, one unique difference to be noted in comparing what is said here and what is said in the letters to the church. In the letters John wrote: *He that hath an ear, let him hear what the Spirit saith unto the churches.*

The statement here is simply; *If any man have an ear, let him hear.*

There is no reference to the Spirit, nor to the churches. We do not think that the Church is still here, so there would be no warning to them at this point. But there is a warning given to anyone who will hear that they should not worship the beast nor join his system if they expect to be saved. To do otherwise is to doom one's soul eternally!

While the beast and his cohorts - his P/R men - will be pressuring everybody to join in with his plans, as he promised to have the answers to all the problems which are besetting the world; there will be many who will realize the danger of doing so and will refuse to go along.

There will be plenty of warnings mercifully given by the Lord to all who will listen. As mentioned previously, there will be the 144,000 who have been sealed for some purpose. There will be the two witnesses who will be boldly witnessing against the beast.

There will be the angel flying through the air proclaiming his warnings. There will also be those who have been exposed to the Word of God during the time the church was here who will be aware of what is taking place even though they themselves did not heed the message of the church and escape with it.

Verse 10:

He that leadeth into captivity shall go into captivity: he that killeth with the sword must be killed with the sword. Here is the patience and the faith of the saints.

Vincent stated on this verse: "The best text inserts "into" before the first captivity, and omit "assemble," thus reading if any man is for captivity into captivity he goeth."

This statement: He that leadeth into captivity shall go into captivity, reminds us of the words from the law which stated, "an eye for an eye, etc."

While this passage may be a little difficult to fully grasp as to just what is meant, we feel it is a message of hope - and warning to those who have "an ear to hear." It is possible that this verse has a two-fold interpretation as to just what is meant here.

1. A promise to the saints that God will judge those who persecute them. Many of the faithful will suffer martyrdom during this time.

Those who are executioners will suffer execution themselves.

2. A warning to the saints that they must not try to take matters into their own hands. They cannot fight their own battles. God will do the fighting for them. If they resort to the sword, they will suffer for it. If they put their trust in the Lord, they will ultimately be the winners.

Here is the patience of the saints... Those who will heed the words of God at this time will find the security they are looking for. It will be a time which will call for great patience to wait on the Lord.

These saints will have a wonderful example which they can look to during this time of testing of their patience: *who for the joy that was set before Him endured the cross*, (Hebrews 12:2).

There is no doubt that this will be the darkest time that any people have ever faced. The people of Abraham have faced a lot of dark periods of time in their long history, but none can be compared to this one! Even the dark days of the holocaust during World War II was not as dark as these days will be during the last half of the tribulation week. We have the warnings of Daniel 12:1, as well as Jesus Himself, to emphasize this (Matthew 24:21).

ANOTHER BEAST... THE FALSE PROPHET

Verse 11:

And I beheld another beast coming up out of the earth; and he had two horns like a lamb, and he spake as a dragon.

Throughout history we have always had the religious element of any power struggle. Each empire of men had their religious element. The religious element is an attempt to unify men under one power or controlling force. Religion is that force which bonds men together for one common cause. Nebuchadnezzar realized the influence of religion in his day, and he attempted to bring all in his vast empire under one religious-system. Nebuchadnezzar had invaded and conquered many nations, including the people of Israel. All these nations represented many kinds of religion. Nebuchadnezzar realized that to be able to control the people he would have to get them to worship one god and be directed by one religion. He realized the tremendous influence which religion has upon people. So, we have the story in chapter three of Daniel of his attempt to get all the people in his vast domain to bow to his god and surrender to his state religion.

Nebuchadnezzar was, in the days of Daniel, the first of the Gentile rulers who would govern the people of Israel. The last such ruler is the one under study in this thirteenth chapter of Revelation. Nebuchadnezzar attempted to do what the man of sin will also attempt to do in the last days; get all people under one religious-system. Nebuchadnezzar was just a little premature with his attempt.

The other beast... It is of interest to note that this second character brought to our attention in this chapter is also described by John as *a beast,* (This is the Greek "therion", "dangerous beast.") Now we know from the description given to us here that this is the religious

element of the system headed by the man of sin. This beast is called the *false prophet* elsewhere (such as 19:20; 20:10). Although he is a religious man, he is labeled as a Beast.

Nothing is as dangerous as a false religion! Thousands are placing their eternal security in a religious system. Hoping that because they embrace some religious system they will be saved eternally.

Paul spoke of those *who would believe a lie...* and be damned. Jesus spoke of those whom He classified as the Blind leading the blind. And who would all ultimately fall into the ditch.

A person can escape putting his trust in some broker, only to wind up losing his shirt off his back when the market takes a turn against his investments. A person can survive waiting for a certain time to plant some seeds, because the weather man said the weather was going to be such and such at a certain time, only to find that it doesn't turn out that way. But when it comes to your eternal soul, only a fool would place his trust in a religion that was not supported by the Word of God!

This "beast" is going to present to the world the religious element of this new system. It will be a religious element which will sound attractive because of the manifestations of what seems to be the supernatural accompanying it; but it will also be a religion in which people will be compelled to join or suffer the consequences!

It is also interesting to note that the "false prophet" is never mentioned alone. He is always mentioned in the company of the beast. On the other hand, the Beast is mentioned by himself without any reference to the false prophet (11:7), for example.

Two horns like a lamb... The apostle John spoke of the antichrist's which would come into the world (1John 4:1-3). The spirit of antichrist, John informs us, was already in the world in his day, and would continue to manifest itself. This will be the last great manifestation of the spirit of antichrist in the world.

Jesus Christ is spoken of several times in the Revelation as "Lamb." Here the false prophet has this reference made of him as well. While Jesus, however, is the true Lamb of God, the false prophet will be the false lamb. He attempts to influence people with his lamb-like appearance when he comes with a message of death!

And he spake as a dragon... Although he appears as a religious man with a religious message for the world, when he opens his mouth, the message which he presents will be directly from Satan himself! Again, we find it difficult to fathom that anyone would use religion as a cloak of deceit to destroy lives, but this will happen. Men's hearts will be so hardened that surrendering their worship to something wicked and evil, and something inspired by Satan, will not faze them!

Verse 12:

And he exerciseth all the power of the first beast before him, and causeth the earth and them which dwell therein to worship the first beast, whose deadly wound was healed.

We are not given any details as to how this couple are united under one cause. Somehow their paths cross and they become united in their purposes of controlling the world. They form an unholy alliance which continues to the very end. In fact, they are both cast into the lake of fire together when the Lord returns at Armageddon!

He exerciseth all the power of the first beast... This statement informs us that the false prophet must be influenced and controlled by the man of sin. He is not his own man! He is only mouthing the message and intentions of the man of sin. He is the "hireling." Yet at the same time he is a powerful force because he has the man of sin behind him. Men will tremble at his sight!

And causeth the earth... to worship the first beast... If nothing else about the man would reveal his real nature, this would! No true prophet of God would direct people to worship another man. This is the sin of idolatry which thing God hates!

He causeth - that is his influence, as well as the power to inflict harm to all who do not comply with his demands to worship the beast - will result in people bowing to his demands rather than suffer the consequence.

<u>**Verse 13:**</u>

And he doeth great wonders, so that he maketh fire come down from heaven on the earth in the sight of men,

The false prophet, in fulfilling his role as "prophet" to the man of sin, seems to perform miracles before the people.

With more and more emphasis being placed on the occult phenomenon of today; with more and more interest in things supernatural; emphasis on UFO's, etc., the minds of men are being conditioned to accept anything which smacks of supernatural.

Just what happens when the false prophet makes fire come down from heaven is not clear.

Possibly causing something like this to take place would be an effort on his part to deceive people into thinking that he is sent by God. That heaven is sanctioning what he is doing. In reality it will probably be nothing short of some more lying wonders which are to deceive people into believing "the lie" which will result in them being swallowed up in this system of evil and thus doom their soul to hell.

If the false prophet is making these demonstrations at the same time the two Witnesses are preaching to the people, do we have another Moses and the magicians of Egypt confrontation? Or another Elijah and the prophets of Baal confrontation?

We know that the magicians of Egypt certainly did not manifest the power of God when they sought to duplicate the miracles of Moses. Neither will the powers demonstrated by the false prophet be a manifestation of the power of God.

The false prophet is attempting to show that he possesses the same kind of power as the two witnesses. Or he is trying to get the people to believe that he is the messenger of God by such manifestations. It is not likely, however, that it is the latter, as the man of sin defies God! So, it does not stand to reason that his associate would claim that his power was from God.

<u>**Verse 14:**</u>

And deceiveth them that dwell on the earth by {the means of} those miracles which he had power to do in the sight of the beast; saying to them that dwell on the earth, that they should make an image to the beast, which had the wound by a sword, and did live.

And deceiveth them... This statement is a key to the understanding of what is taking place here.

The manifestations are to deceive. Even today it seems that people are more gullible to take in what some charlatan says than what a man of God says about the Word of God.

The past few years has witnessed a tremendous increase in interest of things occult. More and more the number of people who admit to being Satan worshipers is increasing. Millions are spent annually on the occults by this generation. The media gives prime time to exposing this message about the occult wonders of the universe.

Satan comes with great wrath to bring havoc to this planet and those who dwell on it. He knows his time is short and he will work continually and feverishly in his attempt to bring about the deception, and destruction, of every life he can. The beast will be his "lie." The false prophet will be his messenger who proclaims that the beast is the answer to the world's woes. The great "deceiver" has arrived on planet earth!

Let us remember the words of Jesus when he was speaking of these very days, in Matthew 24:24: *For there shall arise false Christs, and false prophets, and shall shew great signs and wonders; insomuch that, if {it were} possible, they shall deceive the very elect.*

It will be a time of tremendous trials by fire. The power which Satan's henchmen will manifest will seem so convincing to those who are not spiritually alert.

Many will fall victims to this show of power and miracles by the false prophet. Many are already falling victim to the show of the "miraculous" by todays false prophets.

That they should make an image... Throughout the years since the first idolatrous practice was instituted, men have sought to identify with their god by erecting some image of that god. In the many different classes of people there have been witnessed various idols which depicted to that people their god. The god was oft times part human and part animal in appearance. We not only have reference to some of these gods in the Old Testament, but we also have the strict commandment from God that His people were not to worship these gods. Nor were they to erect any type of image that would depict Him to them.

This practice has come down to this twentieth century intact, but under different guises. It has invaded the religious world, where we find the many statues (idols) in different religions of the world.

Whether it has a religious title to it or not, it is still idolatry! And it is still forbidden by GOD!

As to just what this image is which is erected, we are not informed. There are differing views. Many today feel that the image could be a computer-type image.

Verse 15:

And he had power to give life unto the image of the beast, that the image of the beast should both speak, and cause that as many as would not worship the image of the beast should be killed.

- The ramifications of this verse are awesome! To say the least.

The false prophet has an image of the Beast erected and then commands the image to manifest "life" expressions by speaking! Now, we know from the Word of God that only God can create life. Life comes only from God! The "lie" which the false prophet gives to this image is a very convincing lie!

First, what is this image which is erected? Then, where is this image erected? Next, how can the demand to worship this image go out to them that dwell on the earth?

It would be foolish to create a law if you did not have some way to enforce that law. Supposing that the image is erected in Jerusalem - where the beast has entered the Jewish temple and declared himself god and demanded their worship - how will this demand be enforced upon people living in Medora, IN?

Today the tiny silicon chips half the size of a fingernail are etched with circuitry powerful enough to book seats on jumbo jets, keep the planes working smoothly in the air, help children learn to spell and play chess well enough to beat all but the grandest masters. The new technology means that bits of computing power can be distributed wherever they might be useful. This "computational plenty" is making smart machines easier to use and more forgiving of unskilled programming. Machines are even communicating with each other.

It is quite possible that what we have described for us in Revelation thirteen is not only a computer with a tremendous capacity to handle any problem which is programmed into it, but it is also a union with something living. Could it be possible that Satan will dispatch one of his angels to indwell this creation of man, seemingly giving it life?

Worship the image... The creation of man is to receive the worship of men. Let us notice that the command is that they would make an image. The "they" are those who dwell on this earth. The great minds of technology are called upon to create the super wonder. But it is to be made in the "image" of the beast! And then man is commanded to worship that which he has created. Again, the humanistic philosophy comes through. Man is great. Man is his own god. Man can create, and so man can worship his own creation.

In verse twelve we have the command to worship the beast. Now the command is given to worship the image erected to the beast.

Regardless of whether one worships the beast or the image, the results of either will be the same according to 19:20; 20:4.

Should be killed... Again, we are faced with the questions. If someone refuses to worship this image, how will it be known they do not? And how will the death sentence against such an offense be carried out? I think we are again confronted with the computer system. There is no way that a police force could police every person to see if they were following the orders to worship this image. The only thing that could make this possible is the computer.

The word *worship* which is used in this passage is the most frequently employed word in the New Testament regarding worship. It means to "make obeisance, do reverence to," It is from words which mean; "pros," towards, and "kuneo," to kiss, It is an act of homage or reverence to someone or something. So, the command to worship this image involves the people in giving reverence to this creation of man. To submit to it in homage and respect.

It has been pointed out that the day when the planned computer system is fully implemented, it will be possible to control who buys and who functions in that society by them being programmed into the system via the computer. It would be possible then to pull a rebels name - or number - from the computer, or mark their number some way so that if they attempted to purchase something a warning light would go off, or something, thus making it impossible for them to function. A Reader's Digest article on the subject referred to such a person as a "non-person."

Verse 16:

And he causeth all, both small and great, rich and poor, free and bond, to receive a mark in their right hand, or in their foreheads:

The false prophet enforces the system which is in the making right now! More and more the computers are taking over the business affairs of men. Even the smallest of businesses are now using a computer to help them stay abreast of what is taking place in their business world, as well as to help them keep better and more accurate records.

When all systems are in place, then the economy as it is presently known in these nations will be completely revised. We will no longer transact business with dollars and cents. Such a society has been projected for the last several years now. The planners of such a society have been warning us that it is coming. We have seen their warnings with the computer system. See how quick your name, and information about you, can be called up on the computer. They have been warning us with the use of the UPC (Universal Product Code) on just about everything you buy now. (Those funny looking lines and numbers underneath on items).

With the introduction of the credit card system; With the introduction of the Social Security system with its identifying number; With the advancements being made with the computer; with the introduction of the various codes, etc., that only a computer can read; it would seem we are being conditioned for the ultimate system!

He causeth all... Remember our comments on verse seven regarding the term ALL, which would apply here as well. The term does not mean that everyone on this earth at this time will accept the mark. When the edict is given for all to take the mark and join the system of the beast, there will be a great number who will refuse to accept this demand. They will choose to suffer the consequence, even if it means their life, rather than accept the mark and join the system and thus doom their soul eternally.

Better to die even the death of a martyr, than to die an eternal death in hell!

It is evident from reading 20:4 that there will be those who will not accept the mark and will give their life rather than do so.

Small and great, rich and poor, free and bond... The implication is that the system that will be introduced will affect all walks of life. This, in fact, may be one of the tactics employed by those who propose the system that everyone is joining it! None are excluded because of their social or financial position.

Nebuchadnezzar said: *To you it is commanded, 0 people, nations, and languages... fall down and worship the golden image,* (Daniel 3:4,5). None were to be excluded in his vast domain. The same will hold true for those under the influence of the man of sin.

To receive a mark in their right hand, or in their foreheads... The 144,000 received a mark in their foreheads which declared to the world the Name of Jesus Christ (7:3; 14:1). Now we have the declaration for all to receive a mark in their hand or forehead which identify them with the beast and his system.

It is registration time for the empire of the beast! All are commanded to register and receive the identification mark which will identify them with the beast.

This term is found some eight times in the Revelation, and only one time outside of Revelation in the book of Acts (17:29) about idols. The practice of marking is an old practice which was prevalent in John's day. Slaves were marked by their masters.

The groundwork - like the printing in advance of the UPC marks - is being laid now. When the machinery is in place, the order will be given.

<u>Verse 17:</u>

And that no man might buy or sell, save he that had the mark, or the name of the beast, or the number of his name.

The issuance of this Number, or Mark, or Name, will not take place until the middle of the week.

For people to think someone may have already received the mark is a misunderstanding of what the Bible is saying about it.

In verse sixteen the demand was that all must receive a mark in their right hand or forehead, Here we have mention of a *mark, name, number.*

Mr Morris suggested: "Evidently the brand may take anyone of three forms, perhaps based on certain further categories into which the emperor wishes to divide his followers - say, perhaps, military, government, and civilian, with different types of privileges and duties applied to each. One group receives the mark, some peculiar design (or logo) which is appropriate for the beast, and this is

probably applied to the bulk of the population. Another group is imprinted with the beast's own name, probably the group associated most closely with his purposes and actions. The third group is marked with a number, that number which is peculiarly fitting for both his character and for his own name. Unless a person can display one of these three brands, thus marking him permanently as committed to Satan, he is marked for privation and death."

Until the government started using the Social Security number for identification purposes, many Americans were identified with different numbers and ways. They were known by their name, first. They were identified by their serial number, etc. Now, everyone is identified by their Social Security number.

Some have suggested that the three forms of identification issued by the beast could represent the three forms of his system; 1). Mark = Government. 2). Name = Religion, 3). Number = Monetary.

The Mark... Not only because the mark is listed separately here, but we also find it listed separately elsewhere, such as; 14:9; 15:2; 20:4, does it appear that the mark is not the same as the *name* or the *number of his name.* As to just what the mark is, we do not know. It would be pure speculation on anyone's part to conjecture just what it will be.

The Name... There has been a lot of speculation as to who he will be, even to him being Judas Iscariot resurrected from the dead. But there is no scripture that we can turn to that will give us his name.

We do not know who he is, and the world will evidently not know who he is until the time of his proper introduction (2Thessalonians

2:3-8).

The Number... The number of his name is the number of a man. Like the foregoing, as to just what this statement means we are not given the understanding at this time.

<u>**Verse 18:**</u>

Here is wisdom. Let him that hath understanding count the number of the beast: for it is the number of a man; and his number {is} Six hundred threescore {and} six.

This verse has probably raised more speculation and produced more differing views and theories than any other verse in the Bible.

To continue the symbolism of the Revelation, this verse as well contains some symbolic numbers. Numbers which identify a character of utmost importance for the last day. What an advantage people would have if they were able to identify this Satanically influenced character before he came on the scene! First, let us consider that John probably wrote the Revelation in the language of his day - Greek. We are reading what he wrote in our own language, English. If we knew the language of John, we might could better grasp what he is saying here. The Greek language is unlike our English in that we have numbers we use separate from our alphabet of letters. The Greek language was not like this. Certain of their letters stood for numbers as well.

That the man of sin will come and rise to power, there is no doubt. But his rise to this position will be a gradual one. He will "work" his way to the top through his subtle approach of flatteries, and smooth talk. While we believe the church will be removed prior to the man of sin rising to this position of power, we could none the less be caught up in the spirit which is preceding his rise to power and control. If one is caught up in the spirit of this system, he could lose his identity with the church and Christ and thus be swallowed up in the system and miss the rapture!

So, we have the warning to Watch ye therefore, and pray always, that ye may be accounted worthy to escape all these things that shall come to pass, and to stand before the Son of man, (Luke 21:36).

Men through the years have taken the number 666 and the statement here that it is the number of a man and applied it to men whose name in numerical value equaled 666.

Now the number six seems to be the number of man. As six is short of seven, God's number of perfection and completeness, this points out the limitations of man. Man, being created on the sixth day, identifies man with this number.

One thing, however, remains; the signs are all about us, The Word of God is being fulfilled. Plans are being laid to bring into existence a system - or systems - that fit the pattern as described for us in the Revelation. It is only a matter of time!

CHAPTER FOURTEEN

What a contrast we find when we enter chapter fourteen from chapter thirteen! All that we witnessed in chapter thirteen was beastly! death! horror! depravity! blasphemy! Satanic! etc. Now, when we come to this chapter we come to a scene of beauty; of peace; of hope and life! It is like the difference between night and day; between the horrors of a great storm and the singing of the birds after the sun is shining again.

It seems that chapter thirteen is telling us; This is how dark and dismal the tribulation will be. Then, chapter fourteen seems to be telling us; This is how tranquil life with the Lord will be when victory is attained over the beast and his system of evil.

While chapter thirteen seems to present a picture of doom and gloom, chapter fourteen presents to us a picture of hope and promise. Chapter thirteen speaks of bondage under a system in which all are demanded to be marked by the name, number or mark, of the beast. Chapter fourteen speaks to us about a people who are also marked; but it is with the name of the Lord Jesus Christ. Chapter thirteen speaks of a system in which people are forced to join with the threat of death to all who do not. Chapter fourteen is about a group of people who gladly follow their Master, the Lamb, where ever He leads.

These contrasting views of these two chapters are evident without trying to strain anything out of the context to make certain statements symbolize certain things. They not only depict for us the contrast between the system of the beast during the tribulation, and the wonderful victory which all who do not join his system will enjoy, but it also depicts the contrast between those who follow the spirit of the age and those who follow the Spirit of God, regardless of the age.

Considering these two chapters in this manner will give one a perspective view of the future. It should make one to realize the utter folly of listening to the voice of the flesh and the world, which seeks to influence all to follow the path of lust and pleasures of this world. And it should give one the joyous feeling of victory as we see that those who choose to walk with God are those who will come out with joy and eternal life in their possession. It should not be difficult deciding which group we will follow!

THE LAMB ON MOUNT SION

Verse 1:

And I looked, and, lo, a Lamb stood on the mount Sion, and with him an hundred forty {and} four thousand, having his Father's name written in their foreheads.

The history of the two beasts that we were studying about in chapter thirteen is interrupted for a while as John shares with us something of great interest that he witnesses taking place on mount Sion.

We will pick up the story of the beast again when we get to chapter sixteen.

This chapter presents to us seven interesting things which will take place during the tribulation.

Seven being the number of completeness and perfection, this chapter seems to present to us a complete picture of the events which will take place during this seven-year period of time called tribulation.

• 1. The Lamb with the 144,000 on mount Sion, verses 1-5.

• 2. The angel proclaiming the everlasting gospel, verses 6,7.

• 3. Another angel declaring that Babylon will fall, verse 8.

• 4. The third angel proclaiming doom to all who will worship the beast and take his mark, verses 9-12.

• 5. The blessing pronounced on all those who die in the Lord during this time, verse 13.

• 6. The vision of the Son of Man on a cloud with a sickle for reaping the earth, verses 14-16.

• 7. The angel from the temple with a sharp sickle to reap the vintage of the earth, verses 17-20.

If we interpret this chapter in this manner, then we can see the order in which the events will take place during the tribulation.

1. The 144,000 are sealed at the beginning of the tribulation. By them being sealed with the name of Jesus in their forehead, they must have a special mission during the tribulation. Many feel they will be witnesses to their Jews - as well as to the world - against the beast and his system. By having the name of Jesus in their forehead,

they will obviously be objects of hatred by the beast. We are not informed, that we are aware of, in the Revelation what happens to the 144,000. That is, are they martyred? Or are they preserved through what would evidently be bitter persecution against them?

2. The Church having been raptured sometime before or at the beginning of the tribulation period, there is no longer any saint - minister or otherwise - to witness to people, warning them of what is coming. So, God, who is rich in mercy, dispatches His angel to fly through the air with His message of warning to people to fear God - not the beast.

3. Babylon, that great city which represents everything and all that is evil; the headquarters of the beast, no doubt during this time; the city which has affected the entire world with her influence and power, will fall. The angel of the Lord declares her doom. Her fall will take place sometime just prior to the Lord's return at the battle of Armageddon. It is described in detail in chapter eighteen, where there we learn it falls in one hour! We are not informed how she falls (there may be a hint of a nuclear destruction involved!), nor are we informed who brings about her fall.

4. Yet another angel comes with a warning to those who dwell on this earth, that they must not accept the mark of the beast nor worship the beast and his image. The doom of all who do is graphically depicted for us in verse eleven, where it states: *And the smoke of their torment ascendeth up for ever and ever:*

5. Heaven declares that those who die during these dark days will be blessed people - that is those who die refusing the mark of the beast. They will come forth at the Lord's coming back to this earth, to live during the millennium reign.

6. The one who is like unto the Son of man is told to thrust in his sickle and reap the earth; for the time is come for thee to reap. The One who has been blasphemed by the beast is now bringing judgment upon the blasphemer.

7. Yet another angel is informed that he should reap the vineyard of the earth. The clusters of the vine of the earth - Armageddon has arrived!

AND I LOOKED, AND LO, A LAMB STOOD... As most all - if not all - commentators agree, this should read The Lamb.

Jesus Christ is the One whom John is witnessing here.

STOOD ON THE MOUNT SION... This is where there are differences of opinion drawn. Some look at this passage as taking place in heaven. That mount Sion refers to heaven. Others feel that it has reference to earthly Mount Sion: Jerusalem.

First of all, let us consider that John had been witnessing the events which are taking place on this earth as the beast rises up out of the sea, and his cohort, the false prophet, rises up out of the earth, and the events which begin to transpire as they rise to power. It would appear to us that what he is witnessing now is also taking place on the earth. When the scene changes from earth to heaven in other places in the Revelation, you will find that John identifies where the vision is taking place (note for instance; 12:1; 10:1; 13:1).

John stated: I looked... This term or one similar to it, is employed by John when he is introducing something different and exciting about the Revelation. You will find John using a term like this, some ten times in the Revelation. What he is now witnessing is certainly exciting, to say the least!

Mount Sion is oft times spoken of in the Scriptures, and it would seem that it always has reference to Jerusalem. Psalm 132:13: *For the Lord hath chosen Zion; he hath desired {it} for his habitation.*

Psalm 48:2: *Beautiful for situation, the joy of the whole earth, {is} mount Zion, {on} the sides of the north, the city of the great King.*

The writer of Hebrews states; 12:22,23: *But ye are come unto mount Sian, and unto the city of the living God, the heavenly Jerusalem... To the general assembly and church of the firstborn.* That there is a city in heaven is evident from other passages, and this city is a heavenly Jerusalem; that is a City of Peace. Paul spoke of *Jerusalem which is above is free, which is the mother of us all* (Galatians 4:26). John witnesses this city coming down from God out of heaven in chapter twenty-one. Just as the Tabernacle in the wilderness and its furnishings were patterned after a heavenly pattern, even so do we have a heavenly Jerusalem which will be the home of the redeemed.

But as John does not identify any change in the locations of what he is witnessing, it would seem that this Mount Sion has reference to the Jerusalem on this earth.

AND WITH HIM AN HUNDRED AND FORTY-FOUR THOUSAND... Again, we are confronted with differing views as to who this number is. Some feel that the term 144,000 is a symbolic number representing the whole company of the saved. That the twelve times twelve is the signature of the eternal city, the home of the redeemed. That this number is a governmental number, speaking not of exactly this many people, but a symbolic number speaking of all the redeemed.

While we certainly feel that the views of others are worthy of our consideration; and we would not attempt to dissuade them from their views; we none the less are of the opinion that the 144,000 spoken of here by John are the same 144,000 which he spoke about in chapter seven.

We know of no place where the saved, whether it be the church or the tribulation saints, are referred to by a specific number. Whereas the chosen from among the tribes of Israel are selected by a specific number.

HAVING HIS FATHER'S NAME WRITTEN IN THEIR FOREHEADS... The center column reference in the Scofield Bible, as well as other versions and commentaries, conclude that this should read: His name and His Father's. George Ricker Berry, in his Interlinear Greek-English New Testament, translates it: having the name of His Father written on their foreheads.

The purpose of many commentator's translating it "His name and His Father's name," is an attempt to give them support for their Trinitarian dogma. (Or at least it is one of the reasons.) If the proper translation is "His name and His Father's name, it would seem that would be the proper translation; not one of the translators or commentators attempted to supply the name of the Lamb and His Father's name. As it is evident from other references in the Revelation, there is mention of but one throne in heaven, and One sitting on that throne. And as Jesus said; *"I am come in my Father's name,"* (John 5:43); it would seem evident that there is but one name under consideration here. There is but one New Testament salvation name (Acts 4:12), and that is the peerless name of Jesus Christ. The name of the Lamb, which is written in their foreheads, is the name of His Father.

It is said of the 144,000 in chapter seven; till we have sealed the servants of our God in their foreheads. While there is no mention of a name being inscribed in their foreheads in chapter seven, the reference to the "seal" would no doubt be referring to the Name. A "seal" could denote ownership. Having the name of Jesus written in their forehead would denote they belonged to Jesus Christ, and not to the beast.

If this group is sealed at the beginning of the tribulation, then they will have this seal on them long before the beast issues his edict that all must wear his name, or mark, or number, on their forehead.

Possibly this will be an effort on the beast's part to show open opposition to this group who have been witnessing against his system.

The use of the term "*Lamb*" identifies with the Jewish nation. Lamb is not a Church term. We find the term "Lamb" some 27 times after we get past the Church chapters, two and three. It is never employed in any of the letters to the seven Churches of Asia. Paul never employed the term in any of his epistles to the Churches. Outside of the book of Revelation it is only found in John 1:29,36; Acts 8:32 and 1Peter 1:19, and that of the Messiah of Israel, and as the anti-type of the Jewish sacrifices. So, the 144,000 standing with the Lamb seems to also emphasize that they are the same 144,000 Jews who were sealed in chapter seven.

Verse 2:

And I heard a voice from heaven, as the voice of many waters, and as the voice of a great thunder: and I heard the voice of harpers harping with their harps:

I HEARD A VOICE FROM HEAVEN... This further attests that John is witnessing these events as they take place on the earth. If he was in heaven, as in some previous experiences in the Revelation, he would not employ this term regarding the voices.

If the scene before John is that of the 144,000 standing with the Lord Jesus in Jerusalem at the end of the tribulation in a time of victory and rejoicing, then it would seem that those in heaven who were caught up at the time of the rapture are aware of what has taken place on earth at this time and express their feelings of joy and victory.

There appears to be some difficulty in getting the proper order in all that is taking place here. If the 144,000 are actually standing on Mount Sion in Jerusalem with the Lord, and it is actually the end of the tribulation, then we would have some problems:

1). The time period in which this chapter is found in the Revelation is during the middle of the week, or shortly into the last half.

2). Jesus does not appear on this earth until He returns with His Church at the time of Armageddon.

3). The redeemed are going to return with Christ when He returns to this earth, so they could not be in heaven and the Lord on this earth at the same time.

As Revelation is filled with symbolism's - things which mean something else - there are things which are spoken in one place in the account which takes place historically at another time. One good example of this is 11:15. The last time that John witnessed the Lamb was in chapter 7:17. He is seen in the midst of the throne with those who have come through the tribulation and *washed their robes, and made them white in the blood of the Lamb,* standing around Him involved in that record as well. They were sealed in the first part of the chapter. Then, this number that John could not number are seen coming forth from the tribulation. Are they there because of the 144,0007 This scene in chapter 7 is also a scene in which John is ushered forward in time - and then returns to the present. The group who stand before the throne are those who have come "through" the tribulation. The event actually takes place, possibly, seven years later than chapter seven. It is quite possible that the scene of the 144,000 standing with the Lamb on Mount Sion should also be treated in the same manner. It speaks of the ultimate triumph which they shall know. Heaven witnessing this triumph rejoices for the victory which shall be known by them.

AS THE VOICE OF MANY WATERS, AND AS THE VOICE OF A GREAT THUNDER... This reminds us of what John heard in chapter nineteen (vs. 1-6). It is no doubt the redeemed who are sounding forth praises for what the Lord is doing on this earth.

Verse 3:

And they sung as it were a new song before the throne, and before the four beasts, and the elders: and no man could learn that song but the hundred {and} forty {and} four thousand, which were redeemed from the earth.

AND THEY SUNG... Who sung? The 144,000? No! The voices heard from heaven with their harps.

It was called a new song. We are not told what the song is. Some have referred to chapter fifteen and said it is the song of Moses and the Lamb. But chapter fifteen is speaking about another group and another song. The song of Moses is not a new song, either.

There is mention of songs being sung in three places in the Revelation; 5:9; 14:3; 15:3. The first one, 5:9, is the song sung by the redeemed - the raptured. The second song here; 14:3, is sung by the redeemed and only the 144,000 are able to learn it. It must be a song which speaks of their victory and being sealed. The last song, 15:3, is sung by those who had endured and gotten victory over the beast and his mark. Each song speaks of a victory in some manner.

There is a lot of singing going on in the Revelation, and in the Word of God, relative to our worship of the Lord. Reading the accounts in the Old Testament concerning the Temple services and those who were appointed to be worshipers of God, to praise Him on their instruments, and to sing their songs of worship, inspires and challenges us to SING UNTO THE LORD! There is not a lot said about singing in the New Testament relative to the Church. Paul in his epistle to the Ephesians (5:19), did say, *Speaking to yourselves in psalms and hymns and spiritual songs, singing and making melody in your heart to the Lord.* Singing has been a very important part of worship throughout the ages. It is even recorded in Job 38:7, in reference to a time before the earth was ever formed; *When the morning stars sang together, and all the sons of God shouted for joy.*

Songs are utterances of Praise and Worship to the Lord for His bountiful blessings and goodness.

Songs are expressions of victory that are expressed by those who have endured some temptation or difficult problems or tests. If any do not like music and singing, they would surely not feel at home in heaven!

<u>Verse 4:</u>

These are they which were not defiled with women; for they are virgins. These are they which follow the Lamb whithersoever he goeth. These were redeemed from among men, {being} the firstfruits unto God and to the Lamb.

These are a unique group! Chosen by the Lord and sealed with His name in their forehead. They must have been so chosen for a special purpose. While it is not spelled out in the Revelation, there are many who feel they are special witnesses during this period. Some feel that they will fulfill Matthew 24:14; *And this gospel of the kingdom shall be preached in all the world for a witness unto all nations; and then shall the end come.*

THEY WHICH WERE NOT DEFILED WITH WOMEN; FOR THEY ARE VIRGINS... Some choose to spiritualize this statement as meaning they did not commit spiritual idolatry. "Women" having a reference to a false religious system. We do not choose to follow this line of reasoning. A unique responsibility calls for a unique group of men. It is not without reason to suggest that this group of men are a special class who have felt the urging of the Spirit of God in their life and have dedicated their life to His work, and His work alone.

John the Baptist was such a man. From all indications John never knew a woman. His calling was a very special calling - and it called for a very special man. John fit the bill! Paul spoke to the Corinthian church; 1Corinthians 7:7, *For I would that all men were even as I myself (*unmarried). Jesus said, Matthew 19:12 *For there are some eunuchs ... which have made themselves eunuchs for the kingdom of heaven's sake. He that is able to receive {it}, let him receive (it).* The work of God during these dark days of tribulation calls for men who will not be tied down to a wife and children. Men who will have but one dedication, and that is to fulfill the will of God with their life. Paul said: *But he that is married careth for the things that are of the world, how he may please his wife* (1Corinthians 7:33).

Paul also said: *He that is unmarried careth for the things that belong to the Lord, how he may please the Lord.* This is not to imply that married people cannot please the Lord or do a work for Him. It is evident that the apostle Peter was married, and the Lord gave him the keys to the kingdom of heaven!

But the urgency and seriousness of the hour calls for a unique dedication - a unique class of men - and that unique group are the 144,000 sealed by the Lord.

Some feel that this number is made up of special saints throughout the ages who have stood out in their commitment to God. To this we would disagree as well, for we do not believe there is any indication elsewhere to support this supposition. Besides, among the many who stand out historically that have lived committed lives of dedication for the Lord you could find a number of women as well as men. This group are all men.

THESE ARE THEY WHICH FOLLOW THE LAMB... Being married would not permit one to follow in any direction and to any place, the bidding of the Lord. The Word of God has already commanded us that if one *provide not for his own, and especially for those of his own house, he hath denied the faith, and is worse than an infidel,* (1Timothy 5:8).

Again, I do not think we are to take this statement in a literal sense. The Lamb is not on this earth at this time, so it would not be possible for the 144,000 to literally be found walking behind the Lord.

They are following the Lord in the same manner which we are following Him, by being obedient to His will for our life.

THESE WERE REDEEMED FROM AMONG MEN... This statement has prompted some to think this group is different from the group in chapter seven. They take the statement to mean that this group of 144,000 were taken from among men in the sense that they are from all nations, tongues, and people. Not just from among the Jewish people. Such a statement is made in chapter five in regards to the redeemed that are part of the raptured ones (5:9). For, the redeemed in the rapture are certainly from the various races and nations of people on earth. We do not choose to take this statement to mean that it is necessarily a reference to all, or different, races of people they have been purchased from, but that this group has been purchased from among men, in contrast to them being a host of angelic beings with Him on Mount Sion. They are men taken from among men. Twelve thousand from each of the twelve tribes of Israel.

BEING THE FIRSTFRUITS UNTO GOD AND TO THE LAMB... Being firstfruits implies that there will be more to follow. Just as Jesus Christ is the "firstfruits," of those to come forth from the dead, afterward they that are Christ's at His coming (1Corinthians 15:23).

When Israel prepared to harvest their crops, they would bring the first of the harvest - firstfruits - and offer it to the Lord as an offering of thanksgiving. The firstborn among the cattle and flocks were offered to the Lord, being firstfruits.

They are a sampling of what is to come later. It is possible that the influence of the 144,000 which they had on others during the tribulation is seen in chapter seven by the great multitude which no man could number! They will not be the only ones who will be living for God and refusing to accept the beast and his system of evil.

Verse 5:

And in their mouth was found no guile: for they are without fault before the throne of God.

The Psalmist, long ago, stated; Psalm 15:1,2: *Lord, who shall abide in thy tabernacle? who shall dwell in thy holy hill? He that walketh uprightly, and worketh righteousness, and speaketh the truth in his heart.* James wrote; 3:2: *For in many things we offend all. If any man offend not in word, the same {is} a perfect man, {and} able also to bridle the whole body.*

It was said of Job, 1:8: *{there is} none like him in the earth, a perfect and an upright man, one that feareth God, and escheweth evil?*

It was said of Noah that he was *a just man and perfect in his generations* (Genesis 6:9).

There have only been a few men down through the course of history that such things were said about them. We know that they were not without sin - *for all have sinned, and come short of the glory of God.* But they were unique men who had been given a special role in life to play. Paul said of himself, that God had; separated me from my mother IS womb, and called me by His grace, in reference to the call of God on his life (Galatians 1:15). Even John the Baptist was filled with the Holy Ghost while yet in his mother's womb!

These are four very special men who were used in a very special way during their lifetime.

It is quite possible - if not probable - that the 144,000 were chosen by God from birth; protected by God through the years; called and ordained of God during the tribulation to fulfill a very important role. It is not beyond reason to think that God would choose such men from birth and lay His hand upon them, like He did John the Baptist, keeping them through the years for this specific calling during the tribulation.

John the Baptist's ministry only lasted a few months, before being beheaded, after giving way to the ministry of Jesus Christ. The ministry of these will be but a few years at the most. Again, we are not given any specifics as to just how long they do witness, whether it is for the entire tribulation, or until the beast moves on the scene. We do not know for sure what happens to them; whether they are killed by the beast (which we doubt seriously); or, they are present to greet and welcome the Lord when He returns at Armageddon.

THE EVERLASTING GOSPEL

Verse 6:

And I saw another angel fly in the midst of heaven, having the everlasting gospel to preach unto them that dwell on the earth, and to every nation, and kindred, and tongue, and people,

This verse strengthens the argument that the Church must not be here during this period of the tribulation, as we find an angel proclaiming the gospel to the world. If the Church was still here her ministers would be proclaiming the gospel! During this Church age, only the people of God; men who have been called and anointed of the Spirit, are carrying the gospel message to the world. The angels desire to look into this gospel message which men are declaring to the world (1Peter 1:12), but they do not have the privilege of proclaiming the gospel.

This is another tremendous statement emphasizing the mercies of God during this dark period of time on earth. God does not shut up the heavens for seven years and refuse to listen to the cries of His creation. His mercy is seen here, as we have witnessed it during our journey through tribulation to this point.

What kind of tremendous affect must this have on people who are battling their mind as to which way they should go. Should we take the mark and join the system of the beast? as he offers so much to us? We will be free from want, so he tells us, if we will just take his mark and join his system. He claims to have the solution to the woes which beset the world. On the other hand, there are these "witnesses" who keep warning everybody not to believe the smooth words of the beast and his cohort, the false prophet. Now an angelic being - as it is obvious he must be to be able to fly through the air - is proclaiming an everlasting gospel.

It is not beyond reason to think that by this time the beast has taken over the entire media. Newspapers will be publishing what he wants the people to read. Radio and Television will be employed to propagate his message to the masses. There is no way that anyone could use the air waves, nor the printed page of the newspapers and news magazines, to publish a warning to people on earth about the real plans of the beast. While the beast may control the air-waves in the sense that no radio or television broadcast may be made without his approval, this does not prevent an angel from flying through the air with his message to the world. This angel becomes a heavenly satellite system with a message of hope and warning to the world.

TO EVERY NATION, AND KINDRED, AND TONGUE, AND PEOPLE... No one is left out of hearing the message of this heavenly messenger.

It is no wonder that John saw a number that could not be numbered who came out of the great tribulation and washed their robes in the blood of the Lamb. Consider the tremendous influence of mercy which the world will have exerted upon them at this time. First of all, the rapture is not a hidden fact to the people. It is obvious to the vast majority that something shocking has taken place, which no doubt does not take long to conclude it was the rapture of the redeemed. This will have a tremendous effect on anyone who has any feelings whatsoever about being saved. This would probably prompt a lot of praying; a lot of Bible reading; and a lot of soul-searching. The churches of the redeemed are left behind as mute witnesses to all about them. Their Bibles and publications are as well left for all to see.

Then, here are 144,000 who are witnessing against the rise of this smooth-talking, very persuasive, person who is having such an effect on the world. Then the arrival - from somewhere, no one knows just where, though! - of the two unique men who demonstrate such tremendous power and authority.

Though attacked, none are able to hurt them! And then in the midst of all this the sky above reveals a startling sight as obviously an angel is seen flying all over the world - just above the people - proclaiming an everlasting gospel. Oh yes, there will be a whole lot of people who will heed the message and save their soul eternally.

Verse 7:

Saying with a loud voice, Fear God, and give glory to him; for the hour of his judgment is come: and worship him that made heaven, and earth, and the sea, and the fountains of waters.

Mr Morris wrote: "It is significant that the first time the word is used (Matthew 4:23), it is in reference to "the gospel of the kingdom," looking forward to the great day when Christ will be universally acclaimed as King of kings. The final occurrence is here in Revelation 14:7, where it looks back to the creation. The gospel of Christ ("the good news about Christ") is that He is the Creator of all things (and therefore able to control and judge all things), the Redeemer of all things (and therefore able to save to the uttermost them that come to God by Him), and the heir of all things (therefore able and certain to bring the kingdom of God to earth as it is in heaven). The creation is the foundation of the gospel, the second coming is the blessed hope of the gospel, the cross and the empty tomb constitute the power of the gospel. A gospel without the creation and the consummation is as much an emasculated gospel as one with the cross and empty tomb. One does not really preach the gospel unless he places and teaches all these together in their true majesty and fullness."

FEAR GOD... The man of sin has been bringing fear into the hearts of mankind with his threats, and with his judgments of death The natural reaction to threats against one's person is to have fear. The reality of death is a fearful thing.

The words of Jesus were: Matthew 10:28, *And fear not them which kill the body, but are not able to kill the to destroy both soul and body in hell.*

The wise man said: Proverbs 9:10, *The fear of the Lord {is} the beginning of wisdom.* This is not a fear in the sense of recoiling at His presence, but a godly fear of respect for His power and glory. Solomon concludes his remarks in Ecclesiastes by stating; *Let us hear the conclusion of the whole matter: Fear God and keep His commandments: for this is the whole duty of man.*

There will be a lot of fear manifested toward the man of sin and his cohorts because of the death that follows in their wake. But the judgments of the man of sin will soon pass. The judgments of God will be forever.

GIVE GLORY TO HIM... The one thing which the beast does not want is for someone to honor God at this time. He who has made his claim that he is god, will be incensed at hearing someone worship the true God.

Regardless of the conflict in life that one must be called upon to face, he will be wise to give God the glory regardless of the conditions.

FOR THE HOUR OF HIS JUDGMENT IS COME... What a spine-chilling reaction this must produce to hear this angel flying through the air bellowing out this warning in the ears of the inhabitants of this earth! We have but to recall the Antediluvian world, or the world of Sodom and Gomorrah, to be reminded of the judgments which God brings to a rebellious society!

WORSHIP HIM THAT MADE HEAVEN, AND EARTH, AND THE SEA, AND THE FOUNTAINS OF WATERS... Four objects of God's creation are here mentioned. In verse six we also have reference to four objects; *Nation, kindred, tongue, and people.* The numeral four seems to point to the four directions of the earth; North, south, east and west. The gospel goes into all the world. It touches all of His creation. It reaches every race of people. He is the God of all creation. Unlike the beast who is acknowledged as god only by those who follow him.

Verse 8:

And there followed another angel, saying, Babylon is fallen, is fallen, that great city, because she made all nations drink of the wine of the wrath of her fornication.

We are here introduced to Babylon, that great city of sin and debauchery. This angel, following the one with the message of the gospel, shouts out in his wake that Babylon will fall. This statement, like some of the others we have been considering in the Revelation, speaks of something as though it had already happened, when the time has not fully arrived yet. But the certainty of Babylon's fall is found in the words of this angel.

The pronouncement of the fall of Babylon here also seems to add emphasis to what we previously mentioned that this chapter seems to be a chronological order of the events which transpire during the tribulation. The fall of Babylon being near the end of the tribulation. The fall of this city is given to us in detail in chapter eighteen. We will wait until then to go into detail concerning this city of wickedness. We will say here, however, that Babylon is the headquarters of the beast as well as the headquarters of sin and ungodliness. What Jerusalem represents to the people of God, Babylon represents to the ungodly. And it is that capital of sin that is going to fall!

Verse 9:

And the third angel followed them, saying with a loud voice, If any man worship the beast and his image, and receive {his} mark in his forehead, or in his hand,

It would appear that we have one angel after another flying through the air with their own unique

message to deliver to those dwelling on this earth at this time. Again, we are reminded that there is mercy mingled with judgment during the tribulation!

This one as well is said to have a loud voice to declare his message to all earth-dwellers. None will stand before God in judgment with the excuse I did not hear. I did not know.

Let us notice the continuity of these messages by these three angels; The first comes with the everlasting gospel; that which will save those who obey it. The second angel comes with his warning about Babylon is fallen, as if to declare that righteousness will prevail. Obeying the gospel will assure one of victory as well. Babylon will seek to keep the gospel from men and men from the gospel; she shall fail.

Now, the third angel proclaims doom to all who accept the beast and his system.

If any man worship the beast... If any man worship his image... If any man receives his mark... The judgment is the same to all regardless of the extent of their involvement. It will not justify anyone to say, I took the mark, but I never did worship him. The judgment will be the same!

We don't want to sound redundant, but, again, there will be no excuse accepted from anyone. There are plenty of warnings given to all as to the consequence of joining the system of the beast. Today one may claim ignorance by saying I was never told the gospel message (not that it will hold up in judgment); but here we have angels flying through the air proclaiming in a loud voice the messages of warning. ALL ARE WARNED!

Verse 10:

The same shall drink of the wine of the wrath of God, which is poured out without mixture into the cup of his indignation; and he shall be tormented with fire and brimstone in the presence of the holy angels, and in the presence of the Lamb:

The warning has been made concerning the wine of the wrath of her fornication which Babylon has made nations to drink during her time of power over the nations. Now, in contrast to this, God is shown causing those who drink the wine of Babylon to drink His wine, which is judgment! This statement reminds us of Psalm 75:8: *For in the hand of the Lord {there is} a cup, and the wine is red; it is full of mixture; and he poureth out of the same: but the dregs thereof, all the wicked of the earth shall wring {them} out, {and} drink (them).*

It would be better to have the whole world mad at you for a lifetime than to have God mad at you for five seconds! The angel pronounces the sentence which God will mete out to those who have rejected His call of love and mercy, and who have committed spiritual fornication by worshiping the beast and accepting his mark. The sentence meted out is fearsome - to say the least!

Men do not stumble into hell blindfolded! They are warned again and again. This is the third angel who has cried out to the inhabitants of earth concerning the beast and the judgment which will fall upon him and those who follow him. Considering these angels, along with the 144,000, along with the two witnesses, along with the available Word, there will be many witnesses against the beast and to the people concerning what is taking place and what is going to happen to all who follow the man of sin.

POURED OUT WITHOUT MIXTURE... Mercy has sounded forth her voice. Those who hear her voice and follow her call, will know the blessings of security which she will grant. Those who refuse to heed her voice, and instead walk on in their own stubborn ways, will find that mercy will be lifted.

There is an end to mercy! Here is mercies end! Up till now, the judgments of God have always been mixed with mercy. Eight souls were saved when the first great judgment of God fell upon the world. In a later judgment, three souls were saved from the fires of judgment. Now there will be no mercy mixed with the cup of wrath. Judgment is final!

SHALL BE TORMENTED WITH FIRE AND BRIMSTONE... This is speaking, again, of the judgment which will come to those who follow the beast. The judgment is described for us in chapter twenty by John, as he witnesses the dead stand before God at the White Throne judgment. The awful doom to depart into the lake of fire echoes eternally in the ears of those who receive that awful fate.

Theologians can argue the authenticity of the lake of fire and the eternality of the fate of those who enter that place of judgment; but the fact remains this judgment is pronounced upon all who reject the message of salvation and accept the message of the beast.

The argument of some that God is a God of love and would never send someone does not have scripture to support the argument. It is not a matter of God sending anyone anywhere; it is a matter of men sending themselves to this place of torment because of their refusal to accept the mercies which God has offered to them again and again in their lifetime.

IN THE PRESENCE OF THE HOLY ANGELS, AND... THE LAMB... This is a very interesting, as well as puzzling, passage of scripture. It is not likely that we are to think that the Lord Jesus and His angels will watch the torment of those confined to this place of fire and brimstone. But, like the rich man in Luke sixteen, confined to "hell," he was in torment, and yet could see Lazarus in a place of peace and rest. If there is anyone looking at anyone else, it is likely those in this place of torment would be looking at the Lord and His angels - not the other way around.

Probably one of the most "tormenting" things about the lake of fire could be that men will retain their faculties of remembrance; tastes; feelings, etc. If it is possible for the lost to view, somehow, the bliss of the saved; how much more this would add to their torment.

Verse 11:

And the smoke of their torment ascendeth up for ever and ever: and they have no rest day nor night, who worship the beast and his image, and whosoever receiveth the mark of his name.

The modern liberal theologians argue there is no such thing as eternal punishment for the wicked.

The message of annihilation of the wicked is not a new message. It has been taught by many through the years. One well known minister of our generation argued that souls would not be in hell for an eternity, because that would mean they would be in possession of eternal life. That the lost will burn-up in the lake of fire. That only the saved will know eternal life. And for the lost to be in hell eternally would mean they would possess eternal life.

The error he makes - as well as others like him - is his argument that the unsaved would know eternal life in hell if hell is eternal. No! They will know eternal death! Not eternal life. Revelation 20:14 speaks of it as "the second death."

If hell was not eternal; if those who go to that place soon burn up; then why does it say here that *the smoke of their torment ascendeth up for ever and ever?* If it is not eternal, what makes it burn for ever and ever? If those who go to that place are not there eternally, why would smoke come from that place eternally?

The term for ever and ever is "unto ages of ages." Ages rolling upon ages. The Greek rendering for eternity.

Even if we were to assume that no human mortal body could stand the fires of such a judgment; that the mortal flesh would have to be consumed in such a place of fire, the Bible fact remains that we are eternal beings. Our bodies might die and cease to function; we may have to bury the body of a loved one, but we never bury the soul or spirit of the individual. So, while one may argue that the body would be consumed in such a fire, the same argument could not apply to the soul and spirit! Just supposing that the body does burn-up in the flames, the soul remains in that place of torment eternally!

THEY HAVE NO REST DAY NOR NIGHT... One of the wonderful things about heaven and the place of the redeemed is the emphasis which is placed upon the rest and peace which will be enjoyed by all who enter that blissful place. What a contrast! Here in this place there will be no rest. None whatsoever! This may not have reference altogether to a physical nature. What is more restless than a soul under conviction? What is more tormented than a soul that knows they are lost? What could be more restless in that place than knowing that during their lifetime they rejected the message which would have caused them to avoid that place? Recalling all the messages they heard; all the altar calls they spurned; all the opportunities to live for God squandered, will certainly be cause for restlessness.

Regarding the eternity of this place, consider the words of Mr. Morris: "Modern science has demonstrated the principle of conservation of matter and energy to be the most certain and universal principal of science. Matter and energy can change forms but can be neither created nor annihilated. And if mere physical matter cannot be annihilated, the far more important entity of the human soul/spirit complex (in particular the created "image of God" in man - note Genesis 1:27) can surely not be destroyed, as claimed by the so-called "annihilationist's," or believers in "conditional immortality." Every human being ever conceived, possessing a divinely-created human soul and spirit, will exist forever somewhere."

There will be more said about the lake of fire when we get to chapter twenty.

Verse 12:

Here is the patience of the saints: here {are} they that keep the commandments of God, and the faith of Jesus.

Jesus had said during His discourse on the tribulation; Matthew 24: 13, *But he that shall endure unto the end, the same shall be saved.*

The church has been confronted with persecution and trouble through the years since Pentecost.

Many have become martyrs rather than recant their testimony. But no period has been as dark as this one. The pressures which will be exerted against all who refuse to join the system of the man of sin will be tremendous - even to death!

One thing which will make this decision such a challenge will be the lifestyle that people will have been accustomed to living, and then, suddenly, to be faced with the loss of everything - or join the system!

The attachment to materialistic things is a very strong attachment. Many will no doubt try to retain these materialistic, worldly, things, and in so doing doom their soul eternally.

HERE... John writes, as if to point out the obvious difference between this group without the mark of the beast and the majority who do have it. This separation has always been obvious. You cannot blend in with the world and retain your identity with Jesus Christ.

THE PATIENCE OF THE SAINTS... This passage has puzzled some. If the church is not going through the tribulation, then why do we have this reference here in what is obviously taking place far into the tribulation period?

There are 13 times the word saints is found employed in the Revelation. The first time in 5:8, which refers to the prayers of the saints; and the last time in 20:9, which speaks of the camp of the saints.

Looking back into the Old Testament we find that there are at least four different Hebrew words which are translated saints. The words mean; "Pious, godly, good, holy one, sacred things or places, hallowed. "

When we get to the New Testament, we find there is only one Greek word which is employed and translated saints, "hagios." It is used some 61 times in the New Testament.

So, the term found in this verse is not necessarily referring to church members. The term saint is not used exclusively of members of the church. It is referring to anyone whom the Lord considers pious, holy, godly, etc.

The first place we find the word employed in the New Testament is interesting; Matthew 27:52, *And the graves were opened; and many bodies of the saints which slept arose.* Obviously, this is referring to the Old Testament saints - not New Testament - as the church has not even come into existence yet.

And the last place the term is employed is likewise interesting; Revelation 20:9, *And they went up on the breadth of the earth, and compassed the camp of the saints about...* Obviously, this is not a reference to the church, as this is something which takes place after the millennium. Even if the church would go through the tribulation they would have been raptured long before this and would have received their glorified body and would not be in any danger of anything Satan could bring against them. This is evidently a reference to those who are saved at the end of the millennium.

HERE ARE THEY THAT KEEP... The message has been *"If you love me ... keep."* Paul wrote in his final recorded epistle; *I have kept the faith...* How important it will be at this time to keep the Word of God. This term implies an obedience to the commandments of God.

AND THE FAITH OF JESUS... Salvation is through the blood of Jesus Christ, without faith in the atoning power of His blood, there will be no salvation.

Again, how interesting when we consider the Jews who refuse the mark and accept that Jesus Christ is Messiah. The One whom their father rejected two millenniums ago, has now become the means of salvation to their children.

<u>Verse 13:</u>

And I heard a voice from heaven saying unto me, Write, Blessed {are} the dead which die in the Lord from henceforth: Yea, saith the Spirit, that they may rest from their labours; and their works do follow them.

WRITE... BLESSED ARE THE... This is the second of the seven beatitudes that we find the book of Revelation;

• 1). "Blessed is he that readeth ... " (1:3)

• 2). "Blessed are the dead which die ... " (14:13)

• 3). "Blessed is he that watcheth ... " (16:15)

• 4). "Blessed are they which are called ... " (19:9)

• 5). "Blessed and holy is he that hath part ... " (20:6)

• 6). "Blessed is he that keepeth the sayings ... " (22:7)

• 7). "Blessed are they that do his commandments ... " (22:14)

This beatitude is particularly interesting as it pronounces a blessing upon those who die during this dark time of the tribulation. Usually we think of people wanting to live; here it will be a blessing to die!

This emphasizes to us the dark days which the people will face during this period of time.

But the message is not to just anyone dying; it is directed to those who die in the Lord. There will be many who will die who will not be "in the Lord" at this time. But to die in the Lord is a blessing at any time regardless of the period in which we live. But particularly is a blessing given to those who die during this time because of the tremendous persecution they are facing.

The darkest three and one-half years the human race has ever known is facing those living during this time. Death will be a blessed relief. People are prone to want to cling to life because of their possessions; or because of their friends and family ties, etc. To those who die during this time, there is nothing on this earth anymore which makes them want to stay.

During this period of time it will be an effort, no doubt, just to keep body and soul together. With the beast rising to power and declaring that all must worship him and receive his mark, pressures have been placed against all who have heard and believed the messages delivered to them against the beast and his empire of evil. Those who do not die during this time will face tremendous persecution and pressure against them and their family.

This is also a message which has been given to all the people of God through the years. In our walk with God we are to be "laborers" in His kingdom. Paul informs us that *our labour is not in vain in the Lord* (1Corinthians 15:58). We know that rewarding day is coming to every child of God. Your labor in the Lord will not go un-noticed.

Jesus lets us know that our labor here is a basis of our service there in Matthew 25:21. We are also warned (1Corinthians 3:14,15), if we are lazy and indifferent and do not take care how we labor for the Lord, we will come up short and embarrassed on that day of judgment!

The message is that it will be much better to die "in the Lord" and then at His coming reign with Him for one thousand years, than to "reign" with the beast for three and one-half years, and be lost eternally!

THEIR WORKS DO FOLLOW THEM... We can look at this statement in two different ways:

1). It is a blessing to know that our life can be a blessing while we live, and then, after we are gone, what we did during our lifetime can continue to bless people. This could certainly apply to many of those who die during this dark time. There will no doubt be a lot of brave people who will leave a great impression on the mind of others as they die rather than bow to the demands of the beast. So, many of the martyrs during this period of time will leave a tremendous testimony behind them to encourage and bless others who follow.

2). According to Vincent the Greek word here translated "follow" should be "accompany." The Revised Version has it "follow with them." The thought being that their works go with them into the presence of the Lord. One cannot take houses and land; stocks nor bonds; friends nor family, with him when he dies; but he can take his labors! Your works, your record of labor, is one thing you can take with you to the Lord's presence.

• **THREE MORE ANGELS....**

THE GRAPES OF WRATH AND HARVEST TIME ...

Verse 14:

And I looked, and behold a white cloud, and upon the cloud {one} sat like unto the Son of man, having on his head a golden crown, and in his hand a sharp sickle.

A WHITE CLOUD... There seems to be little argument that this is a vision of the Lord Jesus Christ Himself. The "white cloud" is identified with Him. John had already written (1:7) of this; Behold, He cometh with clouds. Jesus speaking of this event in Matthew 24:30, said; And that they shall see the Son of man coming in the clouds of heaven with power and great glory.

The following verses (14-20) take us forward to the time of Armageddon when the Lord Jesus shall come with vengeance and judgment upon the beast and his empire and all those who follow him.

It would seem that this vision is of the Lord Jesus because:

• 1). The white cloud identifies with Him in fulfillment of the above passages relating to His coming again.

• 2). The reference to this being the Son of man is a title Jesus was called. Also, John 5:22 states: *For the Father judgeth no man, but hath committed all judgment unto the Son.*

• 3). The white color of the cloud speaks in typology of Jesus Christ

- "pure and holy."

• 4). The "golden crown" on His head speaks of Jesus Christ as King of kings and Lord of lords.

A Golden Crown... This vision of the Lord's return to this earth at the battle of Armageddon. For He will return at that time to reign over this earth as He establishes His kingdom upon this earth and the earth enjoys one thousand years of peace and great glory. John states at that event (19:12), *"on His head were many crowns."*

The man of sin has usurped authority to reign as king of this earth. He has made his boast in the Jewish temple that he is god. He has demanded that all should worship him as if he was god. All of this is soon to change as the rightful King is soon to appear on this earth again and claim that which is rightfully His. At that time, He shall come with crowns on His head, signifying that He is King of ALL nations and peoples.

IN HIS HAND A SHARP SICKLE... A sickle speaks loudly of a harvest. It is almost harvest time for planet earth. And the One who has the sickle in His hand is the Lord Jesus Himself! He is the *"Lord of the harvest,"* (Matthew 9:38), and He is getting ready to harvest the fields.

The scene seems to be a fulfillment of the prophecy of Joel (3:12,13): *Let the heathen be wakened, and come up to the valley of Jehoshaphat: for there will I sit to judge all the heathen round about. Put ye in the sickle, for the harvest is ripe: come, get you down; for the press is full, the fats overflow; for their wickedness {is} great.*

Some have mistakenly interpreted this passage as a reference to the rapture. The Lord is thrusting in His sickle to gather the Church out of the earth, they say. But the language does not fit the language of prophecy relative to the rapture of the Church. The vision of the sickle is evidently a scene of judgment of sin and wickedness, not a reaping of righteous fruit into the Lord's garner.

<u>Verse 15:</u>

And another angel came out of the temple, crying with a loud voice to him that sat on the cloud, Thrust in thy sickle, and reap: for the time is come for thee to reap; for the harvest of the earth is ripe.

Again, referring to the words of Joel, this is an almost direct quote of the reference in Joel mentioned above. And it is evident from Joel's words that the harvest that is being mentioned is not the rapture of the church, but a reaping of wickedness from this earth!

The prophet Isaiah seems to be referring to this same occasion in his prophecy: Isaiah 63:1- 4, *Who {is} this that cometh from Edom, with dyed garments from Bozrah? this {that is} glorious in his apparel, travelling in the greatness of his strength? I that speak in righteousness, mighty to save. Wherefore {art thou} red in thine apparel, and thy garments like him that treadeth in the winefat? I have trodden the winepress alone,· and of the people {there was} none with me: for I will tread them in mine anger, and trample them in my fury; and their blood shall be sprinkled upon my garments, and I will stain all my raiment. For the day of vengeance {is} in mine heart, and the year of my redeemed is come.*

Three angels are coming forth now, it would seem in rapid succession, as the events of the closing hours of man's day is fast coming to an end. John said this angel came out of the temple. He does not specify whether this is the temple he saw opened in heaven (11:19), or the temple the beast has previously entered on this earth. We are not to take the statement of this angel, directed to the One sitting on the cloud, as being a command. No angel would consider making such a command to the Lord Jesus! It is no doubt an appeal. There must be an appalling feeling among the angelic host at the conditions which are now existing on this earth. The only solution to the world's woes lies in the hands of the One who has the sharp sickle. So, the appeal thrust in your sickle and reap the harvest, for the wickedness of the world is fully ripe.

Sinfully wicked conditions will have by this time reached epidemic proportions. The Antediluvian world could not be compared to the conditions of this age when the beast and his systems of wickedness is unleashed upon this world. While sin and ungodliness has always been rampant in the human race since the fall of man and his expulsion from the garden of God, no generation has witnessed the conditions of depravity that this last generation witnesses!

The age-old question of Why? has been asked again and again, as men have witnessed the wicked conditions that have prevailed from time to time. Why do the wicked prosper? Why aren't the wicked judged? Why are the wicked permitted to continue their wickedness unchallenged by God? When God was making His covenant with Abraham (Genesis 15.), God told Abraham what would happen to his seed in later years. How that although the land belonged to them, they would not possess it for some four hundred years. That in later years his descendants would have to go down into Egypt, and then come forth to take their land at last. The reason for this delay? *For the iniquity of the Amorites is not yet full* (v. 16). God, in His justness, gave the Amorites four hundred more years, during which time they did not change their ways. They were among the many "ites" that were marked by Joshua for extermination when the people entered the land of promise (Joshua 3:10). So, sin and the sinner may not be dealt with immediately; but truth will triumph in the end. Judgment will come to this wicked world in the time that God has appointed - not before!

Verse 16:

And he that sat on the cloud thrust in his sickle on the earth; and the earth was reaped.

We have under consideration in these closing verses of this chapter, two scenes of a sharp sickle reaping the harvest of the earth. One seems to be done by the Lord Jesus Christ Himself, as seen in the past two verses, the other that of a special angel coming forth from before the altar. There are some who are of the opinion that they are both referring to the same time; Armageddon. There are others who feel they refer to two types of harvesting which will take place. One by the Lord Jesus, the last by the angels. The first is referred to as the "Harvest of the earth;" the other as the "Vintage of the earth."

The words of Morris seem appropriate here: "The 'reaping of the earth' is apparently something different than' gathering the vine of the earth' (V. 19), though the great sickle of judgment is used in both. The one precedes the other, and the latter is clearly a reference to the gathering armies of the beast and his followers to Armageddon. The first reaping is apparently a "harvest" of grain, the second a "vintage" of grapes. The first is cut and threshed, the second is gathered for the winepress. Probably the first refers to all the worldwide judgments of the second half of the tribulation, unleashed when the seven bowls of wrath pour out over the earth (Revelation 16), climaxing in the utter destruction of Babylon, the capital, and the entire Babylonish world-system. The second refers more specifically to the final judgment of the beast and all his followers at Armageddon."

Let us keep in mind that it is the Lord Jesus who opens the seals of judgment upon this world. The judgments which are falling upon the beast and his followers during this time are at His command and directions. The last of the judgments upon the beast and his followers are about to begin falling upon the earth, as the seven angels with their bowls of wrath get ready to pour out their contents upon the beast and his followers in chapter fifteen. This is the final - and most horrible - judgment upon the beast and his followers prior to Armageddon. The sharp sickle of Jesus Christ is getting ready, at this point, to make its sweep through the earth!

While Jesus Christ is the one who brings the judgments of His wrath upon the beast and his followers, it is evident from Matthew 13:39, for example, *"the harvest is the end of the world; and the reapers are the angels."*

Verse 17:

And another angel came out of the temple which is in heaven, he also having a sharp sickle.

In this age of corruption and sinful wickedness, only the brave and determined will remain faithful to God and refuse to join the beast and his crowd. But there will be some who will refuse to go along with the beast, even if it means their life! When Babylon's judgment is falling upon her we hear the voice of mercy calling out, Come out of her, my people, that ye be not partakers of her sins (18:4).

Again, we have an angel coming from the temple to bring judgment upon this wicked world. The temple is the sacred dwelling place of God. The angels, guardians, as it were, of the holiness of this place, are involved in bringing judgment against those who have brought so much wickedness to the human family.

Verse 18:

And another angel came out from the altar, which had power over fire; and cried with a loud cry to him that had the sharp sickle, saying, Thrust in thy sharp sickle, and gather the clusters of the vine of the earth; for her grapes are fully ripe.

This is the sixth angel introduced in this chapter. He is seen coming from the altar - the place of judgment! The altar was where the sins of the people were brought in the form of animals and sacrificed.

It is said of this angel that he "*had power over fire.*" We know from chapter eighteen that Babylon will burn with a tremendous fire. Also, we have witnessed in our study some references to judgments of fire. Is this the angel which has brought these judgments about?

We get a glimpse in reading the Revelation of some of the various responsibilities of the angelic host. We know there are myriad of angels, and they each have their own responsibilities, but here we have some of those special responsibilities spelled out for us.

The appeal is made to the angel with the sharp sickle, like was made to the Lord Jesus, to thrust in thy sickle. Sin and ungodliness has raised its ugly head long enough! Sin and ungodliness has affected enough people long enough! The beast and his followers have had their day, and it is now finished!

This angel is then to thrust in his sickle to *"gather the vine of the earth. "* The *"grapes"* are now *"fully ripe."* The time for harvest has come. Armageddon is about to begin!

Verse 19:

And the angel thrust in his sickle into the earth, and gathered the vine of the earth, and cast {it} into the great winepress of the wrath of God.

The harvesting process brings together the grain which is cut down by the sickle. This angel brings together the "grain" of wickedness - the tares of the world - to a place of final judgment. Chapter sixteen, verses 13 and 14, inform us that three unclean spirits go forth to the kings of the earth to gather them together for Armageddon. Specifically - politically - what brings the leaders of the world's nations, and their armies, to this place of final showdown is a matter of interpreting to one's own satisfaction the prophecies concerning

this final battle.

We have such passages as Zechariah 14:2: *For I will gather all nations against Jerusalem to battle.* Or Joel 3:2: *I will also gather all nations, and will bring them down into the valley of Jehoshaphat.*

The "winepress" is the "valley of Jehoshaphat," the place of

Armageddon. The "plains of Megiddo."

It will be the place of final showdown for all the armies of this earth who will be gathered there. The One who brings about the victory to all that is good, and defeat to all that is evil, will be the Lord Jesus Himself (19:11-21).

Verse 20:

And the winepress was trodden without the city, and blood came out of the winepress, even unto the horse bridles, by the space of a thousand {and} six hundred furlongs.

In the middle eastern countries, it was the custom to gather the harvest of grapes into a great vat, or enclosure, and people would get in with their bare feet and walk, dance, and sing, as they tread upon the grapes, squeezing the juice out into containers. This is the picture we get of the Lord Jesus in Isaiah 63, as He is seen treading the winepress alone, and He has His garments stained from the grapes He has treaded down.

Isaiah chapter 34 gives a descriptive view of the scene which is taking place as he mentions, *The sword of the Lord is filled with blood... For it is the day of the Lord's vengeance, and the year of recompenses for the controversy of Zion.*

Armageddon will not be a pretty place! The judgment upon sin cannot be pretty because sin is not pretty!

There is no way we can accurately describe what takes place at this battle. The nations of the world are brought together to this place. How many people would be involved in the armies of the world?

"Nothing less than the sudden spilling of the blood of all the unnumbered multitudes massed together in a great phalanx extending through the whole land of Israel is the terrible sight entrusted to him (John). The bloodshed is so massive and so quick that the only apt comparison is the spurting of the juice from tremendous clusters of ripe fruit beneath the feet of the grape-tramplers in a winepress. The hordes of soldiers and civilians, many, many riding horses, no doubt many on foot, perhaps others on vehicles of one sort and another, thronging together as in a great trough, unable to flee, their gaze transfixed on an amazing scene in the heavens, suddenly explode like bursting grapes, and the blood pours from a billion fountains." (Morris)

The reference to the blood as it came out of the winepress, even unto the horse bridles, by the space of a thousand and six hundred furlongs, presents thought provoking questions. Does this statement mean that the blood from the dead reaches this deep - to the horse bridles? Does it mean blood this deep flows 1600 furlongs - about 180 miles? There are various comments on this passage, and others do not comment on it specifically. It is evident that the carnage at this battle will be tremendous. So great, in fact, that the vultures are invited by the Lord to come and clean up the carnage. If Ezekiel 39:12 has reference to this battle, then it will take "seven months" to bury the dead. This in its self is mind-boggling!

The sixteen hundred furlongs - a furlong is about 607 feet in length - would come to about 180 miles. This is about the distance of the length of the land that Israel possesses today. So, it would seem the entire land will be bathed in the blood of Armageddon.

If the armies gathered for this battle number 200 million - which they could possibly be that many gathered there - and if each one of them shed his blood that day at the appearance of Jesus Christ from heaven, that would amount to about 300 thousand gallons of blood!

No other battle in all recorded history can compare with the one which will take place at this time. There have been references in times past of wars to end all wars, which, of course, did not! but this will be the final war. (There is reference to Satan gathering sinners together to battle, in 20:8, but this will not be a battle per se, as the Lord will cause fire to come down from heaven and destroy his host. There is no real fighting that goes on.)

- ***One thing we can be certain about regarding this battle; The victor will be the Lord Jesus Christ and all those who will be in His army!***

CHAPTER FIFTEEN

We come to the shortest chapter of the entire book, only eight verses long. It is as if it was the preface to the events which will transpire as the final seven angels bring forth their judgments on this earth, bringing to a conclusion the events which have been so earth-shattering during this seven-year period of time.

The seven seals and the seven trumpets have lasted for the first three and one-half years of the tribulation. The seven vials - or bowls, as some versions have it - shall last the last three and one-half years.

The seventh seal brings the seven trumpet judgments; the seventh trumpet brings the seven bowls of judgment. The time element involved in the bowl judgments seem to add significance to them.

Before they are poured out, however, John gets another glimpse of something glorious. Before the final dark days of the Beast are brought about, John is shown there will be those who will overcome regardless of the pressures put against them.

The last three and one-half years of the tribulation are actually the Tribulation the Great. The first three and one-half years serve as a preparatory time for the Beast in reaching his pinnacle of power.

Then, also Satan comes down in the middle of the week to enter the Beast - which actually turns the man of sin into the Beast! So, while there will be trouble all during the seven years, the darkest period of time will be the last three and one-half years.

Verse 1:

And I saw another sign in heaven, great and marvellous, seven angels having the seven last plagues; for in them is filled up the wrath of God.

Another sign... As noted in our Study on chapter twelve, where there the word is "wonder," both words are the same. John had been witnessing events which were transpiring on this earth, and now his vision is directed to the heavens where there he beholds another wonderful sign.

Great and marvelous... When we consider what John had been witnessing up to this point in the Revelation: all the havoc, the deaths and bloodshed among those who have been persecuted and slain by the Beast and his system of evil, what could it possibly be that would prompt John to exclaim that what he was now witnessing was great and marvelous? He had been witnessing the terrible upheavals of nature as judgments fall on this earth from God. What a beautiful change to witness now the beauty and glory which unfolds before him in the heavens.

Mr Morris points out that it is interesting how that God has oft times sealed His revelation to His prophets and ministers by a threefold sign. Joseph is the first one to receive such a confirmation from God; Genesis 37:5-11; 40:8-22; 41:15-40. Then Joshua received a three-fold confirmation; Joshua 4:22-24; 6:20; 10:10-14. Gideon also witnessed such a confirmation; Judges 6:36- 40; 7:13-15. Saul received a threefold notice; 1Samuel 10:1-7. Then, it was Elijah; 1Kings 19:9-13. Elisha; 2Kings 2;14,22,24, received such a confirmation. Then there was Hezekiah; 2Kings 19:20,29-35; 36:8-11.

And Ezekiel; Ezekiel 1:1; 3:22,23; 8;4. So John joins the elite group who are so informed of great events which are about to transpire.

Seven angels having the seven last plagues... "These seven angels will not be ordinary ones but seven redeemed men who will be already in heaven with glorified bodies at the time of this fulfillment of the book. Such is entirely possible as proved in chapter two, point 5. According to Revelation 17:1, one of the angels showed John the judgment of the great whore and the beast that carrieth her. In Revelation 21:9, one of them, perhaps the same one, came to show John the Holy City. After showing him the Revelation, John fell down at his feet to worship him, but was told "See thou do it not: for I am thy fellowservant, and of thy brethren the prophets and of them which keep the sayings of this book: worship God," Revelation 19:9,10; 22:8,9. This proves that one of them is a redeemed man, for he is expressly called "a man" in Revelation 21:17; and if one of them is a man, the other six must be also. It seems entirely reasonable that God would permit redeemed men to take part in executing His vengeance upon His enemies." (Dake).

Mr Dake offers some interesting, as well as strong arguments, concerning these being redeemed men, and not angels in the sense that we usually associate the name. The term "angels" comes to us from the word "angelos," which means "a messenger."

While it is debatable as to whether these are actually men or angels, it remains interesting to note the many places in the Revelation in which it would appear that men are involved in the events which are taking place during this period of time. Who knows just what God has in store for those whom He will redeem from this earth at the time of the rapture!

SEVEN LAST PLAGUES... Again, we are confronted with the numeral "seven" in our journey through this interesting book. Here it has unique meaning as it refers to the final judgments which God will bring on this earth. They will not only be the final judgments; they will also be the darkest!

God has forewarned through His prophets that such an hour was coming on the earth. One such warning is lifted from the words of Zephaniah 3:8; *Therefore wait ye upon me, saith the Lord, until the day that I rise up to the prey: for my determination {is} to gather the nations, that I may assemble the kingdoms, to pour upon them mine indignation, {even} all my fierce anger: for all the earth shall be devoured with the fire of my jealousy.*

What stirring, thought-provoking, words! There are many other similar warnings from the pen of God's prophets. Like the Antediluvians of old, this world will have been warned many times over before the dark clouds of God's wrath engulfs them!

When we hear the word "*plagues*" we are quickly reminded of Moses in Egypt and Pharaoh. We are not to think of this word in the sense of sicknesses or similar ailments. In fact, the word is also translated "*stripes*" in Luke 12:47, where we read; *and that servant, which knew his lord's will, and prepared not (himself}, neither did according to his will, shall be beaten with many stripes.*

The Lord is here speaking of the judgment which will be brought upon those who do not prepare for His coming again. The judgments of the last three and one-half years will be the judgments which God brings upon a fore-warned world! It is a judicial judgment! They have sinned; they have ignored the warnings of God's messengers; they must suffer the judgment!

FILLED UP THE WRATH OF GOD... There are a lot of troubles which men bring upon themselves by the way they live and conduct themselves. It is true that men sometimes blame the devil for a lot of their troubles, when in reality it is nothing but their own doings which causes them their troubles.

In this instance, though, it is God who is bringing these judgments of His wrath upon this sinful world.

After we get to this chapter it does not appear that we witness any more of God's mercies which have been sprinkled throughout the book thus far, as we have noted. From here on to Armageddon mercy does not seem available. The world at this time will have reached such a condition of rebellion against God, and such ungodliness will prevail over the earth, that the only alternative will be the judgments which God will bring upon this world.

Verse 2:

And I saw as it were a sea of glass mingled with fire: and them that had gotten the victory over the beast, and over his image, and over his mark, {and} over the number of his name, stand on the sea of glass, having the harps of God.

AND I SAW... These words signify that John witnesses something different from what he has just described in the preceding verse. Having witnessed the seven angels with the bowls of wrath in their hands, waiting for instructions to pour them out on this earth, he now witnesses another strange and wonderful sight.

SEA OF GLASS... We saw the term "sea of glass" when we were in chapter four. There it was before the throne. This as well seems to be a symbolic expression.

Some have taken the sea of glass in chapter four and this sea of glass as referring to the same thing, except noting that this one is referred to as being" *mingled with fire.*" We hesitate to conclude that they are both referring to the same place. It would appear that what John is here witnessing are events which are taking place on this earth, at the end of the tribulation. While what he witnessed in chapter four took place in heaven before the throne of God.

"The beautiful "sea of glass like unto crystal" in Revelation 4:6 is not really explained, but its purpose is at least partially clarified in its symbolic representation here. It has a memorial signification of great import to all the people of God through the ages, as seen in the next verse. It also speaks, through the mingled fire, of coming judgment." (Morris).

MINGLED WITH FIRE... The scene is at the end of the tribulation. The people seen by John are the ones who have been through, or died during, the tribulation at the hand of the beast. The reference to the "fire" speaks of those times of trouble through which they have come.

We should especially note that it does NOT say that what John is witnessing here is taking place in heaven before the throne of God. By the reference to the "sea of glass," many are prone to connect the two references, and the two locations. It is true that John had just witnessed seeing the angels in heaven with the seven last bowls of judgment in verse one; but this verse begins with a new vision; *And I saw...* It is evident from chapter twenty where we have reference to the same group, these are the tribulation saints and martyrs who have endured - and died - during the tribulation. They are called forth at the end of the tribulation and Armageddon.

AND THEM THAT HAD GOTTEN THE VICTORY OVER THE BEAST... What a tremendous testimony these shall have in that day! Against such tremendous pressures and such great persecution, there are those who refuse to give in to the demands of the beast, and thus doom their own soul. It is a decision of physical death and eternal life! Instead of temporary life and eternal death!

Like Moses of whom it was said: Hebrews 11:24, By faith Moses, when he was come to years, refused to be called the son of Pharaoh's daughter.

One of the key words in the above passage is *"for a season,"* That is the best this world can offer anyone. True, their pleasures which they offer may be filled with a lot of interesting and exciting things; but the end result is death - eternal death! And the best the world could ever offer is only temporary pleasures and enjoyment.

While suffering is not the most pleasant thought to have about life; nor would it be an easy decision to make, no doubt, but when one seriously considers the consequence of their decision, then it certainly makes more sense - eternally, at least - to choose pain and suffering, and even death if necessary, as opposed to eternal death. Now John said they had gotten the victory over the beast. He does not inform us how they were victors. If this is the same group we witness in chapter twenty, then it is through death. Even through death there is victory for those who live for God. The beast may not inform us how they were victors. If these are the same group we witness in chapter twenty, then it is through death. Even through death there is victory for those who live for God. The beast may consider it his victory each time one of these saints die at his command; but in reality, it will be deliverance for them from the beast and his tormenting ways, and ultimate victory at the Lord's return in glory!

It is probable to assume that there will be some who will remain alive at the end of the tribulation.

Let us recall the remnant of the woman in chapter twelve. There will probably be others as well who, because of the remote area in which they reside, that will be able to endure to the end of the tribulation and will be alive at the time of the Lord's return at Armageddon.

Remember the words of Paul when he was speaking about death; *For me to... die is gain.* (Philippians 1:21)

Like these saints, death can be victorious to those who are prepared for it! And we have just read in the preceding chapter; Blessed are the dead which die in the Lord from henceforth (v. 13), So there certainly is victory in death to the child of God!

OVER HIS IMAGE... HIS MARK... HIS NAME... The implication seems to be that any allegiance to the Beast and his system marks one. So, for one to claim the excuse in that day, "I took his mark, but I never did bow to his image," will not be justifiable. The stain of sin, though small, permeates the entire fabric of the human soul. Sin in any form contaminates the soul. With sin you can't just go part of the way and stand guiltless. *For whosoever shall ... offend in one point, he is guilty of all* (James 2:10).

HAVING THE HARPS OF GOD... A reference to the "*Trumpets*" of the angels, and this reference to the "*Harps*" of the saved, as well as in chapter five, are the only references to musical instruments (other than those mentioned in the city of Babylon in chapter eighteen) mentioned in the Revelation among the redeemed and inhabitants of eternity. Music will accompany the victors as they sing praises unto the Lord for bringing them home to victory!

<u>Verse 3:</u>

And they sing the song of Moses the servant of God, and the song of the Lamb, saying, Great and marvellous {are} thy works, Lord

God Almighty; just and true {are} thy ways, thou King of saints.

This gathered host, having come through the darkest period of time the world has ever witnessed, many of them have been slain for their testimony of faithfulness to God, stand now by this "*sea of glass*," singing their song of praise. There is some difficulty with respect to this "*sea of glass*" as to just what it has reference to. If it is to be taken symbolically, like so many other things in the Revelation, then what does it represent? If we say that it has reference to masses of people, then would we not have a double reference to the same people here? The sea of glass referring to the masses who have gotten victory over the beast, it is mingled with fire to show the tribulation aspect of it; plus, the reference to those singing by this sea - or, "on the sea", as in the King James. Although it would appear that the majority are of the opinion the word should be "BY" the sea, instead of standing "on" the sea.

The prophet Isaiah employed a metaphor with the sea and those who are wicked before God. He said the wicked were *like the troubled sea, when it cannot rest,* (57:20). If applied in this manner here in the Revelation it would be appropriate, for these have just come through a troubled time. The sea could speak of the boiling turbulent troubles which they have endured.

We also note in Revelation 21:1, that there will be no more sea when the new earth is brought through the fires of renovation which shall burn the present earth up (2Peter 3:10).

THEY SING THE SONG OF MOSES... We are not informed as to just what song this has reference to. Moses seemed to have sung a song in Exodus fifteen, at the deliverance through the Red Sea from the armies of Egypt. He sang a song in Deuteronomy thirty-two. The ninetieth Psalm which has also been attributed to Moses, could also be referred to as his song. The most appropriate song, and the one which would apply to what we have just said concerning the "sea" and what it refers to, seems to be the one in Exodus fifteen. It is a song of deliverance: *I will sing of the LORD, for He hath triumphed gloriously; the horse and his rider hath he thrown in the sea.*

This group, as well, stand by their "sea" of trouble and deliverance to sing praises and honor to the Lord.

Why the song of Moses? Why not a song of David? or, one of the many others who are found singing praises to the Lord in the Bible.

Moses seems the appropriate one for he was the one who delivered Israel from the iron furnace of Egypt; a time of terrible persecution during the time of Pharaoh. Their deliverance was found with angels accompanying them and assisting them in their deliverance, which will also be found - as we have seen - during the time of tribulation.

AND THE SONG OF THE LAMB... Some take the reference to Moses and the Lamb to be speaking of the fact that both Jew and Gentile will be saved during this time of tribulation. While this is no doubt true in respect to both classes of people being saved, at the same time consider that the song of Moses would identify the Jewishness of the singers (at least a group of them), and how appropriate that they are singing the song of the Lamb - Jesus Christ! How appropriate that Jews are singing praises to the Lamb - Jesus Christ!

SAYING, GREAT AND MARVELOUS... The expressions of praise which are here attributed to Jesus Christ are exciting to consider! The rest of this verse and the next ascribe expressions of praise as to who and what the Lord is. Mr Morris expressed it very well: "He is the "Lord God Almighty" (a term used five times in Revelation, and nowhere else). "Almighty" (Greek pantokrator) is a synonym for "omnipotent." He is also long-suffering, desiring men to come to repentance, but one day soon He will assume His great power and reign (Revelation 11: 17). He is Creator of all - therefore Sovereign of all!

"But also, He is "King of saints." This title is used in no other passage, and a few of the manuscripts render it "King of nations," others "King of ages." However, neither of these two titles appears anywhere else either, and the King James rendition, based on the Received Text, best fits the context.

As King of all the saints (a term applied in the New Testament uniquely to true believers in Christ), the Lord Jesus will soon lead them forth to battle (Revelation 19:7-16). At this juncture, He has not yet become King over all nations (note the next verse), but the saints all gladly acknowledge His role, knowing from full experience that He is both just and true."

These expressions directed to the Lord Jesus Christ, spoken of here as the "Lamb of God," are certainly descriptive of Who and what He is. How can anyone read this passage and then come away stating

Jesus Christ is a second person in a Trinitarian godhead! Although Mr. LaHaye is a Trinitarian in his belief on the godhead, he spells out in his comments on this passage that Jesus Christ is Almighty God. He, like others among the Trinitarian camp, speak of the Deity of Jesus Christ in one place, and then make Him a second person in another. But here Mr LaHaye stated: "The fact that they combine this song and the song of the Lamb can only be explained on the basis that Jesus Christ is Almighty God. The song of Moses and the Lamb in verses 3 and 4 clearly identify Jesus Christ with the attributes of God Himself. No man or created being has ever been addressed like this. Note the characteristics attributed to Him:

1. Creation - *Great and marvelous are thy works, Lord God Almighty.*

2. Justice - *Just and true are thy ways.*

3. Object of worship - *...thou King of saints. Who shall not fear thee, 0 Lord, and glorify thy name?*

4. Holiness - *For thou only art holy.*

5. Omnipotence and eternity - *...for all nations shall come and worship before thee;* for thy judgments are made manifest. This song is a prophetic fore glimpse of the true treatment of Jesus Christ at the end of the tribulation that will exist for the entire millennium and eternal order.

The most pitiful people in all the world are the religionists who, representing modernistic liberalism or the cults and isms, do not understand who Jesus Christ is. The book of Revelation certainly clarifies His identity, and, if for no other reason, it is worthy of our study because it does what its introduction predicted. Chapter 1, verse 1, announces "The Revelation of Jesus Christ." It is the only book in the world that truly presents Jesus Christ as He really is."

GREAT AND MARVELOUS ARE THY WORKS... God's Judgment upon sin and wickedness may not come when we think it should come, but when it does come it is final! The Lord who is *longsuffering to usward not willing that any should perish, but that all should come to repentance* (2Peter 3:9), waits on sinful man to tum from his wickedness. When man refuses to, there remains but one alternative - judgment!

Before these seven years are expired the greatest rebellion against

God and man will be put down, Satan will have been cast out of heaven - then bound in a bottomless pit. The most wicked man who ever lived, along with his cohort who is just as ruthless and without mercy, will have been taken and cast into the lake of fire. Sin which had raised its ugly head so high for so long, will bite the dust as the King comes bringing vengeance and victory with him. The works of the Lord are GREAT and MARVELOUS!

LORD GOD ALMIGHTY... This expression of praise is directed to the Lord of glory. Only one person could have such a statement made about him and to him - the Lord Jesus Christ! It would be folly to claim there were three persons to whom such an expression could be made. There is but ONE who is the Lord God Almighty!

<u>Verse 4:</u>

Who shall not fear thee, O Lord, and glorify thy name? for {thou} only {art} holy: for all nations shall come and worship before thee; for thy judgments are made manifest.

We note here the words of the prophet Jeremiah (10:7): *Who would not fear thee, O King of nations? for to thee doth it appertain: forasmuch as among all the wise {men} of the nations, and in all their kingdoms, {there is} none like unto thee.*

It is ironic that when the Beast is introduced to us in chapter thirteen, the people are heard proclaiming; *Who is like unto the beast? Who is able to make war with him?* (v. 4).

Who shall not fear thee...? Only the foolish would dare not fear the Lord God of heaven. Only the foolish will shut their eyes and ears to the Word of God and the warning found therein concerning the awesomeness of our God. The fear of the Lord is the beginning of wisdom, So, to not fear the Lord places one in the category which is directly opposite of wise!

Above all names is the name of Jesus! This name was received by inheritance (Hebrews 1:4). It is the name of the eternal God which has been made manifest in this dispensation (John 5:43). Throughout the Old Testament God was known by several names, from Elohim (Genesis 1:1), to Jehovah-Shammah (Ezekiel 48:35). But in these last days God has made Himself known through the name Jesus. To all those who have taken on that name in baptism - and thus become identified with Him through the baptismal rite - we have glorified that name. The time will come when every knee will bow to that name which is above all names (Philippians 2:9-11).

The Jewish nation, who through the years since Bethlehem, have refused to acknowledge that name as the name of their Messiah, will on that day bow in reverence and honor to that peerless name. The atheist who has denied the very existence of God, will bow in that day to that wonderful name.

The Trinitarian, who through the years, since 325 A.D., have relegated Jesus to a second-person status in a triune Godhead, will on that day acknowledge Him as Lord alone!

The so-called Jehovah's Witnesses, who through the years, since their founder Charles Taze Russell, founded this group about 1872, have relegated Jesus to the level of the archangel Michael, shall bow before Him as Lord in that day!

FOR THOU ONLY ART HOLY... Jesus told the rich young ruler, *There is none good but God* (Mark 10:18). Here, in essence, There is none holy but thee! If there were two other "persons" in the Godhead, they would not be considered holy, for only One is holy! He is the only one who can make such a claim to holiness. While we may use the expression "Holiness" in reference to our lifestyle, none can use this reference personally. If any are holy it is because of Him - not us! If we could be considered holy, it is not "our" holiness, it is His!

COME AND WORSHIP BEFORE THEE... It is not so now! It has not been so through the years.

But it will be so when that day comes to this planet when the King Himself reigns!

When He establishes His kingdom on this earth, and for one thousand wonderful years, reigns as King of kings, and Lord of lords, all nations will be expected to come and worship Him. Micah speaks of that time in a wonderful manner in chapter four. After the storm of Armageddon is past, life will continue on this earth. There will be, of course, one unique difference - Satan will be bound. But nations and countries will continue to exist, and industry and the other things which go into making a society exist, will continue. But there will be one central gathering place for all nations and people to worship God, and that will be before the King's throne in the country that is presently referred to as Israel.

People which for years learned of atheistic communism will then learn of Jesus Christ. People who had been under the influence of Rome and her false religious truth concerning Jesus Christ. For one thousand years people will be exposed to the truth in its purest form.

FOR THY JUDGMENTS ARE MADE MANIFEST... The words of J Vernon McGee are appropriate here: "Thy righteous acts comes from the lips of those who passed through the Great Tribulation. This testimony, coming from witnesses of this period, is inexpressibly impressive, and should settle in the minds of believers the fact that God is right in all that He does."

All that God does is right! Even that which appears to be so dark and gruesome, will be revealed as proper and deserved, when all things are weighed in the balances of eternity. GOD NEVER MAKES A MISTAKE!

"His judgments (that is, His "righteous deeds and righteous words) shall soon be universally acclaimed as such. Someday everyone will understand and acknowledge that even God's punishments are deserved and righteous in the fullest degree. The terrible plagues that are about to burst on the earth are incalculably destructive but arraigned for God's righteous purpose." (Morris)

<u>Verse 5:</u>

And after that I looked, and, behold, the temple of the tabernacle of the testimony in heaven was opened:

It would appear that the phrase *and after that...* signifies that John's eyes are moved from one scene to another. It would appear to us that his vision shifts from heaven (v. 1), to the earth and the end of the tribulation period (vs. 2-4), and now, back to heaven.

TEMPLE OF THE TABERNACLE... This is an interesting expression. We are familiar with both of them - but as a reference to two separate structures! The Tabernacle in the wilderness, erected during the wilderness journey of Israel, by Moses; then, many years later, the erection of the Temple of Solomon, during the reign of Solomon as king over Israel.

Vincent, the Greek scholar, states; 'The sanctuary at the Tabernacle."

The term "TABERNACLE," whether it be from the original Hebrew or Greek word, speaks to us of being a "Dwelling place." In both the Tabernacle in the wilderness and the Temple of Solomon, there was an inner sanctuary which housed the Ark of God. The Ark of God represented God's presence with the people of Israel. God told Moses that he would Meet with thee, *and I will commune with thee from above the mercy seat, from between the two cherubims which are upon the ark of the testimony* (Exodus 25:22). The Tabernacle and Temple became the "dwelling place" for the Ark of God. And, in essence, the "dwelling place of God." What John witnesses being opened in heaven is the "dwelling place" of God.

"Every time these words (words translated from the Hebrew and Greek to Temple and Tabernacle) are used they are to be taken in their plain and natural sense unless there is an explanation that they are used differently. What kind of temple would the heavenly one be if not a literal material one? If this be not the meaning of these passages, then upon what basis can there be any other meaning? These facts with those in chapter nine should prove conclusively that the temple and all things seen in be opened at different times and that beings will come out of it, shows that the temple is literal. The Greek word "ek" translated "Out" in Revelation 14:17,18; 15:6; 16:1-17), etc., denotes motion from the interior and means "Out from" as distinguished from "away from." Such could not be possible if there were no temple and if it were impossible to go into and out of it as with other buildings." (Dake)

Mr. Vine, in referring to the word "Testimony" states: "... the testimony is the witness to the rights of God, denied and refused on earth, but about to be vindicated by the exercise of the judgments under the pouring forth of the seven bowls or vials of Divine retribution. "

John makes reference to the term "temple" some sixteen times in the Revelation. So, from this we can see the significance of this term. This, however, is the only place in which it is referred to as "temple of the tabernacle."

Our comments on chapter eleven pointed out the importance the Ark of the Covenant had in the history of the people of Israel. We pointed out in our study there that, from what we glean from the scriptures relative to the time of the invasion by Babylonian forces, and Israel being carried away captive, while there is mention made of some of the vessels of the temple, there was no mention made of the Ark. An item as important to God and Israel as the Ark (at one time over fifty thousand were slain because they dared look into it!) would have surely been mentioned among the spoils of Nebuchadnezzar if he had stolen it out of the most holy place when he destroyed the temple. If not then, it would surely have been mentioned later when Belshazzar had his drunken feast and called for the vessels which had been taken from the temple to be brought out. As we mentioned in chapter eleven, it is our opinion that God took the Ark Himself to prevent the hands of the heathen from getting control of it.

The Ark was "threatened" by the first Gentile ruler of Daniel's day. When time began to click off regarding the four empires of the image of Nebuchadnezzar, he was the first ruler of the first empire.

Three more would follow him, the last one being headed by the man of sin, the beast of Revelation. If God took the Ark to keep it out of the hands of the first heathen ruler, it is interesting to notice that we have mention of it now - many centuries later - in connection with the anti-type of Nebuchadnezzar.

The Ark contained the law of God given to Israel from Sinai by His own hand, written on tables of stone by His own finger. This law was broken by Israel which resulted in them being taken into captivity to Babylon. Now, many years later, the anti-type of Nebuchadnezzar and Babylon, stand condemned before God as breaking His divine ordinances.

Verse 6:

And the seven angels came out of the temple, having the seven plagues, clothed in pure and white linen, and having their breasts girded with golden girdles.

There was mention made of seven angels in connection with the seven churches of Asia to whom John wrote his letters. Then there were the seven angels who had the seven trumpets to blast forth the judgments of God. Now, these seven angels line up as soldiers awaiting their orders to go forth from the very presence of God Himself to bring His judgments of wrath upon this earth.

SEVEN PLAGUES... We are told in verse one these are the "seven last plagues." We are getting close to the end of the tribulation period and close to the return of the Lord Jesus Christ to this earth.

Again, seven speaks to us of completeness, and how significant it is at this time. These plagues of judgment will bring to an end the tribulation.

OUT OF THE TEMPLE... They are coming from the presence of the Lord Himself. God is sending these angels forth on their mission of duty for Him. By the fact they are coming forth from the temple of God - the place of the Ark and Mercy seat - seems to be speaking to us that they are leaving mercy behind and coming to this earth bringing God's judgment of wrath upon an ungodly people. A people who have gone beyond mercy's limit.

CLOTHED IN PURE AND WHITE... The type of garment that John saw the Lord dressed in his vision of Him in chapter one, and Daniel's vision of Him (10:5-7). Pure and white speaks of the holiness and purity of Jesus Christ and His kingdom. The angels in their purity of dress are coming to a world that is dressed in "black," wicked, sinful, darkness.

HAVING THEIR BREASTS GIRDED WITH GOLDEN GIRDLES... The careful description given to these seven angels seem to add emphasis to their mission from God and His temple. No such minute description was given of the previous seven angels.

Again, the reference here speaks of the description which John gave of his vision of the Lord Jesus in chapter one.

If, as Mr Dake contends, these are redeemed saints that are called upon to administer the final judgments of God upon this earth, they are appropriately dressed. Who would be better qualified to dress in pure and white linen than those who have been redeemed. Who could better represent Jesus Christ in bringing His judgment upon this earth than those who have been redeemed by His blood! And also, the white Linen, John informs us in 19:8, is the righteousness of the saints.

Verse 7:

And one of the four beasts gave unto the seven angels seven golden vials full of the wrath of God, who liveth for ever and ever.

The last time we saw these four beasts was when the seals were being opened, and as they were opened one of the beasts would say:

Come and see... So, they are involved with the opening of the tribulation, and here they are involved with the closing of the tribulation.

The term "*golden vials*" is usually translated "*bowls*" by most other translations and commentators.

Whatever they may be, they are "*full of the wrath of God.*"

The "seals" introduced the man of sin and his moves in reaching for the top. They spoke of the troubles he would bring on the world to reach this position of power and control of the world. The "trumpets" involved atmospheric as well as demonic powers which were brought upon the world. The results being cataclysmic. The "bowls" will introduce judgments of wrath from God! What happens when these angels pour out their bowls directly from the hand of a God who is angry at a world that has gone mad? A world that has made man his god? A world that has ignored and spurned His calls of mercy?

Before the final bowl is poured out the entire world will be affected!

Men who have laughed at God will now stare into the face of His judgments. Men who have denied His existence will now feel the sting of His wrath. Sin, which for so long has been enjoyed by so many, will now become loathsome to those who feel the sting of God's wrath.

FULL OF THE WRATH OF GOD... The events which are about to happen upon this wicked world will be directly from God Himself. The angels who will pour out these "bowls" of wrath are coming from the temple in heaven. Up to this point in the tribulation men may have been able to explain, to the satisfaction of the populace, that what had taken place was due to atmospheric pressures, or due to some other phenomenon which they explain away. But when these judgments fall upon mankind it will not be such an easy thing to explain away.

The world has experienced to a degree the judgments of God's wrath upon them in past generations.

The two which stand out are the Antediluvian world, and Sodom. But they are not to be compared to that which is going to come upon the world during the next three and one-half years of tribulation!

WHO LIVETH FOR EVER AND EVER... The Beast, like many of his predecessors, has no doubt promised a rosy future to all who would follow him. Hitler promised his thousand-year Reich.

Other despotic rulers have made similar promises of a long and glorious future, just by following them.

Well, they all failed miserably in their attempt at a millennium. There is only One who will bring about that long-awaited millennium of peace and glory, the Lord Jesus Christ. He and His kingdom will not be a fly-by-night, temporary thing that will leave people shaking their heads in confusion. Only God can make such a promise of peace - and fulfill it. That is just exactly what He is going to do. But first, before this time of peace can come to this earth, there is one matter which must be taken care of - the Beast and his kingdom of wickedness; sin and its ugliness, all must bite the dust. Sin must be taught a lesson. It has raised its ugly head long enough. Now the sting of God's wrath will reach to the beast himself, as well as those who are a part of his company of wickedness.

Verse 8:

And the temple was filled with smoke from the glory of God, and from his power; and no man could enter the temple, till the seven plagues of the seven angels were fulfilled.

FILLED WITH SMOKE... There were two other times in which the glory of the Lord was so mightily present that man could not enter God's sanctuary 1). When the Ark and other furniture was placed in the Tabernacle. Exodus 40:34,35.2). When the Ark was brought into the Temple of Solomon, 1Kings 8:10,11. In those instances the glory of the Lord filled the place because the Ark was finding it's resting place. In those instances, the glory associated with the buildings have been referred to as the "Shekinah" of God.

Isaiah also witnessed "*the house was filled with smoke*" when he saw the glory of the Lord (6:3,4).

So, the Lord seems to be wrapped in a cloud of glory, which is manifested on occasions when His power is emphasized.

Smoke seems to be associated with judgment from God. We find it some ten times in the Revelation, and it is associated there with judgment; 8:4; 9:2,3,17,18; 14:11; 15:8; 18:9; 19:3.

Smoke from countless numbers of sacrifices during the Old Testament era ascended, billowing, as it were, up to God. The smoke of their sacrifices spoke of judgment upon the sin of the sinner, in whose stead the animals were sacrificed. The smoke now billows out from the temple, as judgment upon sin and sinners is meted out by a holy God.

NO MAN WAS ABLE TO ENTER INTO THE TEMPLE... This is an interesting statement!

Nothing has been said up to this point concerning man entering the temple. Is this an indication that men have been entering the temple. Is this an indication that men have been entering the temple in heaven up to this point? Is this an indication that these "angels" who are seen coming out with their seven bowls are men who have been glorified from this earth?

This statement as well reminds us of the Tabernacle in the wilderness when the cloud filled it. No one - not even Moses - was permitted entrance until the cloud was lifted. Then, later, when the Temple of Solomon was dedicated, and the Ark brought into the Holy of holies, the cloud filled the Temple, and no one was able to enter until the cloud lifted. In these two instances it seems that God was sanctioning the works of men and anointing with His Spirit those two dwelling places upon earth where He would dwell among His creation. Here, however, God is bringing judgment upon this earth. God, as it were, comes out of His Temple to bring judgment upon man for his wickedness. And for three and one-half years, the Temple will be shut up till this judgment of tribulation is over.

TILL THE SEVEN PLAGUES... WERE FULFILLED... It will take three and one-half years, approximately, to bring about the cleansing of sin from this earth. The bowls of God's judgments will rain down upon a sin-drenched world. During this time the Temple will be off-limits. While there is no mention of the time element involved with the glory filling the Tabernacle and the Temple, preventing the priests from entering, it would not appear that is was very long. At least, nothing like three and one- half years!

The seven plagues of God's judgment are the final judgments upon the beast and his empire of wickedness. When the last bowl is emptied upon the earth, the Lord Jesus will appear Himself, bringing with Him righteousness which shall at that time fill the earth.

It is for this time that the whole of creation anxiously waits: Romans 8:22,23: *For we know that the whole creation groaneth and travaileth in pain together until now. And not only they, but ourselves also, which have the firstfruits of the Spirit, even we ourselves groan within ourselves, waiting for the adoption, to wit, the redemption of our body.*

CHAPTER SIXTEEN

• The Bowls are poured out...

Jesus stated in Matthew 24:13; *But he that shall endure unto the end, (*of the tribulation*) the same shall be saved.* There will be those who will refuse the mark of the beast down to the very end of the tribulation. There will, no doubt, be many who will be alive at the end of the tribulation, and the coming of the Lord Jesus Christ in the clouds of glory and power.

This period our study is taking us into with the beginning of chapter sixteen seems to be emphasizing, not the mercies of God, but His wrath. There is no mention made in the following passages up to the Lord's return at Armageddon regarding mercy, or salvation, being extended to mankind, although there will be those during this period that will no doubt continue to reject the beast and his system and commit their life to be a testimony to the Lord. But the attention we have in the record of John is concerning the wrath of God being poured out upon the wicked upon this earth. It is certainly a very dark period for those dwelling on planet earth.

Verse 1:

And I heard a great voice out of the temple saying to the seven angels, Go your ways, and pour out the vials of the wrath of God upon the earth.

Man's day has run its course. The cup of sin is now filled to the brim, and overflowing. So is the bowls of God's judgment for sin and sinner alike! The great voice out of the temple, must be the voice of the Lord Jesus Christ Himself. For six thousand years, He has permitted man to do his own thing. HE HAS PERMITTED Satan to do his thing upon this earth, in his attempts to bring about the fall of man - God's creation. Man has reached the lowest gutter in his refusal to obey God and his willingness to listen to Satan and his plans of evil. Now, the master plan of Satan, and the master of Satan's final thrust during this time, the man of sin, will meet their

doom.

- • The voice of justness cries out against the injustice of man and his system.

- The voice of holiness cries out against the ungodliness of man's system.

- The voice of Godliness cries out against all that is ungodly in this world and among mankind.

- The voice of righteousness cries out against all that is not right among the plans and actions of mankind.

- The voice of vengeance cries out in vengeance for all those who have lived for Him through the ages, whose righteousness will be vindicated by the judgments of God upon that system which persecuted and killed the righteous through the years.

So, the seven angels are given their "marching orders" from the Commander in Chief Himself, to go forth with their bowls of judgment which they are to pour out upon this world of sin and corruption.

That which they are to pour out upon this world is in direct contrast to the promise of another "pouring out" He spoke of in Joel 2:28, *I will pour out my Spirit upon all flesh* ... The mission of these angels is to pour out the vials of the wrath of God upon the earth. It is not His Spirit of love and salvation which is now being poured out, but His wrath upon sin and the sinner.

These bowls of wrath are poured out upon the beast and his empire of wickedness. It does not appear that the bowls of wrath affect any primarily but those who are part of the beast and his kingdom. What took place with the opening of the seals, and the sounding forth of the trumpet's, that everyone in their judgment could have been affected. The water being turned to blood, for instance, would evidently affect everyone in that area. The sea being affected with wormwood would likewise affect everyone in that sea. But these bowls of judgment seem to be directed toward the beast and his kingdom only.

Verse 2:

And the first went, and poured out his vial upon the earth; and there fell a noisome and grievous sore upon the men which has the mark of the beast, and upon them which worshipped his image.

This seems to be a repetition of the plague which fell upon Egypt during the days of Moses. Dr Wilbur Smith points out that the same word found here in reference to these "*grievous sores*," is the same word used by the Old Testament translators of the Greek Septuagint for boils when referring to the story of the Egyptian plague of boils. Most all agree that what took place in Egypt during the days of Moses was literal, and not something symbolic. Yet, there are those who would make these judgments in Revelation symbolic in meaning. If the "boils" of Exodus and among the Egyptians were literal, then it would appear that these "sores" which fall upon the beast and his followers are as well literal.

Poured out his vial upon the earth... There is no definite reference in the Revelation passages relative to these bowls of judgment as to their geographical coverage. Some have assumed that they cover the entire earth. (Which may be what takes place!) Others assume that they cover only the area of the beast's kingdom. As he does not control the entire earth - that is every nation - then the judgment would not affect every people on the earth.

There fell a noisome and grievous sore... Dake has an interesting comment on this statement; 'The word "fell" refers to anything suddenly falling and shows that the plague is a sudden one causing men, before they can hardly realize it, to break out with sores and ulcers. The words "noisome" and "grievous" are from two Greek words meaning "depraved, bad in nature" and "full of labours and pain in working mischief' and are used here to show that the ulcers will be very painful and corrupt."

There is no record as to how these sores are produced, other than as the result of what the first angel pours out from his bowl of wrath. Mr Morris suggests that it is possible the sores are a result of them being made susceptible because of having been marked by the system of the beast, thus causing their skin to not only be marked, like a tattoo, but also the system which produced the tattoo could also cause something to enter the bloodstream making them susceptible to some agent which produced a quick reaction resulting in the boils.

While the suppositions may abound as to just what causes the boils, it remains that it is a direct result of the wrath of God being poured out from the first bowl of judgment by the angel.

Upon the men which had the mark of the beast... This statement emphasizes as well that it would appear that only those who are followers of the beast and his system will be affected. Like the "locusts" from the abyss who sought out only those who did not have the seal of God upon their foreheads (9:4), this judgment falls only on those who have the mark of the beast upon them! Again, we are not informed as to how the distinction is made. If the angel is pouring out something which rains down on the earth, like dust - or rain - how can it be that only certain ones are affected? While we may not know for sure the answer, God knows those who are His own, and He is able to direct judgment against those who are not!

By the fact this judgment falls upon those who have received his mark also helps to identify the time period involved in these bowls of judgment. Again, some have sought to make the judgments; "seals," "trumpets," and now these "bowls," as all happening simultaneously. It appears, from other passages, that the mark is not issued until the middle of the week. That seems evident from chapter thirteen. So, the bowls could not be poured out until after the mark has been issued in order for this statement to apply. From this it appears that the bowls of wrath are poured out during the last half of the week.

And upon them which worshipped his image... Mr Dake seemed to think this statement should read; "Those worshipping his image." That is, while many are in the act of worshipping the image erected to the beast, "this judgment falls upon them and the sores begin to appear, filling them with pain."

What a thought! If this would happen as he suggests, what a terrible reaction will come from those who are bowing before this image to suddenly be covered with boils and filled with pain!

By the fact this judgment is poured out upon those who are worshipping the image also indicates that it is during the last half of the week, as the image is not erected until chapter thirteen - or the middle of the week.

Verse 3:

And the second angel poured out his vial upon the sea; and it became as the blood of a dead man: and every living soul died in the sea.

Again, we are reminded of what happened under one of the trumpet judgments. The only difference is that the trumpet judgment resulted in a third of the sea becoming blood (8:8). This was the result of some meteor-like mountain being hurled into the sea. There is no mention of a mountain - nor anything else - being hurled into the sea here. Just that the angel poured out his vial upon the sea.

It is not clear that we should think that this judgment affects all the "Seas," and oceans of the world.

It is possible that what is in reference here is the Mediterranean Sea. The sea used in scriptural prophecy usually has reference to the Mediterranean Sea.

"It should be remembered that, chemically speaking, the composition of sea water is almost identical to that of blood, so that only a relatively small modification would be necessary ... In no way could sea water substitute for the blood of the living flesh, but in this case the waters of the sea become as the blood of a dead man. It is merely a chemical solution, water containing iron and other chemicals which give it a blood-red appearance, but there is no longer life therein. In fact, it brings death to every living creature in the sea." (Morris)

Whether this death is brought just to the Mediterranean Sea or to all the large bodies of water on the earth, the result for the immediate areas will be catastrophic! Imagine the teeming millions of sea life that will die and float to the top of the water, much of it washed to shore, the dead remains putrefying and spreading stench and disease to the surrounding areas. The results are unimaginable!

We know that on the new earth which will be brought into being after this earth is cleansed by fire (2Peter 3: 10-13), there will not be any seas. Some feel this could be the beginning of that transition.

Remember when the trumpet judgments were being brought upon this earth a third of the sea was turned to blood because of that judgment (8:8). Again, the reference is made to the sea, which would seem to have more of a reference to the Mediterranean Sea. This

being the Sea in prophecy. This judgment, however, brings death to ALL the Sea!

Verse 4:

And the third angel poured out his vial upon the rivers and fountains of waters; and they became blood.

Man can live much longer without food than he can without water. As man is made up largely of liquids, he must have liquid to sustain his life. Without fluids, the body will begin to dehydrate quickly.

With the sea turned to blood, God now turns the rivers, which flow into the sea, and the fountains into blood. Man is without water!

If, as we suggested, the two witnesses are witnessing during the last half of the week, one of the things they had power to do was to cause it not to rain during their ministry. If it has not rained for some time when this bowl of judgment is poured out, the lakes and ponds have either begun to dry up or are already dried up. The rivers are drying up as well. Now what water is left in the lakes and rivers turns to blood.

Now whether this is actual blood or a chemical reaction which causes the water to appear blood red, it really does not matter, the end result is the same - man is unable to drink the water!

The first judgment brought boils to those in the kingdom of the beast, which would result in fever, which would in turn cause them to become extremely thirsty. The stench of dying carcass's from the sea fills the air around the shorelines of the sea. Disease spreads inland. Now, with feverish brews, they seek the thing a feverish person would want above all else - water - only to find blood instead!

Verse 5:

And I heard the angel of the waters say, Thou art righteous, 0 Lord, which art, and wast, and shalt be, because thou hast judged thus.

In chapter seven, verse one, we saw the four angels which controlled the winds which blow upon the earth. Here we witness the angel of the waters. In this we see that angels are appointed to positions of authority and responsibility. This angel has authority over the rivers and water ways of the earth.

Someone called him the Superintendent of the water department here on earth.

While the judgment of God in turning the waters into blood might seem very harsh to those living on the earth at this time, the angel cries out that such a judgment from God is "righteous."

Swallowing up an entire population in a great deluge; raining fire and brimstone upon entire cities, destroying all living there, all may seem like something which is foreign to God, whom we identify as being a God of mercy and love; But the judgments of God are not without righteousness. Witnessing this action on Good's part, the angel of the waters praises God for the actions taken. Every one of us should seriously consider what is taking place here. God is righteous. God will judge righteously. Sin and sinners will be judged by a righteous God. God is not playing games here! Sin and ungodliness is not a game with God!

Verse 6:

For they have shed the blood of saints and prophets, and thou hast given them blood to drink; for they are worthy.

This statement seems to answer the questions which could have been posed till this point in regards to the awful dark days of tribulation. There is a reason for these judgments falling upon mankind. They are reaping what they have sown. God's law of reaping what you sow is being carried out here.

These are they who have persecuted so severely those who refused to accept the mark and their system. Many of them were killed because of their refusal to go along with the system of the beast. They probably made great boasts about killing the rebels against their system, using their deaths as a threat to others. Now they are being judged for their actions, and the judgment is just as severe as that which they meted out.

They shed the blood of the saints, now they are given blood to drink. The angel states that such a judgment is righteous.

You recall what happens when the two witnesses are killed by the forces of the beast; there is rejoicing in the world of the beast. They throw a big party. While the majority were not actually involved in the death of these two men; and were probably not personally involved in the death of the thousands of others, but they were guilty by being a part of the system.

The history of the church is filled with references to those who were bitterly persecuted - some even unto death - down through the years.

But no period of history can compare with the awful atrocities which are perpetrated against the saints during this period, as the beast issued his edict to destroy anyone who stands in his way of dominion.

Verse 7

And I heard another out of the altar say, Even so, Lord God Almighty, true and righteous are thy judgments.

Remember the souls under the altar (6:9). We note here that it does not identify the origin of this voice. It does not say, Another angel, although all of the angels in heaven without doubt echo this type of response to what is taking place in this judgment from God.

We are told that the words *another out of* should be omitted from this verse. That the statement should read; *And I heard the altar...* We know, of course, that an altar per se cannot speak, but metaphorically the altar cries out as well that the judgments of God are righteous and true. The Altar reminds us of those who were seen under it in chapter six. Many have died on the "altar" of sacrifice rather than surrender their devotion to the beast and his system of evil. Now their testimony of dedication cries out, as the blood of Abel cried out from the ground.

"The appropriate name they ascribe to the great Judge is "Lord God Almighty, " the same as in the great song at the glassy sea (15:3) and in the song of the cherubim (4:8). Seven times in Revelation is Jesus called both "Lord" and "Almighty. " In the first (1:8), He introduces Himself as "the Lord, which is, and which was, and which is to come, the Almighty. " In all the others (4:8; 11 :17; 15:3; 16:7; 19:6; 21:22), He is simply addressed in praise as "Lord God Almighty, " or "Lord God Omnipotent" (same Greek word). Because of who He is, His judgments and ways are what they are - true and righteous altogether Psalm 19:9)." (Morris)

The saints have suffered terribly during this period of persecution by the beast. Now, however, their suffering is over with. They enter a place where there will be no more suffering, but eternal joys instead. On the contrast, however, those who have meted out the persecution are now suffering for what they have sown to others. But their suffering will never cease! When their life is finished on this earth they will then be ushered before the Judge, Then His judgment will continue for them eternally!

Verse 8

And the fourth angel poured out his vial upon the sun; and power was given unto him to scorch men with fire.

When the fourth judgment fell upon the world a third of the sun was smitten that it should not shine for one third part of the day. Here, the fourth bowl of wrath poured out results in the sun becoming so hot as to scorch men because of the tremendous increase in heat from the sun. Up till now the other bowls have been directed to this earth and those living on it. Now God directs His wrath to include the sun as well. While the sun is not part of the earth, it is part of the planetary system of which the earth is a part.

Again, we are not informed as to how the sun becomes hotter. The other judgments are not explained in detail; neither is this one. It would be left to our imagination and speculation as to how this could happen.

Today when the temperature rises to 90 or 100 degrees Fahrenheit, we hear a lot of complaining about the heat. One hundred degrees is nothing compared to what it will be when the fourth angel pours out his bowl of wrath upon the sun.

Note that the verse states that this angel is given the power to "scorch men with fire." It would appear from this statement that more is involved here with this judgment than just the temperature rising several degrees!

There has been much talk and warning from the scientific world concerning the Ozone layer which surrounds the earth, and which protects us from the radiation which comes from the sun. We are being told that the Ozone layer is thinning in some areas, which in turn results in radiation leaking through.

Some have suggested that this is one reason for the increase in skin cancers, and other maladies of the skin.

We have been introduced to an angel of the winds; an angel of the waters, and now we are introduced to an angel of the sun.

The prophets spoke in the Old Testament concerning the judgment God would bring upon the world through the sun. Note some of them:

Malachi 4:1 ,2, *For, behold, the day cometh, that shall burn like an oven, and all the proud, yea, and all that do wickedly, shall be stubble; and the day that cometh shall burn them up, saith the Lord of Hosts, that it shall leave them neither root nor branch. But unto you that fear my name shall the Sun of righteousness arise with healing in His wings; and ye shall go forth, and grow up like calves of the stall.*

Isaiah 24:6, *Therefore hath the curse devoured the earth, and they that dwell therein are desolate: therefore the inhabitants of the earth are burned, and few men left.*

As if preparation for the time when these evil men will be cast into the lake of fire, God causes the sun to scorch them till they cry out in pain and agony for the terrible judgment falling upon them.

The intensity of the judgments seems to increase with each succeeding angel who steps forward from the temple with his bowl of wrath to be poured out upon the beast and those in his kingdom. It would appear that those who do not have the mark of the beast, like was noted in verse two, will be exempt from this judgment as well somehow.

Mr. Morris made an interesting observation regarding this verse: "However, the intense heat of the sun will also produce another effect which will, at least for a time, somewhat compensate for oceanic evaporation. That is, the great ice sheets on Greenland and the continent of Antarctica will melt. There is enough ice stored in these great reservoirs, it is estimated, to raise the world's sea levels about 200 feet if it were all melted.

"Such melting is imminent even under present environmental conditions, as the global greenhouse is being augmented by the burning of fossil fuels. It is probable that the ice sheets would melt before the sea level could be lowered much by evaporation. Thus, the most immediate hydrologic effect of this fourth bowl of wrath would likely be a rapid rise of sea level, to be followed later by the great drop in level already suggested.

"This phenomenon may be intimated in certain scriptures. He casteth forth his ice like morsels ... He sendeth out his word, and melteth them ... (Psalm 147:17,18). Hast thou entered into the treasures of the snow? or hast thou seen the treasures of the hail. which I have reserved against the time of trouble, against the day of battle and war? (Job 38:22,23). The word "treasures" in the latter passage could as well be translated "storehouses," so the verse refers to great storage reservoirs of snow and hail which have been reserved for the "time of trouble " (the period of tribulation?)."

If we consider the scenario to this point it is not very nice to look at! Men have been stricken with sores over their body. The adjoining sea has turned to blood, resulting in everything in it dying, rising to the top and floating to shore, bloated, decaying, stinking! Then, with feverish brews they find out that their water supplies have also been turned into blood. There is no water to drink! Now the sun beams down with intensity until it scorches their skin!

It would appear that even nature itself is turned against these who are going around with the mark of the beast on their person. But, when the sun scorches them, there is no speculation as to what has caused this to occur. It would appear that men now realize and acknowledge that it is the judgment of God which has fallen upon them, for we note the next verse;

<u>Verse 9:</u>

And men were scorched with great heat, and blasphemed the name of God, which hath power over these plagues and they repented not to give Him glory.

When Moses brought the judgments of plagues upon Pharaoh and Egypt, Pharaoh's magicians at first performed the same things. Then there came a time when they were unable to produce similar results. It was then they acknowledged that it was a greater power than their own. Instead of these judgments turning the heart of Pharaoh and Egypt to Jehovah God, they hardened their hearts, and refused to yield to the demands of Moses. Thus, they were faced with such excruciating pain; such horrifying judgments; such evident judgments from GOD, that you would think they would turn to God with a plea for mercy and humble themselves in repentance before God. God listened to the cries of repentance which came from Nineveh, would He not listen to the cries of repentance from people of another generation and time? But instead there is open rebellion against God. Men do not repent. What has driven men to this degree of depravity? We are once again reminded of the words of Paul; *Because they received not the love a of the truth, that they might be saved. And for this cause God shall send them strong delusion, that they should believe a lie (the lie!) that they all might be damned who believed nor the truth.*

It is of interest to note that the record states that they blaspheme the name of God. They have heard His Name mentioned many times, without doubt, as the two witnesses have declared His name to them.

The 144,000 are bearing His name in their foreheads. Those who have rejected the mark of the beast, by their rejection, if not audibly, have declared the name of the Lord. Men today are guilty of rejecting that lovely name as well. The vast majority of religions in the world deny their converts the privilege of bearing the Name of Jesus Christ through the act of baptism by employing the paganistic, Romish, term of the trinity when baptizing them.

- Why is it that men will reject the very thing which will help them?

Verse 10:

And the fifth angel poured out his vial upon the seat of the beast; and his kingdom was full of darkness; and they gnawed their tongues for pain.

There is no indication as to how long any of these plagues last once they are poured out. Any suggestion of time would be purely speculative. But whether it is one day - one week - one year, or for the rest of the tribulation, it will be a horrible time regardless!

There are differing views as to just where the throne of the beast will be situated. There is one group which contend that Babylon will be rebuilt (in fact, they inform us that it is being rebuilt right now with the plans in mind of restoring it to its original condition as it was in the days of Nebuchadnezzar!), and it will become a major city during the time of the tribulation. Whether this is the case or not remains to be found out when that day arrives.

By the reference to the "seat (throne) of the beast" we have confirmed for us that the beast is a man. That there will arise a man of great power and influence who will fill the role outlined here in REVELATION. While the power which will arise will be a political governing force, there will also be a man at the head of it. A man whom Paul refers to as "the man of sin."

We are reminded of the wisdom and power of God in this verse as we have in previous verses. How is it that only the kingdom of the beast is filled with this horrible darkness while the rest of the world is not affected? The same way that God separated the judgments in the days of Pharaoh when Israel was exempted from the plagues, while the land of Egypt was covered by them!

Having only the kingdom of the beast filled with this horrible darkness, which is so thick that men gnaw their tongues for pain, will add emphasis to the fact that this judgment is from God! He who said, Let there be light, and there was light; Is the One who controls that which he created. If He decrees that this light shall only shine where He wants it to shine, that is just exactly what will happen!

The same kind of judgment fell upon Egypt when the ninth plague was brought upon the land. We read in Exodus 10:23; They saw not one another, neither rose any from his place for three days: but all the children of Israel had light in their dwellings.

God pulls the shades down over the kingdom of the beast as if to say, I shut you out from among the living! You deserve only darkness, because your heart and life is darkened with evil and wickedness.

This is a miraculous mystery! How is it that the sun not only quits shining, but there is darkness which drops over the kingdom of the beast that is so thick that people gnaw their tongue for the pain.

Again, we emphasize that this judgment is evidently to the beast and his kingdom only. The rest of the world does not seem to be affected by this judgment.

While the beast has made his boast of being god, and demanded that people worship him as such, the darkness which envelopes his kingdom seems to be saying that he is of the dark one - Satan. God is the One who dwells in the light which no man can approach unto, (1Timothy 6:16). The beast is of the wicked one, and the darkness which covers his kingdom identifies him with the kingdom of darkness.

Again, we have the prophets speaking of this day, referring to darkness in their prophecies: Joel 2:1,2,31: *Blow ye the trumpet in Zion, and sound an alarm in my holy mountain: let all the inhabitants of the land tremble: for the day of the LORD cometh, for it is nigh at hand: a day of darkness and of gloominess, a day of clouds and of thick darkness, as the morning spread upon the mountains: a great people and a strong; there hath not been ever the like, neither shall be any more after it, even to the years of many generations. The sun shall be turned into darkness, and the moon into blood, before the great and terrible day of the LORD come.*

Amos 5:18, *Woe unto you that desire the day of the LORD! to what end is it to you? The day of the LORD is darkness, and not light.*

The pain which the people are filled with which results in their gnawing on their tongue could be a mental pain as well as a physical pain. Having these judgments fall upon them from God - and it would appear they now realize that it is God who is bringing these things upon them - would cause one to be filled with tormenting fear and pain.

Verse 11:

And blasphemed the God of heaven because of their pains and their sores, and repented not of their deeds.

Men readily acknowledges that it is "God in heaven" who is bringing these judgments upon them.

While blaspheming God, they acknowledge that He is *"the God of heaven."* They have been guilty of worshipping the "god of this world," but now they acknowledge that the High and exalted One is the God of heaven.

It seems so unreal that men, enduring such tormenting pain and suffering would, instead of calling upon God for mercy, blaspheme Him! Is it because they know there is no hope for them now, with the mark stamped upon them which identifies them with the beast and his system?

One dogma of the church of Rome is that sinners will go to a purgatory, where there they will do penance and be purged from their sins. Some also feel that after men have been in hell for a while they will turn their heart to God in repentance. Here men are feeling the pains of "hell" upon this earth, and there is no indication that they are thinking anything about repenting of their sinful past! While God is rich in mercy (Ephesians 2:4), at the same time these are those who have trampled His mercies under their feet. These are those who have refused the message from the angel; from the two

Witnesses: from the 144,000, and from whoever else is on the Lord's side at this time!

Verse 12:

And the sixth angel poured out his vial upon the great river Euphrates; and the water thereof was dried up, that the way of the kings of the east might be prepared.

Some five times we find the term "the great river Euphrates" employed in the Bible. This verse is one of those places. This emphasizes the importance of this river to this area. In ancient Bible times the two rivers which held great influence in the affairs of kingdoms of men was the Nile River and the Euphrates River. Ancient Babylon was built on the Euphrates River. In fact, the River ran through the city.

Like some of the other judgments we have studied about in the tribulation, this could be brought about through the efforts of mankind. We do know that Turkey has finished another dam project upon the Euphrates River which could, in effect, stop the flow of the river. This is not the only dam along the 1800 miles long River, but this one is close to its source and could conceivably have the greatest effect on the flow of the River.

The Euphrates River is the natural eastern boundary of the territory which God gave to Abraham's seed. They have never possessed territory which extended this far east before, but this is the eastern boundary of their promise land. The river was also the eastern boundary of the Babylonian Empire. So, the river has played, and will play, an important role in the affairs of man.

As to what this vial of judgment is which will result in the Euphrates being dried up, we are not informed. One thing to consider is the fact that high up in the area of Ararat is Mount Ararat, and the source of the river Euphrates. This huge mountain is capped with an ice cap. These high mountainous areas which are covered with snow and ice provide most the water for the Euphrates River. If it has not rained now for some time, at the command of the two witnesses; and considering that the fourth vial caused the sun to get so hot that it scorched men, then we could conclude that the Euphrates has probably already been greatly reduced in volume. If this vial of judgment caused something to happen to the Mount Ararat region, such as an earthquake, this could result in the river's source being shut off.

There is an interesting prophecy in Isaiah 11:15,16 which seems to allude to this judgment; *And the LORD shall utterly destroy the tongue of the Egyptian sea; and with His mighty wind shall He shake His hand over the river, and shall smite it in the seven streams, and make men go over dryshod. And there shall be a highway for the remnant of his people, which shall be left, from Assyria.*

Now as to who these kings of the east are we are not informed. We do know that there is a great host of people who live east of the Euphrates. We have but to consider the great hosts in China, India, Japan, and other oriental countries east of this river to realize that there is a vast horde of people east of the Euphrates. And at the same time, we are reminded of the warlike nature of these people. In our own generation's time, we have witnessed the destruction of millions among the Chinese and among the people in Vietnam and Cambodia. Something happens which prompts this vast host of people to invade the middle east.

Looking at the drying up of the Euphrates for a military invasion purpose is somewhat puzzling.

Crossing a river like the Euphrates presents no problem to an invading army. Rivers like this have been crossed many times in time of warfare. So, drying up the river for these forces to cross leaves us a little confused. So, we would think that there is more involved here than just drying up a river so an invading army can cross it to do battle.

Verse 13:

And I saw three unclean spirits like frogs come out of the mouth of the dragon, and out of the mouth of the beast, and out of the mouth of the false prophet.

An unholy alliance, in an unholy conference, come to an unholy conclusion. John seems to be witnessing a meeting of the heads of the empire of evil during the tribulation. The real boss of this system is present. One more decision is made by this unholy trinity. That decision will result in earth-shaking results.

Morris wrote: "With one voice they speak, and all the principalities and powers of darkness spread out from the darkness at Babylon into the nations of the world. As when darkness settles on a quagmire, and suddenly the clamorous croaking of frogs pierces the night air in every direction, so these three evil spirits. ...like frogs - go forth to lead an innumerable multitude of lesser spirits out into all the world, rasping out their guttural messages in the world's dark night. These "seducing spirits," with their "doctrines of devils" (1Timothy 4:1), spread lies and deceptions, as they have for millennia, one more time. And the kings of the earth, already irrational with their drug-distorted perceptions and with the pain of God's plagues, listen to their deceptions one more time."

The vision of this trinity of Satan emphasizes to us that the man of sin along with his cohort, the false prophet, are obviously tools in the hand of Satan. It is, it would seem, not a matter of deception by Satan, as is the case in many instances, but it seems to be a matter of an unholy union by the man of sin and his cohort with Satan in order to gain power and position. It has been said that men would sell their soul to the Devil for power and position, and this seems to be a good example of just that!

Verse 14:

For they are the spirits of devils, working miracles, which go forth unto the kings of the earth and of the whole world, to gather them to the battle of that great day of God Almighty.

The world, at this time, is on a course which will lead to utter destruction. There is no turning back!

The leaders of the nations of the world, here referred to as the kings of the earth and of the whole world, are in the unenviable position of being persuaded and motivated by forces of darkness.

Jesus, in speaking of the last day events, spoke of how false Christ's and false prophets shall rise, and shall show signs and wonders, to seduce, if it were possible, even the elect (Mark 13:22).

We don't fully understand just what is meant by these evil spirits working miracles, unless it is accomplished somehow through some influential parties in the governments of the world, which in turn causes the leaders; presidents, premiers, kings, etc., to order their armies into action to the Middle East.

Joel writes: *Prepare war, wake up the mighty men, let all the men of war draw near; let them come up: Beat your plowshares into spears:*

let the weak say, I am strong. Assemble yourselves, and come, all ye heathen, and gather yourselves together round about: thither cause thy mighty ones to come down, 0 LORD. Let the heathen be wakened, and come up to the valley of Jehoshaphat: for there will I sit to judge all the heathen round about. (3:9-12)

It is interesting to note that this verse states it is the *"battle of that great day of God Almighty."* If the kings of the earth were asked what they were going to battle for they would probably respond that it was their idea and that they were going to war to defend their country, and to bring an end to the usurpation of the beast and his empire of evil.

The sight must be awesome! To witness the vast hordes of armed personnel making their way to the Middle East. Coming from all directions, heading for a final showdown in the plains of Esdraeleon.

There has never been such a gathering of forces in the long history of warfare!

Verse 15:

Behold, I come as a thief. Blessed is he that watcheth, and keepeth his garments, lest he walk naked, and they see his shame.

This verse seems like a pause in the exciting actions which are taking place. Verse sixteen obviously continues the story of the events which are taking place. This verse seems to be just dropped in here between the record of actions which are taking place.

It seems obvious that this statement would not be directed to those who are headed for the battlefield. There is no stopping them, they

are being influenced by demonic spirits to go to their doom on the battlefield.

This verse seems to emphasize to us that even in this darkest hour of the tribulation there are still those who are remaining true to their convictions and resisting the pressures exerted against them by the beats to join his system.

While the armies of the world hasten to the battle site, bent on bringing down their enemy; complementing themselves that they will enjoy victory on the battlefield, little do they realize what is awaiting them.

The Israelites, gathered for their first Passover observance in Egypt, were warned to eat the Passover meal with their shoes on their feet and their staff in their hand, prepared to leave without delay as soon as the command was given. These weary pilgrims, who have endured the hardships of the tribulation, are encouraged to remain alert, for at any time now the Lord will appear and deliverance will come.

Verse 16:

And he gathered them together into a place called in the Hebrew tongue Armageddon.

Somehow, we do not fully understand just how, these armies have been convinced by these demonic spirits which have come forth from the Satanic trinity, to gather here to fight against Christ Himself. Have they been convinced that the real enemy standing between them and ultimate world dominion and world control, is Christ?

John states in 19:19, where we have the actual battle taking place; *And I saw the beast, and the kings of the earth, and their armies, gathered together to make war against him that sat on the horse, and against his army.* What fools are mortals!

Armageddon is taken from "Har-megiddo," or the "Mountain of Megiddo." Megiddo is a town that is located some sixty miles north of Jerusalem. The town overlooks the plain of Megiddo and the plain of Esdraeleon. It is called the valley of Jezreel as well. Through the years many battles have been fought on this site. And the final one will be fought here as well. The vast host which will gather here will fill this valley. It has been stated that Napoleon said of this place: "This is the ideal battleground for all the armies of the world."

M R Vincent stated in his Word Studies in the New Testament: "Megiddo was in the plain of Esdraeleon, which has been a chosen place for encampment in every contest carried on in Palestine from the days of Nabuchodonozor, king of Assyria, unto the disastrous march of Napoleon Bonaparte from Egypt into Syria, Jews, Gentiles, Saracens, Christian crusaders, and anti-Christian Frenchmen; Egyptians, Persian, Druses, Turks and Arabs, warriors of every nation that is under heaven have pitched their tents on the plain of Esdraeleon, and have beheld the banners of their nation wet with the dews of Tabor and Hermon."

Larkin had an interesting statement to make about the gathering of these forces for this battle: "The power of a delusive and enthusiastic sentiment, however engendered, to lead to destruction great hosts of men is seen in the Crusades to recover the Holy Sepulchre at Jerusalem. If a religious fanaticism could, at nine different times, cause hundreds of thousands of religious devotees to undergo unspeakable hardships for religious purpose, what will not the miracle working wonders of the "froglike demons" of the last days of this Dispensation not be able to do in arousing whole nations, and creating vast armies to march in all directions from all countries, headed by their kings, for the purpose of preventing an establishment of the Kingdom of the King of kings in His own land of Palestine!"

Verse 17:

And the seventh angel poured out his vial into the air; and there came a great voice out of the temple of heaven, from the throne, saying, It is done.

The previous bowls of judgment had been poured out upon the land, upon the sea, on the various waterways, and as well on the sun, and the kingdom of the beast, and the last one on the river Euphrates. Now this one is poured out into the atmosphere, which will result in affecting the entire planet.

IT IS DONE! This statement coming from the temple in heaven, reminds us of the voice from the cross which said, **IT IS FINISHED.** The voice form Calvary spoke of the redemption and the fact that the Lord's death on Calvary brought about the payment for redemption for all mankind. This statement signifies the end to

the long and troublous times of the Gentiles. An end to the long reign of Satan and sin and terror over this earth. This is the final showdown, and the victor will be the Lord Jesus Christ and all those who have joined forces with Him.

This statement will be made yet one more time. We find it in 21:6. It will be spoken then after the millennium, and the final White Throne judgment, and just as John begins to describe for us the New heavens and new earth. The ultimate final act of God will result in making all things new and bringing His creation into a new creation *wherein dwelleth righteousness* (2Peter 3:13).

Verse 18:

And there were voices, and thunders, and lightnings; and there was a great earthquake, such as was not since men were upon the earth, so mighty an earthquake, and so great.

John has recorded a similar statement before three times; 4:5; 8:5; 11:19. Just before the seals were opened; just before the trumpets sound forth their judgments, and just before the bowls of wrath are poured out. The first time there is no mention made of an earthquake, but the other two times there is mention of an earthquake. But none seem to compare with this one. The last two, along with this one, seem to emphasize the judgments of God upon an ungodly world.

While the two previous statements about the voices, thunderings, and lightnings and an earthquake, announce the judgments being brought upon the ungodly, this one emphasizes that this will be such as was not since men were upon the earth, so mighty an earthquake, and so great. History bears out the record of some mighty devastating earthquakes. The record we have by John records some shocking earthquakes which will shake the world. But this states that it will be the greatest the earth has ever experienced. The effects of this earthquake will change the entire earth it appears.

Verse 19:

And the great city was divided into three parts, and the cities of the nations fell: and great Babylon came into remembrance before God, to give her the cup of the wine of the fierceness of his wrath.

Is this the earthquake that Zechariah is speaking about in 14:4,5, when he describes the return of Jesus Christ to this earth, as He steps

His feet on Mount Olivet, from where He left over nineteen hundred years ago?

From what we read in Ezekiel 47:1-12, it appears that this earthquake will raise the Dead Sea level so that it will once again flow into the Red Sea and bring life back into it. The topography of the earth will be changed by this tremendous earthquake.

Reference to *the great city* being divided into three parts, is evidently a reference to the city of Jerusalem. It is interesting to note that, while Jerusalem will suffer from the earthquake by being divided into three parts, it is not destroyed as the other cities of the world are.

John states *the cities of the nations fell.* If we are to take this statement to literally mean that all the great cities of the world fall because of the effect of this earthquake, then this is awesome, to say the least. Think of the great cities of the world, many of them with teeming millions dwelling in them; with their mighty skyscrapers penetrating the clouds, and they will all come tumbling down. What chaos!

- What a judgment!

The fact that Jerusalem alone seems to be exempted from this horrible destruction, brings to mind such passages as;

Psalm 125:1, *They that trust in the Lord shall be as mount Zion which cannot be removed, but abideth for ever.* Jerusalem has a special place in the Kingdom Age, while the cities of the world are symbols of all that is wicked and evil. The breeding grounds of every wicked and evil devise of mankind.

Morris writes; "The fate of great Babylon, however, is diametrically different. All the other cities of the nations fell, evidently lying in ruins but potentially renewable and rebuildable during the millennium. Babylon is not so, She is the very special object of God's wrath and must be made to serve as an object lesson to all mankind forever. She must be made to drink the wine from the trampled grapes of the wrath of God and will be thrown down with violence and so dismembered as to leave no remains at all."

Verse 20:

And every island fled away, and the mountains were not found.

Is this what the prophet Isaiah was speaking about when he wrote in 40:4,5; *Every valley shall be exalted, and every mountain and hill shall be made low: and the crooked shall be made straight, the rough places plain: and the glory of the LORD shall be revealed, and all flesh shall see it together: for the mouth of the LORD hath spoken it.*

We can only imagine what the earth will look like after this cataclysmic event transpires. The shaking of the earth results in such topographical changes as to cause the islands to disappear beneath the oceans and seas, and the mountains which have loomed so high and challenged so many to climb them, to be brought down level with the plains.

Is the Lord preparing the earth for His millennium by this action? Was the earth like this prior to the great deluge and cataclysm which befell the antediluvian world?

There is no way of estimating the number of those who will be swept away from the islands, and buried by the tumbling down of the cities, during this great deluge of God's judgment upon this wicked world.

Verse 21:

And there fell upon men a great hail out of heaven, every stone about the weight of a talent: and men blasphemed God because of the plague of the hail; for the plague thereof was exceeding great.

Larkin wrote: "Here we have a repetition of the seventh Egyptian plague. Hail has been one of God's engines of destruction. He used it to discomfit the enemies of Israel at Beth-horon in the days of Joshua. The Law required that the blasphemer should be stoned to death (Lev. 24:16), and here these blasphemers of the end time shall be stoned from heaven."

It is possible that we are not to consider this reference to great hail as being identified with the kind of hail that is common to us during summer storms. The hail we are used to is the result of violent updrafts in atmospheric storms, which results in ice being produced and dropping to the earth. The expression used here is "stone," which is the word employed elsewhere in reference to rocks, or stones.

Possibly this is the result of the great heaving the earth is undergoing from the mighty earthquake, which in turn could cause the volcanoes to erupt with mighty force as the mountains are crushed down, and they in turn belch forth with tremendous force, resulting in hurling huge stones into the air, and thus raining down upon the earth as if raining from the sky.

One of the awesome things about this hail is that the stones are not just small golf-ball size hailstones; but huge stones weighing as much as one hundred pounds!

- *The result of all of this must be horrifying, to say the least!*

Morris wrote: "It may be that this is the meaning of the graphic figure in Revelation 14:19,20, where these masses are said to be cast into God's great winepress of wrath, there to be trodden without the city until blood flows even to the horse bridles. Perhaps the men and their mounts are the grapes, and the boulders the treading feet. Possibly intense cyclic waves of atmospheric high and low pressures resulting from the earth shocks also contribute to the bursting of blood vessels and spilling of blood. Whatever the details may be, the utter horror of the scene is beyond imagination. God is long-suffering, but the day of the Lord will come. 'Thou shalt break them with a rod of iron; thou shalt dash them in pieces like a porter's vessel."

When this day is over those who remain alive on this earth will witness the establishment of the Lord's Kingdom upon this earth and will be granted the privilege of entering the millennium, to live under a reign of peace. For the past seven years, they have experienced anything but peace! Now the true Prince of pace has arrived, and true peace will at last come to planet earth.

- Blessed will be those who enter this Kingdom!

Is this the ultimate conclusion to the message being propagated today by many who are preaching the kingdom now theology? That is, that we will establish the kingdom of God on this earth through our own efforts and bring the Lord down to this earth because of our efforts.?

CHAPTER SEVENTEEN

THE POWER STRUGGLE

Revelation seventeen presents to us an interesting view of the religious system which will be prevalent in the time of tribulation, and the great political system which will be in power. As they both aspire for the same goal = world dominance; there must necessarily be a power struggle between the two of them.

We are confronted with Babylon again in the Revelation, this time in a more definitive manner. In fact, this chapter and the next one, give us great detail about Babylon. There are differing views as to whether the Babylon's which are mentioned in these two chapters are one and the same, or they are two different Babylon's.

Babylon, representative of man's glory and power, is mentioned significantly SIX times in the Revelation; 14:8; 16:19; 17:5 18:2,10,21. Six being the number of man, this emphasizes that the best man can manufacture is still short of the ultimate of perfection which God offers mankind.

Mr Hislop, in his book, The Two Babylons, has some interesting comments concerning this system which Babylon represents; "The Babylonians, in their popular religion, supremely worshipped a Goddess Mother and a Son, who was represented in pictures and in images as an infant or child in his mother's arms. From Babylon, this worship of the Mother and the Child spread to the ends of the earth. In Egypt, the Mother and the Child were worshipped under the names of Isis and Osiris. In India, even to this day, as lsi and Iswara; in Asia, as Cybele and Deoius; in Pagan Rome, as Fortuna and Jupiter-puer, or Jupiter, the boy; in Greece, as Cere, and Great Mother, with the babe at her breast, or as Irene, the goddess of Peace, with the boy Plutus in her arms; and even in Thibet, in China, and Japan, the Jesuit missionaries were astonished to find the counterpart of Madonna and her child as devoutly worshipped as in Papal Rome itself: Shing Moo, the Holy Mother in China, being represented with a child in her arms, and a glory around her...

"The original of that mother, so widely worshipped, there is reason to believe, was Semiramis, already referred to, who, it is well known, was worshipped by the Babylonians, and other eastern nations, and that under the name of Rhea, the great goddess

"Mother."

"It was from the son, however, that she derived all her glory and her claims to deification. That son, though represented as a child in his mother's arms, was a person of great stature and immense bodily powers, as well as most fascinating manners. In scripture, he is referred to (Ezekiel 8:14) under the name of Tammuz, but he is commonly known among classical writers under the name of Bacchus, that is, "The Lamented one." To the ordinary reader the name Bacchus suggests nothing more than revelry and drunkenness, but it is now well known, that amid all the abominations that attended his orgies, their grand design was professedly the "purification of souls," and that from the guilt and defilement of sin. This lamented one, exhibited and adored as a little child in his mother's arms, seems, in point of fact, to have been the husband of Semiramis, whose name, Ninus, by which he is commonly known in classical history, literally signified "The Son." As Semiramis, the wife, was worshipped as Rhea, whose grand distinguishing character was that of the great goddess "Mother," the conjunction with her or her husband, under the name of Ninus, or "The Son," was sufficiently diffused among the nations of antiquity; and this, no doubt, is the explanation of the fact which has so much puzzled the inquirers into ancient history, that Ninus is sometimes called the husband, and sometimes the son of Semiramis."

The first city mentioned in the Bible is Enoch (Genesis 4:17). Babylon is the next one. The founder of Babylon was Nimrod. It was built in the plains of Shinar, along the Euphrates River plains. Man had been told to Be fruitful, and multiply, and replenish the earth, (Genesis 9:1). The building of this city after the flood and after this command, seemed to be in open defiance to this command from God.

Nimrod, the rebel against God involved in the first rebellion against God after the flood, and also involved in a religious system which till this day continues to dominate the lives of people in bringing them in opposition to the will and purpose of God for mankind.

The rise to power, and the system which is advocated by the Beast during the tribulation, is the continuation and culmination of the old Nimrodic, Babylonian, system which has been prominent in the religious systems of the world since the days of Nimrod. Nimrod was a member of the original trinity.

Which trinity was adopted many years later at the council of Nicea by those who established the Church of Rome in the religious world. The decision made at this council to embrace the trinity and to baptize converts in the titles, Father, Son and Holy Spirit, was an effort to influence the pagan world which surrounded Rome to join their religious system. In succeeding years, when Rome would take over a pagan temple, the temple was not destroyed, nor were the gods found in the temples destroyed, their names were merely changed, and it became a church of Rome. Not only was the trinity borrowed from paganism, but also many of the other practices which are today found in the Churches of Rome were borrowed from pagan customs handed down through the years from Nimrod, and the Chaldean Mysteries religious system.

One of the first pagan rites to be introduced into the religious system of Rome was the worship of saints, especially of the virgin Mary. The worship of Mary was set up in 381 A.D., three years after Damascus became head of the Babylonian cult. Just as the Babylonian Cult worshipped the "Queen of heaven" and her "son" and did not worship the Father, because He, supposedly did not interfere with mortal affairs, so the Roman church has a similar worship in that they worship Mary as the "Mother of God."

The sign of the cross had its origin in the mystic "Tau" of the Babylonian Cult. I of Tammuz (Ezekiel 8:14).

Christmas was kept centuries before Christ was ever born. The Chaldians called it "Yule Day, or "Child Day." The Christmas tree so well known now was equally pagan and was common to all the heathen in those lands.

Easter also sprang from the fountains of Babylon. It is not even a Christian name, since its derivation is from Ishtar, one of the Babylonian titles of the Queen of Heaven. It was the worship of this woman by Israel which was such an abomination to God, 1 Samuel 7:3, Jeremiah 44.

The Easter eggs, which playa great part in this day's celebration, were common in the heathen nations. The fable of the egg affirms that an "egg of wondrous size fell from heaven into the river Euphrates, the fishes rolled it to the bank, where the doves settled upon it and hatched it and out came Astarte, or Ishtar, the goddess of

Easter.

Lent which is observed for forty days, ending with Easter, is derived from the Babylonian system as well. For many years, it was also observed by the Devil worshipers of Kurdistan, who obtained it from the same source as did Rome.

These systems which are here exemplified for us in this chapter and the next, will come to their end. One, it seems to us, will meet its doom at the hand of the power force she is using; the other will meet her doom in a fiery judgment as described in chapter eighteen.

There are several who strongly feel that the city of Babylon, which is presently being rebuilt by the Iraqi government, along with help from Japan, will be the headquarters of the Beast during the tribulation. This, along with many other things presented to us in the Revelation, is something which there is no way of knowing at this point in time. Like so many other things that are surrounded with symbols, and hard to understand statements, as the time draws nearer a clearer understanding will be seen.

According to a statement from the Ministry of Antiquities in Bagdad, the city being rebuilt will also include the Tower of Babel spoken of in Genesis eleven; "Although it will not "reach unto heaven," as its original builders intended, it will - nevertheless - provide the tourists with a splendid observation tower more than 300 feet high, from this height, the sight-seers will have a panoramic view of the site of Ancient Babylon. The reconstruction of the Tower of Babel will be carried out - as far as possible - according to the original dimensions found in ancient documents."

Dr McGee pointed out:

"Ecclesiastical Babylon is destroyed by the will of the beast.

"Commercial Babylon is destroyed by the return of Christ.

"Ecclesiastical Babylon is hated by the Beast (17:16).

"Commercial Babylon is loved by the world (18:9,19).

"Ecclesiastical Babylon is destroyed at the beginning of the last 3 1/2 years of the Great Tribulation (17:15-18).

"Commercial Babylon is destroyed at the end of the last 3 1/2 years of Great Tribulation (18:8; 19:11-16)."

The building of the city of Babylon with its tower which was to reach into the heavens, called for one of the greatest manifestations of unity that we have record of in the history of mankind. It would seem from what is said in Genesis eleven that they would have accomplished what they had set out to do if it had not been for the intervention of God. Their plans were premature. They were the type of what will take place in the last days when the Man of sin, along with his cohort, the False Prophet, bring together the great unification of religion and state for a common purpose.

"To build a tower so high that it reaches to heaven seems such an obviously impossible dream that no one would take it seriously. Of course, the builders of Babel were serious, and so are billions of followers of thousands of religions that today still offer heaven in exchange for human gifts and efforts.

This basic goal and the delusion it breeds', can be seen everywhere in our modem world. Even the atheistic scientist hopes to conquer the atom, space, and disease, and to enthrone man at last as king of the universe, captain of his own destiny. This is the theme of science fiction. And here we find a fascinating connection.

"God took Babel's seemingly absurd project seriously. In fact, God declared that "nothing will be restrained from them, which they have imagined to do." That has proven to be true. The most exotic technology we now enjoy (television, space travel, computers, etc.) was first of all conceived in the fertile imaginations of science fiction writers.

"The hope of the world is still in man's ability to achieve whatever he can imagine.

"The song "We are the World" depicts the spirit of Babel, once again uniting earth's inhabitants. One of the lines boasts, "We will tum stones into bread." This is the very thing that Christ was tempted of Satan to do but refused, drawing His sustenance from obedience to the Father's will. Now it is foolishly imagined that modem technology aligned with Eastern mysticism can transform this world once again into a paradise." (Dave Hunt)

THE APOSTATE CHURCH

Verse 1:

And there came one of the seven angels which had the seven vials, and talked with me, saying unto me, Come hither; I will show unto thee the judgment of the great whore that sitteth upon many waters.

One of the seven angels reveal to John the mystery that he witnesses concerning this one which he called "the great whore." We will also see one of these seven angels - possibly the same one - later showing John the beautiful city, New Jerusalem.

Here he is to be shown "*the judgment of the great whore.*" Anytime we find reference to a woman in the Bible, relative to prophecy, it is either speaking of the redeemed, such as the wife of the Lamb (19:7), or it is speaking of a false religious system. So, it has reference either to a true religious system, or a false one. It is evident here that what John is witnessing is a false - wicked, immoral - religious system.

The great "harlot" referred to here is that religious system which prevails during the time of tribulation. The true church has long since been removed from the earth. Now the religious system which remains is a conglomeration of the religious systems which were left behind. They have formed a unity (?) to band together under one common cause. They each have something in common - they are each lost! They join forces with the man of sin in their quest for world dominion. At last they will have their world church!

The description of this religious system as "*the great harlot*" emphasizes for us the spiritual condition this religious system is in before God. It has been said that the reference to this system as a "mother" emphasizes that she has children, i.e. daughters. It stands to reason that if she is referred to as a mother then she must have children in order to bear this title. We shall not attempt to identify who those children may be which have been born by this woman, but we will say that if the mother is a false religious system, then it is likely that her children are as well a part of that false religious system.

What John is to witness here is the "*judgment*" of this false religious system which has had such a tremendous effect upon the world. This seems to be what chapter seventeen depicts for us; the judgment of this system.

We do not know nor understand, with our finite minds, the will of God in regards to such things.

Evidently this system is the same one which has caused so much persecution to the True Church through the past several centuries. Even here it is mentioned that she is "*drunken with the blood of the saints,*" (V. 6). Going under the guise of being the voice of God to this world, she has systematically persecuted and destroyed those who opposed her. If we would have our way we would probably have brought about her judgment long before now. But there is a time for all things in God's eternal plan of things - and this is the time for her judgment!

This "*great whore,*" is depicted as sitting "*upon many waters.*" This must be a symbolic reference to masses of people. This religious system which prevails with the beast during this time, has control over great masses of people. She is living at the height of her glory. Jesus, speaking of those who among the Pharisees made their long prayers to be heard of men, said they have their reward. This religious system, whatever name may be placed upon it at this time, will have her glory days - but they will be short-lived!

A NAME FOR THE WOMAN

To name this woman by a name of one of the religious systems known to us today, would not be totally accurate. While no doubt the systems which today operate under the guise of the banner of Christ, will play an active part in the system that will join company with the beast, it will probably not be just one single church system which exists today, but a coming together of the various religious systems that will unite as one Super Church. It is evident that the Catholic religious system today is the strongest and most influential among the world's religions, it is not likely that she alone could be identified as the "*whore*" of this passage.

So, it would be impossible to identify her within one entity. As a "woman" she represents a church or religious system. But she is more than that. As a "whore 11 she is the FALSE CHURCH. As a "city" she reigns over the kings of the earth. This gives her the structure and co-equal power of a "political" entity. As an "abomination" she has every ungodly characteristic of evil, symbolizing everything that is wholly revolting to a Holy God. As a "mystery" she is shown to carry within her system the mystical religious rites that date back to Nimrod and the ancient Chaldean mysteries. It is said that the papal crown once bore the word "Mystery" on its frontlet for some time, but was later removed by Julius III, after having his attention called to the accusation of this passage.

The Babylon of this chapter does not appear to us to be the same Babylon mentioned in the following chapter. The "Woman" of this chapter, and the "City" of chapter eighteen, seems to be speaking of two different systems. What is said of the woman does not apply to the city, and vice versa.

There are several points that woe dealing with a "political, or commercial," system.

There are, however, some similarities between the two Babylons;

• 1. Both commit fornication with the kings of the earth; one in a religious manner, the other in a commercial manner; 17:2, 18:3,9.

• 2. Both shed the blood of the saints; 17:6, 18:24.

• 3. Both have a cup of abominations; 17:4, 18:6.

• 4. Both are called a city; 17:18, 18:10.

• 5. Both are called "Babylon the Great;" 17:5, 18:2.

Verse 2:

With whom the kings of the earth have committed fornication, and the inhabitants of the earth have been made drunk with the wine of her fornication.

This verse seems to affirm the unholy alliance which will be made between church and state during this time. A state which rejects the God of the Bible, and whose leader claims to be god; and a religious system which claims monopoly on religion. Both aspiring for the same goals; they join forces.

FORNICATION, is no doubt speaking of spiritual fornication which has been committed by this religious system, and which in turn has influenced the world to join her in this disregard of obedience to God in worshiping the Lord alone. The one religious system which has influenced the kings of the earth through the years is that which originated with Nimrod and the Chaldean religious mysteries. No other religious system has so permeated the nations of the world as has Babylon. The past sixteen hundred plus years that influence has been coming from Rome. While our nation's leaders scream about separation of church and state, they at the same time appoint ambassadors to this religious system.

have been made drunk... The influence of this system is so tremendous that the head of this system - the pope - receives special recognition where ever he goes. He is wined and dined as a president or king would be when he comes to any country. The pomp and display which Rome displays to the world fills the mind with awe and wonderment. But it is all "fornication" in the eyes of God!

Verse 3:

So he carried me away in the spirit into the wilderness: and I saw a woman sit upon a scarlet-colored beast, full of names of blasphemy, having seven heads and ten horns.

John was told he would be shown the *"judgment of the great whore"* and was taken into the wilderness where he saw a woman sitting on a scarlet colored beast! We are informed that the article is not found before the word wilderness in the Greek. So, we could read the statement: "into wilderness. "

We have read about John being taken into heaven with his visions, and then back to this earth, but this is the first time we have a reference to him being taken "in the Spirit" into the wilderness. As so many other things in the Revelation is symbolic, it is likely that this reference to Wilderness is likewise to be taken symbolically. Both the woman and the beast are in this wilderness. How symbolical this could be of the spiritual condition both stand in before God. Neither one of them, the woman nor the beast, can offer to mankind direction to the kingdom of God. They are both 'lost" in the wilderness!

WHO IS THIS WOMAN?

We have already been introduced to the Beast which the woman is riding on. We met him in chapter thirteen. But this is the first time we have come upon this type of introduction to this woman. We have several references to her identity given here for us;

SHE HAS A NAME ON HER FOREHEAD, MYSTERY, BABYLON THE GREAT. This title connects her to the ancient Chaldean system from the days of Nimrod. This shows the impact this system has had on the world! She is nothing more than the modern day idolatrous system of Babylon.

All one would need do is to visit one of her services and the pagan traditions handed down through the centuries would be evident.

SHE HAS A NAME ON HER FOREHEAD, THE MOTHER OF HARLOTS. This name means, according to Dake, "One who has forsaken the true God and His worship, to follow idols and false gods. "By her name "mother" we are to understand she has children. She is the "mother" by Rome's leaders today as "separated brethren. "Rome speaks of the day when they will return to the fold. The ecumenical movement of the past few years has seen an increase in interest among the world's religions of joining forces with Rome. The vast majority will no doubt return to "mother" during this time of tribulation.

SHE HAS A NAME ON HER FOREHEAD, THE MOTHER OF THE ABOMINATIONS OF THE EARTH. An examination of the pagan practices of Rome through the years certainly qualifies her for this title! An abomination in the Word of God speaks of something which is detestable to God. The teachings of this system are repulsive to anyone with a godly mind and understanding of the Word of God! Even one of their own, Cardinal Newman, in his book "The Development of the Christian Religion" plainly admits that; "Temples, incense, oil lamps, votive offerings, holy water, holidays and seasons of devotions, processions, blessing of fields, sacerdotal vestments, the tonsure (of priests and monks and nuns) and images are all of pagan origin."

SHE IS CALLED, THE GREAT WHORE. Borrowing some words from Finis Dake; "The word "fornication" refers to her illicit practices and superstitious pagan ceremonies appealing to the religious nature of men which give her influence over the many peoples. She has long kept people in drunkenness of superstition and ignorance of the true teachings of Christ and held an unbelievable influence over the masses, who are afraid of eternal damnation without her blessing. This term not only refers to physical, but also to spiritual harlotry, Jeremiah 3:6-9; Ezekiel 16:32; Hosea 1:2; Revelation 2:22. This woman is the peerless harlot."

SHE IS CALLED, THE WOMAN. This reference to her as a woman speaks of her false religious condition before God. A reference to a woman in the Word of God relative to prophecy is speaking of a false system. This religious system is anything but a propagator of the truth!

SHE IS CALLED, THAT GREAT CITY... She is called this in verse eighteen. This speaks of her headquarters, from which she influences the nations of the world. She is not a political system, but she has tremendous influence over the political systems of the world. This reference could have a symbolic as well as literal meaning. We know for instance, that the Church is referred to as a city: New Jerusalem. So, this city could also have reference to the religious system as well as a literal city. It is not likely that she could affect the rulers of the nations unless she had some physical headquarters from which to operate. Rome certainly has her city, but her influence is also felt throughout the world!

AN UNHOLY UNION

The woman is seen sitting on the beast in this verse. In verse one John was told that the woman was sitting upon many waters. But when he IS taken in the spirit to view the woman she is seen on a scarlet-colored beast. The term "sitting" must speak of a relationship. They "sit" together, in their plans to dominate the world, both politically and religiously.

"As the dragon empowers the beast, so the beast supports the harlot. The woman in turn makes the beast appear outwardly beautiful, thus making it easier for him to attain the control he seeks over mankind. Instead of following the true spiritual bride, the Jerusalem which is above, the mother of us all (Galatians 4:26) most men prefer to pursue the spiritual harlot, the false bride, Babylon, the deceiver of us all. The harlot Babylon is a contrasting type of the chaste Jerusalem and, in one sense, the whole course of history is essentially a tale of these two spiritual cities. Thus, as the beast represents political Babylon, the great whore is religious Babylon. The one is governmental rebellion and confusion, the other is spiritual rebellion and confusion. As Jerusalem is the City of Peace, Babel is the City of Confusion." (Morris).

Men can choose strange bed partners when it comes to aspiring to power and position. What an unlikely duo this makes; the beast, who seeks to dominate the world from a political position, and who has already made his boast in the Jewish temple that he is god; and the harlot, who likewise aspires for worship of the people of God on this earth. The fact that the woman accepts the claims of the beast emphasizes what kind of system she is. If she was the Church of God on this earth as she claims she is, she would not join company with someone who has just claimed that he is god and demands that all worship him as such!

While such a union does bring these two together, it cannot - and will not - last for long. They both are bidding their time till they can claim the whole prize for themselves. One part will win out over the other, and they both will lose out before God!

Verse 4:

And the woman was arrayed in purple and scarlet color, and decked with gold and precious stones and pearls, having a golden cup in her hand full of abominations and filthiness of her fornications.

"Purple was the predominant color of Roman imperialism. Every senator and knight wore a purple stripe as a badge of his position, and the emperor's robes were purple. Scarlet is the color adopted by Roman Catholicism. Popes and cardinals are clothed in scarlet." (McGee)

"Scarlet (17:3,4), color of the Beast and the Harlot, and also of the Dragon (12:3), is the color of the Papacy. The Papal Throne is scarlet. It is borne by twelve men clad in scarlet. The Cardinals' hats and robes are scarlet. Originally the Devil's color (12:3), it has now become the color of Atheistic Communism: they are commonly spoken of as Reds, Red Army, Red Territory, the Red Square in Moscow, the Devil again marshaling his hosts from without." (Halley's)

When it comes to pomp and splendor, the mother church and her daughters are no match. Her finery has blinded the eyes and minds of a lot of people through the years. Foolish men have been caught up in the outward show of this system, without giving serious consideration to the inward deceitfulness that lurks behind the tapestry.

Proverbs 5:3-5 pretty well describes this woman; *For the lips of a strange woman drop as a honeycomb, and her mouth is smoother than oil: but her end is bitter as wormwood, sharp as a two edged sword. Her feet go down to death.; her steps take hold on hell.*

People are kept in poverty in some of the underdeveloped countries, while the Roman churches are decked out in gold and precious stones.

Reference to the cup in her hand which is full of abominations and filthiness of her fornications, speaks of her spiritual condition in the eyes of God. Abominations is found employed many times in the Word of God, especially in the Old Testament, where there it has reference to the idolatrous practices of the people which was many times associated with demon worship, witchcraft, etc., which was found prevalent among the pagan heathen neighbors of Israel.

Thus, the outward show of religious pomp and splendor is acceptable to the masses. There is an outward show of religious traditions, but there is no contact with things Godly and holy.

While the long flowing robes; the brightly decorated garments; the richly designed buildings, etc., may fill the eyes and mind with wonderment, the spiritual substance is nil. There is no Spirit of God in these rituals. The swinging censures; the sprinkling of the holy water, the chanting of prayers, are not Bible related - but, rather, pagan related.

Verse 5

And upon her forehead was a name written, MYSTERY, BABYLON THE GREAT, THE MOTHER OF HARLOTS AND ABOMINATIONS OF THE EARTH.

It has been said that in ancient times the harlots displayed their names on tags worn on their forehead. Vincent, in speaking of this practice, wrote; "As was customary with harlots, who had their names on a ticket. Seneca, addressing a wanton priestess, ''Nomen tunum pependit a fronte,' thy name hung from thy forehead."

Her name is interestingly referred to as "MYSTERY," which certainly fits the pattern of the church of Rome. For years, the mass was always conducted in Latin, which the vast majority of the people did not understand. Many things about the entire system is kept secret to the public. It also carries the title mystery because of its association with its ancient past; Babylon and the Chaldean mysteries.

While we continue to refer to the Roman Catholic church, we do not mean to imply that she alone is the woman described to John here in this chapter. She no doubt is very much involved in this system spoken of here, but she alone is not the woman spoken of here. We note a comment from Morris in conjunction with this;

"Many Bible teachers have identified this harlot not only as spiritual Babylon but also, more explicitly, as the Roman Catholic Church, noting that many of the doctrines and sacraments of the Babylonian religion were transmitted to pagan Rome and thence ultimately to papal Rome... There is no doubt that many of the doctrines and practices of the Roman Catholic Church, as well as the various Orthodox churches and similar ancient churches, are based on tradition rather than scripture... But to say that spiritual Babylon is either Rome or the Roman Catholic Church is to grossly underestimate the age-long global impact of this great mystery, Babylon the Great. Babylon is the mother of all the harlots and abominations of the earth. From her have come ancient paganism, Chinese Confucianism, Asian Buddhism, Indian Hinduism, witchcraft, spiritism, Sikhism, and all the world's vast complex of 'gods many, and lords many' (Corinthians 8:5)."

We are witnesses of the coming together of the religious systems of the world right now. One of the encroaching spirits which is swaying a lot of people is the spirit of humanism. This spirit is found in many places. Their message on the surface seems plausible, and many gullible people are swallowing the message. The bottom line, however, remains the same - it stems from Babylon. If it is not supported by the Word of God, and if it does not exalt the Lord Jesus Christ, then avoid it like the plague!

Verse 6:

And I saw the woman drunken with the blood of the saints, and with the blood of the martyrs of Jesus: and when I saw her, I wondered with great admiration.

The *"blood of the saints,"* could have reference to the Old Testament saints who suffered bitter persecution under the hand of those who were influenced by Babylon. There has never been a time, since the Babylonian system came into being, when the people of God have not felt the sting of persecution from some system connected to the Babylonian system.

There is something about the people of God, whether they be Old Testament saints, or members of the New Testament church, that has brought persecution upon them where ever they have gone. Today countries refuse to allow the Gospel to be preached in their country. And those who do allow it, many of them, do so only under strict control. The very thing which will bring people out of poverty and depression; the very thing which will liberate those who have been so long held down in the bondages of tradition, is the thing which is refused.

'The horrors of the Inquisition, ordered and maintained by the Popes, over a period of 500 years, in which unnumbered millions were tortured and burned, constitute the MOST BRUTAL, BEASTLY and DEVILISH PICTURE in all history... It is not pleasant to write these things. It is inconceivable that any Ecclesiastical Organization, in its mania of power, could have distorted and desecrated and corrupted, for its own exaltation, the beautiful and holy religion of Jesus, as the Papacy has done. But facts are facts. And History is History. And, most amazing of all, it seems exactly pre-figured in Revelation. No wonder John's vision made him sick at heart (10:10)." (Halley's)

There is no way that anyone could accurately number the lives which have been destroyed through this system. It has been estimated that Rome has slain more than 200,000,000 people in the past because they would not bow to her system of religion and submit to the Church and her pope. In one of the darkest periods of time the people of God have ever endured, the inquisition, hundreds of thousands were killed in the name of religion! From Halley's Bible Handbook; "The Inquisition, called the "HOLY QFFICE," was instituted by Innocent III, and perfected under the second following pope, Gregory IX. It was the Church Court for the detection and punishment of heretics. Under it everyone was required to inform against heretics. Anyone suspected was liable to Torture, without knowing the name of his accuser. The proceedings were secret. The Inquisitor pronounced sentence, and the victim was turned over to the civil authorities to be imprisoned for life or to be burned. The victim's property was confiscated and divided between the Church and the State. In the period immediately following Innocent III the Inquisition did its most deadly work in Southern France, but claimed vast multitudes of victims in Spain, Italy, Germany, and the Netherlands. Later on, the Inquisition was the main agency in the

Papacy's effort to crush the Reformation. It is stated that in the 30 years between 1540 and 1570 no fewer than 900,000 Protestants were put to death, in the Pope's war for the extermination of the Waldenses. Think with heartless cruelty and inhuman brutality, the work of

Torturing and Burning alive innocent men and women, by the direct order of the "Vicar of Christ." The INQUISITION is the MOST INFAMOUS THING in history. It was devised by the Popes and used by them for 500 years to maintain their power. For its record, none of the subsequent line of "Holy" and "Infallible" Popes have ever apologized."

When John witnessed the sight of this great harlot which was bloodied with the blood of hundreds of thousands of martyrs, he was filled with "great admiration. "Now, let us not consider this statement in the same manner we would employ the term today. John did not admire the woman. He was filled with "AWE!" or, "AMAZEMENT!" at what he saw. It is amazing how such a system can be permitted to exist and thrive in the world for so many years, and have the sanctioning of kings, presidents, and rulers of countries upon her!

She not only continues to exist, but she is a highly honored system in the world today. Her bloody past is ignored or explained away. If circumstances were changed, and the conditions would find this church system with the same controlling power which she enjoyed during those bloody years of her "inquisition" the same results would come about. In fact, that is just exactly what happens during the tribulation. She once again enjoys this power, and she becomes drunken on it to the extent that once again blood flows in the streets.

Historians have a way of liberally applying the paint brush of white-wash on those events which mark the cruel and dark history of the Church of Rome, but they have not been erased in God's record book. It is difficult for us to imagine the atrocities which were perpetrated against the people of God during those dark years. At the same time, it is difficult to imagine people by the millions being swallowed up in such a system today!

Verse 7:

And the angel said unto me, Wherefore didst thou marvel? I will tell thee the mystery of the woman, and of the beast that carrieth her, which hath seven heads and ten horns.

We today are not unlike John was in his day, we many times and in many ways, fail to recognize the formation of the nations and their significance to prophetic time tables. We fail to see behind the scenes in the political arenas of our world and generation. Who could imagine a religious system, professing to be the body of Christ on earth, carrying out such atrocities against those who opposed her and her dogma?

Let us note together in his statement. While they may represent different aspects of the scene unfolding in the last days, they are classified in the same category; enemies of God. One of them a political enemy, with the leader professing to be god: the other a religious enemy, with the leader professing to be the infallible spokesman for God on earth.

The fact that they both have deceived the masses into believing and accepting their message, is a mystery. Their systems which have brought them to the forefront in this hour, is shrouded in mystery. Their origin - Babylon - is connected to the mystery of Babylon of the Old Testament.

Verse 8:

The beast that thou sawest was, and is not; and shall ascend out of the bottomless pit, and go into perdition: and they that dwell on the earth shall wonder, whose names were not written in the book of life from the foundation of the world, when they behold the beast that was, and is not, and yet is.

As mentioned previously, we have studied about the beast when we were considering chapter thirteen, but with this verse we are presented with some information which we did not receive when we were studying chapter thirteen. The beast on which the woman is here identified to John as one who was and is not; and shall ascend out of the bottomless pit. In In other words, the beast existed on this earth prior to John's time (was); and during the time of John he no longer was on the earth, (and is not); yet the time will come when he shall once again come forth upon the earth (shall ascend out of the bottomless pit.)

The identification of this beast has produced a lot of speculation by Bible commentators. One spent a lot of time pointing out that this could be Judas, because of what was said about him by our Lord (one of you is the devil); and by the apostles (that he might go to his place, Acts 1 :25). Others have been suggested including Nero, Napoleon, and many others.

Some contend that the beast will be someone, such as Judas or Nimrod, who will be reincarnated.

The Bible certainly does not teach reincarnation!

LET'S IDENTIFY THE BEAST

First of all, let us notice that the beast stands for three things;

1). **He is an individual; a human being.** It is said of him in 13:18, for it is the number of a man. He will sit on a throne, which has been given to him by Satan.

There are passages which speak of the time of his defeat at the hand of Christ, which emphasizes that he is a human being. Paul states in 2Thessalonians 2:8, Then shall that Wicked (antichrist - beast) be revealed, whom the Lord shall consume with the spirit of His mouth and shall destroy with the brightness of His coming. Daniel, evidently speaking of the same one, states; I beheld even till the beast was slain, and his body destroyed, and given to the burning flame. (7:11) This evidently has reference to what we find recorded in Revelation 19:20; And the beast was taken, and with him the false prophet that wrought miracles be/ore him, with which he deceived them that had received the mark of the beast, and them that worshipped his image. These were cast alive into a lake of fire burning with brimstone.

2). **The beast is also an empire**. The description which is given by John in chapter thirteen concerning the beast being like a leopard, a bear, and a lion, are symbols employed in reference to kingdoms. Daniel makes mention of these animals in one of his visions (chapter 7), which are evidently representative of kingdoms or empires. Also, the beast of Revelation is seen to have seven heads, which, again, are representative of kingdoms, or nations.

3). **The beast is also some supernatural being**. This is evident from the fact he is seen corning from the abyss. Now, we need to elaborate some on this statement. In point one we stated that the beast is human. There is no scriptural support, however, that any human has ever - or ever will - descend into the abyss, nor ascend out of it. The only reference we have concerning those who inhabit that place is that Satan and his angels inhabit that place. This is the place where Satan will be bound during the millennium. We noted in our study of chapter nine that this was the prison house of demon spirits, Verse 11.

Evidently, we glean from this fact that what ascends out of the bottomless pit is a demon spirit. He is identified as the beast because of his close association with the beast. He will evidently ascend out at the mid-way point of the tribulation, and will greatly influence the man of sin, bringing about his rise to the position of power and influence which he has sold his soul to Satan to acquire. One could assume that he will indwell the man of sin, thus making the man of sin his puppet, or instrument he employs to gain control of the kingdom and ultimately bring war against Christ Himself. What mortal would be foolish enough to assume that he could war against Jesus Christ?

It is evident that the reference to the beast in this chapter is not a reference to the same beast we were introduced to in chapter thirteen, even though they both are intertwined in their plans and involvement in last day events. When we were introduced to the beast (man of sin) in chapter thirteen we read; 'And I stood upon the sand of the sea, and saw a beast rise up out of the sea. The beast here in chapter seventeen upon which the harlot is seen sitting, is said to ascend out of the bottomless pit. One comes up from among the masses of humanity (the sea), which lets us know he is a mortal human being. The other is seen rising from the bottomless pit, which lets us know he is not a mortal human being, but a prince of Satan. As angels of God, nor their counterparts, angels of Satan, are not witnessed by the eyes of mortals, this prince of darkness will not be seen by men - unless he invades and controls the body of some mortal! Which is evidently what he does and is recognized as the beast.

This would also explain the evident change which takes place in the man of sin during the middle of the week. When we are first introduced to the man of sin we see him riding a white horse (chapter six), and he is given a crown because of his contributions to mankind. Daniel speaks of how he will come in speaking peace and employing flatteries. He will confirm the covenant with Israel (Daniel 9:27), which implies his efforts toward a peaceful solution to the Middle East problems. But when we get to chapter thirteen what we witness there is completely different. He is, first of all, referred to as a beast. His cohort, the false prophet, goes about establishing his authority over those in his kingdom. The order is issued to erect an image to his honor, which the false prophet in turn uses to bring a lying wonder to deceive the people by making the image speak. All who refuse to worship the image are marked for death. The demand is given to become identified with the beast by taking his mark or number or name on one's person.

The dark days of tribulation actually begin with the middle of the week. The great persecution will begin at this time, which would coincide with the coming forth from the bottomless pit of the beast of chapter seventeen; along with the casting out of heaven down to the earth of Satan himself (chapter twelve).

To realize the involvement of angels - both good and bad - in the affairs of this world, we have but to consider such passages of scripture as Daniel chapter ten. There we have a reference to both the good and evil angels. Daniel had been fasting and praying, when he received a vision which greatly stirred him. In fact, Daniel said 'there remained no strength in me: for my comeliness was turned in me into corruption, and I retained no strength. During this time an angel of the Lord touched Daniel and let him know that his prayer had been heard from the first day he began to pray (some three weeks before), but the angel said But the prince of the kingdom of Persia withstood me one and twenty days: but, Lo, Michael, one of the chief princes, came to help me; and I remained there with the kings of Persia. Now, the angel's references to the prince of the kingdom of Persia, and one of the chief princes, Michael, is not a reference to a mortal prince, but, rather, to an evil angel (prince of Persia) and Michael the archangel of the Lord.

We quote here from the commentary of Finis J Dake: "In Daniel 10:1-11: we have the pivot passage of all the Bible concerning the supernatural princes under Satan who rule different kingdoms and concerning God's method of overruling the rulers of these kingdoms to fulfill prophecy. This clearly shows how and why the spirit in the abyss was confined there and incidentally gives his identity. This is not the final reason for this conclusion, but it does settle the fact that there are such supernatural princes over the different kingdoms. Whatever we may conclude about the beast out of the abyss we must associate him with one of the first five kingdoms symbolized by the first five heads on the beast... This spirit then, must be one who has ruled either Egypt, Assyria, Babylon, Medo-Persia or Greece, for they are the first five heads on the beast. Let it be remembered that he was on earth before the sixth, was not on earth during the sixth, that he will come out of the abyss during the seventh and that he will revive a kingdom he once controlled which will become the eighth and the succession of the seventh kingdom ... In Daniel 10:20,21 there is another indisputable reference to supernatural princes over kingdoms. If this is true of these few mentioned, surely it is true of all other kingdoms and principalities in the world that have existed or will exist until all the kingdoms of this world become the kingdoms of Christ at His coming... These passages show that God ordains certain angels and sends them forth to cause the rise and fall of certain kingdoms in order to fulfill prophecy. They also reveal that Satan's princes over these kingdoms try to hinder the rise and fall of kingdoms to hinder God's plan. Daniel 10:12-14 shows that there was war in heaven between the prince of Persia and Gabriel and that Gabriel was detained twenty-one days and could not get through to Daniel until Michael, the prince that protects Israel, came to help him. Together they defeated the prince of Persia. If there was such a war, of twenty-one days in length, over a mere answer to prayer, what kind of wars and how long must they be over the overthrow of a kingdom?"

It is quite likely that the prince of one these kingdoms that existed prior to John's day; Egypt, Assyria, Babylon, Medo-Persia, or Greece, will be the one who is referred to here in verse eight, who shall be permitted to leave his confinement in the abyss, which in turn will bring about the fulfillment of the Word of God concerning the beast and the conclusion of the Tribulation period.

John is told that this beast shall ultimately go into perdition (doom - destruction). We know that at the Lord's return to this earth at the time of Armageddon, the Beast and his cohort the False Prophet shall both be taken and cast into the lake of fire - perdition.

WHOSE NAMES WERE NOT WRITTEN... The change which

which will come upon the man of sin will no doubt be obvious once the demon has entered him and began to control his actions and decisions. This expression is also employed in chapter thirteen where we read; and all the world wondered after the beast. (vs 3). Many today are caught up in the supernatural. There has been a lot of publicity given concerning the fact that President and Mrs Reagan placed a lot of confidence in astrologers and their interpretation of astrology. Many are awed with the subject of reincarnation; astrology; spiritism, etc.

Also, let us note the expression; whose names were not written in the book of life. We have had reference made to those whose names are in the book of life before this, but this is the first time the expression is found in the past tense! Does this imply that all that are going to be saved are already saved! Does this imply that from this point on no one will have their name added to this book?

The people wonder when they behold the beast that was, and is not, and yet is. This is the same statement as the verse begins with. The beast was - he existed on earth before John's day. The beast is not - he was no longer on this earth when John received this vision. The Beast yet is - that is he will return at the time of the end once more to this earth.

Verse 9:

And here is the mind which hath wisdom. The seven heads are seven mountains, on which the woman sitteth.

This reminds us of 13:18, *Here is wisdom. Let him that hath understanding count the number of the beast...* The term "wisdom" here implies understanding. What is said in this verse, as well as the preceding, will be understood only through serious consideration of the symbolism of the Revelation.

This verse has produced differing opinions - like many of the others in the Revelation - as to what is meant by these "seven mountains." One of the common interpretations of this verse is to say it is speaking of the city of Rome. Those who interpret it this way state that Rome sits on seven hills. Well, no doubt Rome does have seven hills (in fact, we are told that Rome has MORE than seven hills!), but the word for hills is the Greek word bounos. While the Greek word for mountain is oros. And it is the latter word which is employed here in this verse. Besides this, there are other cities in the world which are situated among seven or more hills.

If we interpret something symbolically in one place in the Revelation, it is likely that when we come upon the term again we should interpret it symbolically there as well. And this is what it has reference to in this passage as well.

We have already seen in verse one that the harlot sitteth upon many waters; and in verse three she is seen sitting "upon a scarlet-colored beast. "And, as we have already pointed out, the beast is a kingdom as well as a person. The kingdom of the beast is made up of nations which have cast their allegiance to him and his system. What this harlot is doing is joining forces - sitting - with this alliance.

The next verse will point this out:

Verse 10:

And there are seven kings: five are fallen, and one is, and the other is not yet come; and when he cometh, he must continue a short space.

From this verse we see that the seven mountains are seven kings. Some versions of these two verses have it; *The seven heads are seven mountains... and are seven kings.*

The use of the term mountain in symbolically referring to a kingdom is evident in such places as Isaiah 2:2, *And it shall come to pass in the last days, that the mountain of the Lord's house shall be established in the top of the mountains and shall be exalted above the hills.* Or, Daniel 2:35, *And the stone that smote the image became a great mountain and filled the whole earth.* Or, Micah 4:1, *But in the last days it shall come to pass, that the mountain of the house of the Lord shall be established in the top of the mountains, and it shall he exalted above the hills; and people shall flow unto it.*

So, we have seven mountains, which represent kingdoms. We have seven heads, which speaks of these kingdoms as well. And we have seven kings now referred to, which in tum represent the seven kingdoms. Many times, the king is referred to in representing the kingdom over which he rules.

Now, if the reference to the seven mountains refers to the city of Rome, as some contend, then according to this verse five of those hills would have to have been fallen by the time of John, and another one would someday be flattened. It is obvious, of course, that this statement does not refer to natural mountains.

The question which arises now is which nations - or kingdoms - do these kings - or mountains - represent. Five of them existed prior to John's day but were not in power in his lifetime. When we turn to Daniel two, we are helped tremendously in our search for these five kingdoms. The king Nebuchadnezzar had a dream. Daniel was called to tell the king what his dream was and the interpretation of the dream. His dream consisted of a great image which consisted of four different metals. The head of gold; shoulders and arms of silver; thighs of brass, and the legs of iron. Daniel let the king know the image represented four kingdoms, beginning with the Babylonian kingdom of which Nebuchadnezzar was the head of gold. We know from the Bible and history that the succeeding three kingdoms were; Medo-Persia; Greece and Rome. Rome was in power in John's day. So, the three before Rome; Greece; Persia and Babylon, would be three of the five which were part of this system which John is writing about in the Revelation. Who would the other two be?

There have been several great kingdoms or empires before John's day. China; India; Edom; Syria. But to qualify for what John is witnessing and writing about, the kingdom would have to be a continuation of the system that Babylon is identified with; and they would have to be involved with the nation Israel. There are two empires which fit this category of enemies of the people of God and the Word of God, as well as fitting the description outlined in this chapter; Egypt and Assyria.

Mr Morris wrote concerning these six kingdoms: "Furthermore, all six of these were not only legitimate heirs of political Babel but also of religious Babel as well. Babylonia, Egypt, Assyria, Persia, Greece, and Rome were all strongholds of the world religion of evolutionary pantheism and idolatrous polytheism. Thus, they appropriately are represented as six heads on the great beast that supports the harlot."

the other is not yet come... he must continue a short space. John said there would come one more after these six have moved off the scene. This one which is to come would also, it seems, correspond to the image of Daniel chapter two. For the interpretation included down to the toes which were mixed with iron and clay. These ten toes would correspond with the ten horns which are noted here on the beast. This would also identify the one to come with the kingdom which was in power in John's day; Rome, because the material of the image continues down to the toes; Iron, only it is now mixed with clay. Although though the empire of Rome split into two divisions, east and west, represented by the two legs of the image, and eventually toppled as a ruling empire, the influence of Rome continues to this day.

"The Revised Roman Empire is the only one of the seven kingdoms that is yet future. It will become a relentless persecutor of Israel under the leadership of the great whore, which will rule the ten kingdoms of Revised Rome until the middle of the week. Mystery Babylon, the great whore, will seek to suppress every religion that is not her own, and will murder the saints of Jesus until she will be drunk on their blood during the first three and one-half years of the week.

We have many scriptures revealing the persecution of Christians and Israel by the great whore and the ten kings before Antichrist gets full power over them, Matthew 24:4-13; Mark 13:4-13; Revelation 6:9-11; 17:3-6. Antichrist will continue the persecution of Christians and will break his seven-year covenant with Israel, being determined to exterminate them from the earth" (Dake).

The previous six empires which greatly affected Israel and the world, enjoyed their glory days of power and control for differing lengths of time, lasting hundreds of years each. But the one which is to come will have a very short life-span in which they will enjoy their moment of power. When the beast finally rises to the top in his quest for power, he will bask in that position for only a short while. At the most three and one-half years.

Verse 11:

And the beast that was, and is not, even he is the eighth, and is of the seven, and goeth into perdition.

This verse presents an interesting, and intriguing, statement. Just what is it saying, anyway? We have been told that the beast only had seven heads, and yet here we have a reference to an eighth head! What is the meaning to all this?

The beast that was, could take us back to verse 8, where there we had reference to the beast coming forth from the abyss. Which beast we identified as being a ruling prince of darkness under the influence of Satan, and who was ruler of evil influence over one of the previous empires (possibly Greece).

At some point in the tribulation - probably in the middle of the week - he shall come forth from the abyss and take control of the man of sin.

While the man of sin has been identified as the seventh and final head that would come, the prince of darkness will conquer and control him, and, in essence, be the eighth head, while at the same time being part of the seventh.

It appears that the empire which the man of sin will have under his control, is here spoken of as the seventh. Then, the prince of darkness from the abyss will step in, taking control not only of the man of sin, but his empire as well. From this he will seek to enlarge the empire in his efforts to control the whole world. In this we could see that it will be in essence the eighth, while at the same time out of the seventh.

Mr Morris had some interesting comments here: "Since it is "of the seven," it partakes of the character of all of them, in a sense marking the resurrection of all these ancient nations, from Babel to Rome. This is not surprising, since all manifest the same characteristics, political and religious, and all together are identified as Babylon the Great in mystery form.

"In various Old Testament prophecies, this final Antichrist is identified in one way or another with all six of these ancient empires. He is identified with the Romans in Daniel 9:26, which notes that "the people of the prince that shall come" are the people who will destroy Jerusalem and the temple after Messiah's rejected by the Jews. The head of one of the four divisions of the Greek empire which preceded Rome was Antiochus Epiphanes, the "vile person" of Daniel 11 :21, whose wickedness and violence against Jerusalem are taken as a type of the beast of the last days (Note Daniel 8:23-25; 11:31-33).

"Among the Persians, the traditional "enemy of all the Jews" was Haman the Agagite (Esther 9:24), whose plot to annihilate them makes him also an appropriate type of the beast (compare Esther 3:8-10,13 and Revelation 12:17; 17:14). The Egyptians, likewise, were enemies of God's people from the time of Abraham to the time of Jeremiah and especially in the time of Moses. The Pharaoh of the Exodus, who also attempted to destroy all the children of Israel, becomes thereby also a type of the Antichrist. Pharaoh is called the great dragon that lieth in the midst of his rivers in Ezekiel 29:3, and is said to be like in glory and greatness among the trees of Eden (Ezekiel 31:18), but he and his people (like the beast) will be brought down to "the nether parts of the earth." More directly to the point, the Antichrist is specifically called "the Assyrian" in a number of passages (e.g. Micah 5:5, 6; Isaiah 30:31; 31 :8), possibly because of the close association of Assyria with Babylon in their origin and history (note Isaiah 23: 13; Micah 5:6). As far as Babylon is concerned, not only is Nimrod a type of the beast and Nebuchadnezzar's image (Daniel 3:1-7) a type of the beast's image, but the beast himself is here directly identified with Babylon the Great."

Verse 12

And the ten horns which thou sawest are ten kings, which have received no kingdom yet; but receive power as kings one hour with the beast.

The explanation of the beast continues with the explanation of the ten horns seen on the beast. When we first see the beast, we note there are seven heads, but ten horns. When trying to reconcile the number of horns with the number of heads, we have a problem. But the seven heads, as explained in verses 9 and 10, point out that they represent kingdoms or leaders of those seven kingdoms. Kingdoms and leaders which, at the time of the tribulation, six of them have already moved off the scene, leaving only the seventh and last one. It is on this seventh and last head that we have the ten horns, which represent ten kings to be. John is told they are not in possession of their own kingdom at first but share the power of kings with the beast for just a short while. There will evidently be a confederation of power during the rise of the beast which he will employ to gain control of the empire.

Evidently this is what Daniel saw in one of his visions in chapter seven; *And the ten horns* (Revelation 17:12) *that were in his head,* (of the last beast Daniel saw - Revelation 13:1) *and of the other which came up, and before whom three fell; even of that horn that had eyes,* (the man of sin - the beast of Revelation 13:1) *and a mouth that spake very great things, whose look was more stout than his fellows. I beheld, and the same horn made war with the saints, and prevailed against them. And the ten horns of this kingdom are ten kings that shall arise: and another shall rise after them; (the man of sin) and he shall be diverse from the first, and he shall subdue three kings. And he shall speak great words against the most High and shall wear out the saints of the most High, and think to change times and laws: and they shall be given into his hand until a time and times and the dividing of time (last three and one-half years of the tribulation). But the judgment shall sit, and they shall take away his dominion, to consume and to destroy it unto the end.* (Verses 20,21,24,25,26.)

The political scene of the world will be greatly altered by this time. In fact, the political world has greatly changed in our own generation! Nations which were once our allies are no longer in the same camp with us. The encroachment of humanism is changing the world drastically. We are continuing to be witnesses of changes which are taking place in our world politically. These changes will continue to take place, until the time of this great tribulation, which will see the greatest shake-up of nations ever.

The man of sin will make his moves that will ultimately place him at the head of the confederation of powers which will seek to dominate the political scene during this time. Those who are in influential positions, and who have selfish ambitions of their own, will join allegiance with the man of sin in order to share in his limelight for a while.

Verse 13:

These have one mind, and shall give their power and strength unto the beast.

As to the identity of these ten powerful men and nations, we are left to our own speculation. Much has been said concerning the alignment of nations into the European Economic Community. Many of us thought that when they reached ten in number this would be in fulfillment of the ten horns of the beast. But after Greece was added in 1981, making their total ten, the number did not stop there. Other nations have been added since then as well.

This is not to say that this bloc will not have something to do with the end time events, they will in all probability be actively involved in whatever takes place during the tribulation period.

These have one mind - that is they agree to surrender their will and plans to the beast. They permit his plans to control their own. They surrender their sovereignty to him.

They give their power and strength - which could speak of their armaments (power) and their sovereignty or authority (strength) to the beast. This is a total surrender or commitment to the beast and his authority.

All of these events will not take place over night.

Daniel suggests there is a power struggle when he states, and he shall subdue three kings (7:24).

So, there will be some political maneuvering going on, along with some arm twisting.

Let us not forget that during this time the judgments of the seals and trumpets will be coming upon the earth. So, the nations of the world will be in trouble. Leaders of these nations will be feeling the pressures of their constituents crying for solutions to their many problems which will beset their countries. Hearing the brazen promises of the man of sin could be persuasion enough to join affinity with him in his power struggle to gain control of the world's governments and bring his solution to their myriad of problems. The result will be an unholy alliance which will in turn seek to control the entire world scene. One of their great problems will be they will not stop in their selfish ambitions to gain control of the worlds governments, they will also join forces with this demon controlled leader to attempt to destroy God completely from the picture.

Verse 14:

These shall make war with the Lamb, and the Lamb shall overcome them: for He is Lord of lords, and King of kings: and they that are with Him are called, and chosen, and faithful.

As utterly preposterous as this all seems, men, when they have sold out to Satan, will do anything!

The master of the prince of darkness who has ascended from the abyss to conquer and control the man of sin, brought about his own fall when he made his boasts many millennium's ago; *I will ascend into heaven, I will exalt my throne above the stars of God: 1 will sit also upon the mount of the congregation, in the sides of the north: I will ascend above the heights of the clouds; I will be like the most High.* In his selfish ambitions Satan, instead of reaching beyond the stars, found that he not only could not displace God from His throne, but that he experienced a demotion. *Yet thou shalt be brought down to hell, to the sides of the pit.* (Isaiah 14:13-15).

Power is intoxicating! The man of sin, and those who have joined allegiance with him, have become intoxicated on their power. Like some drunk man, they are seeing things and thinking things that no sober, sane, mortal would consider.

By this time the man of sin will be sitting at the top of the most powerful military force the world has ever known. He will have under his control the latest technological weaponry the world has ever known to this point. The nations which at the first opposed him, have either joined forces with him, or are rallying their forces, waiting for the time when they will have to deal with him. The final showdown will come at Armageddon!

Ever since Satan's fall and his entrance into man's world, he has been an antagonist against all that is like God. There has been, in reality, a warfare going on between the kingdom of God and the kingdom of Satan since his expulsion from heavens inner circle. But this will be the final battle, and it will be a personal battle, which will bring about the demise of the kingdom of the man of sin, and he, along with his cohort, the false prophet, will become the first inhabitants of the lake of fire as they are cast into it after their defeat at Armageddon.

The man of sin has professed to being lord over the world, but the Lord of lords is coming on the scene! The man of sin has sat on his throne as king of his vast empire, but the King of kings is coming to dethrone him!

We are not clear as to how this battle will come about. We are informed that it will be at Armageddon - the plains of Jezreel, or Megiddo. And we know it will be at the time of the Lord's return to this earth. But we do not know the details as to what brings these great armies to this battle sight - except for the fact that they are influenced to come by the *three unclean spirits like frogs...* for they are *spirits of demons... which go forth unto the kings of the earth, and of the world, to gather them to the battle of that great day of God Almighty* (16:13,14).

Let us recall that Jesus promised that the days would be shortened for the elect's sake (Matthew 24:22). There is a limit as to how long the Lord will allow the beast to triumph and make his boasts about what he is going to do with the world - and then with God Himself! When he has run his course, God will step in and declare it is enough. God will tear up his playhouse and bring his kingdom tumbling down about him.

THOSE WITH THE KING

John records, and they that are with Him are called, and chosen, and faithful. Jesus does not return alone to this earth. We have the description of this return to Armageddon in chapter nineteen. He is bringing the "armies in heaven" with Him! The description of this army fits the description of the redeemed who were raptured from this earth some seven years prior to Armageddon! Again, we are not informed as to details who all are in this great army which descends from heaven with their Great Commander in Chief. Is it ALL of those who were raptured previously? Or, is it a select group from among them which are referred to as the armies of heaven? To what extent will this battle be engaged?

The weapons involved? On the side of the beast; the latest in scientific technology. Nuclear arsenals are at his disposal. Who knows where we will stand in advanced warfare technology at that time? On the side of the King; Armor of light! Fine linen, clean and white.: the righteousness of the saints! Who wins this great confrontation? Just read the back of the book and you will see!

Verse 15:

And he saith unto me, The waters which thou sawest, where the whore sitteth, are peoples, and multitudes, and nations, and tongues.

The angel having explained to John in detail about mystery Babylon, now explains to John who is involved with the woman; who is supporting this system of evil, as well as her defeat.

In verse one we have the reference to her sitting on many waters; in verse three we see her sitting on a scarlet colored beast. They are referring to the same thing. Here John is informed as to what these waters refer to. So, here we have an explanation of a symbol given to us in the Revelation.

Waters are employed in the Bible to refer to the masses of humanity. The words of Jesus Himself, in speaking of the last day events, stated; upon the earth distress of nations, with perplexity; the sea and the waves roaring. (Luke 21:25)

At this point in the course of the history of humanity, the world as a whole - the masses of humanity - have become deceived into thinking the harlot, along with the system she is associating with, the beast, has the answers to all their woes. She has succeeded into deceiving the multitudes which are here depicted as waters.

The harlot has been successful in deceiving people down through the years, and she will continue this deception into the tribulation. But her days of deception are numbered at this point in time...

Verse 16:

And the ten horns which thou sawest upon the beast, these shall hate the whore, and shall make her desolate and naked, and shall eat her flesh, and burn her with fire.

Her greatest goal ever seems to be within grasp - and then defeat! This proud, haughty, self-righteous, religious system, which through the years has brought so much distress and anguish to so many people, will at last meet her final doom. And to think, she will meet it at the very hand of the one she has joined in an unholy wedding of super powers seeking to gain ultimate control of the world's populace.

The demise of this harlot will take place sometime during the last half of the week, as we have reference to the ten horns bringing about her destruction, and they will only come on the scene during the last half of the week, as a power bloc with the beast.

The beast in his attempt to gain control of the world realizes the significance of religious influence regardless of the fact that it is humanistic religion which is now at the forefront. Employing his manipulating ways, he gets the harlot to join forces with him, and, along with him, gain control of the people of the world. The harlot, wanting the same recognition, accepts his proposal and joins forces with him. It is not beyond reason to assume that the harlot has the same thing in mind - that is, she will put up with the beast long enough to gain control, and then she will make her moves to get rid of him. He beats her to the punch!

We can only imagine what will happen to the thousands of cathedrals which dot the landscape across the world, once the harlot is brought down. Will they remain empty for a while as a mute reminder of a system which went awry?

With the joining together of the ten-nation confederacy, the ten kings receiving power for one hour with the beast fills them with their own selfish motives, there is now the completed bloc of power which feels confident they can overcome any obstacle in their way to world dominion. The first obstacle is the harlot, whom they dispose of right away!

Verse 17:

For God hath put it in their hearts to fulfill His will, and to agree, and give their kingdom unto the beast, until the words of God shall be fulfilled.

How astounding! Man thinks all the time that he is doing what he wants to do! That it is really his idea to get rid of this system which they despise! They think: We oppose God and anything closely related to God, so we will destroy this religious system, and in so doing we will show our defiance to God. When all the time they are working for God!

How puny is man! How puny and insignificant are his plans! How foolish of man to think that he can oppose God and His eternal will. All that has been happening, and all that is happening to this point, is all in fulfillment of what God determined millenniums ago!

God has used men - carnal ungodly men - to fulfill His will down through history.

The kings have come together because the Word of God declared they would. There has been an alliance of power under the dominant head of the beast because God's word declared there would be. They have in turn destroyed this harlot and her system of religious evil because the Word of God declared they would. The world may seem out of control at this point because of what is taking place, with all the havoc and blood shed, etc., but it is not! All things are working out according to the eternal plan and will of God. Those involved in the events during this time are merely players in the great game of life and fulfillment of prophecy.

Jesus had declared, *Heaven and earth shall pass away, but my words shall not pass away.* (Matthew 24:35) What God has decreed will come to pass. No force that Satan can muster together will be able to prevent the Word of God from reaching its prior ordained and predestined goal.

Men have rejected God and His Word, so they in turn accept the lie of Satan. Paul said; *...because they received not the love of the truth, that they might be saved. And for this cause God shall send them strong delusion, that they should believe a lie: that they all might be damned who believed not the truth, but had pleasure in unrighteousness* (2Thessalonians 2:10-12).

Men have passed the point of no return. They have believed the lie of Satan and God has turned them over to a reprobate mind. The world at this point - as far as those involved in what is being described in this chapter - is without hope of salvation!

Verse 18:

And the woman which thou sawest is that great city, which reigneth over the kings of the earth.

That great city! What city is this? The woman has been identified as a harlot, as a great religious system, as a companion of the beast, and now she is called a city! What city is it that reigneth over the kings of the earth. The city must have reference to the title she bears in verse five, MYSTERY, BABYLON THE GREAT. Babylon, who through the years has held sway over world leaders. Her system is seen all over the world, and all through history. This religious system has caused more wars and more bloodshed and more lost souls, than all other systems of men put together!

Now she has met her doom as for as her influence on this earth is concerned. Those who have been actively involved in furthering her system will come up before the great White Throne for judgment and to hear the awful doom pronounced upon them - Depart into outer darkness!

Religious Babylon has run her course. Religious Babylon is now history. Now our attention will be focused on political Babylon and her ultimate fall.

CHAPTER EIGHTEEN

THE SECOND BABYLON...

Having spent chapter seventeen dealing with Babylon and witnessing there her destruction at the hand of the kings who had joined allegiance with the beast, we could think we were through with Babylon; but here we are studying again in chapter eighteen about Babylon. Is this the same BABYLON? There are those who feel that this is the same Babylon. However, there are also many who do not feel that we have the same Babylon under consideration here as we had in chapter seventeen.

Dr McGee wrote: "Ecclesiastical Babylon is destroyed by the will of the beast. Commercial Babylon is destroyed by the return of Christ.

"Ecclesiastical Babylon is hated by the beast (17:16). Commercial Babylon is loved by the world (18:9,10).

"Ecclesiastical Babylon is destroyed at the beginning of the last 3 1/2 years of the Great Tribulation (17:15-18). Commercial Babylon is destroyed at the end of the last 3 1/2 years of the Great Tribulation (18:8; 19:11-16)."

Finis Dake also concurs that there is a difference to be noted between the two. In fact, he makes these distinctions between the two:

"1. One of the seven angels shows John the complete mystery of the woman (17:1,7), while another angel begins the other message, 18:1.

2. The woman and the beast are symbolic in Rev. 17:1-18. Nothing is symbolic in Rev. 18:1-24.

3. Everything is explained in Rev. 17:1-18. Everything is clear in Rev. 18:1-24, and therefore needs no explanation.

4. The woman and the beast are mysteries in Rev. 17:7. Nothing is mysterious in 18:1-24.

5. In Rev. 17 the angel talks to John, while in chapter 18 he simply hears various voices announcing certain facts, Rev. 18:1,2,4,10,16,18,21. This would be entirely out of place if the two Babylons were to be the same, for the angel in Rev 17 promised John this: "I will tell thee the mystery of the woman."

6. In Rev 17 only one angel speaks, 17:1,3,7,15. In Rev. 18 both men

and angels speak, Rev. 18:1,2,4,10,16,18,20. If the two Babylons are the same why did not the angel of Rev. 17 continue speaking to John in Rev. 18, especially so, when he said, "I will tell thee the mystery of the woman?"

7. The Babylon in Rev. 17 will dominate the nations (17:1,9,15,18), while the Babylon of Rev. 18 will not.

8. One is called "the woman"; the "great whore"; etc. The other is not.

9. One is on a scarlet colored beast. The other is not.

10. Names are written on the forehead of one, but not on the other, for one is symbolized by a woman and the other is not.

11. John wonders "with great admiration" over the one 17:6,7, because he has never seen nor heard of her before, while there is no such wonder over the other. (He was well acquainted with the existence of the literal city of Babylon).

12. There is no announcement in Rev. 17 of the fall of mystical Babylon, while there is of literal Babylon in both Testaments, revealing its complete destruction in the latter days, Isa. 13:19-22; 14:4; 21:9; Jer. 50:39-41; 51:6-11,24-29,36-57; Rev. 14:8; 16:17-21; 18:1-24.

13. No merchants are to be enriched through the commerce of one, while they are with the other, Rev. 18:3,9-19. Cf. 17:4.

14. No voice will warn people to come out of one. But a warning will be given of the other, Rev. 18:4.

15. There is no boasting by one, while there is by the other, Rev. 18:7.

16. Plagues, mournings, famine, and fire from God are not to be in one. They are in the other, Rev. 18:8. Cf. 17:16,17.

17. Men do not stand afar off for fear of the destruction of one, while they do of the other, Rev. 18:8. Cf. Rev. 17:16,17.

18. Merchandise is not described in one. It is in the other, Rev. 18:11-14.

19. No definite period of destruction is mentioned of one, while it is of the other, Rev. 18:8,10, 17-19.

20. Man destroys one, Rev. 17:16,17. God destroys the other, Rev.

18:5-8,20.

21. God will put it into the hearts of the ten kings to give their kingdom to the beast for the purpose of destroying Mystical Babylon 17: 14, -17. While this is not true of the other.

22. The beast and the ten kings will rejoice over the destruction of Mystical Babylon, Rev. 17: 16,17. They will mourn over the destruction of the other, Rev. 18:9-19."

First of all, let us note how John begins this chapter; "*And after these things.*" Our first question would be, of course, What things'! The answer must be the things he has just described in chapter seventeen. This would emphasize for us that the two Babylon's mentioned in these two chapters must not be the same! For the first one was destroyed as emphasized in verses 16 through 18. That Babylon was destroyed. This Babylon of this chapter must be referring to a different Babylon.

The word "Babylon" is employed some 283 times in the Word of God, and it is generally employed in connection with Israel. There is perhaps one exception to this rule, which we will discuss later in our study. It seems there is one time that it is employed in a symbolic manner in the Revelation, and that is in chapter seventeen where we have reference to "MYSTERY, BABYLON THE GREAT, THE MOTHER OF HARLOTS".

The prophet Isaiah seems to come to our rescue in pinpointing the time of the destruction of Babylon when he speaks of it as the Day of the Lord, (13:9). He goes on to state that it will be when The stars of heaven and the constellations thereof shall not give their light; the sun shall be darkened in his going forth, and the moon shall not cause her light to shine, (13:10). Connecting this with the words of Jesus in Luke 21:25-27, as well as the record we have for us in Revelation, it seems that this will be during the last of the tribulation period. When the original Babylon was overthrown by Cyrus nothing like this happened. Nor did anything like this happen later when Babylon was destroyed.

The apostle John tells us that the destruction of Babylon shall be in "one hour," and she shall be made desolate (verse 19). And to emphasize this, an angel took a stone and threw it into the sea saying; Thus, with violence shall that great city Babylon be thrown down and shall be found no more at all, (Verse 21). We are also informed that she would be destroyed by fire (Verses 8,9,18). This is in harmony with the words of the prophet Isaiah 13:19; *And Babylon, the glory of kingdoms, the beauty of the Chaldees' excellency, shall be as when God overthrew Sodom and Gomorrah.* The prophet Jeremiah makes a similar statement in 50:40; *As God overthrew Sodom and Gomorrah and the neighbor cities thereof...*

The destruction of this great city is not to be protracted over a long period of time, but her glory is to disappear in a few hours. From this it would seem that the prophecies of Isaiah and Jeremiah have not been completely fulfilled, and there must be a future city which will meet the doom which these prophets pronounce upon her.

Verse 1:

And after these things I saw another angel come down from heaven, having great power; and the earth was lightened with his glory.

The expression *And after these things*, suggest that what is about to take place is after what has happened in chapter seventeen. That the Babylon of chapter seventeen and the Babylon we are introduced to here in this chapter are NOT the same Babylon! What happens in chapter 18 does not take place until AFTER chapter seventeen.

The term another angel seems to take us back to chapter fourteen where we were introduced to so many angels coming forth bringing the judgments of God upon the earth. The angel which spoke to John in chapter seventeen was one of the seven angels who poured out the bowls of wrath upon the earth. But this angel, like those in chapter fourteen, remains unidentified, except for being referred to as another angel, of the many who are involved in these events.

Notice that it is said of this angel the earth is lightened with his glory. Consider the condition of the earth at this time as the bowls of judgment have been poured out and the results as described for us in the preceding chapter sixteen. The fire and the smoke, the darkness which covered the land of the beast, the cities which have toppled at the pouring out of the final bowl of judgment. Now, through the clouds of darkness which must be hanging over the earth, there is a radiant light (the word lightened could also be translated, radiant), which bursts forth upon the scene.

We are informed in 16:19, the cities of the nations fell. Somehow

Babylon did not fall at that time. It seems as if God preserved her for a special judgment which was to come upon her alone. Now her hour has come, with a strong voice, saying, Babylon the great is fallen, is fallen, and is become the habitation of devils, and the hold of every foul spirit, and a cage of every unclean and hateful bird. That which had been spoken of prophetically in 14:8 - at the midpoint of the Tribulation - is now becoming a reality.

In our study of chapter seventeen we noted the comparison of the church of Rome with the Mother of Harlots riding the scarlet colored beast. But that Mystery Babylon was destroyed by the very power she had joined allegiance with. This is evidently another Babylon for our consideration in this chapter.

But what does this Babylon speak to us about?

NATIONS IN PROPHECY

Verse 2

And he cried mightily with a strong voice, saying, Babylon the great is fallen, is fallen, and is become the habitation of devils, and the hold of every foul spirit, and a cage of every unclean and hateful bird.

It is not difficult to notice some nations that exist today in ancient prophecy. A good example of this is the Communist Bloc countries. Ezekiel seems to point them out clearly in his prophecy of their invasion of Israel in the last days (38: 39:). There are other nations which we may identify in prophecy as well; Egypt, Ethiopia, Libya,

Persia, European nations, to mention a few. But none of these nations, are as powerful and world-influencing as the United States. Why don't we find the greatest and most powerful nation in the world in the prophetic word? Or, do we? Consider for thought the following scenario found in the words of the prophets Isaiah and Jeremiah.

Isaiah 18: 1; *Woe to the land shadowing with wings...*

What nation in the world has as her national emblem the Bald Eagle! The eagle with extended wings!

Let us keep in mind that when the prophets spoke, they were not aware of any country beyond the great Sea, except the nations around the Mediterranean. They could speak of Egypt; they could speak of the nations to the east; they could speak of the nations to their north, because they were all nations with which they were familiar. They were - or had been - nations of power in their day. But the United States of America was known only in the mind of God at the time of Isaiah.

which is beyond the rivers of Ethiopia... Is it possible that this could speak of America? The fact that the message is directed across the sea from Israel, and far from Ethiopia, would eliminate Europe; Asia and Africa. To a nation shadowing with wings could certainly refer to America.

Isaiah 18 :2 *...to a nation scattered and peeled.*

Could this have reference to the land mass which is far-reaching? America is certainly one of those lands which enjoys some wide-open spaces.

To a people terrible from their beginning... This could have reference to the fact they are a people to be reverenced and respected because of their power. Again, this could apply to America.

A nation meted out and trodden down... To realize the various states and counties and cities which are so carefully measured out in America; to look down on this vast and wonderful country from the heights of an airplane, would certainly make this statement come alive to us! So carefully is the entire land mass measured and marked out.

Whose land the rivers have spoiled... The experts of ecology would agree with this statement of the prophet concerning what is taking place in America, if one is to take the words literally.

Is the prophet Isaiah speaking to us about America, our beloved land?

Turning to the prophet Jeremiah we also find some interesting statements made prophetically by this prophet of God. Noting particularly chapters fifty and fifty-one, we find some interesting prophecies we examine what the prophet has to say about this country it would seem that the Babylon which he is referring to is not the one we most often think of when this word is employed.

the hold of every foul spirit... Considering the United States again in the light of this place, what nation has opened the flood gates of filth such as America has? Pornographic garbage which was banned in other countries have found an open market in America. Also, what country has so many different religious elements; cults; sects, etc., as America?

This does give us something to think about regarding this Nation being referred to here by John, that will reap what she has sown in turning her back on God and His Word.

Robertson made reference to the repeated declaration: "is fallen, is fallen," as being "like a solemn dirge of the damned."

The event, though future, is described as past, being predetermined in the counsels of God.

The words here are also found in Isaiah 21:9: *Babylon is fallen, is fallen; and all the graven images of her gods he hath broken unto the ground.*

Verse 3:

For all nations have drunk of the wine of the wrath of her fornication, and the kings of the earth have committed fornication with her, and the merchants of the earth are waxed rich through the abundance of her delicacies.

Comparing this statement with 17:2, we note the comparison between the two Babylons which are involved in these last day events; Political Babylon and Religious Babylon. The results being the same as the people of the world are affected by the influence of both. The two powerful forces which have such great effect on mankind is that of religion and riches.

"The religious worship of the ungodly world is no longer focused on mystic rituals and demonic doctrines, but is frankly fixed on the great god Mammon, and Babylon lives! The international bankers and the corporation directors and the mercantile barons and the shipping magnates and all their host of money-worshiping, power-seeking underlings, who once traversed their orbits around New York and Geneva, London and Paris, Moscow and Berlin, Johannesburg and Tokyo, now find it gloriously profitable to center it all in great Babylon. Babylon is the great capital of the world, and all the capital of the world flows in and out of Babylon. Even in the midst of all the terrible plagues of the tribulation, it is business as usual for the merchants of the world. Shortages abound, and inflation is rampant, but the money kings know how to turn it all to their advantage, and their riches increase still more. It will not be for long, however." (Morris)

Paul informs us that *the love of money is the root of all evil,* (1Timothy 6:10). James has this to say about those whose god is money; *Go to now, ye rich men, weep and howl for your miseries that shall come upon you. Your riches are corrupted, and your garments are moth-eaten. Your gold and silver is cankered; and the rust of them shall be a witness against you, and shall eat your flesh as it were fire. Ye have heaped treasure together for the last days,* (5:1-3).

Again, when we consider America in relation to this verse, what nation has set the pace for the rest of the world in the matter of finance? What nation has enriched the rest of the world with her abundance as America?

<u>Verse 4:</u>

And I heard another voice from heaven, saying, Come out of her my people, that ye be not partakers of her sins, and that ye receive not of her plagues.

The voice must be that of the Lord Jesus Christ Himself, as He makes an appeal to His people to leave this place of confusion.

This is a difficult passage to deal with. At this late date, why are there still people of God residing in this place? Has the appeal for recognition; the appeal for power and all that Babylon can offer been so strong as to override the wisdom of getting out of this place which has become such a den of demons!

Some are of the opinion that what is taking place at this time occurs somewhere around the middle of the week. A time when God has also dispatched angels to warn His people of the beast and his system. One angel flies through the air proclaiming the "everlasting gospel," and to warn people to worship God not the beast. Now God Himself issues a special warning to all who remain in this wicked city, to get out before the final judgments of His wrath fall upon it bringing it down in total destruction.

Let us consider the statement in verse two which proclaimed that *Babylon is fallen...* From this statement, it would appear that what is taking place is at the end of Babylon's reign. She is about to feel the wrath of God falling upon her which will bring her down in "one hour!"

We have a similar warning given by the Lord through Jeremiah in his prophecy concerning Babylon (51:5,6), *For Israel hath not been forsaken, nor Judah of his God, of the Lord of hosts; though their land was filled with sin against the Holy One of Israel. Flee out of the midst of Babylon, and deliver every man his soul: be not cut off in her iniquity, for this is the time of the Lord's vengeance; he will render unto her a recompense.*

Before Lot was brought out of Sodom, God sent His angels there to warn him of the pending judgment upon the city, and to give him opportunity to flee. We are informed that warning was given to the saints who dwelt in Jerusalem at the time of Titus' invasion and subsequent destruction of the city and temple, that they should leave the city, which it seems that they did and their lives' were spared.

Philip Mauro has an interesting comment to make on the calling out of Babylon of the people of God: "The call to depart from Babylon is first heard in the prophecy of Isaiah, and is heard seven times in all, the last being in Revelation 18:4. It is a significant fact also that, in each of these seven instances, the city of God, Jerusalem (or Zion) is in the context. Thus, the Scriptures remind us repeatedly of the rivalry between the city of man and the city of God. The passages are these:

1. Isaiah 48:20 "*Go ye forth of Babylon, flee ye from the Chaldeans, with a voice of singing declare ye, tell this, utter it {even} to the end of the earth; say ye, The Lord hath redeemed his servant Jacob.*"

"Even in this first passage the note of exultation is heard, as God contemplates the redemption of His people, and their deliverance from Babylon. In the context we read that "He will do His pleasure on Babylon, and His arm shall be on the Chaldeans" (V.14). Also we find in verse 2 a reference to "the holy city."

2. Isaiah 52:11 "Depart ye, depart ye, go ye out from thence, touch no unclean {thing}; go ye out of the midst of her; be ye clean, that bear the vessels of the Lord."

"Babylon is not mentioned here by name; but she is the subject of the passage. For in verse 4 God speaks of the sojourn of His people aforetime in Egypt, and of the subsequent oppression by the

Assyrian; and then He asks, "Now therefore, what have I heard, that My people is taken away for nought?"

This refers to the coming captivity in Babylon, which is the general subject of this part of the prophecy. Zion is named in verse 8, and Jerusalem in verse 9.

3. Jeremiah 50:8,9 "Remove out of the midst of Babylon, and go forth out of the land of the Chaldeans, and be as the he goats before the flocks. For, 10, I will raise and cause to come up against Babylon an assembly of great nations from the north country: and they shall set themselves in array against her; from thence she shall be taken: their arrows {shall be} as of a mighty expert man; none shall return in vain."

"In verse 3 it is said concerning the people of God, "They shall ask the way to Zion with their faces thitherward". The punishment of Babylon is foretold in verses 13,15,18,23, etc.

4. Jeremiah 51:6,8 Flee out of the midst of Babylon, and deliver every man his soul: be not cut off in her iniquity; for this {is} the time of the Lord's vengeance; he will render unto her a recompense.

Babylon is suddenly fallen and destroyed: howl for her; take balm for her pain, if so be she may be healed.

"The call here is very urgent, and the similarity of the language to that of Revelation 18:2-4 will be noted. In verse 10 Zion is named.

5. Zechariah 2:6,7 Ho, Ho, {come forth}, and flee from the land of the north, saith the Lord: for I have spread you abroad as the four winds of the heaven, saith the Lord.

Deliver thyself, 0 Zion, that dwellest {with} the daughter of Babylon.

"This is the vision to which reference has already been made, wherein Jerusalem is being measured with a view to her being inhabited again (vv. 1-4).

6. 2Corinthians 6:17, 18 Wherefore come out from among them, and be ye separate, saith the Lord, and touch not the unclean {thing}; and I will receive you. And will be a Father unto you, and ye shall be my sons and daughters, saith the Lord Almighty."

Babylon is not named in this passage, but it is implied in the confusion and mixture of believers and unbelievers, Christianity and paganism, described in verses 14-16. Moreover, the first part of the passage is a direct quotation from Isaiah 52: 11, cited above. Neither is the holy city of God mentioned by name; but that too is implied in the words, "And I will receive you, and be a Father unto you." The family relation implies the family home.

7. Revelation 18:4-8 "And I heard another voice from heaven, saying, Come out of her, my people, that ye be not partakers of her sins, and that ye receive not of her plagues."

"This sevenfold call of God to His people to come of great Babylon is most impressive. The call to come out implies that the way is open for them to depart. And such is the case, for Christ gave Himself for our sins that He might deliver us out of this present evil world, according to the will of God and our Father" (Gal. 1:4).

As an interesting thought in connection with this warning from the Lord, and considering the possibility of America being the "Babylon" under consideration, what city in the world contains the largest population of Jews? The answer, of course, would be New York!

Verse 5:

For her sins have reached unto heaven, and God hath remembered her iniquities.

When we first come upon the building of the city of Babylon in Genesis eleven, we note that the purpose of the erection of such a place was to build a tower which would reach into heaven. The haughty spirit which prevailed among the builders was to not only defy God in their building of such a city, but also to develop their own worship system which would elevate man to a position of being god.

When Nebuchadnezzar began to feel great in his own eyes, the Lord permitted him to have another dream (Daniel 4:). In this dream Nebuchadnezzar was depicted as a great tree which grew, and was strong, whose height reached unto the heaven. (Verse 20).

The judgment which fell upon the building of the city of Babylon and the tower which was to reach into heaven; the judgment which fell upon Nebuchadnezzar, who was consequently driven out to eat grass as an ox, will ultimately fall upon anyone and any system which makes man his god, and leaves God out of his plans.

Again, our comparison; No country in all the world is filled with the vices and sin any more than this country. America has become a haven for those who are peddlers of the vices and corruptions of sin.

Verse 6:

Reward her even as she rewarded you, and double unto her double according to her works: in the cup which she hath filled fill to her double.

There is a universal law. A law which applies to nations and families. To races and individuals. That is the law of sowing and reaping. Paul quoted the law for us in Galatians 6:7, Be not deceived; God is not mocked; for whatsoever a man soweth, that shall he also reap.

None are exempt from this law. Whether it be Israel or Babylon. It has now come Babylon's turn for this law to be applied to her.

It is of interest to note that this is the sixth time that we have reference to the "cup" of wickedness that Babylon and the nations of the world are involved with; (14:8; 17:2,4,6; 18:3,6).

According to some authorities the word "you" should not be included in this verse. That it should read like; *Render unto her as she also rendered...* We are not for sure whether this statement is coming from the Lord or from the saints, who are imploring God's judgment upon this wicked system for all they have suffered because of her.

The angel had declared in verse two, "*Babylon is fallen, is fallen,*" and here we have reference to "*double unto her double.*" The judgment upon this wicked system will be complete and final.

The prophet Obadiah (1:15), speaks to us of the judgment which is meted out upon the ungodly: *For the day of the Lord (is) near upon all the heathen: as thou hast done, it shall be done unto thee: thy reward shall return upon thine own head.*

We have the exiles in Babylon bemoaning their fate in the 137th Psalm. We also have the judgment which was to be meted out against Babylon, which could certainly be applicable here as well; *0 daughter of Babylon, who art to be destroyed,' happy (shall he be), that rewardeth thee as thou hast served us.*

There is an interesting prophecy found in the book of Zechariah,

(5:5-11), which seems to shed some light on this matter; *Then the angel that talked with me went forth, and said unto me, Lift up now thine eyes, and see what (is) this that goeth forth. And I said, What (is) it? And He said, This (is) an ephah that goeth forth. He said moreover, This (is) their resemblance through all the earth. And, behold, there was lifted up a talent of lead: and this (is) a woman that sitteth in the midst of the ephah. And he said, This (is) wickedness. And he cast it into the midst of the ephah; and he cast the weight of lead upon the mouth thereof Then lifted I up mine eyes, and looked, and, behold, there came out two women, and the wind was in their wings; for they had wings like the wings of a stork: and they lifted up the ephah between the earth and the heaven. Then said I to the angel that talked with me, Whither do these bear the ephah? And he said unto me, To build it an house in the land of Shinar: and it shall be established, and set there upon her own base.*

An ephah was the largest dry measure of the Hebrews. It is employed as a symbol of commerce. By a woman sitting in the midst of the ephah seems to indicate there is a religious involvement connected with this system. Out of the wickedness which the prophet witnessed he saw two women coming out, which could possibly be a reference to the wedding of the religious systems of both the protestant and Catholic religions which even today are making efforts to unite. The women are lifted with the ephah (commerce), and with the wings of a stork (which was an unclean bird to the Hebrews), they are borne forth, which seems to indicate a world-wide movement. When asked where they were going with the ephah, the prophet is informed they are going to build it (commerce) a house in the land of Shinar - or Babylon.

Verse 7:

How much she hath glorified herself, and lived deliciously, so much torment and sorrow give her: for she saith in her heart, I sit a queen, and am no widow, and shall see no sorrow.

The prophet Isaiah (47:1-9), seems to speak of this time and the conditions which shall suddenly fall upon this proud city: *great abundance of thine enchantments. Come down, and sit in the dust, 0 virgin daughter of Babylon, sit on the ground: there is no throne, 0 daughter of the Chaldeans: for thou shalt no more be called tender and delicate. Sit thou silent, and get thee into darkness, 0 daughter of the Chaldeans: for thou shalt no more be called, The lady of kingdoms. And thou saidst, I shall be a lady for ever: (so) that thou didst not lay these (things) to thy heart, neither didst remember the latter end of it. Therefore hear now this, (thou that art) given to pleasures, that dwellest carelessly, that sayest in thine heart, I (am), and none else beside me; I shall not sit (as) a widow, neither shall I know the loss of children: But these two {things} shall come to thee in a moment in one day, the loss of children, and widowhood: they shall come upon thee in their perfection for the multitude of thy sorceries, (and) for the*

The pride of the haughty against God will be brought down to the dust. The beauties which have been glorified by those who have boasted of this wicked city will suddenly be made ugly and despicable.

Those who are foolish enough to place their trust in commercialism or politics shall find themselves in the same boat as Babylon. This world and all that it offers will someday meet the judgments of God!

Verse 8:

Therefore shall her plagues come in one day, death, and mourning, and famine; and she shall be utterly burned with fire: for strong {is} the Lord God who judgeth her.

It would appear that verses seven and eight are imprecatory prayers, prayed against this wicked city and system. If that is the case, then this would also be an indication of the involvement of the Hebrew people. We have such prayers prayed by the Hebrew people in the Old Testament against their enemies. One good example of this type of prayer is found in the thirty-fifth psalm.

The reference to her judgment coming in one day seems to be an indication of the suddenness of her judgment from God. In fact, we are informed that the same word is employed in 2Peter 3:10, and in both instances it is speaking of something happening suddenly.

Babylon is referred to as "she" as she has referred to herself in verse seven as a "queen." This proud queen is about to bite the dust!

The judgment of fire reminds one of the judgment which God brought upon the wicked cities of Sodom and Gomorrah. They too were burned with fire. What or how Babylon is burned is not pointed out to us. What could possibly burn such a great city in such a short time! By the reference to this judgment being from God Himself, we are tempted to consider that the fire is of supernatural origin. This seems to be emphasized by the reference to strong is the Lord God who judgeth her.

The burning of the Babylon of chapter seventeen is done by the kings who have joined allegiance with the man of sin (v. 16). The burning of the Babylon of this chapter seems to be a direct judgment from God Himself.

Verse 9:

And the kings of the earth, who have committed fornication and lived deliciously with her, shall bewail her, and lament for her, when they shall see the smoke of her burning,

Dake wrote on this verse: "What a contrast to the result and destruction of the Babylon in Rev. 17:16, 17! Such language is too literal for one to mistake the reference as being anything else than to a material city, for the inhabitants of it, as well as others, will lament over its destruction. The kings are to be the instruments of the destruction of Mystical Babylon and vent their wrath on her freely. If there were no other proof that the two Babylons will be different, this one would be sufficient. These kings will commit fornication, and live in luxury with Literal Babylon right up to the time of her destruction, while, as seen in the other chapter, they will tire of Mystical Babylon before her destruction and rejoice over her fall."

The kings who had committed fornication with this wicked city, and who had waxed rich on her abundance, bemoan her fate. Sad is the day when men bemoan the destruction of that which is wicked and evil! Terrible is the day when men call evil good and good evil! In a march on Washington it was estimated that 300,000 were involved in the march for pro-abortion. It is a sad epithet on the history of the United States of America when she opens the doors for such atrocities on her unborn.

Dr McGee, in his unique manner, had this to say about this verse: "In this day Babylon will dominate and rule the world, she will have the first total dictatorship. The stock market will be read from Babylon; Babylon will set the styles for the world; a play to be successful will have to be a success in Babylon. And everything in the city is in rebellion against Almighty God and centers in Antichrist. No one dreamed that this great city would be judged. Yet by the time the sun went down, Babylon was nothing but smoldering ruins. When the news goes out the world is stunned, and then begins the wail.

The whole world will howl when Babylon goes down. You will have to tune down your earphones if you are on the moon."

The mighty Titanic was reported to be unsinkable - but it did! That mighty unsinkable ship did go down in just a short while after striking one of God's icebergs. The mighty Babylon which will be hailed as such a mighty and powerful city, will as well go down in a short while at the hand of God.

THREE CLASSES OF PEOPLE WHO BEWAIL

First we have the KINGS of the earth crying for the city's destruction. Kings who had shared in the pomp and glory of that wicked city. Kings who had no doubt benefitted from the power which emanated from Babylon. Power which in turn made their own position more powerful over their own country. Now with Babylon gone their own power base is threatened.

Next we have the MERCHANTS (v. 11) who will cry because Babylon is destroyed. Merchants who have been made rich because of the commercial system which Babylon headed up. Now their business is ruined.

Thirdly we have the MARINERS (v. 17) who had been made rich by importing and exporting goods from this the richest market basket of the world. Now their ships will set idle, and they are ruined. So much and so many depended on Babylon. Now so much and so many wail and are ruined because Babylon is ruined.

Verse 10:

Standing afar off for the fear of her torment, saying, Alas, alas, that great city Babylon, that mighty city! for in one hour is thy judgment come.

We are not for certain just what is meant by them standing afar off. There are differing views and opinions from others. It is felt that because of their narrow escape from the judgment of God upon this wicked city, they look back in horror as they flee from the destruction which is bringing the city down.

It is also felt that possibly these kings, with their armies, are right then on their way to the valley of Jehoshaphat, and witness, possibly through the means of satellite coverage, the destruction of this city.

If the reference in 16:18-21 to the seventh bowl of judgment being poured out resulted in Babylon's destruction, as verse nineteen seems to state; *And the great city was divided into three parts, and the cities of the nations fell: and great Babylon came in remembrance before God, to give unto her the cup of the wine of the fierceness of his wrath.* then possibly they are standing afar off to escape the buildings which are tumbling down all over this wicked city.

The expression ALAS is the same word which is translated woe in other places in the Revelation, such as 8:13. It speaks of grief and terror. The destruction of Babylon seems to leave little doubt, if any, that her destruction is a result of God's judgment.

The expression "one hour" is evidently a relative term speaking of not sixty minutes necessarily, but that the destruction is so quick. The city seemed so strong and powerful, and yet in a short while it is gone!

THE MERCHANTS

<u>Verse 11:</u>

And the merchants of the earth shall weep and mourn over her; for no man buyeth their merchandise any more:

Morris wrote: "The word for "merchants" (Greek emporos) is used only here in Revelation 18 (four times) and refers particularly to wholesalers, those who deal in large quantities of trade items involved especially in international commerce. It is highly appropriate to list these two categories of world leaders (kings and merchants of the earth) in such close juxtaposition. Such international magnates and financiers constitute, more often than not, the power behind the throne. Kings and presidents often attain and keep their authority by sufferance of those who finance their undertakings. In turn, these great men of the earth receive land grants and trade monopolies and tax loopholes and innumerable other favors from those whom they establish in political power, all to enrich themselves still further."

Let us remember that when the beast sits at the control of this system as the god of this system, his order is that none can buy or sell in this system without the mark, or number, or name. Those who have gladly lined up to receive their special number or mark, which would authorize them to do business with this system, now stand with their mark or number, but without their system. Their source of supply is now dried up!

The people of this world have reached such a condition spiritually at this time that the weeping which is taking place is not for the loss of some spiritual liberty; it is not because some martyr has just died; it is because of a city of untold immorality is destroyed! They who have given their soul to the beast and his system have no feeling for things godly or spiritual.

Verses 12, 13:

The merchandise of gold, and silver, and precious stones, and of pearls, and fine linen, and purple, and silk, and scarlet, and all thyine wood, and all manner vessels of ivory, and all manner vessels of most precious wood, and of brass, and iron, and marble, And cinnamon, and odours, and ointments, and frankincense, and wine, and oil, and fine flour, and wheat, and beasts, and sheep, and horses, and chariots, and slaves, and souls of men.

In these two verses we find a remarkable listing of those things which were to be found in this city of commerce. It was certainly a place where one could find anything and everything desired.

The words of Dr McGee are appropriate here:

"Everything listed here is a luxury item. Babylon will make these luxury items necessities. You will not find a cotton dress or a pair of overalls anywhere in this list.

"And the merchants of the earth weep and mourn over her, for no man buyeth their merchandise (cargo) any more: merchandise (cargo) of gold, and silver, and precious stones, and pearls.

"Then we move from the jewelry department to the ladies' ready-to-wear: ... and fine linen, and purple, and silk, and scarlet;

"Then to the luxury gift department;

... and all thyine (citron) wood, and every vessel of ivory, and every vessel made of most precious wood, and of brass, and iron, and marble;

"We move on to the spice and cosmetic department:

... and cinnamon, and spice (amomum), and odours, and ointments, and frankincense,

"To the liquor department and the pastry center:

... and wine, and oil, and fine flour, and wheat (this is the food of the rich, see 6:6, barley was the food of the poor),

"On to the meat department for T -bone steaks and lamb chops:

... and cattle, and sheep,

"The merchandise covers every phase of business. The articles are for a society accustomed to the better things of the material universe. Even men were bought and sold - including their souls.

.. . and merchandise of horses, and chariots, and slaves (bodies), and souls of men."

From gold, which has governed nations through the years in their monetary standards, to souls of men, the listing of things bartered for in this wicked city are emphasized and wept over by those who will no longer bargain for the soul of a man, or the price of an ounce of gold. While certain things may seem to apply specifically to John's day, how applicable are many of the things when considered by our standards today. While the mention of precious metals of gold, silver, and precious stones, were something of value and beauty in John's day, they are also very important in our commercial world as well.

We have plenty of advisors who will inform us how to invest in the markets of today regarding gold and silver and precious metals.

The reference to oil in John's day would probably have been a reference to olive oil. But when applied to our day how applicable it becomes. Nations run on oil today. The oil cartels have sought to blackmail the entire world market of oil. We have become so dependent on oil that if it were possible for any power to control the oil supply of the world he could in turn bring the world to their knees before him.

The reference to the chariots could also be applied to our own automobile industry which is so important to our society today. If it were not for the planes and automobiles that get us from place to place today, we could never function as we do today.

The reference to slaves, and souls of men, is especially descriptive of the sinful immoral condition of our own society today. Untold numbers of both girls and boys are being herded into the ugly world of prostitution. They are bartered on the market like cattle. The filthy world of sexual abuse is lower than the lowest gutter!

Verse 14:

And the fruits that thy soul lusted after are departed from thee, and all things which were dainty and goodly are departed from thee, and thou shalt find them no more at all.

All that has been enjoyed; all that has been making men rich; all that has been so immoral and wicked in the eyes of God and holiness, is suddenly no more! Those who were never satisfied, but always looking for something more to satisfy their lustful cravings, suddenly find themselves without their source of pleasures.

The utopia which man was aspiring to build - without God - is now nothing but ashes. Like his ancestors, they set out to build themselves a city which would have a tower that would reach into the heavens, so that they could build for themselves a name on the earth. And like their forefathers, it seemed that they were about to accomplish their mission - until God steps into the picture!

This wicked city which had plans of ultimately sitting as queen of the world, and out of which the man of sin would rule the world, now sits in ashes. Their dreams are gone up in smoke! They have foolishly attempted to defy God and this has resulted in their own

defeat.

The fruits which they hoped to reap has been taken from them before they could enjoy them. Before they could be harvested, they are all gone!

THE MERCHANTS

Verse 15:

The merchants of these things, which were made rich by her, shall stand afar off for the fear of her torment, weeping and wailing,

Mr Morris wrote: "For what is a man profited, if he shall gain the whole world, and lose his own soul? the Lord had said (Matthew 16:26). Men accustomed to dealing in profit-and-loss calculation should have spent more care with that calculation. They had carelessly added wrong, mistakenly thinking they had been made rich, placing far too small a valuation on God and their own souls.

Now that these are lost forever, the enormous deficit in their accounts confronts them and they know they have entered eternal bankruptcy, never to rise again."

The merchants which have been made rich in their business dealings with this wicked system, now join the kings of the earth in their bewailing the destruction of Babylon. This is worse than the crash of 1929 and the fall of Wall Street. There was a future after the fall of 1929, but there will be no future to the demise of Babylon! Her destruction, along with that of those who have joined in with her wicked system, is eternal!

Both the kings and the merchants are referred to as "standing afar off." We are not for sure just what this statement implies. We are of the opinion that Babylon is a literal city that shall become the headquarters of the Beast during the tribulation. How these are able to stand "afar off" and witness her destruction we are not informed. It is possible they are witnessing her destruction by means of satellite TV.

Verse 16:

And saying, Alas, alas, that great city, that was clothed in fine linen, and purple, and scarlet, and decked with gold, and precious stones, and pearls!

Witnessing the destruction of this great city leaves the merchants with feelings of tremendous loss. There are no expressions of repentance, nor cries for mercy for their condition. They are beyond such feelings and actions! Their expression; "Alas, alas!", could also be translated as "Woe, woe!"

Those who have placed their future in the securities of this world, are faced with feelings of tremendous losses when they are no longer within their grasp. Those who have their future secured through the blood of Jesus Christ will suffer no loss nor feelings of loss when this old world and its treasures are destroyed.

The Lord said to the man who had placed his trust in his barns and his fields and purposed to erect new and bigger barns to take care of his harvests, *"Thou fool!"* There may be no audible voice echoing from the heavens in that day, but they who have placed their trust in Babylon will surely feel like fools when their security is destroyed before their eyes.

The prophet Zephaniah (1:18), was possibly speaking of this day when he said: *Neither their silver nor their gold shall be able to deliver them in the day of the Lord's wrath; but the whole land shall be devoured by the fire of his jealousy: for he shall make even a speedy riddance of all them that dwell in the land.*

MARINERS

Verse 17:

For in one hour so great riches is come to nought. And every shipmaster, and all the company in ships, and sailors, and as many as trade by sea, stood afar off,

The third party of those who bewail the fall of this wicked city now join in bemoaning the destruction of Babylon. Those who had plied the seas bringing to and from the merchandise of Babylon, now witness their future going up in smoke. They too are described as witnessing this destruction from "afar off." Possibly some ships are coming toward this city while others are departing from the city laden with their goods, and witness the smoke billowing up in the air as the city falls in just a short time to the judgments of God.

Verse 18:

And cried when they saw the smoke of her burning, saying, What {city is} like unto this great city!

To all three classes of men who bewail the destruction of Babylon, there is no city like Babylon!

The city had come to signify so much to them. Now it is going down in ashes!

The very fact that these men make such a cry over this wicked city is a clear indication of where they had placed their hope and security. How foolish it is for men to place their trust: the trust of their material benefit, as well as their spiritual benefit, in such a wicked place and system. Those who do deserve what happens to them!

Verse 19:

And they cast dust on their heads, and cried, weeping and wailing, saying, Alas, alas, that great city, wherein were made rich all that had ships in the sea by reason of her costliness! for in one hour is she made desolate.

The psalmist makes a statement which seems applicable here: Psalm 52:7, Lo, {this is} the man {that} made not God his strength; but trusted in the abundance of his riches, {and} strengthened himself in his wickedness.

The foolish acts of these men are an indication of how extreme their feelings of loss really are. Their actions may appear to be that of children, but it also emphasizes the utter helplessness which they feel at the loss of their city.

We have yet another reference to the destruction of this city taking place in one hour.

This verse concludes the expressions of remorse coming from those who bemoan the fall of Babylon. It is evident that all they are concerned about has been their financial security, regardless if it meant the loss of their eternal spiritual security.

Verse 20:

Rejoice over her, {thou} heaven, and {ye} holy apostles and prophets; for God hath avenged you on her.

The judgments of God are sure and righteous judgments. Babylon represented all that was contrary to God and what He represented. Babylon had ensnared the souls of millions, bringing them down to eternal loss and destruction. The demise of this city, and the system which she represented, is something which brings cause of rejoicing to the hosts of heaven.

Who is encouraging the hosts of heaven to rejoice we are not for sure. Probably the same voice which is referred to in verse four which cried for the people of God to come out of Babylon.

The expressions which are heard coming from heaven are the opposite of those which we have been considering coming from those three classes of men who have witnessed the destruction of Babylon.

To them it was a great loss; to those of heaven it is a great victory for all that God represents and stands for. There are no tears of sorrow shed by this heavenly group at the destruction of this wicked city - just the opposite, there is rejoicing.

The reference to ye holy apostles and prophets, seems to connect both the Old Testament and the New Testament together. We usually connect the apostles with the New Testament and the prophets with the Old. If this is the case here, then it is an indication that there are both Old and New Testament saints residing in heaven at this time.

The admonition to rejoice seems to be given to all who inhabit the heavens at this time, which would include the angelic host as well. Let us not forget that the angelic host has also been affected by what Babylon represented. They too have been engaged in a conflict with the forces which ruled through Babylon. So, to them this is also a time for rejoicing.

Verse 21:

And a mighty angel took up a stone like a great millstone, and cast {it} into the sea, saying, Thus with violence shall that great city Babylon be thrown down, and shall be found no more at all.

We have here yet another angel which is involved in the affairs of the tribulation. This could possibly be the same angel who declared in 14:8 that Babylon would fall.

To emphasize the certainty and finality of the fall, the angel takes a millstone and hurls it into the sea. In the same manner Babylon has "been brought down. Like a stone which would sink to the depths of the waters, never to be raised again, even so has Babylon been cast down in destruction, never to rise again. The wickedness of this evil place will never effect the affairs of men again.

The prophet Jeremiah seems to be speaking of this time when he predicts in Jeremiah 51:63,64: *And it shall be, when thou hast made an end of reading this book, {that} thou shalt bind a stone to it, and cast it into the midst of Euphrates: And thou shalt say, Thus shall Babylon sink, and shall not rise from the evil that I will bring upon her: and they shall be weary. Thus far {are} the words of Jeremiah.*

She which had caused so much violence to the lives of others, is now violently taken off the face of the earth! The city which has been identified with evil and wickedness for millenniums, is now brought to judgment by a vengeful God!

Dake wrote: "The phrase "no more at all" is used six times. It is an expression showing the absolute truthfulness of the statement as well as the utter destruction of the city. This corresponds with the many passages above in the Old Testament concerning the destruction of Babylon, thus showing that after it is rebuilt and destroyed under the seventh vial that it will be utterly ruined and made desolate forever."

Verse 22:

And the voice of harpers, and musicians, and of pipers, and trumpeters, shall be heard no more at all in thee; and no craftsman, of whatsoever craft {he be}, shall be found any more in thee; and the sound of a millstone shall be heard no more at all in thee;

Babylon was a city of many vices, and also a city of pleasure. It was a city of commerce as the reference to craftsman points out. The music is no doubt wild and sensual in its nature. Whatever the desire of man longed for could be found in this wicked city of many vices.

The reference to musicians as well as the reference to millstones could speak of the affluence that could be found in the city.

That which has been so prevalent, and which attracted so many, is now suddenly silent and still. The judgment of God has been pronounced and the vices which once flourished are now deathly silent!

The prophet Isaiah, in speaking of the judgment which would be brought upon the earth because of their sinfulness, could be speaking about Babylon, the representative of all sin and sinners;

Isaiah 24:7-11: *The new wine mourneth, the vine languisheth, all the merryhearted do sigh. The mirth of tabrets ceaseth, the noise of them that rejoiceth endeth, the joy of the harp ceaseth. They shall not drink wine with a song; strong drink shall be bitter to them that drink it. The city of confusion is broken down: every house is shut up, that no man may come in. {There is} a crying for wine in the streets; all joy is darkened, the mirth of the land is gone.*

While Babylon is not mentioned here by name, what is said in this entire chapter concerning the sins of the earth would certainly apply to Babylon. Also, verse ten speaks of the "city of confusion" which would certainly apply to this city, for this is what the name Babel implies.

Verse 23:

And the light of a candle shall shine no more at all in thee; and the voice of the bridegroom and of the bride shall be heard no more at all in thee: for thy merchants were the great men of the earth; for by thy sorceries were all nations deceived.

Mr Morris had an interesting comment to make on this verse; "For some time prior to this final judgment, Babylon had been in darkness. Under the judgment of the fifth bowl of wrath (Revelation 16:10), the throne of the beast and his kingdom had been plunged into unrelieved darkness. No doubt the city will have been designed with ultramodern illumination facilities, but the probability is that the power stations serving the city will malfunction under the impact of the plagues. Any hydroelectric plants will be helpless as the water supplies are exhausted, climaxed by the complete drying up of the river Euphrates. Solar-energy plants will be useless with the city in perpetual darkness. Nuclear and oil-driven plants will be unable to function without a copious supply of cooling water. Transmission lines from other regions will probably be rendered inoperative by the intense heat of the fourth plague and then will completely collapse under the shocks of the global earthquake. Thus the city of Babylon, for some period of time at least, will finally have to rely strictly on candlelight or kerosene lamps for its illumination. It will be a miserable and desperate place during its final days."

The judgment of Babylon is not only complete it is also final. What had taken place in the glory days of this great city will never happen again. She had been a great example of ungodliness to the nations of the world, she will never again lead such an example.

The religious system of Nimrod's day - the founder of Babylon - permeated the religions of the world down through the centuries. It found its way into the Roman system of the trinity, for it was there among the Chaldean mysteries that the trinity was first adopted. Through the subtlety of Satan himself, millions have since been swayed into accepting this false religious dogma which stemmed from paganism.

The reference to sorceries in this verse, as a reason for the fall of this wicked city, involves more than just witchcraft, which no doubt flourished in that place as well. We borrow another comment from Mr Morris here: "Furthermore, as noted before the "sorceries" actually involve inducement of religious visions and states of altered consciousness by use of drugs. The Greek word translated "sorcery" and "witchcraft" is pharmakeia, meaning "drug" or "potion" or "medication." Thus, this verse states in effect that all nations have been drugged by Babylon, deceived into believing a lie. Whether using actual hallucinatory drugs in the modern revival of occultic super-humanism, or the intellectual soporific of evolutionary humanistic scientism, the Babylonian harlot had deceived all nations into worshiping another God."

Satan is the master of all that is taking place within the system of the Beast. In fact, the Beast is without doubt controlled at this time by Satan himself, or one of his demonic angels. With such a master at the controls, every kind of Satanic occultic practice will flourish in Babylon. It will be a very dangerous time to be living as men are influenced and possessed by the demonic forces of hell which are unleashed upon this world at that time.

Babylon, the last citadel of wickedness and Satanism, has become a memorial to all involved in the system of the Beast in that day. That which has been held up as being so important and so powerful, will fall in complete destruction. Her fall will shock all those who have put their trust in her and her system during the tribulation.

Verse 24:

And in her was found the blood of prophets, and of saints, and of all that were slain upon the earth.

The city may have looked like a queen among all cities, but inwardly she was corrupt and filthy.

Like the religious system which helped to bring about her existence, and her exaltation, she is filthy within although outwardly attractive.

She has a long and bloody history which is hidden from view to the casual observer. Jesus spoke of those in His day who were like "whited sepulchres," who on the outside appeared attractive and peaceful, but He said on the inside they were "full of dead men's bones." Babylon's roots which go back through the religious systems of Rome and back to the ancient Babylonian Chaldean system, are all stained with the blood of those who opposed her and who worshiped the true God.

Mr Dake commented on the statement "and of all that were slain upon the earth": "Rev. 18:24 seems to indicate that Babylon has existed from the beginning of the human race, for in it is found all that were slain on the earth. This is not to be taken to mean that, however, for Babylon was not begun until over two thousand years after the death of Abel. We know that all people have not been slain in Babylon. This would not be so if Babylon were a religious or commercial system. Nor does it mean that the slain in Babylon are the same as the saints slain by Mystical Babylon, for both Babylon's are guilty of slaying saints. This verse should be understood to involve the same principle as that in which Jesus pronounced His judgment upon the Pharisees, saying that they were worse than all preceding generations but prided themselves of being better, Matt. 23:29-36. This shows that Babylon will be the final concentration of martyrdoms and reigns of terror. Therefore, its destruction will culminate the wrath of God, under the seventh vial."

We share also some comments from Dr McGee; "This is Satan's city. He is a murderer - this city murdered. The final crime was the slaying of God's people.

"As we contemplate the destruction of Babylon, we think of other great cities and civilizations of the past that have fallen."

Mr Edward Gibbon wrote that interesting and well-read work, "The Decline and Fall of the Roman Empire." His book was published in 1788 and has become an interesting example of what happens to a nation which brings about her decline and fall. In his writings Mr Gibbon pointed out certain things which he felt brought about the fall of proud Rome;

• 1. The undermining of the dignity and sanctity of the home.

• 2. Higher and higher taxes.

• 3. The rise in welfare, spending the tax money for free bread and circuses for the people.

• 4. The mad craze for sports. The more brutal, the more it was enjoyed.

• 5. The building of great armaments, to protect against the unseen enemy, when the real enemy was the one which existed within.

• 6. The lack of religious conviction. Religion lost its appeal to the masses. They found other things they had rather be involved with.

It does not take a great mind to compare what happened to Rome and what is happening in our own nation, as well as other nations in our world today, to come to the conclusion that we are headed for serious trouble.

The fall of Babylon is the fall of the last bastion of ungodliness upon this earth. Her proud haughty ways will be no more. She will influence no one else to fall prey to her enticing ways of evil. This is but one step that God will take in bringing about a complete eradication of Satan and his evil ways from this earth. Eventually the earth will be completely cleansed from Satan and his influence which has permeated it for six thousand years of human history. What a day of freedom that will be!

CHAPTER NINETEEN

We have just witnessed the demise of two great powerful systems which have greatly affected the whole world. We are not for certain as to the exact time during the tribulation that Mystery Babylon, the Mother of Harlots, meets her doom at the hand of those whom she has befriended in her quest for joint control of the world's systems. Nor are we for sure just when the great city referred to as Babylon the great comes tumbling down. Whenever it may be, it is all in preparation for the final showdown which is soon now to take place at Armageddon.

The stage is being set for the greatest confrontation the world has ever witnessed in man's long six-thousand-year history! This confrontation which was referred to in chapter sixteen, is now to unfold for us as John describes it, here in chapter nineteen.

VERSE 1:

And after these things I heard a great voice of much people in heaven, saying, Alleluia; Salvation, and glory, and honour, and power, unto the Lord our God.

After these things... We have come upon this statement before in our study in the Revelation. Like before, we must conclude What things? The obvious answer here as well is those things which John just finished writing to us about in chapter eighteen; the destruction of Babylon.

Now that Babylon is finished and will no longer inflict her will upon the people of the world, we are prepared for the final and last conflict between good and evil. Between darkness and light. Between God and Satan.

THE HALLELUJAH CHORUS...

Here we come upon the great Hallelujah chorus. We have had reference to it in such places as 5:8-12, but for the first time we have a clear reference to the praises which shall come forth from those who have been redeemed from this earth, and who now stand in the presence of the Lord Jesus.

It would appear that the first series of Hallelujah praises come forth in recognition and praise to God for the judgment which has been brought upon the harlot of chapter seventeen.

The second Hallelujah praise seems to be directed to God for the destruction which has been brought to the wicked city of Babylon described in chapter eighteen.

This is the first time we come upon the term Hallelujah in the New Testament, although spelled here alleluia. It is employed four times in this passage of scripture. And this is the only place it is found in the New Testament, and how appropriate that it is employed in connection with the final victory which the Lord will bring against the enemy of the people.

It is the compound Hebrew word Hallal and Yah, or Jah. It means; PRAISE YE JAH, or PRAISE YE THE LORD.

It is one of those words like Amen, which is the same in many languages. The word is found in the Psalms some twenty-two times. Interestingly we find it employed several times in the concluding Psalms, as if the final Psalms depict the ultimate victory which the Lord will bring to His people. It is translated there Praise Ye the Lord. The last five Psalms open and close with this exclamation. In this the last book of the New Testament and Bible, we find this wonderful expression coming forth from those who have witnessed the defeat and destruction of these two wicked systems, and the anticipation of the ultimate victory which will be wrought at Armageddon.

Let us recall what was stated in 18:20, *Rejoice over her, thou heaven, and ye holy apostles and prophets; for God hath avenged you on her*. It is here that we hear - through John the apostle - these shouts of victory echoing from heaven.

The Archbishop of Canterbury, of many years past, stated the word "Hallelujah" was the language of the angels. Augustine said that it contained everything belonging to the praise of the Eternal God. From the Apocryphal writings, we note, Tobias 13:20,21, that the doors of Jerusalem will be built of sapphire and emerald and her walls round about of precious stones. Her streets will be paved with white and pure marble, and "Hallelujah" will be sung in the streets.

Another remarkable thing about this great noise of praise coming from heaven, is the fact that the destruction of the two Babylon's has just taken place, and when the last one fell as described in chapter eighteen, it was said, *And the voice of harpers, and musicians, and of pipers, and trumpeters, shall be heard no more at all in thee; and no craftsman, of whatsoever craft he be, shall be found any more in thee; and the sound of the millstone shall be heard no more at all in thee.* What a contrast between the two groups and the two chapters! Deathly silence falls over the remains of the wicked city Babylon.

Now, in the presence of Christ in heaven, there is a great swelling of voices which ring out reaching the ears of John of praise and thanksgiving unto the Lord God.

Verse 2:

For true and righteous are his judgments: for he hath judged the great whore, which did corrupt the earth with her fornication, and hath avenged the blood of his servants at her hand.

God is not as man. His judgments are not out of human reasoning. They are not mere retaliation for harm brought. His judgments are unbiased and final. His judgments are pure and holy. What has taken place on this earth at this time, with the destruction of these systems of evil that have brought so much havoc and sorrow to the inhabitants of this planet, has been a holy judgment. A righteous vindication of all that God represents through His people.

When it comes to the judgment of our enemies we want the judgment to be swift and instant. When it comes to us wanting forgiveness of our sins and mercies extended for our wrong doing, then we want God to have patience and wait on us for a while. So, we should thank the Lord for His patience. While the Lord is slow to anger, and His judgments may not come when we think they should, we do know that His judgments are final. With this in mind we should rejoice to know that God understands everything which comes upon us. And while judgment may not come to those who wrong us when we would want it to come, the day will come when God's judgment will be issued. There may, consequently, be a period of time when we will be called upon to suffer for a while before deliverance is known. But let us rejoice in knowing that God is faithful, and He will bring His own out to ultimate victory.

"We are taught in the Word that there is such deep sympathy between heaven and earth, and that there are emotions of tenderest Pity felt in heaven towards man below. And yet in this series of symbolic visions we have the representation that heaven is made glad by that which brings wailing on earth. How is this to be accounted for? Observe: (1) It is not the wailing itself at which there is rejoicing, nor yet at its immediate cause. (2) It is not from any vindictive feeling. All such feelings are, we are sure, dead in the completely sanctified character. But (3) there are matters of immensely greater importance than the happiness or misery of individuals. It may be a grievous thing to see a human being with a tear in his eye; it is much more so to see him in rebellion against God. And if there are those who need to be taught this, it is better to see them weeping over the bitter fruits of rebellion than to see them at ease in the revolt itself. (4) That may be joyous in one aspect which is sad in another. It may be a sad thing to see so many precious things perishing. It is good to find that when aught is poisoned by sin it is not allowed to continue. (5) As the great multitude in heaven often grieved over the burden of sin which the earth was carrying, how can they but rejoice that from it the earth is freed? (6) While angels in heaven have sympathy with man, they have no sympathy with his sin, but much, very much, with God. (7) Hence they see that while man's sin is the blight of earth, God's righteous judgments against sin as the guard of righteousness. Especially when (8) the Divine vengeance is a perfectly righteous one, never erring by excess or defect." (Pulpit Commentary)

Verse 3:

And again they said, Alleluia. And her smoke rose up for ever and ever.

The second Hallelujah rises from the throng of heaven! We are not for sure, as mentioned previously, whether those whose voices John hears coming from heaven, actually are witnesses of the destruction of Babylon. These statements seem to imply that if they are not witnesses of Babylon's destruction, they, at least, are informed of her destruction. With this awareness there is rejoicing that this system of evil has come tumbling down.

The expression, her smoke rose up for ever and ever, is no doubt a reference to her eternal doom.

The smoke of a literal city would not, of course, burn on for ever and ever. But the judgment which God renders to her is eternal!

This reminds us of what was said about those who receive the mark of the beast and join his system (14:11), *And the smoke of their torment ascendeth up for ever and ever.*

436

The judgment of God upon sin is eternal. The judgment which comes upon the sinner is eternal!

Verse 4:

And the four and twenty elders and the four beasts fell down and worshiped God that sat on the throne, saying, Amen; Alleluia.

We first saw the twenty-four elders in chapter four. There they were noted sitting on thrones, round about the throne of God. We have not seen them since we entered the time of the tribulation in chapter six. Now, at the ending of this dark seven-year period, we have our attention once again directed to them.

As we mentioned in our study of chapter four, we feel the twenty-four elders are representatives of the redeemed from both Old and New Testament. Witnessing what God has done in judgment against Babylon, they fall down to worship Him. The term worship as employed in the Word of God signifies to "fall down before in acknowledgment of sovereignty." Worshipping the Lord signifying an acceptance of what has taken place. Accepting what has happened to Babylon as being the will of God.

How many through the years have joined with the Psalmist in wondering why it was that the wicked seemed to get by with their wickedness, while the child of God was oppressed for his righteousness (Psalm 73.). If we could have our way, we would mete out judgment upon the enemies of the Church long before God does, in many instances. But the ways of the Lord are best. And we will be the wiser for it if we acknowledge that God knows what is best regarding the judgment which will come against those who oppose the Church.

The term "Amen; Alleluia" is an expression stating: *So be it! Praise the Lord!* Our acknowledgement of the sovereign will of God must begin here in this life as a child of God, whose life has been surrendered totally to His will and His will alone. It is only when one has thus surrendered their life to the Lord that he will be able to accept completely those things which come into his life during his sojourn on this earth. Otherwise we will find ourselves continually questioning those things which happen to us.

Verse 5:

And a voice came out of the throne, saying, Praise our God, all ye His servants, and ye that fear Him, both small and great.

We have been confronted with many "Voices" through our study of the Revelation. On some occasions, we have been told who the voice or voices were, but, like here, there were other times we were not informed as to the source of the voice.

We are informed that the voice comes from the area of the throne of God. Those who are around the throne at this time are the redeemed, as well as the angelic host. It would appear by the exhortation to *"praise our God"* that this could be one of the redeemed.

We have been informed that God dwells in the midst of praise. We are confronted with many Praises in the Psalms. The psalms, in fact, seem to be made up mostly of praises unto God. There are seven great Hebrew words employed to express praises unto God.

The great joy which is known by the child of God in this life through praising the Lord, will be continued after the rapture, as we receive our glorified body in which we will be able to praise Him as we were never able to in this life!

To those who feel that worship and praise should be reserved and solemn, they would surely feel ill at ease in that group and that atmosphere which John is here describing for us. Heaven will be anything but a calm, sedate, reserved place when the children of God enter it. That is evident from the following verse.

Verse 6:

And I heard as it were the voice of a great multitude, and as the voice of many waters, and as the voice of mighty thunderings, saying, Alleluia: for the Lord God omnipotent reigneth.

As if in response to the exhortation to Praise the Lord, there resounds the great ovation of praise to the Lord God, which to John sounded like many waters. Millions upon millions pouring forth praises in unison rolls and reverberates across the vast expanse of heaven.

As mentioned, the expression Alleluia, is found employed several times in the Psalms, where there it is translated *Praise the Lord.* It is of interest to note that when we first come upon it in Psalm 104:35, we read; *Let the sinners be consumed out of the earth, and let the wicked be no more. Bless thou the Lord, 0 my soul. Praise ye the Lord.* The prayer which began here is thus consummated in Revelation nineteen, as judgment is brought upon the enemy.

It is interesting to note that it has been said of the Lord Jesus Christ that *"His voice as the sound of many waters"* was heard by John (1:15). Now, those who have been redeemed, and who have been delivered to His side, and who have been made like Him, are identified with voices that sound like many waters.

With this Alleluia, we have the fourth and final Alleluia. We are now about to be introduced to the great wedding which is going to take place.

THE MARRIAGE OF THE LAMB

Verse 7:

Let us be glad and rejoice, and give honour to him: for the marriage of the Lamb is come, and his wife hath made herself ready.

Paul, in speaking to the church at Corinth, stated, *For I have espoused you to one husband, that I may present you as a chaste virgin to Christ* (2Corinthians 11:2). The relationship between Christ and His church is compared to the relationship which exists between a man and his wife. Paul in his epistle to Ephesus, employs this analogy, especially in chapter five. It is here we find Paul stated: *For this cause, shall a man leave his father and mother, and shall be joined unto his wife, and they two shall be one flesh. This is a great mystery: but I speak concerning Christ and the church,* (verses 31,32).

After the expressions of praise unto the Lord, now comes the wonderful expressions of great joy as the marriage of the Church with the Bridegroom finally arrives. From the context, it is as if those who had been praising the Lord for the judgment He has brought upon the great whore, is now turned to expressions of joy for the events which are getting ready to transpire. After all, who would not rejoice at such an event as a wedding!

Verse 8:

And to her was granted that she should be arrayed in fine linen, clean and white: for the fine linen is the righteousness of the saints.

Becoming the Bride of Christ is something which has taken great effort. For almost two thousand years this bride has been preparing herself for this grand event which is, at last, about to take place.

Appropriately the bride is seen dressed in the finest of attire, for this, her grandest, event.

Considering these two verses together, we find an interesting fact; she hath made herself ready, and here, to her was granted. In one point, we find the wife prepares herself, in the other, she is given this preparation. While it is true we must live for the Lord, at the same time we only live a life of righteousness because of His Spirit which indwells our life.

We note the reference to the fine linen in the Old Testament in reference to the Tabernacle and Temple worship. It spoke typically of righteousness. Here it refers to the righteousness of the saints.

Mr Morris stated: "The word is plural and could be better translated "the righteous deeds of saints." Here is a paradox, yet a paradox which is utter reality. No believer is saved, or made fit to enter his Savior's presence, by virtue of his righteous acts. Yet, once having been saved by grace through faith, he then is both enabled and constrained to walk in righteousness, and these righteous deeds in some marvelous transmutation become the clean and white linen robe of righteousness provided by the Savior for His people."

Verse 9:

And he saith unto me, Write, Blessed are they which are called unto the marriage supper of the Lamb. And he saith unto me, These are the true saying of God.

The "he" is evidently the same voice heard in verse five. The voice is not identified, but it is assumed that it is probably a mighty angel of God.

We assume that the marriage and the wedding feast takes place in heaven, as soon afterward we find the Lord returning to the earth for the judgment which He will bring upon the beast and those gathered at Armageddon.

We are confronted with yet another intriguing question in our study of Revelation, Who are those invited to the marriage supper?

In the Lord's teachings, He referred on different occasions to weddings, we have the story of those who were invited to the marriage of the king's son, and many refused to come and made excuse. In Matthew 25, we have the story of the virgins, five which were classified as being foolish and did not properly prepare themselves for the bridegroom's appearance.

We have differing views as to just who these are that are called to this great feast. It is evident that this statement could not apply to the Church for the bride is not invited to her own wedding! Nor do we feel, as some do, that this has reference to those in other religious systems - our trinitarian friends - who, though not in the rapture, are invited to the wedding feast.

We have an interesting statement in John 3:29, *He that hath the bride is the bridegroom: but the friend of the bridegroom, which standeth and heareth him, rejoiceth greatly because of the bridegroom's voice: this my joy therefore is fulfilled.* This is John the Baptist speaking of his relationship with Jesus Christ. John referred to himself as a friend to the Bridegroom. Do we conclude from this that John, along with Old Testament saints, should be considered as the friends of the Bride and the Bridegroom, and are those in reference in this verse? It would appear that only the redeemed of the New Testament could properly qualify to be addressed as the Bride. For the New Testament plan of salvation alone can bring about the righteousness of the soul which the Bride is here referred to as possessing. The Church being the Bride, all those who are saved outside the church, both Old and New Testament, are those who have been invited to share in the wedding activities.

THE MARRIAGE SUPPER

"It is not the wedding itself. The "Marriage Feast" is the supper that follows after the Marriage has been solemnized. There is one thing about this Feast it will be such an honor to receive an invitation, and to be present, that the angel said to John, "Write," put it down in black and white lest you forget, do not trust to tradition lest the world never hear about it, but - "write, Blessed are they which are called unto the marriage supper of the Lamb." What a supper it will be. As a Feast, the Feasts of Belshazzar and Ahasuerus will be but a poor meal in comparison." (Larkin)

Verse 10:

And I fell at his feet to worship him. And he said unto me, See thou do it not: I am thy fellow servant, and of thy brethren that have the testimony of Jesus: worship God: for the testimony of Jesus is the spirit of prophecy.

Here we are confronted with an interesting question: Who is this that John falls down before? Why did John feel so impressed by this one who had been talking with him to fall down to worship him? John had been an eye witness of Jesus Christ during His ministry on this earth. John had also received a vision of the Lord which he describes in chapter one. So, it would appear that John would not mistake this one as being the Lord Jesus.

The majority of commentators feel that this was an angel which John was falling down before. That John, so carried away with what the angel had been showing him up to this point, is so overwhelmed with feelings of thanksgiving, that he falls down to pay honor and worship this angel. Which, of course, the angel refuses to accept.

This may the case. He may be some mighty angel who has been showing John all these things. The expression "I am thy fellow servant," could also be applied to angels, for they too are servants of God just as we are. But the statement "*and of thy brethren that have the testimony of Jesus,*" does not seem to apply to an angelic being. The term "*Brethren*" seems to speak to us of the relationship which exists among the people of God in the Church.

We have indications before this that would appear to be glorified saints doing the talking to John, so it would also be possible that this one as well is one of those glorified saints.

The problem we do have with this theory is that John did fall down to worship him. It does not seem likely that John would make such a move toward another person! There was something about this one that prompted John to bow before him in a worshipping attitude.

We know that Jesus Christ did receive the worship of men (John 20:26-29) during His visit on this earth. The reply of the angel (?) directing John to worship God instead of him, is indirect proof that Jesus Christ is God. Only God is to be worshipped. If Jesus Christ

Therefore, received worship, then this must point out that He is God!

The testimony of Jesus seems to have special reference to the fact that Jesus Christ had come in the flesh. John had warned of those who would deny His coming, and those who do he termed "Anti-Christ."

It is those who have the "Testimony of Jesus Christ" that Satan has brought his fury against during the tribulation (12:17).

"Prophecy is not solely the prediction of the future, as some say, nor is it only the declaration of ethical principles, as others claim. Prophecy receives its value and meaning from its relation to Christ, whether that relation be direct or indirect. The first prophetic utterance of God, Genesis 3: 15, to the last prediction of the Revelation, the heart of prophecy, has been directed to the person of Christ. Errors of interpretation of details may be inescapable, but there need be no error in understanding the direction and purpose of prophecy; as a whole, it points to Christ" (LaHaye).

During this time of tribulation, the world has witnessed the rise of the false prophet with his claims of miraculous power, along with the man of sin who has made his boast of being god. Their system and their dogma is false. The testimony of Jesus Christ is the true spirit of prophecy. If prophecy is not centered around Jesus Christ, then it is false prophecy.

THE KING IS COMING!

<u>**Verse 11:**</u>

And I saw heaven opened, and behold a white horse; and He that sat upon him was called Faithful and True, and in righteousness He doth judge and make war.

This is His second advent! This is Jesus Christ coming as Jesus described in Matthew 24:30, *And then shall appear the sign of the Son of man in heaven: and then shall all the tribes of the earth mourn, and they shall see the Son of man coming in the clouds of heaven with power and great glory.*

John had witnessed heaven being opened on different occasions before this - but never to reveal what he witnesses now!

The last time John described one riding a white horse was in chapter six. That one evidently was the great imposter, who promised peace but brought war and destruction. He came to destroy all that God stood for and represented on this earth. Now the Lord Jesus is appearing to bring him down in bitter defeat.

What John is describing for us in simple, yet profound words, is the great climax of the ages. The final show-down between good and evil; between light and darkness; between God and Satan.

He is called Faithful because He is bringing to pass the promises which have been given down through the centuries concerning the ultimate victory of good over evil. He is the fulfillment of the promises that God has given to the righteous since Eden.

He is called True because in Him alone is absolute truth. He is the One who claimed: *"I am the way, the truth, and the life,"* (John 14:6).

He is coming in Righteousness to bring an end to all unrighteousness which has prevailed upon this earth, especially that which has prevailed for the past seven years.

He is coming to Judge and make War upon those who have gathered at Armageddon. He is not coming this time to die on a cross. He is coming to bring judgment. Isaiah spoke of this event when he said; *Who is this that cometh from Edom, with dyed garments from Bozrah? this that is glorious in his apparel, traveling in the greatness of his strength? I that speak in righteousness, mighty to save. Wherefore art thou red in thine apparel, and thy garments like him that treadeth in the winefat? I have trodden the winepress alone; and of the people there was none with me: for I will tread them in mine anger, and trample them in my fury; and their blood shall be sprinkled upon my garments, and I will stain all my raiment. For the day of vengeance is in mine heart, and the year of my redeemed is come* (63:1-4).

HIS RETURNING

There are four Greek words which are employed in the New Testament which speak of the Lord's returning:

Parousia... (par-oo-see'ah). This word means "personal coming, immediate presence, arrival, advent or return." It is found in Matthew 24:3,27,37,39; 2Thessalonians 2:8; 2Peter 3:4. It speaks of the personal return of Jesus Christ to this earth. Some confuse this reference to be referring to the Lord's return for His church.

Phaino... (fah'-ee-no). This word means "to shine, be apparent, to appear publicly, be manifest and be seen." It is found in only one place, Matthew 24:30. This reference is also speaking of the time when the Lord shall return to this earth.

Erchomai... (er-khom-ahee). This word means "to go or come." It is used generally relative to the second coming of Jesus, as in Matthew 25:13; Acts 1:11.

Epiphaneia... (ep-if-an'-i-ah). This word means "advent, appearing, brightness, to give light or become visible." It is used in 1Timothy 6:14; 2Timothy 4:1,8; Titus 2:13.

Verse 12:

His eyes were as a flame of fire, and on His head were many crowns; and He had a name written, that no man knew, but He Himself.

When John saw the glorified Lord in chapter one, he said, "*His eyes were as a flame of fire.*" There is no doubt as to who this One is that John witnesses riding forth from heaven on a white horse.

Solomon had spoken of how *The eyes of the LORD are in every place, beholding the evil and the good* (Proverbs 15:3). These are eyes of judgment. Eyes of wrath, which search out the wicked of this earth for judgment. None can hide from His all-seeing eyes. The purpose of our Lord's coming at this time is not for redemption - but for judgment. He is not coming to bless - but to judge.

- **Many crowns.**

John sees the Lord coming with many diadems on His head. He does not come to receive them. He comes wearing them! Every king and every ruler and every president and every queen, will bow to His sovereignty. He will come to be King of the earth!

It is of interest to note that the reference to the crowns which are cast at His feet by the twenty-four elders (4:10), are not the same as He is seen wearing here. Those in chapter four are from the Greek term *stephanos* (stef'-an-os), while this reference to crowns is from the Greek word *diadema (dee-ad'-ay-mah)*. It is the same word which describes the crowns which are worn by the red dragon (12:3); the beast (17:9-12). It is a reference to the type of crown which has been usurped by Satan and the beast, and those kings who follow them. They have usurped control of this earth during these dark days of tribulation. This control is just about to be taken from their hands. The real King is coming!

Verse 13:

And He was clothed with a vesture dipped in blood: and his name is called The Word of God.

As with many other things which we find recorded in the Revelation, we have a mixture of symbolism and reality here. The horses John sees coming forth from heaven are no doubt symbolic. The blood dipped vesture worn by our Lord is probably also symbolic. But the great battle which is engaged at the place called Armageddon is very real! The blood which will be shed there, as the enemies of righteousness are slain, is very real!

His name is called *"The Word of God."* When John introduced us to Jesus Christ with his gospel account he let us know that Jesus Christ was the Word of God in human form (1:14).

Verse 14:

And the armies which were in heaven followed Him upon white horses, clothed in fine linen, white and clean.

This army in heaven is not identified for us by John. We assume they are the redeemed of about seven years previous to this event which are now returning in victory with their Commander in Chief, the Lord Jesus Christ. Their attire "clothed in fine linen," (note verse 8) seems to identify them for us.

Let us recall here the words of Enoch, as recorded for us by Jude in verse 14; *Behold, the Lord cometh with ten thousands of His saints.* This must be the time of which Enoch was prophesying.

John must have been overwhelmed with this tremendous sight, as he witnessed the heavens opening and the Lord of glory coming forth arrayed in conquerors garments, astride a tremendously white horse. And then to witness the great host following Him on white horses. It must have been a breathtaking experience for the aged apostle.

Verse 15

And out of his mouth goeth a sharp sword, that with it He should smite the nations: and He shall rule them with a rod of iron: and He treadeth the winepress of the fierceness and wrath of Almighty God.

We have references, such as Hebrews 4:12, to the Word of God being a sharp sword. We also have references to the judgment which will issue forth from the mouth of the Lord; He shall smite the earth with the rod of His mouth, and with the breath of His lips shall He slay the wicked (Isaiah 11:4). *The Lord shall consume with the spirit of His mouth, and shall destroy with the brightness of His coming* (2Thessalonians 2:8).

There will not be a physical sword which shall proceed from His mouth, of course. But it speaks of the judgment which He will pronounce and cause to come forth upon the wicked at this time. It will be by His command - the sound of His voice - which will bring judgment upon the ungodly at this time.

He is coming to *"smite the nations."* The nations are the Gentile powers which have joined allegiance with their ungodly leaders in opposing the people of God and the Word of God during the time of tribulation. The forces aligned with the beast will be involved. Those who have joined sides with the Northern Bear will be there. Those from the eastern nations will also feel the sting of His wrath.

Verse 16:

And He hath on His vesture and on His thigh a name written, King of kings, and Lord of lords.

This identification of our Lord is not relegated to this place only in the Revelation - nor in the Word of God. In speaking of this coming event, we note in 17:14, *These shall make war with the Lamb, and the Lamb shall overcome them: for He is Lord of lords, and King of kings.* Paul, also speaking of this very event, stated in 1Timothy 6:15, *Which in His times He shall shew, who is the blessed and only Potentate, the King of kings, and Lord of lords.*

So, this title of our Lord is not one which is only recognized at the time of Armageddon. He has been called this in anticipation of this very event for many years. He is *King of kings*, in that all rulers of all nations will bow in acknowledgement of who He is. He is their ruler! He is Lord in that He is master of all creation. There is none greater than Him!

Some have also looked at this statement as referring to the fact that we are described as reigning with Him as kings and priests (Revelation 5:10), and He will be King over us. He is King of kings, and the kings are us!

Verse 17:

And I saw an angel standing in the sun; and he cried with a loud voice, saying to all the fowls that fly in the midst of heaven, Come and gather yourselves together unto the supper of the great God.

Why this angel is identified as "*standing in the sun*," we do not really know. Is he the same angel that is seen pouring out his vial in 16:8? Perhaps the sun is his post of duty, and he is given the opportunity to call the fowls that fill the sky to come for this great feast spread for them by the Lord.

It is of interest to note that there is mention of two suppers in this chapter: one is the marriage supper of the Lamb, to which many are invited to help celebrate the wedding of the Bride and Bridegroom.

The other is the supper of the great God. One is a time of great rejoicing - the other is a time of great death and defeat.

Verse 18:

That ye may eat the flesh of kings, and the flesh of captains, and the flesh of mighty men, and the flesh of horses, and of them that sit on them, and the flesh of all men, both free and bond, both small and great.

A similar statement is found in Ezekiel's prophecy of a great battle which will take place in the time of the end. Ezekiel said the battle of which he wrote will involve Gog, and those who join forces with him (38: 39:). In 39:17,18 we note; *Speak unto every feathered fowl, and to every beast of the field, Assemble yourselves, and come; gather yourselves on every side to my sacrifice that I do sacrifice for you, even a great sacrifice upon the mountains of Israel, that ye may eat flesh, and drink blood. Ye shall eat the flesh of the mighty, and drink the blood of the princes of the earth.*

When we consider the statement made in 14:20 about the blood *flowing for a space of 1600 furlongs*; along with the statement of the Old Testament prophet who spoke of the earth being filled with the bodies of the dead, we become overwhelmed with the thought of the number of those who will be consumed during the battle of Armageddon. Many will fall at the hands of the armies fighting against one another; but this will be nothing compared with the number which will meet their doom when the Lord appears bringing

judgments of death upon this great host of ungodly. The numbers which must be involved here are staggering - to say the least!

Verse 19:

And I saw the beast, and the kings of the earth, and their armies, gathered together to make war against Him that sat on the horse, and against His army.

Joel spoke of this day when he said; Multitudes, multitudes in the valley of decision: for the day of the Lord is near in the valley of decision (3:14).

John had stated in 17:14 that the beast, along with the kings who will join forces with him, would *make war against the Lamb*. Here, John is describing that event when it takes place. It is difficult for us to comprehend that anyone, regardless of how powerful they may be in this world, could possibly conceive that they could do battle with the Lord Jesus Christ and not lose! But this is a host which has lost all sense of sensible direction as they join forces with this Satanic leader. Their leader, the man of sin, is evidently empowered by an emissary of Satan himself. And those who have joined forces with him have sold their soul for a moment of glory with their leader. Even to join him as he opposes the Lamb Himself!

Somehow, they have seemingly sold themselves on the idea that they can actually defeat the Lamb in this battle!

Verse 20:

And the beast was taken, and with him the false prophet that wrought miracles before him, with which he deceived them that had received the mark of the beast, and them that worshiped his image. These both were cast alive into a lake of fire burning with brimstone.

The details of this great battle are not given to us here by John. We do not know how long the battle is engaged. We do not know how many have been killed prior to the Lord's coming to the scene of battle. The outcome of the battle now that the Lord is on the scene is not left to speculation.

The great leader with his great powerful influence, whom they have been following for the past seven years, is suddenly no great leader anymore!

The great prophet who convinced many that he was able to perform miracles, and who convinced the multitudes to follow the beast and accept his mark, is suddenly exposed to what he really is.

Just how these two were taken we are not informed either. However, there is one point to be made concerning *the beast* being taken and *cast into the lake of fire*: this emphasizes that the *beast* is not just a system – but an individual! It would not be possible to cast a system into the lake of fire.

Possibly some special angel, like the one commissioned to bind Satan in the next chapter, is responsible for taking these two emissaries of evil and putting them out of business.

These two are cast "*alive*" into the lake of fire. They are not victims of the battle. Although millions are evidently killed during this great battle, these two are not. These two are the only ones who do not ever die - that is a natural death! All others who are cast into the lake of fire later have all died first.

How are they taken? How are they cast into this lake of fire? Are those still living able to witness this event?

Verse 21:

And the remnant were slain with the sword of Him that sat upon the horse, which sword proceeded out of His mouth: and all the fowls were filled with their flesh.

All those left on the battlefield that day are killed by the One sitting on the white horse. This is not to say that everyone living on earth is killed, but those who were among those fighting in this battle of Armageddon. None escape His wrath!

The battle ends with the Lamb coming forth as Victor over every foe. Those who have returned with Him for this great conflict will rejoice in the victory of that great day.

CHAPTER TWENTY

• AND ...

Sometimes we wonder why those responsible for the divisions of verses and chapters in our Bible chose to end and begin a chapter where they did. Here is a case in point.

The events seem to be unfolding hurriedly now for John. He writes chapters nineteen on as if the events are rushing past him now.

Chapter twenty is a continuation of the events described in chapter nineteen. The chapters are divided with the conjunction "*and.*" Chapter twenty is really chapter nineteen continuing. It is interesting to note the continuation of the events which are taking place historically in these chapters as they are continually marked by this conjunction. Note that seventeen of the twenty-one verses of chapter nineteen begin with the conjunction *and.* And thirteen of the fifteen verses of this chapter also begin with the word *and*! It seems to be the unfolding of events which will take place in the time of the end. A succession of events which are not prolonged nor postponed for any period. The events which are described in these chapters unfold one after the other.

If we for a moment disregarded the chapter and verse divisions found in our Bible, it would be evident that what John had been describing in 19:21 is continued in 20:1. There is no pause in the action of events which are transpiring, but rather a continuation of those events!

Two of Satan's most influential servants have been put out of commission: the Man of sin and the False Prophet. Now it comes time for the arch enemy himself to be put out of commission.

• • The Great Binder Is Bound!

Satan, the enemy of the people of God and all righteousness since the very beginning, is at last bound. He who has bound so many people through the millenniums, will now become bound. He who has been responsible for the destruction of so many lives will at last be put out of business.

For six thousand long years, Satan has been the enemy of every inhabitant of planet earth. No one, even Christ Himself, have been exempted from his temptations and snares. If possible, he would have brought Christ down in defeat as well. Look about you at the many lives which he has been responsible for destroying! '

REAL OR FICTIONAL?

There are some, believe it or not, who refuse to believe that Satan is real. That he is just our imagination. He is a character which has been invented by religion to scare people into joining the church.

Well, there are a whole lot of people who worship Satan who will tell you that he is very real! And there are a lot of people who have had their life destroyed by Satan who would tell you he is very real.

- **Ask Judas if he is real!**

If Satan is real, where did he come from? Since God is the creator of all things, why did He create Satan? Or, did He?

There are passages such as that which we find in Ezekiel 28:1-19, which seems to shed some light on this subject for us. It is there that we read such statements as; *Thou hast been in Eden the garden of God... Thou art the anointed cherub that covereth; and I have set thee so: thou wast upon the holy mountain of God...Thou wast perfect in thy ways from the day that thou wast created, till iniquity was found in thee... Thine heart was lifted up because of thy beauty* (13,14,15,17).

WHY?

One could reasonably inquire, why did God permit this enemy of all mankind to have this freedom to tempt and bring destruction to so many lives? Why didn't God merely destroy Satan from the beginning when he first began to bring rebellion against God? If there had never been any contest of wills between Satan and creation, creation would have been nothing more than helpless creatures without a choice. God did not create man without a will of his own. He gave man a will. The privilege of choice.

The contest began in the garden and will not end until judgment! For six thousand years Satan, has been waging his war against the people of God. Many have fallen prey to his influence. On the other hand, there have been many who have refused to give in to the pressures exerted against them by Satan, who have come out with great victory. Such will it be on that day when the righteous shall come forth shining as the noon day sun.

While Satan will have the majority on his side, he will not have everyone on his side! The majority have always followed the easy route. Satan has always had the crowds. It has been the few who have chosen to walk with God. The plan of God never has been to have the majority. There were eight in the ark when the flood came! Israel was the smallest of nations among the many nations about them. The church today is lost in a world which continues to increase in number with every passing day. But she is the pearl of great price, which the Lord knows just where it is, and will someday soon claim that prize for which He paid His OWN life to purchase. The Church was not commissioned to convert the world - contrary to the views which are being propagated by some today, in this time of super churches.

It will be with a feeling of great victory, no doubt, that the Lord shall bring forth His glorious church to reign with Him. A host who have through the years overcome Satan and his influence and remained true to God regardless of the pressures. The event which is about to transpire in verse one will surely be a great time of rejoicing for the people of God.

Verse 1:

And I saw an angel come down from heaven, having the key of the bottomless pit and a great chain in his hand.

Again, this is a continuation of the events spoken about in chapter nineteen. The Beast and his cohort, the False Prophet, have been taken and thrown alive into the lake of fire. The rest of the host gathered at Armageddon are slain by the wrath of God. Now attention is given to the instigator of all this trouble the world has been enduring for the past seven years.

John states that he saw an angel. It is of interest to notice that nothing is said about this angel being a "mighty" angel, or an "arch" angel. It just states that he is "an angel." Satan's host is destroyed on the battlefield. He has attempted to make war against the Lamb through the beast and those gathered with him at Armageddon, and he has failed miserably! His power is gone! He is a defeated foe!

Some are of the opinion this is the same angel which is seen in chapter nine as the fifth angel, who comes down and opens the bottomless pit. He is the angel of the key to the abyss. Now he has the special commission to come back down to this earth to open the abyss again. In chapter nine it was to permit something to come OUT of the abyss. Now he is commissioned to put someone IN the abyss!

Verse 2:

And he laid hold on the dragon, that old serpent, which is the devil, and Satan, and bound him a thousand years.

The titles which are given to Satan are the same as those we found in chapter twelve, verse nine. See our comment on these titles there.

The fact that this angel takes Satan and then binds him with a chain is an indication in its self that Satan is real. T. J. Dake writes; "Thus we see that Satan is literal, his doom is literal, he is to be bound by a literal angel, with a literal chain, cast into a literal place, and sealed with a literal seal for the period of the millennium."

The one who has bound men and women through the ages with his spirits of evil, now finds himself bound with a chain by an ordinary angel of God. Satan, who has boasted through the ages of being so powerful, is now powerless. While some may wonder what kind of chain could bind Satan, it really does not matter. The fact is that he is now bound and will remain that way for one thousand wonderful years. Dr Walvoord says; "The four instances in Scripture of the word for chain in Revelation 20:1 give no reason for interpreting the word in other than its ordinary sense. Whatever the physical character of the chain, the obvious teaching of the passage is that the action is so designed as to render Satan inactive."

This is the first of six times we come upon the term "thousand years" in this passage of scripture. By employing the term some six times in the first seven verses of this chapter it seems that God wanted to emphasize to us the reality of the millennium.

ONE THOUSAND YEARS

Concerning the millennium, we are confronted with some differing views as to whether there will be one or not, and just how long it will be. One commentator put it this way; "What is the period specified? There are four hypotheses respecting the thousand years. One that it is to be taken literally; a second, that on the "day for a year" principle it is equivalent to 365,000 years; a third, that it is an indication of completeness, but not of time; a fourth, that it is a definite expression for a period indefinitely prolonged."

Another stated; "Here, therefore, as in ch. vii. 4, one thousand signifies "completeness." Satan is bound for a thousand years; that is, Satan is completely bound. But, again, in what sense can Satan be said to have been "completely" bound by our Lord's work of redemption? The answer is - In relation to the godly. The purpose of this sentence is that which is one great purpose of the whole book, viz. to encourage the struggling Christian. Thus, this sentence assures Christians that, for them, Satan has been completely bound, and they need not despair nor fear his might" (Milligan).

Well, while many things in the Revelation is certainly symbolic; Many things we have studied about were representative of something else; There is no reason for us to think that what is being described for us here is not real. The casting of the beast and the false prophet into the lake of fire was real. The battle which took place called Armageddon is real. And what we have here is also real, without a doubt.

Many of those who spiritualized many of the things in the Revelation were those who lived before the present age in which we are living. A time when much of the things spoken of in the Revelation seemed so far-fetched to their world. But in our computerized age we are realizing that what John has written is indeed things which will surely come to pass.

WHY A THOUSAND YEARS?

There are those who strongly feel that the days of creation were each seven thousand years long.

That is the first day equaled seven thousand years; the second day, seven thousand years, etc. Man was then created on the sixth day, or the sixth seven thousandth day of creation. Man's day has now almost lasted for six thousand years. Soon six thousand years will expire. It would appear that the Lord will come for His church, and the days of tribulation will occur, before this six thousand years have expired.

The thousand years of the Kingdom Age, a time in which Satan is bound and Jesus rules and reigns as King of kings and Lord of lords, will complete man's sixth day, bringing it to its seven thousand years of duration. Thus, man's day will be completed, then judgment will be set, the earth burned up with a new earth and new heavens coming forth, in which there will dwell righteousness. A time of new creation will then be enjoyed by the people of God without any fear whatsoever of Satan bringing his temptations against them.

If we look at the days of creation, along with man's day, in this manner, then we can see that the thousand years will conclude this day of man. What lies beyond man's day? We know from the study of types and shadows that we have an interesting study in the book of Leviticus concerning the Feast days of Israel. Each of them have their fulfillment in the New Testament period. It is in the twenty-third chapter of Leviticus where we find the many Feast Days of Israel. It is also there where we have reference to the "morrow after the Sabbath," which many have included in their study of types and anti-types. Also, in chapter twenty-five we have the interesting study of the Year of Jubile! If the other Feast Days, and matters pertaining to the Tabernacle and Temple, were types of something yet future in a more glorious manner, would not the Jubile also be a type of a yet future time of a great Jubile which God will share with His creation: Only eternity will reveal, of course, all the things which God has in store for those who live for Him, it will certainly be worth it all to live for Him so that we might live WITH Him in that glorious future which is planned for His creation.

MILLENNIUM!

There is more prophecy found in the Word of God concerning the Millennium than any other period. The Old Testament prophets are found making many references to the Kingdom that they looked for with great hope.

Daniel, while interpreting the dream of Nebuchadnezzar, informed him that *in the days of these kings shall the God of heaven set up a kingdom, which shall never be destroyed,* (2:44). Daniel must have been referring to the time of Armageddon and then the Millennium.

KINGDOM CONDITIONS

Micah spoke with great hope of that time in chapter four. He said there would be a time *when many nations shall come, and say, Come, and let us go up to the mountain (kingdom) of the LORD, and to the house of the God of Jacob; and He will teach us of His ways, and we will walk in His paths: for the law shall go forth of Zion, and the Word of the Lord from Jerusalem.*

Jerusalem will become the center of not only the kingdom of God for the nations of the world, but it will also be the center of worship for the world.

In verse three, Micah informs us that wars will be a thing of the past; *they shall beat their swords into plowshares... neither shall they learn war any more.* The last great war, Armageddon, which has affected the entire world, will be the last one to curse this earth for one thousand wonderful years.

Verse four speaks of the peace which will prevail during this period; *But they shall sit every man under his vine and under his fig tree; and none shall make them afraid.*

Isaiah speaks of the conditions which will prevail during this time when he wrote; *The wolf also shall dwell with the lamb, and the leopard shall lie down with the kid; and the calf and the young lion and the failing together; And a little child shall lead them. And the cow and the bear shall feed; their young ones shall lie down together: and the lion shall eat straw like the ox. and the sucking child shall play on the hole of the asp, and the weaned child shall put his hand on the cockatrice's den. They shall not hurt nor destroy in all my holy mountain (kingdom): for the earth shall be full of the knowledge of the LORD, as the waters cover the sea.* (11 :6-9)

PEACE - PEACE

Isaiah also describes the conditions which will prevail in that time when the Lord shall reign as King over the earth; *The wolf and the lamb shall feed together, and the lion shall eat straw like the bullock: and dust shall be the serpent's meat. They shall not hurt nor destroy in all my holy mountain, saith the LORD* (65:25).

There are several other passages which speak of the peaceful conditions which will prevail during this time. And no wonder that there will be peace on the earth during this time - for the devil is bound!

While there will be sinners living on the earth during the millennium, they will not be committing their sinful acts because the instigator - the motivator - of sin is bound in the pit. This is evident from the fact that when he is loosed for a while, he is able to gather together a great host who will follow him to their doom.

LONGEVITY OF LIFE

Isaiah seems to inform us that longevity of life will be restored like it was before the great flood of Noah's day (65:20); *There shall be no more thence an infant of days, nor an old man that hath not filled his days: for the child shall die a hundred years old; but the sinner being a hundred years old shall be accursed.*

Looking at this statement through the eyes of two other translations helps us to understand what the prophet is saying here;

The NEB, "There no child shall ever again die an infant, no man fail to live out his life; every boy shall live his hundred years before he dies, whoever falls short of a hundred years shall be despised."

James Moffatt; "No babe shall die there anymore in infancy, nor any old man who has not lived out his years of life; he who dies youngest lives a hundred years. Anyone dying under a hundred years must be accursed of God."

Dying a hundred years of age will be considered dying young during the millennium. Those who do die at that young age, there must be something wrong with them, and God is bringing His judgment upon them.

Among the many adverse things which sin brought into man's world was a shortening of the life span. For with sin came diseases and sicknesses, etc., which brought about a shortening of man's life span.

Verse 3:

And cast him into the bottomless pit, and shut him up, and set a seal upon him, that he should deceive the nations no more, till the thousand years should be fulfilled: and after that he must be loosed a little season.

We are again confronted with language which speaks of a literal being. One would have to stretch their imagination somewhat in order to say that what is being cast into this pit; what is being shut up in this pit, and what has a seal placed upon his prison, is nothing more than an idea; an imagination.

When our Lord was crucified, after they had laid His body in the tomb of Joseph, the chief priests and Pharisees came to Pilate, asking him to make sure that no disciple would come and steal His body and then report that He had resurrected, like He claimed He would do while living. Pilate gave them authority to *"make it as sure as ye can."* Then the record states; *"So they went, and made the sepulcher sure, sealing the stone, and setting a watch."* The difference between this seal placed on the tomb of Jesus Christ and the seal which is placed on the pit in which Satan is cast, is that behind one seal lay the body which God had walked in for thirty-three years; behind the other is an angel which would not keep his anointed position but chose to rebel. One has all power; the other is limited. While this seal will hold Satan in this bottomless pit, no seal - nor death - could hold the Lord Jesus Christ!

His incarceration is for a limited time. Only one thousand years. But it will be one thousand glorious years during which this world will enjoy a utopia of bliss. For those who enjoy this millennium, it will be a wonderful time of peace and tranquility with the Lord reigning as King. For Satan, in that bottom-less pit, it will be one thousand long, lonely, years of confinement, during which time he will no doubt be making plans for when he is let out of his prison house.

WHY LOOSE HIM?

Someone was asked why the Lord would loose Satan once he had been bound, the reply was, If you will tell me why God let him loose in the first place, I will tell you why God lets him loose the second time!

For one thousand years man will be living under ideal conditions. Since the garden of Eden, no generation of man has known such all existence. During this period, however, there will still be many thousands who are not saved living on this earth. Those who were not killed on the battlefield of Armageddon, living in some other place from that battle site, will be among those living during this time. These will live under the same conditions as everyone else, but they are not saved. They are not committing sin during this period because the instigator of their wicked ways is unable to motivate them from his prison house. At the end of the millennium it will be these whom the Devil will gather together and bring against the camp of the saints.

This will show that even under ideal living conditions the heart of man is still set on evil and is corrupt without the blood of Jesus Christ cleansing it.

Verse 4:

And I saw thrones, and they sat upon them, and judgment was given unto them: and I saw the souls of them that were beheaded for the witness of Jesus, and for the word of God, and which had not worshiped the beast, neither his image, neither had received his mark upon their foreheads, or in their hands; and they lived and reigned with Christ a thousand years.

The question foremost in this verse is who are the they that John is speaking of here who sits upon these thrones? Looking back in our study of the book of Revelation, we recall something we noted in chapter five, where there we heard the song which was being sung by the redeemed. Part of that song was, *and hast redeemed us to God by thy blood out of every kindred. and hast made us unto our God kings and priests: and we shall reign on the earth.*

The *THEY* must be these redeemed who have returned to this earth with the Lord from heaven.

They have returned not only to help in bringing down the beast and the false prophet, but also to reign during this one thousand years of the Kingdom Age. We do not know for sure just how the redeemed will reign with Christ during this millennium. While we know that the twelve apostles (again, we are not for sure who will be the twelfth apostle in Judas' place!) will be sitting on twelve thrones, each judge over one of the twelve tribes of Israel, we do not know for sure in what capacity, nor where geographically, the redeemed will reign.

judgment was given unto them... Just how we are to interpret this statement is open for supposition. Are we to interpret this statement to mean that by the fact they are sitting on thrones they have been judged righteous, and thus rewarded by being included in the Kingdom of God by ruling with Him? Or, do we interpret this statement to mean that because of the persecution the redeemed have endured through the years, they are now witnessing judgment falling upon the wicked? We do know that Paul states in 1Corinthians 6:2, *Do ye not know that the saints shall judge the world?*

A RESURRECTION!

John then wrote: *and I saw the souls of them that were beheaded for the witness of Jesus, and for the Word of God, and which had not worshiped the beast, neither his image.* The tribulation is past; the Lord Jesus has come in power and great glory, now those who died during the dark days of tribulation are called forth from their graves. Some of them had been heard crying out (6:9-11) for vengeance upon their enemies. They were informed that they must wait for a little while, until the others who would die during the tribulation would join them. Now they are all called forth to join Christ in a time of rejoicing for one thousand years. These too will receive a glorified body and join the other redeemed and glorified which will include the Old Testament saints and the Church.

OLD TESTAMENT SAINTS AND THE RESURRECTION

John does not give us any clear information concerning the Old Testament saints as to when they are resurrected. Some feel that they will come forth when the Church saints are resurrected and caught up to meet the Lord in the air. If that would be the case, then this would make the Old Testament saints, who are mostly connected with Abraham and the promises related to him and his seed, become part of the Bride of Christ. The Wife of the Lamb.

Daniel seems to inform us as to the time of their resurrection when he wrote; And there shall be a time of trouble, (the tribulation) such as never was since there was a nation even to that same time: and at that time thy people (the Jews) shall be delivered, everyone that shall be found written in the book. And many of them that sleep in the dust of the earth shall awake, (resurrect) some to everlasting life, and some to shame and everlasting contempt.

So, Daniel seems to place the time elf the Old Testament saints' resurrection after the tribulation.

Some place their resurrection at the same time as the tribulation saints. Both coming forth to enter the millennium.

Paul, in speaking about the rapture, specified in 1Thessalonians 4:16, *and the dead in Christ shall rise first.* It would not appear that we could consider the Old Testament saints "in Christ!"

Because of the many references to David and the kingdom age, it would appear that David will come forth in his position as the king of Israel under Jesus Christ, King of kings. It will be a theocratic kingdom established on the earth for one thousand wonderful years.

Jesus said, in Matthew 8:11, And I say unto you, That many shall *come from the east and west, and shall sit down with Abraham, and Isaac, and Jacob, in the kingdom of heaven.* This term "kingdom of heaven," is unique with Matthew and his gospel account. It seems to speak to us of the time of the Kingdom Age and the Millennium. A time when heaven shall rule the inhabitants of this earth. It will be a time when God comes down in the person of Jesus Christ to rule this earth from His throne on this earth.

Daniel spoke of that time when he interpreted the dream of Nebuchadnezzar; *And in the days of these kings shall the God of heaven set up a kingdom.* (2:44). This is referring to the time when Christ shall come at Armageddon, to put down the beast and all those who have sought to conquer and control this earth.

God made a covenant with David, found in 2Samuel 7, which assured David that his house and kingdom would be established for ever. Note especially verses 13 - 17.

Following the wonderful promise of the birth of Jesus Christ, Isaiah goes on to say; Of the increase of his government and peace there shall be no end, upon the throne of David, and upon his kingdom, to order it, and to establish it with judgment and with justice from henceforth even for ever (9:7).

Jeremiah, after speaking of the time of trouble which he referred to as the time of *Jacob's trouble,* speaks of how they *shall serve the LORD their God, and David their king, whom I will raise up unto them* (30:9).

Ezekiel, in referring to the time when Israel would once again be restored in their kingdom, stated; *And I will set up one shepherd over them, and he shall feed them, even my servant David; he shall feed them, and he shall be their shepherd* (34:23).

Hosea prophesied of how that Israel would be without a king or sacrifice for many days. Then he said, *Afterward shall the children of Israel return, and seek the LORD their God, and David their king; and shall fear the LORD and His goodness in the latter days* (3:5).

Amos 9:11 of the Old Testament, and Acts 15:16 of the New Testament, both speak of the time when God will *In that day raise up the tabernacle of David.*

All of these prophecies are referring to the time of the Kingdom Age - or Millennium. Wonderful things are in store for the people of God during this one thousand years of the reign of Jesus Christ. If the New Jerusalem descends at this time, the Church will inhabit the City, and at the same time be involved in the affairs going on during the millennium on the earth. Jesus Christ will have His throne on the earth in the area spoken of by Ezekiel (48:10) which will be allotted from among the inheritance of the people of Israel.

Verse 5:

But the rest of the dead lived not again until the thousand years were finished. This is the first resurrection.

At this point in time it would appear that only those who are not saved remain among the dead. All of the saved, from both the Old and New Testament era, have been resurrected or raptured. It will be one thousand more years before the remaining dead will be called forth for the judgment.

This is the first resurrection... This statement is informing us that the first resurrection is now completed. It does not mean that the martyrs of the tribulation period are the first resurrection, but, rather, the concluding segment of the first resurrection.

The first resurrection is in many segments. Jesus Christ was the *"firstfruits of them that slept,"* (1Corinthians 15:20). It would appear that the first resurrection is in at least five stages;

• 1. Jesus Christ, the first fruits.

• 2. The Church at His coming again.

• 3. The two witnesses of Revelation eleven.

• 4. The Old Testament saints.

• 5. The tribulation martyrs.

Verse 6:

Blessed and holy is he that hath part in the first resurrection: on such the second death hath no power, but they shall be priests of God and of Christ, and shall reign with Him a thousand years.

Those who come forth in the first resurrection will come forth with glorified bodies. Nothing - sin nor Satan - will be able to touch them ever again. Sickness nor death will ever again affect them!

They are the blessed and holy as they will have a unique position in the kingdom of heaven, as they join in a time of reigning with Christ during the millennium.

The second death speaks of the eternal death which those who come before the white throne judgment and do not have their name in the book of life, are cast out into.

They shall be priests of God... The Lord spoke of Israel, after bringing them forth from the bondage of Egypt; *And ye shall be unto me a kingdom of priests, and an holy nation* (Exodus 19:6). Israel sinned before God, breaking the very law they vowed they would obey (verse 8). In so doing they lost their position before God as a kingdom of priests. God instead chose one tribe from among the twelve, and one family from among that tribe, and one household from among that family, to be priests before Him for the people.

Now, at last, Israel shall stand before God in this position of priests of God.

Verse 7:

And when the thousand years are expired, Satan shall be loosed out of his prison.

From one verse to the following one we pass through one thousand years! John does not supply any detailed information for us concerning the conditions which prevail during this thousand years. We must go back to the prophets to find those details.

While we have a glimpse, through the eyes of the prophets, what will be going on during the thousand years of the Kingdom Age, upon this earth, we do not have any information as to what Satan is doing during this time. Except that he is in the abyss for the entire period. This is one place he cannot escape from!

When we read here of Satan being loosed from his prison, there is no mention of his demon associates, as to whether they too are loosed with him.

Verse 8:

And shall go out to deceive the nations which are in the four quarters of the earth, Gog and Magog, to gather them together to battle: the number of whom is as the sand of the sea.

The question has been raised as to how many people could possibly be still living on this earth after the tribulation? We know that during the tribulation we have record of what is evidently millions who have been killed. Many have been destroyed by the beast. Many more have been destroyed by the wrath of God.

Jesus spoke of those who would endure unto the end, (Matthew 24: 13). Zechariah prophesied that *It shall come to pass, that in all the land, saith the LORD, two parts therein shall be cut off and die; but the third shall be left therein. And I will bring the third part through the fire, and will refine them as silver is refined.* (13:8,9). The prophet is speaking here about the Jews in particular.

The prophet also stated; *And it shall come to pass, that everyone that is left of all the nations which came against Jerusalem shall even go up from year to year to worship the King, the Lord of hosts, and to keep the feast of tabernacles.* (14:16).

So, from these two passages alone we note that there will be several Jews who will enter the millennium, along with many of those who did not join the conflict at Armageddon.

We have no way of knowing how many people will be alive at the time of the Lord's return to this earth, but we can assume there will be many thousands across the earth who will be involved in the Kingdom Age.

From the statement made in this verse we can see the population of the world will certainly be great in number. While this is after the thousand years; during which time longevity of life has been restored, and the population has without doubt increased tremendously, it is also an indication of the fact there are many living on the earth at this time.

DECEIVE THE NATIONS.

By John referring to Satan going out to the nations is an indication that the earth is still divided by nations. Again, we do not have any information given to us in the Word of God as to who these nations will be at this time.

By the fact that Satan is able to invade these nations, deceiving masses into following him, is a sad commentary on mankind! For one thousand years they have been living under ideal conditions. The King who has been ruling them is an ideal ruler - the Lord Jesus Christ! The government under which they lived during these thousand years was an ideal government. Yet for all of this, look at the number who yield to Satan and follow him to their doom!

The fact that Satan was able to deceive this host of people is an indication that, although they have not been committing sinful acts during the millennium - because Satan was bound - the seed of sin was there. As soon as Satan is loosed, the spirit which dwells in the heart of the sinner is activated, and he is ready to follow his leader.

"Although the entire book of Revelation deals with last things, especially do these last few chapters. Here is the last rebellion of Satan and man against God. The Millennium is a time of testing of man under ideal conditions - as this passage demonstrates. As soon as Satan is released, a great company, who have been under the personal reign of Christ under ideal circumstances, goes over to him.

From where did such a company come? is a worthy question. The answer lies in the fact that not only do multitudes enter the Millennium, but multitudes are born during the Millennium (see Isaiah 11:6; 65:20). This will be the time of earth's greatest population explosion. Disease will be eliminated; and since the curse of sin will be removed from the physical earth, it will produce enough foodstuff to feed its greatest population. The human heart alone remains unchanged, and many will chafe under the righteous rule of Christ. He will be an absolute monarch, unparalleled by any dictator. This explains why the mob will go over to Satan. The nations of the earth will again come under the spell of Satan, and will plot a rebellion." (McGee)

It appears from such passages as Zechariah 14:17-19, that every nation, although living in such ideal conditions, will not be willing participants in the kingdom. *And it shall be, that whoso will not come up of all the families of the earth unto Jerusalem to worship the King, the LORD of hosts, even upon them shall be no rain. And if the family of Egypt go not up, and come not, that have no rain,' there shall be the plague, wherewith the LORD will smite the heathen that come not up to keep the feast of tabernacles. This shall be the punishment of Egypt, and the punishment of all nations that come not up to keep the feast of tabernacles.*

GOG AND MAGOG

The first time we come upon the term Gog and Magog is in Ezekiel thirty-eight. Magog was the second son of Japheth, grandson of Noah. He founded the great nations north of Israel, the majority of whom today are Russians. Ezekiel is describing the battle which involves Russia and her satellite nations. The reference here to Gog and Magog is not the same thing.

Actually, if you will note the reading of this verse you will note that it does not say that Gog and Magog are the leading forces in this battle - Satan is the leader. Possibly the reference to Gog and Magog is employed more as a symbol, representing those who would come against the people of God.

Like the Northern forces will come against Israel, as Ezekiel describes their invasion, Satan and those who join his forces will come against the people of God.

It is also possible that, since the invading forces were defeated on the battlefields of Israel; such a defeat that only a few of them escaped in humiliation; that those actively involved in this battle will actually be descendants who through the years of Millennium have been rebels.

Mr Morris suggested this thought as well; "The descendants of these, (Russians) however, had multiplied rapidly, so that Russia had soon again become a great millennial nation, possibly even readopting its ancestral name of Magog. One can suppose that after several generations the younger Magogites had begun to rankle over the history of the destruction of their forebears, and especially to resent the Israelites, both because it was in Israel that Gog's empire had been destroyed and because the Israelites now occupied the premier place among the nations. The armies of the other nations had been destroyed in Israel later, at Armageddon, and now their descendants also began to share the same resentment."

AS THE SAND OF THE SEA... Satan has always had the majority on his side. Even at this time, the same will hold true. But victory does not always lie with the greatest number! Victory lies in the hand of the Lord!

The term *sand of the sea* is a term to show a very large number. The term is employed in different places in the Word of God. Abraham's

descendants were compared to the sand of the sea, (Genesis 22:17). The kings who joined together to fight against Joshua and Israel, (Joshua 11:4) their forces were referred to as the sand that is upon the seashore.

Although it is a great host who have joined forces with Satan, it will all be to no avail. They are marching to their doom!

Verse 9:

And they went up on the breadth of the earth, and compassed the camp of the saints about, and the beloved city: and fire came down from God out of heaven, and devoured them.

We have no way of knowing just how much time is involved in all of this. It stands to reason it would take some time to get this great host together for the purpose of coming against the people of God. Who organizes it? Who is the captain of this great host of people? While the beast was on this earth, he was the captain of the forces of evil. We know that Satan is the head, but he must have some mortal under him, through whom he is working to bring about this great number, who are consolidating their forces to come against the people of God.

It would appear from Micah 4:3, that the weapons of warfare have long since been removed from the earth and destroyed. What kind of weapons then does this host bring against the people of God?

With the technology which is available at this time, it is not likely that it would take long to bring about weapons of warfare once again. For one thousand years' weapons of the world have not been employed by war. For one thousand years' weapons of warfare have not existed. Now, just as soon as Satan is loosed, war once again looms on the scene.

CAMP OF THE SAINTS - AND THE BELOVED CITY... It appears that this refers to two sites. The word CAMP is translated elsewhere as "castle." (Such as Acts 21:34). So, it appears that the camp refers to some enclosure or place of fortification where the saints have gathered.

The beloved city is without doubt Jerusalem. The host is so large that they are able to compass both the camp of the saints and the city of Jerusalem, it appears.

Just who are these saints gathered in this camp? John does not identify them other than referring to them as saints. From this we could assume that all who have not joined forces with Satan would fit into this category. How was the division determined? Did the spirit of Satan which has been responsible for enticing men through the ages to follow the path that leads to destruction, prompt the hearts of people to leave family and friends, houses and cities, to make their way to the gathering place for all those who are classified as sinners? And in so doing, leave behind all the righteous, who have themselves gathered together for the final showdown.

With all the activity that must be going on, it would seem evident that Satan is planning his final assault on the people of God.

If the number who have joined Satan in this assault could be listed as sand of the sea in number, how would the number gathered in the camp of the saints be classified? If their number includes those who returned from heaven with the Lord at Armageddon, and all those who were resurrected before the millennium began, then their number as well would be awesome. If when we read "saints" we are to assume ALL the saints of all the ages, then their number as well could be considered as the sand of the seashore!

FIRE CAME DOWN FROM GOD... This is oft times referred to as the "*Battle of Gog and Magog*," but a careful reading will show that John does not call it that. In fact, it is not even called a battle. A battle would be described as when two armies come together in combat against one another. This does not take place here! Note John states; to gather them together to battle. It seems that it is Satan's plans to battle the people of God. But war for the people of God has been over for one thousand years! There is no coming together in conflict here.

We do not even know if Satan's host fired one rocket shell into the camp of the saints. We do not know if one rifle was fired! It does not seem likely that Satan's host inflicted any damage whatsoever upon the people of God. Just as soon as this great host was gathered around the camp of the saints, God steps on the scene bringing down a judgment of fire upon the hosts following Satan.

Some have pointed out that the words from God are not found in some manuscripts. That the record should read fire came out of heaven. The implication is that a nuclear force is employed here to destroy the enemy of the saints. Let's leave it just as we find it in the King James Version! God does not need at this point to employ the weapons of man's warfare to bring about judgment upon the ungodly.

He brought a fire down upon wicked Sodom millenniums before this. He is doing it once again! This time, it involves every sinner who remains alive on the earth.

There is now no living sinner. The only living mortals on this earth at this time are the saints of God.

SATAN'S LAST MOVE

Now that the battle is over, the next step will be the eternal removal of Satan from the scene. God purposely permitted Satan to be held in the bottomless pit during the millennium as He knew there would be a lot of people living during the millennium that would be sinners. He gives the last living mortals upon earth an opportunity to be tested by Satan. Hundreds of thousands fail the test!

Every son of Adam has now been tempted by Satan. None have escaped his subtle attacks. These who are living at the end of the millennium are the last to be confronted by this master deceiver.

For six thousand years Satan, has had opportunity to tempt and ensnare every mortal he possibly could. His greatest prize, the Lord Jesus Christ, escaped his clutches. Millions stand in white linen garments who have been redeemed by the blood of Jesus Christ, as a testimony to his failure against them.

Multiplied millions more stand, ready to enter the new earth, who overcome Satan's greatest salesman - the man of sin. They too represented defeat to Satan and his wicked plans.

Satan's day is now over. It is his turn now to feel the judgment of God.

Verse 10:

And the devil that deceived them was cast into the lake of fire and brimstone, where the beast and the false prophet are, and shall be tormented day and night for ever and ever.

"Here is the final end of the primeval cherub, the highest angel of all, the rebellious "son of the morning" who wanted to exalt his throne above God's throne. The great blasphemer, the idol, the false god, the breaker of God's rest, the rebel against his father, the murderer from the beginning, the robber, the great adulterer, the father of lies, the coveter of divine worship, the one who is the very antithesis of the holy and gracious God, the Devil, will finally be cast forever into outer darkness." Morris

The direct reference found in the words *the devil that deceived them,* is directed to those whom he has brought against the camp of the saints. Those whom he deceived after being loosed from the abyss.

But the greater deception dates back to the first couple in the garden some seven thousand years prior to this.

We assume that the same angel who was called forth to bind Satan and cast him into the abyss is the same one who is called on here to cast him into the lake of fire.

There is much speculation as to the location of this lake of fire. Some have suggested that it is in the center of the earth. We have no scriptural reference to which we can turn to locate it geographically.

But there remains one thing for certain - there is a lake of fire!

The beast and the false prophet were cast into this place one thousand years prior to this, and they are still there! For one thousand years, they have been the sole inhabitants of the lake of fire. Now they receive their first company, and it is Satan!

The fact the beast and false prophet are mentioned by John as still being there emphasizes to us the fact that the lake of fire is eternal.

Those who advocate that the lake of fire is not eternal; that those who are cast into it are burned up, and not there eternally, usually point to this verse and emphasize that the word *are* is in italics. This shows that the word was not in the original writings, and therefore, should not be considered part of this verse. Their argument is that the beast and the false prophet are not still there. That the statement simply means that the devil is cast into the same place where the beast and false prophet were a thousand years before. But they have since long ago been annihilated.

Well, let's remove the word ARE from this verse and see what it does to the teaching that the lake of fire is eternal. It does nothing to destroy this fact. If the word ARE was not considered, we still have the concluding phrase; *and shall be tormented day and night for ever and ever.* If that does not spell eternal, nothing does!

A similar statement is made in 14:11 concerning the doom of those who accept the mark of the beast; *And the smoke of their torment ascendeth up for ever and ever: and they have no rest day nor night, who worship the beast and his image.*

This is the eternal doom of Satan, along with the beast and the false prophet. Never again will they bring havoc to this world, nor to the lives of people. He who blatantly opposed God and sought worship for himself, has now felt the eternal sting of the God whom he opposed. He now - as never before - realizes that it is God who is Sovereign and who rules creation.

AND NOW JUDGMENT COMES

Verse 11:

And I saw a great white throne, and Him that sat on it, from whose face the earth and the heaven fled away; and there was found no place for them.

John's statement *And I saw* signifies yet another awesome vision which comes before him. What John has been witnessing throughout this book has no doubt filled him with great wonderment and awe, but nothing thus far compares with what unfolds before his eyes now.

A great white throne emphasizes the justness of the judgment which will be executed from this throne. It is white because the Judge who sits upon it is just and righteous in judgment.

While the saints have been before the throne of God (2Corinthians 5:10) to be judged, and rewarded for their works in life, none have been before this judgment till now.

When we saw the throne in chapter four we noted there was a rainbow about the throne. The rainbow speaks of mercy mingled with judgment, which the tribulation revealed. But here there is no mention of a rainbow. There will be no mercy issuing from the throne now. It is a time for judgment.

As to the One who is sitting in judgment on the throne, there is no doubt that it is the same One who was sitting on it in chapter four - the Lord Jesus Christ. Paul wrote, 2Timothy 4:1; *I charge thee therefore before God, and the Lord Jesus Christ, who shall judge the quick and the dead at His appearing and His kingdom. Jesus said, John 5:22,27-29; For the Father judgeth no man, but hath committed all judgment unto the Son. And hath given Him authority to execute judgment also, because He is the Son of man. Marvel not at this: for the hour is coming, in the which all that are in the graves shall hear His voice, and shall come forth; they that have done good, unto the resurrection of life; and they that have done evil, unto the resurrection of damnation.* Then Paul also wrote in 2Timothy 4:8, *Henceforth there is laid up for me a crown of righteousness, which the Lord, the righteous judge, shall give me at that day.*

WHERE WILL THIS JUDGMENT TAKE PLACE?

We are not given any specifics as to the location of this judgment. Making some deductions it would appear that it would not take place on this earth, as it is evidently destroyed when the Judge takes His throne to pass judgment. All of those who are called before this judgment have been called forth from their graves, so they are eternal beings. Because of this they could be called before the throne of God in heaven for this judgment. And it is quite likely that this is where this judgment takes place.

The earth and the heaven fled away... The earth which has been corrupted through the seven thousand years that man has lived upon it. The earth which has been corrupted by the influence of Satan through those years, will pass away. It was the prophet Isaiah who wrote; *The earth also is defiled under the inhabitants thereof,* (24:5).

The apostle Peter wrote of this judgment upon the earth and heaven when he said; *the heavens shall pass away with a great noise, and the elements shall melt with fervent heat, the earth also and the works that are therein shall be burned up.* (2Peter 3:10).

Peter also referred to this day when he wrote in verse seven of the same chapter; *But the heavens and the earth, which are now, by the same word are kept in store, reserved unto fire against the day of judgment and perdition of ungodly men.*

It was also Peter who spoke in that chapter about the *new heavens and a new earth, wherein dwelleth righteousness,* Verse 13.

It does not appear that we are to think that the heavens and earth shall cease to exist or be annihilated. It is more proper to think of a complete cleansing by fire.

Mr Dake makes an interesting comment in regards to this; "The word "pass away" is from the Greek parerchomai and means "to go by or away from in the sense of from one condition to another." It never means cessation of existence. It is used over seventy- five times... Thus, we see from the various uses that it never conveys the idea of passing out of existence.

"The word for "melt" is luo, meaning "to loose, put off, unbind, untie or set free," and is so translated in Matthew 21:2; Luke 19:30,33; John 1:27; 11:44; Acts 7:33. It is translated "dissolve" in 2Peter 3:11 and 12. These passages show that all that is to happen to this present heaven and earth in this renovation is the loosing of them from the present bondage into a new state as in Romans 8:21-23."

Verse 12:

And I saw the dead, small and great, stand before God; and the books were opened: and another book was opened, which is the book of life: and the dead were judged out of those things which were written in the books, according to their works.

There is no way in our finite mind that we can grasp the awesomeness of this gathering - where ever it may be taking place! This is the second resurrection (verse six).

This presents us with some questions as to who these dead are that are called forth for judgment.

The dead are all the dead from Adam to the last to die when fire came down from God and destroyed the army which was following Satan to the camp of the saints, who have not been previously called forth. We know that the church will not be there, because she was raptured before tribulation began. The two witnesses will not be there for judgment; they too were raptured. The tribulation martyrs will not be there, for they too were called forth before the millennium began. All of those who were gathered in the camp of the saints won't be there, as they were judged saved by the very fact they were in the camp of the saints, and not following Satan.

This leaves a vast multitude who shall be summoned before God for their eternal judgment.

John said the "*small and great*" were seen there. None are excluded because of their station in life.

- This is where the king and the pauper stand side by side.

This judgment is to judge all who have not been judged. When this judgment is over, every mortal from Adam to the last son of Adam, who died before the camp of the saints, will have been before God and His judgment.

AND THE BOOKS WERE OPENED... There are differing views

as to just what this has reference to. It is evident by the plural term that there is more than one book involved. Some contend that it has reference to the Word of God - the Bible - all sixty-six books.

Others feel that it must have reference to books of record which are kept by God for each member of creation. James Hastings wrote: "Each we are writing ourselves down. We bear about us, in the character we have made, the whole volume of the past, in everything we do and of us writes the book of his own character. Daily and hourly think in the present, in the way we meet every circumstance of life, we go on forming that character. Our book is there, and it will be opened in the hour of judgment."

Malachi 3:16 seems to refer to the writing down of records which will show the activities of those who fear the Lord; *Then they that feared the LORD spake often one to another: and the LORD hearkened, and heard it, and a book of remembrance was written before Him for them that feared the LORD, and that thought upon His name.* If records are kept of those who love the Lord, would it also imply that records are kept of those who do not!

The last phrase of our verse seems to also imply that these books are referring to one's personal record; according to their works.

THE BOOK OF LIFE... Open that day will also be the book of life. The book which contains the names of all those who will be rewarded eternal life.

There are differing opinions as to just how one gets their name inscribed in this book. Some contend that all the living have their name inscribed in the book of life the moment life is given to them.

Then, as they live their life, if they do not commit sins which will cause their name to be blotted out, they will be among those saved eternally. Some feel that only those who are saved have their names written in the book.

Then there are those who feel that there are two books of life. One called the *Lamb's book of life,* in which are inscribed the names of those who have obeyed the Gospel of Jesus Christ. The other book of life contains all those who will live eternally.

Paul wrote: *my fellow labourers,* whose names are in the book of life (Philippians 4:3). He made no specific reference to the Lamb's book of life when he said this. But it is evident that there was an awareness of the book of life to those first century saints of God.

The subject of the book of life, while it is primarily a New Testament teaching, (found referred to at least eight times) it is also found referred to in the Old Testament, although not by name. Moses said; *If thou wilt forgive their sin-; and if not, blot me, I pray thee, out of thy book which thou hast written.* David exclaimed, *Let them be blotted out of the book of life, and not written with the righteous.*

One more note from the words of Morris regarding the judgment; "Then judgments will be pronounced, one after another, as each stand before God for a review of his life. If each were to take an hour, the tribunal scene would last perhaps 5 million years, (assuming 45 billion people to be judged)."

Verse 13:

And the sea gave up the dead which were in it; and death and hell delivered up the dead which were in them: and they were judged every man according to their works.

Death has stalked the steps of every son of Adam. We have record of only two who escaped death prior to the rapture of the redeemed. Consequently, multiplied billions have died across this great globe.

The reference to the sea giving up its dead emphasizes that there is no place where death has taken anyone that they will not be brought forth on the day of judgment. There is no way of knowing the number who have died at sea. Consider first of all, the many thousands of Antediluvians who died in the great flood. They will come forth.

We know that those who have died at sea will soon disintegrate and be scattered by the sea creatures across the sea. Those who died in a fire were annihilated and ascended in smoke and scattered as ashes. But the God who created this earth and all that is therein, is well able to call together again the atoms which made up each body to form again the body which housed each individual originally on this earth.

How will the dead be brought forth? The redeemed who have known resurrection and glorification, all receive a body like that of the Lord Jesus Christ (Philippians 3:21; 1John 3:2). Glorified and free from any pain or sickness or death. To those who are called forth to hear their doom to be cast into the lake of fire, however, while they will be resurrected to stand before the judgment of God, they will not be freed from pain and sorrow. As to whether their body is annihilated in the flames of the lake of fire or not, may be a matter of debate, but their eternal torment is a matter of record.

DEATH AND HELL... Death resulted from Adam's fall (Romans 5:12). Death is the result of sin.

Death is what comes to the physical man. Because of the curse the physical man changes, ages, sickens, and dies. This curse which has troubled every son of Adam will deliver up its victims. Death and the grave are common companions. We refer to the graveyard as the place of the dead awaiting the resurrection. Paul connected the two when he stated: *0 death, where is thy sting? 0 grave, where is thy victory?* (1Corinthians 15:55).

Hell, is "*hades*." Hades is the holding place for the dead. While the body is placed into the grave, the soul of the unsaved goes to hades. So, we have both soul and body called forth and united for judgment.

Again, we have the expression according to their works. The judgment which will be passed upon those gathered before the throne will be just and impartial. Every man will receive only that which his record indicates he is due. None will be judged prejudicially.

<u>Verse 14:</u>

And death and hell were cast into the lake of fire. This is the second death.

We may be prone to think of death as the cessation of life. As far as the living are concerned, that is what it is. But in reality, there is no such thing! The dead do not cease to be! They merely change from one place to another. From one plane to another. Just as we cannot imagine God dying, neither can we think of man - the real man - dying, because the life which lives in man is from God. It is the tabernacle - the body - which ceases to function at death. So, the soul which is cast into the lake of fire will never cease to exist. They will only exist apart from God and His mercy eternally. They will exist with death in an eternal state of death - the second death! The dead will die again after judgment! It will be the "second death!" Just as they did not cease to exist after the first death, because they were called forth to stand in this judgment, they will not cease to exist after the second death.

All graves will be emptied - to be filled no more! There will be no more funerals after this judgment, except the mass funeral into which all the condemned are cast out into the second death.

All souls which have died and have been delivered to hades will be brought forth. Hades will cease to function as a holding place for the departed lost.

The second death is the place of doom for all the lost. All those who are cast out into that place have already died once, but the first death, regardless of how horrible it might have been, was nothing compared to the second death.

It is referred to as death because they will be forever removed from God, who is life.

LAKE OF FIRE... There are arguments put forth to deny the existence of an eternal lake of fire.

Many subscribe to the theory of annihilation. That the soul cast into the lake of fire will be consumed and annihilated by the flames. Many feels that God is too just and merciful to send anyone to such a place. But they fail to accept the fact that it is NOT God who is sending anyone anywhere; those who are cast out into this place have sent themselves by their refusal to obey God!

The word *Hell* is employed some twenty-three times in the New Testament. One of the references has to do with the fallen angels. Ten of the places refer to the grave where the body is placed at death.

The remaining twelve times refer to the eternal abode of the lost! The references to the grave where the dead are placed is taken from the Greek word Hades. The Greek word which is translated hell which refers to the eternal state of the lost is Gehenna. (See my book by that title - Gehenna).

If there were no such word employed in the New Testament as Hades and Gehenna, there would be plenty of references to that eternal state of the doomed to inform us of such a place. Consider these scriptures; Matthew 3:12; 13:40; 15:41; Mark 9:43; 16:16;

John 3:36; 5:29; Revelation 14:11; 20:15.

WHERE WILL IT BE?

Another interesting question is Where will this eternal lake of fire be located? Well, we are not given any specific explanation in the Word of God as to its location. Again, some feel that it is in the center of the earth, as scientists have informed us that the center of the earth is a cauldron of fire. But, let us not forget that this earth is going to be burned up during this judgment! Also, Peter informs us that the new earth will be a place wherein dwelleth righteousness. Would such a place be associated with the new earth of righteousness?

Also, let us recall that Jesus informed us the lake of fire was *prepared for the devil and his angels* (Matthew 25:41). This seems to imply that it was prepared long ago. Possibly shortly after the fall of Satan. So, where ever it is it must have been in existence for millenniums awaiting the devil and those who fell with him from among the angelic host.

Consider the words of Jesus in referring to the doom of those who would be lost as they would *be cast out into outer darkness, there shall be weeping and gnashing of teeth* (Matthew 8:12).

Jude also adds an interesting statement to our search when speaking of those who are lost, he said they would be like *wandering stars, to whom is reserved the blackness of darkness for ever* (verse 13).

Paul wrote to the saints at Thessalonica; *And to you who are troubled rest with us, when the Lord Jesus shall be revealed from heaven with his mighty angels, in flaming fire taking vengeance on them that know not God, and that obey not the gospel of our Lord Jesus Christ: who shall be punished with everlasting destruction from the presence of the Lord, and from the glory of his power* (2Thessalonians 1 :7-9).

The word from is important here. It means "*away from.*"

 We could conclude from these passages that the doomed will be removed far away from this earth and those who inhabit the glories prepared for them by the Lord Jesus. The lake of fire could be located in some far distantly removed area of God's vast creation

Verse 15:

And whosoever was not found written in the book of life was cast

into the lake of fire.

The final test is whether one has their name in the book of life or not. Having been judged by their own works - which condemn them eternally, they are as well faced with the fact that their name is absent from the book of life. Without their name being found in the book of life they are consigned to the eternal doom of the second death.

While the Bible teaches degrees of blessings for the saved, it also teaches degrees of punishment for the damned. The bliss of eternal life will be enjoyed by all those who enter that eternal abode, but there will be differences of positions and rewards given to the saved. Likewise, those who are consigned to the lake of fire will all be cast out into the same outer darkness of fire and brimstone, but with differences in the sense that many will be there who have been among the blessings of the Lord during their lifetime, but who later rejected this type of lifestyle. How they lived in this life, and what they were exposed to, will make a difference as to their feelings in that eternal place. The rich man was reminded of his former life with the words from father Abraham; *Son, remember...* (Luke 16:25).

ARE THERE ANY SAVED?

Another question which is raised about this judgment is whether anyone will be saved at this judgment. Possibly our answer lies in concluding who all have been judged thus far.

The Church we know has been judged already from what Paul wrote in 2Corinthians 5:10.

The tribulation saints we know have also been judged already by their faithfulness in not accepting the mark of the beast, and who are still living at the end of the tribulation and enter the millennium.

The martyrs have been judged to life by their sacrifice of their life rather than accept the mark of the beast.

At the end of the millennium, the many who are gathered in the camp of the saints, will be judged righteous by the fact they are in His camp and have not joined the forces aligned with Satan.

Does that leave any who have not been judged that we could consider saved? It would appear that there would be others who could be considered saved who have not been judged yet.

During the millennium, there have no doubt been many thousands who have been born, and who will die during that time. Although longevity of life will be restored (Isaiah 65:20), it will not be eternal life.

Many who have lived righteous life's will probably die during the millennium who will have to be called before the judgment.

Also, if there is none to be saved at this judgment, then why have the book of life present?

We will have to wait for that day to find the answer to all of our questions concerning this judgment and the question of just who will be rewarded eternal life. It behooves us to make sure that our names are found in that book of life so that we will not stand there that day and hear the awful doom - Depart into outer darkness!

CHAPTER TWENTY-ONE

BEHOLD: I MAKE ALL THINGS NEW.

The judgment of all mankind is now behind us. The eternal destinies of all have been determined.

Satan, along with the beast and his cohort, the false prophet, have been cast into the lake of fire. All those whose names were absent from the Book of Life have also joined them now. The lake of fire, where ever it is located, is now occupied with eternal souls for an eternity away from God.

All that is bad is behind us. All that causes sin and is sinful is behind us now. The dark days of ungodliness is behind us forever. We have stepped, as it were, beyond the veil into a whole new creation of God. The prophet had declared, *For, behold, I create new heavens and a new earth: and the former shall not be remembered, nor come into mind.* (Isaiah 65:17) That day has now arrived. What we are now about to witness is a new creation. The work of the Creator was not finished with the seven days of creation outlined in Genesis. There remains another wonderful act of creation which will result in eternal places and things for an eternal people.

What a great vista of beauty unfolds before us in this chapter!

THE VISION CONTINUES

Verse 1:

And I saw a new heaven and a new earth: for the first heaven and the first earth were passed away; and there was no more sea.

Just as we have found in our study of Revelation many sevens, we come upon another set of sevens in our study of these last two chapters;

- 1. A new heaven... 21:1

- 2. A new earth... 21:1

- 3. A new Jerusalem... 21:2

- 4. All things new... 21:5

- 5. A new paradise of God... 22:1-5

- 6. A new source of light... 22:5

• 7. A new place for the throne of God... 22:3

Again, the prophet Isaiah spoke of the; new heaven and new earth which God would bring into existence after this period of tribulation and chaos; *For as the new heavens and the new earth, which I will make, shall remain before me, saith the LORD, so shall your seed and your name remain.* (66:22) This is the promise which God has made to the people of Abraham. While there will be times when it will appear that all hope is gone for them as a nation, they will somehow be brought through those times to ultimate victory, and an eternal habitation.

The words of Morris are appropriate here: "In both the Old and New Testament passages, the words for "new" mean "new in respect of freshness," rather than "new with respect to existence." That is, "a new heaven and a new earth" could be properly also translated "a fresh heaven and a fresh earth." The new cosmos is not a novel cosmos; it is a renewed cosmos. It is just like the first, except that all its agelong ravages of decay have been expunged and it is fresh and new again. This complete reversal of the universal decay process will require both the creative and formative powers of God for its accomplishments."

AND I SAW... This is the manner in which John has begun several new visions he experienced during this long discourse on Revelation. He had witnessed the rise and fall of a wicked system led by an evil man called the man of sin, the son of perdition. He had witnessed the struggle of the righteous, as they overcame the beast and his system of evil. He also witnessed many who died during this seven-year period. And he witnessed the defeat of this system of evil at the hand of the Lord Jesus Christ. And then the final judgment was witnessed by John. Now his vision is brightened with glories such as he has never witnessed to this point. After seeing the dirty and the ugly, he now is shown the beautiful and glorious. John must have been overwhelmed with what he saw.

The apostle Peter speaks to us of that time when this earth, as well as the heavens, shall pass away: *But the day of the Lord will come as a thief in the night; in the which the heavens shall pass away with a great noise, and the elements shall melt with fervent heat, the earth also and the works that are therein shall be burned up...*

Nevertheless we, according to His promise, look for new heavens And a new earth, wherein dwelleth righteousness, (2Peter 3:10,13).

The result of the destruction which will come to the heavens and the earth will be a new creation.

Completely different from the present world in which we presently live. And different from the world which will be known during the millennium as well. In that new earth, there will never be a sinner seen on the street of any city!

NEW!

That which John is here describing for us as he witnesses it, will be new beyond our imagination.

That which God has in store for His people will without doubt be awesome, to say the least.

"Much that we have known here we shall not know there, for they will no longer be. See the things of which it is here said they shall be no more. 1). The sea. It is the emblem of all unrest. Here there is, indeed, much of this, and its causes are manifold. But there, "no more sea." 2). Death. (verse 4) Here it may be said, "death reigns." His might, past, present, or near at hand, is scarce ever unfelt. What a change, for there to be "no more death"! 3). Pain. "Neither sorrow nor crying." That will indeed be a new world where these are not. Here, where are they not? 4). Night. Twice is it told "there is no night there" (ver. 25 and ch. 22:5). 5). Sin. (Ver. 27). Here sin rushes as a raging river down our streets; but there, "there shall in no wise enter," etc. 6). The curse. (ch. 22:3) Here it is everywhere. On health and wealth, home and friends, business and pleasure; for there is no one of them that may not be a course of sore sorrow to us, and a very fountain of tears. Paradises are still turned into thorn-beds as of old. The curse does it. "I will curse your blessings." But there, no more." (Pul Comm)

Jesus Christ had predicted; Heaven and earth shall pass away, but my words shall not pass away. (Matthew 24:35) This verse is the fulfillment of that prophecy.

NO MORE SEA... The prophet Isaiah spoke of the wicked in comparing them with the sea when he said; *The wicked are like the troubled sea, when it cannot rest, whose waters cast up mire and dirt. There is no peace, saith my God, to the wicked.* (57:20,21)

"A world without a physical sea, we confess, does not strike us as attractive. The sea is one of the grandest and most beneficent parts of this world. It is to the earth what the blood is to the body; it circulates through its every part, animates and beautifies the whole. The negation is to be understood in a spiritual sense. Division, mutation, agitation, are ideas we associate with the sea. In heaven, these things will not be.

"The sea is the great separator. It divides the great family of man into separate sections. The sea forms the boundary of kingdoms, continents, and races. The more fallen the world is the more necessary for such divisions.

"What is so changeable as the sea? A pulse of restlessness throbs through every part. It knows no repose. Sometimes it moves in silence, at other times its march is as the roll of terrible thunders.

"The sea is a tumultuous world. What human agony has its furious billows created! Human life here has many storms. Most men here are driven up and down like Paul in the Adrian, under starless skies, by contrary winds, and through treacherous and unknown seas. In how many hearts does deep call upon deep, and billows of sorrow roll over the souls! In heaven, there are no spiritual storms." (D Thomas)

We do not know for sure just what is meant by the statement that there will be no more sea. If this has symbolic significance, then we know there will certainly not be any unrest, nor wickedness in the new creation. If it is to be taken literally, then think of the tremendous increase of land mass which this will add to the earth. The large bodies of water take up a large percentage of the earth's surface. With them removed, the population of the earth could increase astronomically!

Mr Dake in his commentary on Revelation has an interesting supposition for consideration: "Possibly a few figures in connection with the area of the earth and the many people it might be capable of holding will be interesting here. It is said that the total area of the earth is 196,950,000 square miles. There are now 1,000,000 square miles of lake and river surfaces, not counting, of course, the area of the oceans. Granting that there will be no oceans in the New Earth, let us suppose that 4,650,000 square miles will be necessary for seas, rivers, and lakes and that 2,250,000 square miles will be necessary for the site of the New Jerusalem. That will leave 190,000,000 square miles for man and his activities. If one acre were given to one person there would be room for about 121,600,000,000 people on this earth."

We are not to think that by this statement there will be no waterways whatsoever on the new earth, for we will read in the next chapter of Revelation about the "*pure river of water of life...* "

Verse 2:

And I John saw the holy city, new Jerusalem, coming down from God out of heaven, prepared as a bride adorned for her husband.

This brings us to one of the most marvelous visions recorded in the Revelation. A city coming down from God out of heaven! There is no reason for us to spiritualize this city, as some have chosen to do.

This vision seems so impressive that John, for the first time since chapter one, employs his own name. *And I John...* It must have been a thrilling sight for this aged apostle.

"There is no reason at all why we should not accept it literally, as a real place prepared by Christ in the distant heavens (John 14:2,3) and now finally brought with Him to the new earth. It is the city for which Abraham had looked, one "*which hath foundations, whose builder and maker is God*" (Hebrews 11:10). It is the city which God hath prepared for them which have the faith to believe His Word and follow His will (Hebrews 11:16). It is the city of the living God, the heavenly Jerusalem, where one day will be gathered together the general assembly and church of the firstborn with all the just men whose spirits have been made perfect in the great resurrection (Hebrews 12:22,23). It is that 'Jerusalem which is above... which is the mother of us all' (Galatians 4:26). 'For here we have no continuing city, but we seek one to come'" (Hebrews 13 14). (Morris)

We are not informed when this city was prepared. It could have been part of the original creation.

The majority seem to favor the creation of this city, however, since the Lord ascended. The word *prepared* is the same word employed by Jesus when He told His disciples *I go to prepare a place for you* (John 14:2). It is also the word the apostle Paul employed when he wrote to the Corinthian church, *Eye hath not seen, nor ear heard, neither have entered into the heart of man, the things which God hath prepared for them that love Him,* (1Corinthians 2:9).

If this is the place which our Lord was speaking about that day, then could we suppose that it has been in the making for two thousand years!

PREPARED AS A BRIDE ADORNED FOR HER HUSBAND... Like Israel and natural Jerusalem, the Church and the New Jerusalem are identified together. The city is the Bride; the Bride is the city. The city will be the habitation of the Bride. The Bride has been preparing herself for two thousand years. What splendor will be manifested from this place! Again, it seemed so awesome to John that for the first time since chapter one he makes reference to his own name!

Verse 3:

And I heard a great voice out of heaven saying, Behold, the tabernacle of God is with men, and he will dwell with them, and they shall be his people, and God himself shall be with them, and be their God.

Morris makes an interesting point here: "There was another foreshadowing of this great coming union when God first became man. "And the Word was made flesh, and dwelt among us" (John 1:14). The word "dwelt" (Greek skenoo) is not the usual word for "dwell" but is the same word as used here in Revelation 21:3. It is a direct variant of the word for "tabernacle" (Greek skene), also used in this verse. In the days of His flesh, in other words, the eternal God temporarily "tabernacled" among men and then returned to heaven. In the eternal age to come, however, He will set up His dwelling place on earth and "tabernacle" here forever."

We have been reading in several places of the "voices" which were coming from heaven. We are not for sure as to the identity of the voices, but this one is making a great proclamation to the inhabitants of the earth. The announcement is tremendous in content. God is coming down to dwell among His creation on the new earth.

It is an awesome thought that the throne of God will evidently descend from heaven to the new earth, where God will dwell among His people on this earth. The reference to "*with*" his people, is from the Greek word "meta," which means "*amid*," or "*among*," or it could mean "in company with." Thus, showing that God will come down and live among His people.

The fellowship which was enjoyed in the garden in the very beginning, when man and his Creator knew close fellowship, will once again be restored. God will once again walk among His people.

LaHaye wrote: "Another outstanding characteristic of this new city is that God's tabernacle will no longer be in the third heaven, for He will move His headquarters to the new earth and will literally take up His abode in the new Jerusalem. We simply do not have the mental capacity to comprehend the significance of living in an economy where God Himself exists."

GOD HIMSELF SHALL BE... THEIR GOD... We have lords many and gods many in man's present day society. Not only are there many gods to be found among the idolaters of this generation, but even those who profess Christianity have as well relegated the Godhead into a three-person entity!

They would have God to consist of three persons! Yet at the same time they refuse to acknowledge that such an arrangement would necessarily consist of three gods! Which would in turn make them worshipers of more than one god - or an idolater!

In that day, the issue will be settled once and for all eternity. There will be no more debates among the religious circles as to how many persons there are in the Godhead. Nor will there be any argument as to the number of gods. As the prophet Zechariah put it; In that day there shall be one Lord, and His name one (14:9). The one eternal God who has manifested Himself in various ways to His creation since the days when He walked in the garden in the cool of the day, will in that day come down and dwell among His creation.

Verse 4:

And God shall wipe away all tears from their eyes; and there shall be no more death, neither sorrow, nor crying, neither shall there be any more pain: for the former things are passed away.

In what manner will God wipe all tears from the eyes of those who dwell on the new earth? By what means will this be accomplished? It will be accomplished by the removal of those things which cause the tears in the first place. They are forever absent from the new creation.

The Greek word for wipe comes to us from a meaning of "to smear out, obliterate, or wipe away." Those things which have caused mankind so many tears of sorrow and grief down through the millenniums will be wonderfully absent on that day. The curse which brought the tears in the first place will be removed in that new creation.

THERE SHALL BE...

No More Sea... Restlessness of sin will be no more! Troubled lives will be no more.

No More Tears... The product of the curse will vanish from the faces of all creation in that day.

No More Death... The result of sin and the curse will be absent from that society of blessed.

No More Sorrow... Grief-stricken people will not be seen in that society of tomorrow.

No More Crying... Weeping may endure for the night, but joy cometh in the morning!

No More Pain... The constant companion of so many of us in this life will be wonderfully absent in that day.

No More Curse... That which was brought upon the sons of Adam because of the fall will be for ever lifted (22:3).

We again refer to the words of the prophet Isaiah who spoke of this day so much in his writings;

He will swallow up death in victory; and the LORD God will wipe away tears from off all faces; and the rebuke of His people shall He take away from off all the earth: for the LORD hath spoken it. And it shall be said in that day, Lo, this is our God; we have waited for Him, we will be glad and rejoice in His salvation, (25:8,9).

It is difficult, if not impossible, for us to comprehend such a society as that one will be. Satan is no longer around, so sin is no longer around. Because sin is no longer around, neither are there any of the conditions which sin brings to lives around.

Verse 5:

And He that sat upon the throne said, Behold, I make all things new. And He said unto me, Write: for these words are true and faithful.

All Things New... This reminds us of the original creation as described for us in the book of Genesis. That creation has been contaminated by sin, which has resulted in a marred and corrupted creation.

Again, this was all brought about because of Satan and sin. Both of which will be conspicuously absent from that society. Consequently, there will be no corruption process of that creation. Not only will all things be new, they will remain new! Deterioration will never attack that society.

Mead, in his Apocalypse of Jesus Christ, pointed out some interesting comparisons between the first four chapters of Genesis and the last four chapters of Revelation;

"Genesis I-IV speaks of:

1. The First Creation.

2. The First Sabbath.

3. The first Adam - the head of the old humanity.

4. Eve - the wife of the first Adam sinning, condemned, sorrowing.

5. The garden of Eden.

6. The fall of man.

7. Sin.

8. Communion broken.

9. Death.

10. The promise.

11. Loss of Eden.

12. Exclusion from the Tree of Life.

13. Earth cursed.

14. Satan in the garden, tempting and bruising.

15. The seed of the serpent (Cain and his line), dominant persecuting, building cities, gaining the world.

16. The seed of the woman (Abel and Seth), persecuted, killed, and of no reputation.

Revelation XIX-XXII speaks of;

1. The new creation.

2. The holy rest in the new creation.

3. The second Adam - the Head of the new humanity.

4. The second Eve, - the Bride of Christ holy, exalted, glorious, in exceeding joy.

5. The Paradise of God.

6. Man's full redemption and restoration.

7. Perfect holiness.

8. Communion restored, perfect, eternal.

9. Eternal life.

10. Its complete fulfillment.

11. Restoration to the greater bliss of Paradise.

12. Access to and authority over the Tree of life.

13. Earth's full deliverance from the curse.

14. Satan bruised, and in the lake of fire.

15. The serpent's seed, - the antichrist, the false prophet and the false bride, overcome, dispossessed of the kingdom and cast into the lake of fire.

16. The seed of the woman, - Christ and His bride, risen, victorious, triumphant, in the city of God, possessing the kingdom and the power and the glory, unto the ages of the ages."

There are those among us who would argue about the authenticity of the first few chapters of the book of Genesis. If Genesis is not true, then neither can we place any trust in the hope expressed for the future as found in the Revelation. The first and last books stand - or fall - together!

Let us not fret though, for Jesus Himself set His seal of approval upon the words of Genesis when He quoted from the very first two chapters: *And He answered and said unto them, Have ye not read, that He which made them at the beginning made them male and female, and said, For this cause shall a man leave father and mother, and shall cleave to his wife: and they twain shall be one*

one flesh?

ALL THINGS NEW... We live in a world which continues to grow old. Everything which we touch deteriorates with time. Nothing never wears out! We are even being told by science that our universe is changing, and that someday - although projected to be millions of years away - it too will undergo destruction. The sun will burn-out. The earth will disintegrate. The entire cosmos will undergo a tremendous change. This time will never happen, of course, because first of all, we have no reason whatsoever to think that the coming again of Jesus Christ can be millions of years away! We have every scriptural reason to feel that this verse will be fulfilled; not millions of years from now - but, probably, just over a thousand years from now!

It is beyond our comprehension to grasp living in a society in which all things are new. And, I suppose, we are to assume that not only will all things be new - BUT ALL THINGS WILL REMAIN NEW!

Verse 6:

And he said unto me, It is done. I am Alpha and Omega, the beginning and the end. I will give unto him that is athirst of the water of life freely.

There is no doubt here as to who the *HE SAID UNTO ME* has reference to: It is the Lord Jesus Christ Himself! This is evident from the same statement John heard from the Lord Jesus in chapter one and verse eight.

IT IS DONE... This is the same statement made when the seventh angel had poured out his vial of wrath upon the kingdom of the beast (16:17). It marked the conclusion of the judgments which God was bringing upon the beast and those who were involved in his system.

Now, at the conclusion of the white throne judgment, and the statement that all things are now made new, we again are informed that it is done! It seems to be a reference to the conclusion of the plan of God for man to this point. He now has a new earth on which to live. The redeemed have a new city in which to reside. Satan is forever removed from the scene. At last, man may enjoy the fellowship of his God in complete harmony and peace.

I AM ALPHA AND OMEGA... This speaks of the Lord Jesus Christ. Alpha and Omega being the beginning and ending words of the Greek alphabet emphasize the fact that God is eternal. He is the beginning (Creator) of all things. He is the end (ultimate rewarder and provider) of all things.

WATER OF LIFE... In speaking of those who had come through the great tribulation and washed their robes in the blood of the Lamb, it is said; *For the Lamb which is in the midst of the throne shall feed them and shall lead them unto living fountains of waters* (7:17). We also have reference to the river of water of life in 22:1.

We are not for certain just what this has reference to. We have Jesus at the well of Jacob speaking to the Samaritan woman about; *the water that 1 shall give him shall be in him a well of water springing up into everlasting life* (John 4:14). And, the statement Jesus made at the feast day of Israel; *If any man thirst, let him come unto me, and drink. He that believeth on me, as the scripture hath said, out of his belly shall flow rivers of living water.* John went on to say; (*But this spake He of the Spirit, which they that believe on him should receive ...*) *(*John 7:37-40).

It is evident from the above passages that what Jesus was speaking of was symbolic. The well of water and the rivers of living water are both symbolic references to the Holy Spirit. But the reference in Revelation 22:1 is not symbolic it would seem. It appears that it is speaking of a literal river which will be flowing in that new creation from the throne of God. Alongside that river it speaks of the Tree of Life, which bears fruit which is for the healing -or health - of the nations.

Are we to assume that as the Tree of Life in the garden of Eden would have preserved Adam and his wife, as long as they ate of it, this water and fruit in the new creation will be the means of eternal life to those who dwell in that new creation?

The prophet Isaiah spoke prophetically of the day when *with joy shall ye draw water out of the wells of salvation*, (12:3). He must have been speaking of this time when Israel will once again enjoy the blessings of the Lord dwelling among them.

Verse 7:

He that overcometh shall inherit all things; and I will be his God, and he shall be my son.

The promise to the overcomer will be fulfilled at last! Sweet and lasting victory will be enjoyed by those who have been faithful through the years. Some have come through very trying times. Some have kept their faith by giving their life. Many have endured harsh and bitter treatment by persecutors. All now stand in blessed and glorious victory at last! Surely all of those who are found among this people will be shouting that it was worth the effort to make it to that new creation of God.

Let us recall that when John addressed his letters to the seven churches of Asia in chapters two and three, he spoke to each one of them *to him that overcometh...* To those who are looking at the problems of life, it may appear to be difficult to overcome. To those who are among that number on this day, looking back on their journey to this new creation, their journey will seem as nothing compared to the glory which they will know and enjoy in that day.

INHERIT ALL THINGS... We usually think of the heir as being the son. The children of God are the heirs of God. Heirs of the wonderful riches which heaven holds for them. Paul writes to us in Romans 8:16,17; *The Spirit itself beareth witness with our spirit, that we are the children of God: And if children, then heirs; heirs of God, and joint-heirs with Christ.*

The apostle Peter spoke of how we have an *inheritance incorruptible, and undefiled, and that fadeth not away, reserved in heaven for you* (1Peter 1:4).

Paul informs us that the infilling of the Holy Spirit is *the earnest of our inheritance until the redemption of the purchased possession* (Ephesians 1:14). That which we have now received through the infilling of the Spirit is the down-payment on the fullness of the inheritance which we shall have at His coming. If this joy which fills the soul of the child of God upon being filled with the Holy Ghost, and being born again, is the down payment, what will the fullness of the inheritance be like?

HE SHALL BE MY SON... A reference to the people of God being sons of God is found among the writings of John and also Paul. John wrote in his epistle; *Beloved, now are we the sons of God, and it doth not yet appear what we shall be: but we know that, when He shall appear, we shall be like Him; for we shall see Him as He is* (1John 3:2). Paul wrote: *For as many as are led by the Spirit of God, they are the sons of God* (Romans 8:14). Also, in Galatians 4:6,7, wrote in his epistle; *Beloved, now are we the sons of God, and it doth not yet appear what we shall be: but we know that, when He shall appear, we shall be like Him; for we shall see Him as He is* (1John 3:2). Paul wrote; *For as many as are led by the Spirit of God, they are the sons of God* (Romans 8:14). Also, in Galatians 4:6,7, Paul wrote; *And because ye are sons, God hath sent forth the Spirit of His Son into your hearts, crying, Abba, Father. Wherefore thou art no more a servant, but a son; and if a son, then an heir of God through Christ.*

The unique relationship which is now known through the Spirit will then be known in a wonderful literal relationship which God will have with His creation who enter that new society.

THE OTHER SIDE...

Verse 8:

But the fearful, and unbelieving, and the abominable, and murderers, and whoremongers, and sorcerers, and idolaters, and all liars, shall have their part in the lake which burneth with fire and brimstone: which is the second death.

Having spoken to us concerning the blessings of the blessed, our attention is now taken to those who are absent from this joyous group seen rejoicing in the new creation of God. Somewhere - we do not know for sure geographically - there is another place, and another group. A group who were judged at the White Throne and condemned to an eternity of outer darkness and damnation.

Dr McGee wrote concerning this verse: "There are several amazing features about this passage. First of all, the creation of new heavens and a new earth did not affect or change the status of the lake of fire and of the lost. In the second place, there is no possibility of the sin which made men become fearful, unbelieving, liars, murderers, etc., ever breaking over the barrier into the new heavens and the new earth. Sin and its potential are forever shut out of the new creation. Finally, the lake of fire is eternal, for it is the second death - and there is no third resurrection. It is eternal separation from God."

This entire chapter is taken up with describing the conditions of the new creation of God. The glories which await the child of God in that creation will be overwhelming, without a doubt. In the middle of this wonderful discourse given to John, he is told the words contained in this verse. It is like a solemn warning to all who would read these words. While there is such a wonderful place as the new heavens and the new earth, where there will dwell the righteous eternally, don't forget there is another place. Don't grow careless to the extent that we neglect making sure that we have prepared our life for that new creation. Otherwise, we will find ourselves in that other place, among that other group, which is here so vividly described for us!

What a contrast is seen between verse seven and verse eight! One refers to the blessed who are in that creation referred to as the sons of God. Those who will know and enjoy eternal life filled with the joys which God will personally bestow upon all who enter that creation. In the next verse we have the list of those who are among the lost eternally from God. They are in outer darkness, cursed with the condemnation of being lost for ever and ever. One group enjoys eternal life; the other group is plunged into eternal death!

FEARFUL... This does not have reference to someone who is afraid of something or someone. It is a reference more to those who do not fear God but fear what men will say or do to them if they live for God. It is not a reference to cowardice actions of men necessarily, but a weakness of spirit and desire to live for God. A weakness that causes them to walk in unbelief rather than go against the systems of this world and live for God.

UNBELIEVING... This is a result of fear. Actually, this is the sin which keeps people from living for God, and ultimately will send them to hell. Jesus said; He that believeth on Him is not condemned: but he that believeth not is condemned already, because he hath not believed in the name of the only begotten Son of God (John 3:18). The writer of Hebrews said; *But without faith it is impossible to please Him...* (11:6). Unbelief is sin. The things which we label many times as sin, is really the results of sin in one's life. The habits which people pick up are the results of sin.

ABOMINABLE... Those who would fit into this category would be those who are blasphemers, idolaters. The filthy minded who indulge in the filthy sinful practices that satisfy the flesh, while ignoring morality and cleanness of lifestyle.

MURDERERS... Let us never forget that one could be guilty of murder without ever pulling a trigger to shoot someone down in cold murder. John wrote (1John 3:15) *Whosoever hateth his brother is a murderer: and ye know that no murderer hath eternal life abiding in him.*

WHOREMONGERS... This is from the Greek word pornos. It is translated in other passages as fornicator. It has to do with those who are involved in immoral sexual practices. Those who by their practices make light of the marriage vow.

SORCERERS... This is an interesting word. It is the Greek word pharmakeus. It speaks to us of those who are involved in the use of drugs. This is a very appropriate word which applies so well with the conditions which exist in our generation. The drug problem of today is a major issue with our youth, and is getting out of hand.

IDOLATERS... Mr Morris points out that "A number of Scriptures (Ephesians 5:5; Colossians 3:5) make it plain that even covetousness (inordinate love of material possessions) is idolatry."

The Pulpit Commentary stated; "Sorcerers; those who deceived the heathen. And idolaters; the heathen who were deceived by them."

AND ALL LIARS... How many ways can one lie? Does a lie un-repented of remain a lie forever?

There are many ways one could practice a lie; or tell a lie; or live a lie!

"Although few may wish to acknowledge themselves to be such flagrant sinners as those described here, it must be remembered that idolatry includes covetousness, fornication includes lustful thoughts (Matthew 5:28) and murder includes anger (Matthew 5:21,22). Further, who is there who has never lied or never been fearful? This listing of sinners thus includes all, for all have sinned and come short of the glory of God (Romans 3 :23). " (Morris)

This verse is a list of those who will come up short on that day of judgment. It is those who will hear the awful sentence of *DEPART, YE CURSED, INTO OUTER DARKNESS.* It is those who stood before God in judgment with these sins still on their record. This verse does not say that anyone who was ever guilty of such sins would be cast out into the lake of fire. But it is those who stand guilty of these sins before God on that day of judgment who will be thus cast out.

For we read; *Know ye not that the unrighteous shall not inherit the kingdom of God? Be not deceived: neither fornicators, nor idolaters, nor adulterers, nor effeminate, nor abusers of themselves with mankind, nor thieves, nor covetous, nor drunkards, nor revilers, nor extortioners, shall inherit the kingdom of God. And such were some of you: but ye are washed, but ye are sanctified, but ye are justified in the name of the Lord Jesus, and by the Spirit of our God,* (1Corinthians 6:9 - 11).

THE LAKE - WHICH IS THE SECOND DEATH... If the lake of fire was a place of annihilation, as some contend, then why do we find it referred to here in this chapter? The White Throne judgment is past! The process of change has taken place with the earth and the heavens. Now the new earth is populated with those who will be privileged to live there. Chapter twenty-one is a description of those things which are eternal and glorious. Yet this verse is found among all the verses of this chapter which speaks of the judgment which will befall those whose names are not in the book of life. If the lake of fire was only temporary; a place where the lost were soon annihilated, then why even mention it here in this chapter? It must be here if for no other reason, to remind us that this place does exist!

The wise man said in Ecclesiastes 11:8; *But if a man live many years, {and} rejoice in them all; yet let him remember the days of darkness; for they shall be many. All that cometh {is} vanity.*

Verse 9:

And there came unto me one of the seven angels which had the seven vials full of the seven last plagues, and talked with me, saying, Come hither, I will shew thee the bride, the Lamb's wife.

The last time John was told to come hither was when an angel told him to come so he could be shown *the judgment of the great whore that sitteth upon many waters,* (17:1). It was said of that angel also that he was one of the seven last angels with the seven last plagues to pour out upon the kingdom of the beast. It is interesting that beginning with 17:1, and the angel mentioned there, there are seven angels mentioned altogether in the rest of the Revelation including the one in 17:1; (17:1; 18:1 ,21; 19:10,17; 21:1). Now this one in this verse makes the seventh.

The first of the seven showed John the judgment of the wicked system of Babylon. Now the last of the seven is called upon to show

John the beauty of the New Jerusalem. The first angel told John he would be shown the judgment of wickedness. The last angel informs John that he will witness something beautiful. The first angel informs John of a great city, Babylon. The last angel informs John of a great city, Jerusalem. The first city is thrown down in the wrath of God. The last city comes down from God for His people to dwell in. Babylon spoke of everything which is wicked and ungodly. Babylon spoke of chaos and confusion. New Jerusalem speaks of everything that is altogether peaceful and lovely. New Jerusalem speaks of a place where peace reigns triumphantly.

- John is invited to see **THE BRIDE, THE LAMB'S WIFE.**

"It is believed by many that the bride of Christ is to be made up of only the New Testament saints, but this cannot be true as we shall see below and as is clear from Heb. 11 :8-16, 40. In this passage all Old Testament saints from Abel on were promised the same city as New Testament saints are, so all saints of all ages must be the bride of Christ, Rev. 21:9.

"It is therefore unscriptural to call anyone group of redeemed the bride of Christ. The Church will be a part of the bride, every other redeemed company will be a part, but to call the Church or anyone company of redeemed the bride, is like calling a local church, or anyone person, or any single part of a city by the name of the city of which they are only a part. Anyone who lives in New York City is only a part of that city, so it is with the Holy Jerusalem. Any person or group of persons who go to live in that city are as much a part of the bride as anyone else who lives in that city. Since all saints of all ages go to live in the New Jerusalem, all saints make the bride and not just a select few as taught by some." (Dake)

The word bride is only found four times in the Revelation. One of those is in reference to the city of Babylon (18:23). The only other place the word is found in the New Testament is in John 3:29, where John speaks of; *He that hath the bride is the bridegroom...* There is no place where the word Bride is referred to as the church. We assume it is the church because the church is those who have taken on the name of the Bridegroom in baptism. But there are references to those in the Revelation who have as well become identified with His name; even to having it in their foreheads. The Jews of the Old Testament were the people of the Name. How careful they were in writing and speaking the name of their God.

John is invited to see this bride which is adorned with great beauty for her Bridegroom, the Lord Jesus Christ.

Verse 10:

And he carried me away in the spirit to a great and high mountain, and shewed me that great city, the holy Jerusalem, descending out of heaven from God,

Again, we have an interesting comparison between what John experiences here and what he experienced with the first angel that poured out the vials of wrath. The first one took him into the wilderness to view the judgment of the great whore (17:1-3). Here he is taken up to a great and high mountain to view the Bride the City Jerusalem.

Having been told he was going to be shown the bride, John is shown a city, New Jerusalem. Those who will inhabit that city, the Bride, is identified with the city, and the city is identified with the Bride. Just as Jerusalem on earth was identified with Israel; Matthew 23:37, *O Jerusalem, Jerusalem, (thou) that killest the prophets, and stonest them which are sent unto thee, how often would I have gathered thy children together, even as a hen gathereth her chickens under (her) wings, and ye would not!*

John has been carried away in the Spirit before to witness something which God wanted him to see, but never had he beheld anything which must have been as breathtaking as what he beholds now!

We are not for sure just what is meant by John being taken to a great high mountain to view this city. When we consider the dimensions of this city later, we will see that it is described as being almost 1400 miles high! While the text does not say that from the top of this high mountain John was above the city and could look down upon it, that seems to be our first impression for the reason John was taken to this high mountain.

THAT GREAT CITY... This not just a honeymoon cottage for the Bride and Groom! It is a city of tremendous proportions! It is the city which Abraham looked for; Hebrews 11:10, *For he looked for a city which hath foundations, whose builder and maker {is} God.* It must be the place which Jesus spoke about preparing for us; John 14:2, *In my Father's house are many mansions: if (it were) not (so), I* *would have told you. I go to prepare a place for you.*

DESCENDING OUT OF HEAVEN FROM GOD... It would appear that John is witnessing for the first time this great city. If this is the first time that it appears in the order of events which are described for us in the Revelation, then the city does not appear until after the White Throne judgment, and after the creation of all new things. This would mean that the city is not occupied during the millennium.

We have no way of knowing whether those who are translated into the heavens will be able to see the city prior to its coming down at this time. The assumption would be that it will only be seen at this time when it comes down from God out of heaven for its eternal resting place.

There are various opinions as to just what is meant by *descending out of heaven* ... Will the city become stationary in the heavens above the earth, orbiting the earth? Will it come all the way down and be established upon the new earth? John states in verse 24; ... *and the kings of the earth do bring their glory and honour into it.* Also in verse 26; *And they shall bring the glory and honour of the nations into it.* If we are to consider these statements in the literal sense, then the city would have to be resident upon the new earth.

Seiss' Lectures on the Apocalypse had this to say about the city; "The boundaries would reach from furthermost Maine to furthermost Florida, and from the shores of the Atlantic to Denver, Colorado. It would cover all of Britain, Ireland, France, Spain, Italy, Germany, Austria, Prussia, European Turkey, and half of European Russia taken together!"

While some choose to spiritualize the City, taking it to be symbolic in nature, it does not appear that we have any reason to do this. If God, the mighty Creator of all things, can hang all the planets in their proper orbits and keep them there for eons, why should it be thought that such a city could not be made in the heavens and then brought down at the appointed time to the new earth!

Jesus said He was going to prepare a place for us. It does not seem that He was speaking of preparing a symbol for us! In the book of Hebrews, we have reference to the people of the Old Testament seeking this city; Hebrews 11:16, *But now they desire a better {country}, that is, an heavenly: wherefore God is not ashamed to be called their God: for he hath prepared for them a city.*

Verse 11:

Having the glory of God: and her light {was} like unto a stone most precious, even like a jasper stone, clear as crystal;

Mr McGee wrote: 'The city takes its place as the center of the new creation and the source of light and life for the new universe. In the days of John, men thought that the universe was geocentric (earth centered). Humanism today makes the universe anthropocentric (man centered). The Scripture teaches that today the universe is uranocentric (heaven centered). In eternity the new universe will be Christocentric (Christ centered) and theocentric (God centered)."

THE GLORY OF GOD... We read in Exodus 40:34; *Then a cloud covered the tent of the congregation, and the glory of the Lord filled the tabernacle.*

That same glory would later fill the temple which would be erected during the time of Solomon as they brought the Ark of God into the Holy of Holies. It is the presence of God which has been called the Shekinah of God. A glory which in the time of Moses and in the time of Solomon, was so powerful that the priests were not able to enter into the Tabernacle or Temple until that glory was lifted. A glory which man could not endure in the presence of such power, but in the time of the New creation will come down with the City and shine forth into all the earth.

There have been a lot of beautiful cities in this world in the past six thousand years of man's history, the city of Babylon described for us in Revelation will without doubt be a tremendous city as well, but none can compare with that which God will bring down from the heavens in that day!

John witnessing this beautiful sight exclaimed that her light was the glory of God which shone forth from the city, was like unto a stone most precious, even like a jasper stone. It has been suggested that the jasper stone is probably what we call today a diamond. Catching all the rays of light which shines through her many prisms, the stone glows with an effervescent glow of light which dazzles the beholder. What a place awaits the Church!

Verse 12:

And had a wall great and high, {and} had twelve gates, and at the gates twelve angels, and names written thereon, which are {the names} of the twelve tribes of the children of Israel:

D Thomas wrote of that city:

"SYMMETRY. "And he that talked with me had a golden reed to measure the city, and the gates thereof, and the wall thereof." The metropolis of this commonwealth is not reared capriciously and without plan. Every material is properly measured and put in its right position. The Architect is of unerring skill. Is there any symmetry in our schemes of government, whether political, social, or ecclesiastic? What one generation has constructed, and admired as just and wise, the next, blessed with a higher education, pronounces both unrighteous and unwise. The Architect of this city measured the whole by the "golden rule."

"AMPLITUDE. The city lieth foursquare, and the length is as large as the breadth. The city is of vast dimensions. The walls that enclose it stretch over fifteen hundred miles ... There is nothing limited or narrow in the scheme of social order which God has established for the government of communities; it embraces all, of whatsoever tribe or land, secular condition, or grade of intellect or culture.

"COSTLINESS. Things that men regard as the most precious and costly are here mentioned as belonging to this wonderful social edifice ... The pearl was regarded by the ancients as of all things the most precious."

A WALL GREAT AND HIGH... There is no reason for us to assume that the wall around this blessed City will be for the same purpose that walls were erected around cities in olden times = for protection. There will be no enemies of those dwelling in that City to threaten their safety. Also, we are informed later that the gates to the city are never shut. Possibly the wall speaks to us of the security which will be known and enjoyed by the inhabitants of that eternal habitation of the redeemed.

AND AT THE GATES TWELVE ANGELS... We like to call them the "Welcoming Committee." The angelic host will join those who inhabit that beautiful place, as they continue their service as, ministering spirits, sent forth to minister for them who shall be heirs of salvation, (Hebrews 1:14).

AND NAMES WRITTEN... WHICH ARE THE NAMES OF THE TWELVE TRIBES... If nothing else, this statement seems to emphasize to us that the redeemed of Israel will be included with those who make up the Bride, and who inhabit that City. Israel is thus identified with the City by having the names of the tribes inscribed in the twelve gates.

Mr Morris wrote: "But also the names on the entry gates will be an eternal reminder that it was first of all through the patriarchal ministry of Abraham, Isaac, and Israel, with the twelve sons of Israel, that we Gentiles first entered into the great family and city of God. It was the Israelites to whom {pertaineth} the adoption, and the glory, and the covenants, and the giving of the law, and the service {of God}, and the promises; Whose {are} the fathers, and of whom as concerning the flesh Christ {came}, who is over all, God blessed for ever. Amen (Romans 9:4,5)."

Verse 13:

On the east three gates; on the north three gates; on the south three gates; and on the west three gates.

This reminds us of the encampment of Israel around the Tabernacle during their wilderness travels. Three tribes camped on each of the four sides of the Tabernacle. The order of their encampment is given to us in Numbers chapter two. The order in which they camped was also the order in which they marched, as described for us in chapter ten of Numbers. That is mention is made of Judah first, camping on the east side, and leading the procession during the marches. Here also we have the east side mentioned first in the order of the twelve gates of the city.

Now, in the matter concerning these gates and the names of the tribes of Israel being inscribed in them, we have an interesting puzzle: Whose names will be on the gates? When we consider the tribes in Numbers chapter two, we note that the two sons of Joseph, Ephraim and Manasseh, are included in the twelve, while Joseph is omitted, in favor of his two sons to whom his inheritance fell; and Levi is omitted, as they were made the priesthood of Israel. When we consider the twelve tribes out of which were sealed twelve thousand each, in Revelation chapter seven, we notice a different order as well as different names. Here we find Ephraim and Dan missing who were in the original listing in Numbers two. In their place, we have Joseph and Levi mentioned. Then when we consider the prophecy of Ezekiel as he describes for us; *And these {are} the goings out of the city... And the gates of the city {shall be} after the names of the tribes of Israel* (48 :30,31). The city which Ezekiel is here describing is not the city of Revelation twenty-one, but the city of Jerusalem in the Millennium. Then we have the listing of the twelve tribes and their names on the gates of the city, and in this listing, we have the original twelve tribes, although not in the order of their birth. So, we have three different listings of the tribes, and each one of them different. Now, here in Revelation, we are not informed what names are inscribed on the twelve gates of the New Jerusalem.

Verse 14:

And the wall of the city had twelve foundations, and in them the names of the twelve apostles of the Lamb.

Again, the fact that the names of the apostles listed in the City also emphasizes that the city includes both Old Testament and New Testament saints. Paul made it plain that the foundation of the Church included the Old Testament saints, when in Ephesians 2:20 he said; *And are built upon the foundation of the apostles and prophets.*

Now as to who the twelve apostles are whose names are recorded in these foundations, there is no question about eleven of them, but the one who took Judas Iscariot's place finds room for speculation.

Some contend that it is Matthias, the one chosen by the apostles to replace him. Others contend it is Paul, one born out of due season, and who was the apostle to the Gentiles. John does not indicate by name who they are. Like the names on the gates, we will have to wait until we get there to see that City for ourselves to find out for sure who are listed there.

Like so many other things we have covered in our study of the Revelation, we come upon another area in which there are differing views as to just what is meant by the words of the apostle. Mr Morris stated on this verse; "As the wall has twelve gates, so it also has twelve strong foundations, deep and secure, transmitting the weight of the great wall down to the solid bedrock of the new earth. One foundation at each corner, plus two in each wall (located between the wall's three gates), is no doubt the pattern employed."

We are not for sure just what is meant by John's statement, *The wall of the city had twelve foundations*. I know the singular term is employed in reference to the wall, but a singular term is also employed in reference to the street of gold (v.21), and, as there are twelve gates, it would certainly appear that there would be more than ONE street in a city that is fourteen hundred miles square! More about this later.

Verse 15:

And he that talked with me had a golden reed to measure the city, and the gates thereof, and the wall thereof.

The one in reference here is, of course, the angel which has just carried John to this high mountain to view this great city. The angel produces a golden reed with which he will measure the city. The reed is golden - like the city. He is going to measure for John the city, the gates and the wall. As to how all this was done we are not informed. If you can imagine measuring something which is fourteen hundred miles long, you can imagine how long it would take us to measure such a place! We are not informed as to the manner employed by the angel to measure this city, but what John is about to witness boggles the mind!

Verse 16:

And the city lieth foursquare, and the length is as large as the breadth: and he measured the city with the reed, twelve thousand furlongs. The length and the breadth and the height of it are equal.

Vincent the Greek scholar states the twelve thousand furlongs would be 1378.97 miles. This is where we get the term that the city is approximately fifteen hundred miles long, broad and high. It is the Greek stadia, which is about 600 Greek feet, or approximately 607 English feet.

The city is a cube. Some contend that the city is shaped like a pyramid, not a cube. That the height of the city is equal to its base. We would feel it best to accept what is recorded here by John as being the best description of the city. That is, it is a cube.

The use of the cube in measuring things holy is not something we have not found prior to this in our study of the Word of God. When we consider the Tabernacle and the Temple, we find that the Most holy place of each was a cube. The cube seems to identify with the holiness of God. That inner sanctum where God was pleased to dwell and manifest His glory in the Tabernacle and Temple was cubical in shape. Now the eternal city which is illuminated by the holiness of God is found to be in the same form.

With this verse, we begin to draw in the magnitude of this place where the redeemed of the ages shall live. Referring again to Seiss, we read; "Great was the city of Nineveh, so great that Jonah had only begun to enter it after a day's journey. How long then would it take to explore this city of gold; whose every street is one fifth the length of the diameter of the earth!"

Mr Turner, in his book on Revelation, stated: 'Some think that this city will also be 1500 miles high, from the statement found in the 16th verse "the length and the breadth and the height of it are equal." Other writers think that the Greek word isa which is here translated equal, may mean in proportion; that is the height of the city would be in due proportion to its length and breadth ... Babylon was the largest city of the ancient world and was fifty-six miles in circumference, but the city is over a hundred times as large, being six thousand miles in circumference."

G T Haywood, writing in 1923, had this to say about this city; "This city has twelve foundations (floors), each being separated by a distance of 125 miles. There is nothing said about elevators, or stair cases there. They have no need for such, for they that dwell therein will be equal unto angels. The second floor would be out of sight of the natural eye! Each floor, or foundation, bears the name of one of the twelve apostles of the Lamb.

"Were that city divided into rooms one mile in length, and one mile high and mile long, it would contain three billion, three hundred and seventy-five million rooms (3,375,000,000), each room containing the space of one cubic mile!

"One of the most astonishing features about such a place is the time it would require to visit, or go over that city, visiting each room separately. If we were to begin at the formation of Adam to go through the city, spending one hour in each room for twenty-four hours a day, at the end of 6,000 years we would only have visited 52,570,560, leaving 3,322,529,440 rooms yet to be gone through! This calculation includes all the leap years that occur in 6,000 years, deducting the century year when there is no leap year.

"To bring the calculation down to a smaller point, let us give one minute's time to visit each room of the above dimensions, and at the expiration of 6,000 years one would have visited 3,154,233,600 rooms, leaving 210,766,400 rooms yet unentered. By the time one would have completed his circuit and returned to the point from which he had started "old things" will have become "new." When we carefully consider these things, we are struck with astonishment and are compelled to exclaim in the prophetic words of old, What hath God wrought!"

Haywood was the only commentator who made reference to the city being separated into twelve floors, relating to the twelve foundations. He took the statement twelve foundations as referring to twelve separate foundations, one for each floor of the city.

It is important to note that John wrote *The wall of the city had twelve foundations.* He did not say the city had twelve foundations, which would seem to indicate different levels of buildings. It is the wall which has the foundations, and in which the names of the apostles are inscribed.

Also, if there would be a separation between levels of the city which would be in relation to each foundation, then would there not need to be a wall for each of these levels? And would there not need to be gates for each level?

The record seems to indicate there is but one wall which surrounds this city, and it is under this wall that the twelve foundations are laid.

NO ELEVATORS?

As there is no mention of any means of travel in that city, whether horizontally or vertically, we are to assume that there would be no need of any. The glorified who enjoy the privilege of living in that city will not need this means of transportation, as we will have a body like our Lord which will be able to travel at will. Going vertically will present no greater problem than going horizontally. Whether we choose to travel fourteen hundred miles upward or across the city, neither will present a problem to the redeemed of that city!

Verse 17:

And he measured the wall thereof, an hundred {and} forty {and} four cubits, {according to} the measure of a man, that is, of the

Angel.

You will notice that here the measurement is in cubits, not furlongs, as in the measurement of the city. One hundred and forty-four cubits would equal about 216 feet. A cubit being about 18 inches in length.

Mr Morris contended that this dimension is referring to the width of the wall - not the height! That such a low height for the wall would not relate with the tremendous height of the city.

While it stands to reason we will have to wait until our eyes behold that beautiful city for ourselves, it none the less seems that this dimension is referring to the height of the wall. While it is true the city soars far above the walls height, this would in turn permit the light from that city to shine forth with more brilliance upon the new creation about it. The wall is not needed for protection as there will be no enemies in that society. The wall is for beauty and to eternally declare the names of the tribes of Israel and the apostles of Jesus Christ.

We are confronted again with the numeral twelve. This city emphasizes the number twelve; twelve gates, with twelve angels standing at them, twelve foundations to a city that is twelve thousand stadia (furlongs) square; a wall that is twelve times twelve cubits high. While seven seems to emphasize perfection in God's economy, the numeral twelve seems to speak of completeness. God's plan has now at last come to its pre-determined and promised end.

Verse 18:

And the building of the wall of it was {of} jasper: and the city {was} pure gold, like unto clear glass.

No eyes have ever looked upon such beauty and such wonder as this! There is plenty of architectural beauty in our world today, but there can be found no structure which will even come close to the beauty of this city!

In verse eleven we were told that the glow of light radiating from the city was like a jasper stone.

Here, we are informed that the wall of the city is jasper! The jasper stone is a mystery stone. No one seems to know for sure just what kind of stone this is.

Mr Morris wrote; "The exact nature of the jasper stone is uncertain, but it was renowned in the ancient world. Its name has been essentially transliterated from both the Hebrew (yashpeh) and Greek (iaspis), as well as other languages, but it still is unidentified today. It was one of the stones in the breastplate of the high priest (Exodus 28:20; 39:13) and in the heavenly Eden (Ezekiel 28:13). Its association with the sardine stone (Revelation 4: 3) and with the clear crystal (Revelation 21:11), together with extra biblical references, suggests that it was a fine translucent stone, capable of different colors, primarily radiant white but also with flashing red and purple tints."

Not only does the wall arrest our attention by being built of brilliant jasper stone, but the city itself is said to be of gold!

The two words, pure and clear are both from the same Greek word, emphasizing for us the pure and flawless beauty of this city. It is perfect! Unlike buildings of our era which in a few years will be torn down to make way for more progressive and more modern structures, that city will never be replaced. It is perfect!

Verse 19:

And the foundations of the wall of the city {were} garnished with all manner of precious stones.

The first foundation {was} jasper; the second, sapphire; the third, a chalcedony; the fourth, an emerald;

The farther we read the more glorious and beautiful the city becomes!

Dr Walvoord described these foundations of precious stones in this manner;

"Jasper - gold in appearance but like clear glass in substance, namely, glass with a gold cast to it;

Sapphire - a stone similar to a diamond in hardness and blue in color;

Chalcedony - an agate stone from Chalcedon (in Turkey), thought to be sky blue with other colors running through it;

Emerald - introduces a bright green color;

Sardonyx - a red and white stone;

Sardius - refers to a common jewel of reddish color, also found in honey color which is considered less valuable. The Sardius is used with Jasper in Revelation 4:3 in describing the glory of God on the throne;

Chrysolyte - a transparent stone, golden in color, according to the ancient writer Pliny, and therefore somewhat different from the modern pale green Chrysolyte stone;

Beryl - is sea green;

Topaz - is yellow-green and transparent;

Chrysoprasus - introduces another shade of green;

Jacinth - is a violet color;

Amethyst - is commonly purple.

Though the precise colors of these stones in some cases are not certain, the general picture here described by John is one of unmistakable beauty, designed to reflect the glory of God in a spectrum of brilliant color. The light of the city within shining through these various colors in the foundation of the wall topped by the wall itself composed of the crystal-clear Jasper forms a scene of dazzling beauty in keeping with the glory of God and the beauty of His Holiness. The City is undoubtedly far more beautiful to the eye than anything man has ever been able to create, and it reflects not only the infinite wisdom and power of God but also His grace as extended to the objects of His salvation."

Verse 20:

The fifth, sardonyx; the sixth, sardius; the seventh, chrysolite; the eighth, beryl; the ninth, a topaz; the tenth, a chrysoprasus; the eleventh, a jacinth; the twelfth, an amethyst.

There is no way that we can grasp the beauty and splendor which this city will reveal to those who are privileged to live there.

The stones which are here described by John are not recognized for sure by our generation. This adds significance to the glories which await the child of God as being indescribable.

Some are of the opinion that these twelve stones which make up the foundations of the wall of this city, are equally separated with three being on each side of the city. The record by John does not give this manner of detail. We had rather think that the foundations are in successive layers all around the city. Whether the first foundation stone mentioned, jasper, is the top layer, or the bottom layer, we are not for sure.

Verse 21:

And the twelve gates {were} twelve pearls: every several gate was of one pearl: and the street of the city {was} pure gold, as it were transparent glass.

We have no dimensions given to us concerning the gates. Some suppose that they are as high as the wall. Each a huge entrance of welcome to the city to those who will be privileged to enter there.

We found in verse twelve that an angel stands at each of these twelve gates. Also, that the names of the twelve tribes of Israel are inscribed eternally in the gates.

We are again confronted with an astounding thing concerning the city; the gates are one entire pearl!

- No such pearls have ever been seen by mortal man before!

THE STREET

The singular reference to the street of the city presents some questions. How can there just be one street in such a huge city? The word is taken from the Greek word which is also employed in chapter 11 and verse 8. There it is speaking about the bodies of the two witnesses which shall lie in the street of Jerusalem. We know, of course, that Jerusalem has more than just one street. The same word is translated "streets" in such places as Matthew 6:5; Luke 10:10 and Acts 5:15.

It would appear, because of the twelve gates, that there will be twelve great broadways leading into the city.

The street is of pure gold, like transparent glass. This as well is something which we do not understand in this world and this life, having never witnessed such gold. It has been said that the gold of the city will be so pure that is the reason it is transparent.

Verse 22:

And I saw no temple therein: for the Lord God Almighty and the Lamb are the temple of it.

The one thing which has been prominent to both the Church and the people of Israel, has been their place of worship. To Israel it was their temple. To the church it was their gathering places of worship.

During the millennium there was the beautiful temple, which is described for us by Ezekiel, where people would come from far and near to learn of the Word of God.

The word for temple is taken from the Greek word "naos," which means a dwelling, a shrine, or a temple.

Alford wrote: "The whole city is now the naos (temple), (cf. on verso 16,17, where the shape of the city is that of the holy of holies). The presence of God pervades all the city; (cf. ver. 11); all the redeemed are within the sanctuary, all are now priests (cf. ch. 20:6). There is, therefore, no naos, or temple, within the city, for the whole city itself is the temple. The Object of all worship and the great Sacrifice are there."

Morris wrote: "But then also the Lamb "is the temple of it." Both God in His infinite majesty and God in His suffering humanity are one, both together as God-man, comprising the holy temple in

which He dwells eternally with His own people, His both by virtue of creation and by right of redemption."

There is no temple there because there will be no central gathering place to worship God, as we have now and will have during the millennium. The Spirit and presence of God will permeate the whole city.

Verse 23:

And the city had no need of the sun, neither of the moon, to shine in it: for the glory of God did lighten it, and the Lamb {is} the light thereof.

Let us notice that it states: "the city" had no need of the sun. This does not mean that the sun will cease to shine, but that those who dwell in that New Jerusalem will not be dependent upon the sun or moon for light. It would appear that the sun and moon will continue to shine upon the new earth, but the new city will have a light of its own, provided by the Lord Himself.

Somehow, we do not understand just how, the glory of God will illuminate the entire city. We do not feel that the light is coming from some source of great light which is shining brightly throughout the city. But that the glory of God reaches throughout the city. There is no place in that city where the light of His glory does not reach. We don't expect to see any shadows in that city!

The glory of God illumined the sky for Israel during their wilderness march with a pillar of fire by night (Exodus 13:22). For forty years, the pillar of fire appeared over the camps of Israel, directly over the Ark of God, encased within the Tabernacle, within the Holy of Holies. It is that same glory which, when the Ark was brought into that most holy place filled it till the priests were not able to enter until it lifted. It is that same glory which will fill that City and illuminate it to every comer and square foot.

Verse 24:

And the nations of them which are saved shall walk in the light of it: and the kings of the earth do bring their glory and honour into it.

This is a very fascinating scripture! First of all, this verse lets us know there will be nations of people dwelling on the new earth. Some have explained that the root word for nations employed here is the same word which is translated Gentiles elsewhere. In other words, it is not a reference to divisions of people living on the new earth, but to the fact they are saved Gentiles.

Well, why not accept the scripture as it is presented here to us in the King James Version. We have no scriptural reason to assume there will not be nations of people dwelling on the earth then. Is this what Jesus had reference to when in Matthew twenty-five He spoke of the time when the nations would be separated at the time of His coming back. Some of the nations would be considered Goat nations, and would be lost eternally. Others would be Sheep nations and would be saved eternally. Their salvation had to do with their attitude and treatment of His people; 25:45 *Then shall he answer them, saying, Verily I say unto you, Inasmuch as ye did {it} not to one of the least of these, ye did {it} not to me.*

Did Jesus not promise in, Matthew 5:5, *Blessed {are} the meek: for they shall inherit the earth.*

EDEN AGAIN...

In the beginning God placed man in the beautiful garden of Eden. His first command to man in found in Genesis 1:28: *And God blessed them, and God said unto them, Be fruitful, and multiply, and replenish the earth, and subdue it: and have dominion over the fish of the sea, and over the fowl of the air, and over every living thing that moveth upon the earth.* If man had never eaten of the forbidden fruit he could have lived in that paradise eternally, and his offspring would have lived eternally as well.

Disobedience and sin destroyed that hope and robbed man of ever knowing the joys of living eternally on an earth blessed of the Lord. It would appear, however, that this is just exactly what is happening as this verse describes for us. The renewed and wonderfully changed earth will be the dwelling place of this people who shall walk in the light of the city of God.

By the mention of the kings of the earth I do not think this implies that we are to think that these kings are the kings which ruled over these nations prior to the restoration of all things. Nor are we to think that just because we have a reference to nations here that this implies that entire nations are brought into the new earth. There will in no way enter into that new earth those who were ungodly and sinners before. All sinners have been judged and cast out in to the lake of fire.

WHO ARE THEY?

Just who are these people in reference here? Since we know of no direct statement in the Word of God concerning them, we are left to our own speculation as to their identity. This, needless to say, presents some problems for us. We present the following scenario for our consideration;

At the end of the Millennium, after one thousand wonderful years in which Christ has reigned on this earth as King of kings, and Lord of lords, there have been a lot of people born during this period. There will be, at the end of the thousand years, a lot of people who are saved which are neither a part of the family of Israel, nor part of the Church. We have reference to the camp a/the saints against which Satan brings his host in Revelation 20:9. It is evidently this people who will inhabit the new earth, along with the people of Abraham.

Now this presents the problem of What happens to them when the earth is burned up? Well, we faced the same problem as to what happened to all the people who stand before God during the White Throne judgment. The obvious difference being, the group standing before the White Throne have all been called up from the dead, so they have received their eternal body. But if God can transport an Enoch and Elijah off of this earth in their physical body, why would we think it a thing too great for the same thing to happen to thousands, and not just two!

Their source of life is found in our next chapter where we have reference to the Tree of Life. The same source of life which Adam and Eve knew in the garden until sin entered the picture and they were driven out of the garden and away from the tree.

The reference to the kings could be a reference to positions which will be held by the redeemed. We do have the promise found in chapter five, verse ten; And hast made us unto our God kings and priests: and we shall reign on the earth.

It is not unreasonable to think that the earth will once again be divided into many areas of people, each ruled over by a king from among the redeemed. And as the new earth will be greatly changed from the present condition of the earth, with no more sea, it would appear there would be room for several billions of people to live on this new earth.

WHAT ABOUT CHILDREN?

Can you imagine a society without children? Yet, there is nothing said about children on the new earth. We are again left with our speculation as to whether the marriage relationship will be known in that new economy. We could assume, however, that if God intended such a relationship in that first garden of Eden, why should we think it would be any different in that eternal Eden!

As we have these kings and their nations bringing their glory and honor into the New Jerusalem, this seems to further indicate that the New City will be situated upon the earth, and not suspended in space as another planet.

Verse 25:

And the gates of it shall not be shut at all by day: for there shall be no night there.

The gates and walls of those ancient cities were for protection from invading enemies. Such will not be the case with this city, however. The gates of the ancient cities were open only during the day, and then closed at night to protect the inhabitants. Again, such will not be the case in that New City. There will be no night in that City, for the Lord Himself is the light of the City, and His light never goes out!

Just as the invitation is given by the Lord now to all who are wearied of sin, to enter into His Church, and is available at all times, and to all peoples; the invitation to enter that city will be given to all earth dwellers to enter at any time. The New Jerusalem will stand with Her gates open continually, inviting any who will to enter in and find blessings rich and real waiting for them.

Night, in symbolism, speaks of evil and sinfulness. There will be no evil nor sinfulness in that city. It is beyond the reach of Satan and his emissaries of evil. This new creation will never know the sting of sin.

Verse 26:

And they shall bring the glory and honour of the nations into it.

In verse twenty-four John spoke of the kings bringing their glory and honor into the city, here we have reference, possibly, to the people as well bringing their glory and honor into it.

If the leaders of nations, and the people who make up those nations, would but learn now the blessing and rewards of bringing the glory which is due the Lord what a difference this would make in our world.

Mankind is stubborn when it comes to learning what is best for them. They get it honestly, as the expression goes, for that was the same attitude which Adam had in the garden. He learned belatedly - as his descendants are doing - that it would always be best to follow the Lord's will with their life.

In that society, there will only be godly rulers over the people, and the people will all be godly. The greatest desire for knowledge will be to acquire a knowledge of God and His will for their life.

Verse 27:

And there shall in no wise enter into it any thing that defileth, neither {whatsoever} worketh abomination, or {maketh} a lie: but they which are written in the Lamb's book of life.

We do not assume that this verse is implying that anyone is living who could bring a defilement into the city. John seems to be emphasizing - or the Lord through John - that the city is far beyond the reach of such who would come into it with wicked abominations. That only those whose names are recorded in the Lamb's book of life may have access to that city. And those who are living on the earth at this time are only those who do have their names in the book of life!

The society which will then be known by the people privileged to enjoy it will be the society which is only dreamed about now.

The governments of men have long since failed. Now the government of God is set up which will assure that all who will enter that society will enjoy life and happiness as continual companions. A society which is not brought about by the ballot box, nor by a revolution; but it is brought about by the goodness and mercy of an all-loving and all-kind Sovereign.

To know the joys of that society will be the highest honor!

CHAPTER TWENTY-TWO

EDEN AGAIN!

We now come to the final chapter in this interesting book, which concludes the Book of books, the Bible, the Word of God.

Just as we witnessed the glory of God prevalent in the first chapters of Genesis, in the detailed description of creation, we have the glory of God present in the concluding chapters.

That which God had given man, His creation, in the very beginning, which because of sin had been thwarted for seven thousand years, is now restored. Man, originally was created as an eternal being, and placed on this earth to enjoy the creation of God. Sin enters the picture, and all becomes ugly and dark.

Satan has been the master enemy of mankind for the past seven thousand years. Now, at last, this is all in the past. Satan is removed for ever from the picture, and man is once again placed on an earth which is Edenic in nature. This time, however, it would seem that Eden is not located in one geographic location, but the entire new earth is Eden all over. From here on it will be God and His people - for ever and ever!

THE VISION OF THE CITY CONTINUES

Verse 1:

And he shewed me a pure river of water of life, clear as crystal, proceeding out of the throne of God and of the Lamb.

It would appear from the description given to us by John that the first five verses of this chapter are a continuation of his description of the New Jerusalem which he had been describing in chapter twenty-one.

The word AND which begins this verse seems to point out that he is continuing his description of the city.

Up to this point John had been focusing on describing the city from an architectural viewpoint. The dazzling beauties of the many precious stones, and the shining gold that is like transparent glass, presents an awe-inspiring view, to say the least. But now we are given a view from the inside of the city! What we behold inside the city overwhelms the mind because of the glories which are there to behold.

The psalmist long ago exclaimed; Psalm 46:4 *{There is} a river, the streams whereof shall make glad the city of God, the holy {place} of the tabernacles of the most High.*

The garden of Eden we know had a river which flowed out of it; Genesis 2:10 *And a river went out of Eden to water the garden; and from thence it was parted, and became into four heads.*

Ezekiel forty-seven speaks of a river which would flow out from the temple. It would be a life-giving river which would bring healing to everything it reached. But the river described by Ezekiel is evidently not the same one that John is here speaking of. Evidently Ezekiel is describing a river which would flow from the temple during the time of the millennium. The earth since the millennium has been burned up, and completely renovated. John is here witnessing a new earth, and also witnessing the city of God coming down out of heaven to dwell on the new earth. It is from this City, New Jerusalem, that John is witnessing the flowing forth of this river of life.

The rivers of this world may have their origin from some mountain's base, but the river which John here describes is flowing *"out of the throne of God."* This as well implies that the throne of God is now situated on this earth. At last conditions on the earth are such that God brings His throne down to dwell among His creation. His throne is located in the new city.

While this is evidently a physical river which will flow forth from the throne of God, we are reminded of another river which flowed forth which brings healing to the soul of mankind; John 19:34; *But one of the soldiers with a spear pierced his side, and forthwith came there out blood and water.*

That river has been flowing since Calvary, which has resulted in the cleansing of sin from multitudes of lives.

The fact that this river flows from the throne of God, which is evidently located in the New Jerusalem, presents intriguing questions to us; Just where is the throne located in the City? and how does this river flow out of the City?

"Somewhere on that "Pyramidal Mountain" in the centre of the City, probably on its summit, will rest "The Throne of God," from under the seat of which shall flow down in cascades, from terrace to terrace, the crystal clear stream that shall feed that wonderful River of Life." (Larkin)

"But most notable of all is the source of this mighty river of life and its living waters. There is no sea from which waters are raised by the sun as in the present hydrologic cycle (Revelation 21:1) and thus no rainfall to supply the river with its flow. Rather, it proceeds "out of the throne of God and of the Lamb," high at the central pinnacle of the holy city. Evidently the mighty Creator is continually creating the waters, then sending them forth to give perpetual life and cleansing and beauty to the city and its inhabitants, and then out into the uttermost parts of the new earth. It is water of life, and there is no death. " (Morris)

If the throne of God would be in the apex of the city, then the river would, naturally, flow down from this apex some fourteen hundred miles high, down through the city and out into the earth around it. The imagination of the whole matter is overwhelming, to say the least.

Verse 2:

In the midst of the street of it, and on either side of the river, {was there} the tree of life, which bare twelve {manner of} fruits, ~and} yielded her fruit every month: and the leaves of the tree {were} for the healing of the nations.

There are those who feel that the first phrase of this verse should have been left with verse one. It would then read; *And he shewed me a pure river of water of life, clear as crystal, proceeding out of the throne of God and of the Lamb, in the midst of the street of it. The Revised Version shows it this way.*

We are again confronted with a problem as to how to accurately describe just how it will look. Are we to assume that the river flows down the middle of the golden street? And if that is the case, are we to assume (as in our study concerning the street) that there are actually at least twelve streets; one for each gate? And if that is the case, do we then assume that there are actually twelve branches of that river of life flowing down through those twelve streets?

There will be in that city The Tree of Life. We feel this is the same Tree of Life which was in the garden of Eden, and which after sin entered the picture, man was kept away from. It would appear that

Adam had access to the tree of life in the garden, and it was this tree of life which gave him his source of life. As long as man could eat of that tree he could live forever. This was the reason that God placed the flaming sword of the cherubim at the entrance to the garden. Once man had sinned and had been driven from the garden, man could not have access to the tree of life.

Now that sin and Satan is completely removed from the picture the tree of life is once again given to man.

 Again, we are confronted with the singular term Tree of life. Yet we are informed that it is on either side of the river. One commentary put it; On this side of the river and on that was the tree of life. Like the other singular terms, we have considered in our study, it would appear that we are not to think in terms of one singular tree, but one kind of tree. So far we have the Street of gold, River of life, and now the Tree of life. All of them referred to with a singular term.

These unique trees bare twelve kinds of fruit, one for each month of the year. There is no indication as to what manner of fruit is produced by these trees. Just as there was no indication as to the manner of fruit on either the tree of life in the garden nor the tree of knowledge of good and evil, we are not informed as to the kind of fruits which are produced during the year by these trees.

Another unique thing about these trees is that it states: *and the leaves of the tree were for the healing of the nations.* Now we know that the redeemed have all received glorified bodies, so they are beyond any sickness or disease ever afflicting them. So, these trees would not be for their benefit. The nations referred to here, as we considered in 21:24, does not have reference to the nations of the heathen, but to those who will dwell on the new earth at that time. Why would there be any need of healing if there is never any sickness again in that new earth? Possibly it is more of a preventive measure than an after-the-effect cure. Just as the fruit of the tree affords continual life, the leaves of the trees would afford continual health.

Mead pointed out in his Apocalypse of Jesus Christ, that "The word here used for tree, in the Greek, is not dendron, the ordinary word for tree, but xylon, that is always used of the cross, when that is spoken of as the tree, as in Acts 5:30, 10:29, Gal 3:13 and 1Pet 2:24. It is also the word used in Rev 2:7. Who then can doubt that its use here instead of dendron, is for the purpose of connecting it with the Cross on which the Prince of Life died, which has yielded the fruit of eternal life to all the nations living on the new earth."

Regardless of the tree of life bearing fruit and the leaves giving continual health, the fact remains that the source of life is in the Lord Jesus Christ. He is our health and life.

GEOGRAPHICAL LOCATIONS?

The prophet Ezekiel spoke of the river which flows from the throne of the temple during the millennium; 47:9 *And it shall come to pass, {that} every thing that liveth, which moveth, whithersoever the rivers shall come, shall live: and there shall be a very great multitude of fish, because these waters shall come thither: for they shall be healed; and every thing shall live whither the river cometh.* The implication is that this river flows out across the land of Israel bringing life to every place it touches.

From verse eight of this chapter it seems to be telling us that the Dead Sea will come alive when this river flows into it.

If this would be true of the river which flows from the temple during the millennium, why would the same not be true for the river of life which will flow forth from the throne of God situated in the New Jerusalem! As there will be a completely restructured new earth at that time. An earth in which there will no longer be any seas, and, evidently, no longer any great mountainous ranges, the river could conceivably flow forth into all the earth.

The same could be said of the tree(s) of life. It seems some have assumed that the tree was located only here in the city. Would it not be as logically possible that the tree(s) of life will follow the flow of this river into all the earth? Otherwise, if the tree was the source of continual life in the new earth, men would have to make their pilgrimage to the city on a regular basis in order to continue to know life and health.

One other interesting note from what we glean from this verse; by the reference to the trees bearing fruit every month, twelve fruits, one for each month of the year, seems to be an implication that time will continue as it was set in motion from the beginning. The earth will, evidently, continue to make its orbital rotation around the sun as it has for the past millenniums. While nothing is said about the seasons of the year, nor the differences known today in the various areas of the earth, as to weather conditions, we will have to wait until that day to find out these things.

Verse 3:

And there shall be no more curse: but the throne of God and of the Lamb shall be in it; and his servants shall serve him:

We had been informed in chapter twenty-one of the many things which would be absent in that new creation; things such as death and pain and sorrow. As if to drive this wonderful truth home to us, we are here again informed there would be no more curse. The curse is absent because the Lord is present.

The curse is absent because Satan is absent. He who caused the curse to be brought upon the human race is now for ever removed from the scene, along with all those who followed his pernicious ways.

These being absent only bliss and health and joy is present among those blessed to be inhabitants of that new creation.

Morris wrote: "What has been made evident before, and is obvious in the very nature of things, is here rehearsed again, as though such a glorious truth cannot be contained and must burst forth repeatedly in its wonder. The age-long curse is gone. There is no more death and no more sin. The earth and its inhabitants, indeed the entire creation, are henceforth to thrive in fullest vigor forever. None will ever age, nothing will ever be lost, all work will be productive and enduring. The entropy law, the so-called second law of thermodynamics, will be repealed. Information will nevermore become confused, ordered systems will not deteriorate into disorder, and no longer will energy have to be expended merely to overcome friction and dissipation into nonrecoverable heat. Entropy will from now on be reserved along with energy and mass and momentum. Though time will continue on forever, time's arrow will no longer be directed downward."

His servants shall serve Him. A statement which carries with it such a wonderful thought. What a privilege to be a servant of Jesus Christ in that day and place! It is said of those who come forth from the fires of tribulation; Revelation 7:15, Therefore are they before the throne of God, and serve him day and night in his temple: and he that sitteth on the throne shall dwell among them.

We are not to assume that just because we make it to heaven, or enter a new creation on this new earth, that activities will cease as far as work is concerned. There was to evidently be work for Adam to do in the garden, for God declared; Genesis 2:15: *And the Lord God took the man, and put him into the garden of Eden to dress it and to keep it.* The fact there will be servants present there, serving the Lord, is evidence that there will be work to be done. But the curse of work is gone. It will no longer be eating bread by the sweat of the brow. There will be a pleasant environment to live and work in. The work will not be unpleasant. It will be a great privilege and honor to be able to work for the Master Himself.

Verse 4:

And they shall see his face; and his name {shall be} in their foreheads.

How many times have you wondered what He really looks like? Scanning the faces that the many artists have painted to portray our Lord, we are left wondering just what He really looks like. In that day, we will be privileged to live with Him and look upon His face.

We have been informed about the 144,000 who had His name sealed on their foreheads. We have references made to those who would overcome, in the letter to the church at Philadelphia, 3:12: *I will write upon him the name of my God, and the name of the city of my God, {which is} new Jerusalem, which cometh down out of heaven from my God: and I will write upon him} my new name.*

We are not for sure if this has reference to all who are among the saved in that new creation, are only to those who are classified as servants to the Lord.

We are informed that when the high priest would go into the Most Holy place he wore a name-plate on his forehead which had the name of God upon it. We do know that Aaron wore on his forehead a plate which read "Holiness To The LORD."

Verse 5:

And there shall be no night there; and they need no candle, neither light of the sun; for the Lord God giveth them light: and they shall reign for ever and ever.

We had been informed in 21:23 that *the Lamb is the light thereof* While there it may have been a scene from the outside of the city, here we seem to be standing on the inside, where this fact is repeated.

This verse states that the Lord God is the giver of the light. In chapter twenty-one it states it is the Lamb who gives the light. No problem! They are one and the same!

There are two verses which depict for us the great contrast between those who inhabit this beautiful place and those who enter the lake of fire: Hebrews 4:9: *There remaineth therefore a rest to the people of God.*

Revelation 14:11, *And the smoke of their torment ascendeth up for ever and ever: and they have no rest day nor night, who worship the beast and his image, and whosoever receiveth the mark of his name.* Living and working for the Master in that beautiful City will be a great joy to all who are so privileged. No shadows shall darken any comer of that city. No sadness will be known in that city. This verse actually ends the Revelation with a final reference to conditions which will prevail in that city. We will note that the following verse and those which conclude the chapter, are statements affirming the coming again of Jesus Christ, and the truthfulness of this book.

The study concludes with a reference to the fact that those who are privileged to enter that place shall also be privileged to dwell there for ever and ever.

Mr Turner wrote: "We have in the closing phrase of verse 5, God's unit for the measurement of Eternity; namely, the ages of the ages. There will have been but seven ages from the creation of Adam, to the Judgment of the Great White Throne: The Dispensations or Ages, of Innocence, of Conscience, of Self-will, of Promise, of Law, of Grace, and of the Millennium. The eighth dispensation or age, is the Dispensation of the Fullness of Times, which is the first age in the measurement of Eternity. If then, there are but seven ages from Adam to the last judgment, what must an age be whose unit of time is ages? But even this does not exhaust the meaning of this language; its unit is the AGES of the ages. Age rolling upon age in endless succession. This is God's description of Eternity!"

"The common conception is that, at a certain point, time ceases to be and eternity begins. But the fact is that we are now in eternity, for eternity is the extension of time forever. There never will be a time when there will be no time. The word "time" means "infinite duration, or its measure. A definite portion of duration." The word "eternity" means "infinite duration, or time." Time is commonly contrasted with eternity. This is true as far as things which have a beginning are concerned, but such could not be true of things that have no ending. The heavens and earth and all things therein as originally created are eternal. Since the creation of these things, eternity has been broken up into times periods, and God always recognizes this in His Word. Men generally think of eternity as beginning with the next life, or with the New Heavens and New Earth, but this is not true. When men enter the next life and the heavens and the earth are made new, there is no change made in time or eternity. They remain the same. The change is made in men and in the heavens and earth, in that they enter into a new state which is eternal and unchangeable." (Dake)

THE EPILOGUE

Here begins the concluding statements to John of this marvelous record that he has been given through the Spirit. It is like an epilogue reassuring John that what he has just witnessed, and recorded for the church, is actual. It will all take place just as John witnessed it.

Verse 6:

And he said unto me, These sayings {are} faithful and true: and the Lord God of the holy prophets sent his angel to shew unto his servants the things which must shortly be done.

This takes us back to the very beginning of study in the book of Revelation. Let us note again the very first verse; *The Revelation of Jesus Christ, which God gave unto him, to shew unto his servants things which must shortly come to pass; and he sent and signified {it} by his angel unto his servant John.* Again, the "*he*" in reference to the angel here, is the angel which is mentioned in verse nine of chapter twenty-one. It is one of the angels with the last seven bowls of wrath.

We notice that the phrase *"which must shortly be done,"* in this verse is the same Greek expression in verse one of chapter one. It is from the word "en tachos," which means "in haste." It is interesting to note how God considers time. If this is an expression of what will take place from the time of John, then we are talking about a period of approximately three thousand years (through the millennium). If we are considering from the beginning of the tribulation through the millennium, then we still have over one thousand years. One thousand years compared to God and eternity passes, "in haste!"

Verse 7:

Behold, I come quickly: blessed {is} he that keepeth the sayings of the prophecy of this book.

First of all, we come upon an expression which is employed three times in the closing statements of this book; The Lord is coming quickly. In fact, the concluding statement recorded that Jesus said was I come quickly, as we see in verse twenty. It consequently demands of us a continual watching for that grand and glorious event.

Secondly, we are again taken back to the first verses of the book, to verse three, where there we found a promise given to all who; *readeth, and they that hear the words of this prophecy, and keep those things which are written therein for the time {is} at hand.* The Blessed here is the sixth of the seven beatitudes found in the Revelation. While in verse three of chapter one it was emphasized first of all that all would be blessed who would "hear" the words of Revelation, and then "keep" them. Here the emphasis is on those who keep the sayings of the book.

The term *KEEP* speaks to us about "guarding" what we are witnessing.

Ford C Ottman, in his Unfolding of the Ages, has something interesting regarding this statement; "What is meant by 'keepeth'? The primary meaning of the word is 'to keep guard.' The literal translation of the passage is: 'Blessed is he that keepeth his eyes attentively fixed upon the fulfillment of this prophecy;' or, 'Blessed is he that guards the integrity and force of the words of this prophecy.' The word translated 'keepeth' is used also in commendation of the Philadelphians: 'Thou hast a little power, and hast kept my word, and hast not denied my name.' To all such the Lord says: 'Because thou hast kept the word of my patience, I also will keep thee out of the hour of temptation which is about to come upon the whole habitable world to try those that dwell upon the earth' (Chap. 3:10). What a summons this is to awaken sleepers, and startle those that account prophetic study an indifferent thing!

If the words of prophecy of this book have been fulfilled in past history, there is, then, nothing left for us to keep after the manner implied by this word. We may be sure, however, that the seals and trumpets - much as human history may be shown to have developed in accord with them - shall speak far more definitely than they have yet done. Our place should be, where stood the prophet of old, on the watch tower, to see what He will say in us, and what we shall answer when argued with. (Hab 2:1 Marg.) We should there find, as did he, that 'The vision is yet for an appointed time, but at the end it shall speak, and not lie: though it tarry' (Hab. 1:3). The meaning of this is, plainly enough, that the vision will not tarry beyond the appointed time. 'Behold, I come quickly' are the startling words to such as are being swept away by the trend of modern thought that betrays such an indifference to the glorious fact. But, 'Blessed are those servants, whom the lord when he cometh shall find watching: verily I say unto you, that he shall gird himself, and make them to sit down to meat, and will come forth and serve them. And if he shall come in the second watch, or come in the third watch, and find them so, blessed are those servants.' (Luke 12:37,38)."

The apostle Paul employed the term when speaking of the truth which he had proclaimed to the end; 2Timothy 4:7: *I have fought a good fight, I have finished {my} course, I have kept the faith.*

No one of that first century guarded truth any more than the apostle Paul!

Verse 8:

And I John saw these things, and heard {them}. And when I had heard and seen, I fell down to worship before the feet of the angel which shewed me these things.

John again refers to himself by name, which is only the second time since he had begun writing about the tribulation events. John, the beloved apostle of the first century, verifies what he has recorded by placing his own name to the writings.

The natural reaction of John was to fall down and worship before the angel. John is so filled with awe at what he has witnessed, his reaction is to fall down and worship. John had done this before (19:10), but there is somewhat of a difference in the two passages. In chapter nineteen it clearly states that *I fell at his feet to worship him:* here it states, *I fell down to worship before the feet of the angel.*

Whether John's intentions here was to offer worship to the angel, we do not know for sure. Evidently, he did, because of the reaction of the angel.

John had received what no other mortal had ever received. While the prophets through the ages have received some wonderful visions, none ever received what John has just witnessed, which he has recorded in the Revelation. No wonder his reaction is to fall down and worship!

Verse 9:

Then saith he unto me, See {thou do it} not: for I am thy fellowservant, and of thy brethren the prophets, and of them which keep the sayings of this book: worship God.

This rebuke to John points out; 1. The angel was just that - an angel of the Lord, and therefore not due our worship. 2. This is not Jesus Christ, as He did receive worship during His ministry on this earth - and He still does - as, for instance, we find in John 20:28, And Thomas answered and said unto him, My Lord and my God. John, as mentioned, had previously been rebuked for seeking to worship an angel, so it would appear that John's action here is more of a reaction, but even such a gesture as bowing before any other than God draws correction from the angel.

The statement of the angel is very interesting, to say the least. Just what does he mean by stating that he is of thy brethren the prophets, and of them which keep the sayings of this book? While we could consider the angels brothers in the sense of being part of the family of God, it does not seem that the angels could be spoken of as prophets of God. Unless we take the original meaning of the word and apply it to the functions of angels. Philo writes concerning prophets; "The prophet is an interpreter, echoing from within the sayings of God." If we consider the function of the prophet in this respect and consider the functions of the angels which have been directing John in the Revelation, then, it would seem, that we could say the angels are prophets of God, for they are surely in many instances declaring the word of God.

John is directed to "*worship God.*" This again emphasizes to us the deity of Jesus Christ who freely, without rebuke, accepted the worship of people. Someone said that Jesus accepted the worship of men some ten times without rebuking them.

Verse 10:

And he saith unto me, Seal not the sayings of the prophecy of this book: for the time is at hand.

The vision is now complete. The message has been completely delivered and recorded. The time of the end is at hand. So, the message must not be hidden but revealed, so that those who read, and accept the message may prepare themselves.

Daniel, who received visions which compare with those of John, was told just the opposite; Daniel 8:26, *And the vision of the evening and the morning which was told {is} true: wherefore shut thou up the vision; for it {shall be} for many days.* Also, Daniel 12:4, *But thou, 0 Daniel, shut up the words, and seal the book, {even} to the time of the end: many shall run to and fro, and knowledge shall be increased.*

To Daniel, and those who would read his writings, the events of which he wrote were still in the far distant future, so the command to seal up the writings. The understanding of Daniel's writings was not given at that time. His book remained a sealed book to the time of John. Now that John has supplied the missing links to Daniel's writings, the books are open.

So, the book of Revelation is an open book. It is a book of REVELATION. Revealing the events which will come to pass in the last days, and even beyond the Great White Throne of judgment.

So, we are not to shun the book of Revelation, but we are to open it and read its contents. The book is not a closed book - but an open book. Its name implies such; Revelation. It is a revealing, not a hiding, of God's word for the end time.

One reason the Devil does not want the book of Revelation expounded is probably because it reveals his doom and defeat at the hand of Jesus Christ. As it has been said, Satan hates the book of Genesis - because it reveals he is the reason for the world's woes, and the reason sin and death reigns in the world of mankind. So, he attacks the authenticity of the book. And he hates the book of Revelation because it reveals his doom and defeat. So, he discourages the study of this book by saying we can't understand it, so we should not read it.

There have probably been more books of commentary written on the book of Revelation than any other book of the Bible. So, the writings of Revelation have certainly been opened and expounded to mankind. At the same time, however, there remains so much about this book which we still do not know. And will not know until it is time for it to be revealed unto us by the Lord.

And many of these things will only be revealed after the rapture!

Verse 11:

He that is unjust, let him be unjust still: and he which is filthy, let him be filthy still: and he that is righteous, let him be righteous still: and he that is holy, let him be holy still.

Some feel that the spokesman is the Lord Jesus Christ now. That after verse nine, in which we have the instructions from the angel to worship God, God has been speaking to John. And that it is the Lord who is here speaking.

Mr McGee stated on this verse; "Probably the most frightful condition of the lost is revealed here, ever more so than at the Great White Throne Judgment of chapter 20. The sinful condition of the lost is a permanent and eternal thing; although it is not static, for the suggestion is that the unrighteous will increasingly become more unrighteous the filthy "will be filthy still." The condition of the lost gets worse until each becomes a monster of sin. This thought is frightful."

Morris wrote: "The adverb "still" could even be understood in the sense of "more." "Let him that is unjust, that is 'unrighteous,' become more unrighteous." In contrast, "let the righteous man become still more righteous." Such indeed will often be the result of the study of this marvelous book of the unveiled future, a book which generates fright on the one hand, delight on the other.

"The "*filthy*" ones of whom the Lord speaks are not merely those who are unwashed. Rather, they are morally filthy, the depraved. The "*holy*" are those who are sanctified in both heart and life, consecrated to the will of God by the Holy Spirit."

This verse describes for us the eternal condition of both the saved and the lost. The teaching of purgatory is not to be found in the Word of God. And just as there is evidence here of the continuing condition of the ungodly eternally, the same would hold true for the godly. There will be no such thing as becoming lost after this! The

Eden experience which resulted in the fall of man will not be repeated!

At this point we have passed the point of the temporary. We no longer speak in terms of a "lifetime." Whatever condition one finds themselves in at this time, they will remain in this condition for eternity.

The awesomeness of this verse should cause each one of us to make sure that our heart is prepared before the Lord. Let us not be caught among those who are here described as unrighteous, for if we are we will be *unrighteous still...*

This verse also points out that such conditions exist at this time. The thought that at some point beyond the day of judgment the sins of men will be purged from their life is not supported by this verse, nor any other portion of the Word of God. Just as there will exist those who are holy before God at this time, there will also exist those who are here classified "*unjust*" and "*filthy.*" While they will not exist together, nor ever again rub shoulders with one another, they will continue to exist eternally.

Verse 12:

And, behold, I come quickly; and my reward {is} with me, to give every man according as his work shall be.

The spokesman continues to be Jesus Christ it would appear from this personal reference in this verse.

This is the second of three times that the Lord speaks of His returning in this chapter (7,12,20).

We find the Lord making such a statement six times in the book of Revelation; 2:5,16 - where it is a warning given to the churches of Ephesus and Pergamos. In 3:11, where it is a promise given to those who overcome.

The expression "*quickly*" does not indicate that the Lord was getting ready to come soon after making this statement to John, but, rather, that His return will take place quickly. The rapture of the redeemed will not be a drawn-out affair. Paul spoke of our body being changed in the twinkling of an eye (1Corinthians 15:52). Thus, we are constantly warned to be ready at all times - to "*WATCH AND PRAY*"

Paul spoke in 2Corinthians 5:10 of the rewards which will be given to those who come before the judgment seat of Christ after the rapture takes place. While the greatest of all rewards will be the eternal life which will be given to the children of God, there will also be personal, individual, rewards which will be given to those who have labored faithfully in the vineyard of the Lord. This is indicated not only in the passage in 2Corinthians, but it is also pointed out here that it will be according as his work shall be that the redeemed will be rewarded at the appearance of our Lord Jesus Christ.

Verse 13:

I am Alpha and Omega, the beginning and the end, the first and the last.

Jesus Christ makes this statement which identifies Him as Deity in four places in the Revelation; 1:8,11; 21:6, and now here.

Mr Morris made some interesting comments on this verse; "The Apostle John, in fact, in his five New Testament books refers to "the beginning," in connection with Christ, referring to the creation, no less than twelve times, first of all in John 1:1: "In the beginning was the Word." The Lord Jesus is both Creator and Revelator. The very fact of creation by the Lord leads to the fact of revelation by the Lord, since He would not create without a purpose, nor would He leave that purpose unrevealed to those whom He had created in His own image. The living Word is revealed by the written Word, through human writings in human language, divinely inspired.

In Genesis He is Alpha; in Revelation, He is the Omega, with sixty-four other wonderful "letters" in the books between, all conveying to man the glorious plan and purpose of his Creator. It is foundational to know Him as Maker; it is salvational to know Him as Redeemer, Friend and Lord; it is motivational to know Him as coming King."

The terms Alpha and Omega are the first and last letters of the Greek alphabet. These, along with the other expressions employed by the Lord in this verse, point out His eternality.

Verse 14:

Blessed {are} they that do his commandments, that they may have right to the tree of life, and may enter in through the gates into the city.

This is the last of the seven "beatitudes" found in the Revelation.

This blessing is pronounced upon all who do His commandments. It is not enough to know His commandments. They must be obeyed and kept.

There are some who object to the King James Version reading; Blessed are they that do his commandments. They feel it should read - Blessed are those who wash their robes... Some Versions, such as the New American Standard Version, have it this way. Their argument being that one is saved by grace, not by the keeping, or observing, of commandments. These are they who would have us to believe that we can do nothing ourselves to experience salvation. It has already been taken care of on Calvary by our Lord Jesus Christ. While it is certainly true that we are saved by grace (Ephesians 2:8), it is also true that one must obey the Word of God in order to be saved by grace.

The command to do the commandments of God would apply to any dispensation of time. While the commandments may be different in each dispensation, the command to obey them remains the same.

We may not be saved by the Law given through Moses, we are still commanded to obey the plan for salvation as outlined for the church age.

While we may elect to translate this statement in this verse to wash their robes, we are faced with two other passages in the Revelation which also speaks of keeping the commandments of God; 12:17, And the dragon was wroth with the woman, and went to make war with the remnant of her seed, which keep the commandments of God, and have the testimony of Jesus Christ.

14:12, *Here is the patience of the saints: here {are} they that keep the commandments of God, and the faith of Jesus.*

John made several references in his gospel account as well as his epistle to the keeping of the commandments of God. John said Jesus said: John 14:15, *If ye love me, keep my commandments.* Also, in his epistle, John stated: 1John 2:3,4: *And hereby we do know that we know him, if we keep his commandments. He that saith, I know him, and keepeth not his commandments, is a liar, and the truth is not in him.*

It is those who have done His commandments which have a right to the Tree of Life, and access to the City of God. In this we see the importance of adhering to the Word of God. To fail to obey the Word of God will result in being barred eternally from the City of God and the Tree of Life.

Verse 15:

For without {are} dogs, and sorcerer s, and whoremongers, and murderers, and idolaters, and whosoever loveth and maketh a lie.

First of all, these two verses emphasize to us once again the separation of the saved and the unsaved.

Pointing out once again, just as verse eleven did, that there will remain a separation of the two classes of people in eternity.

The term "*dogs*" in this verse does not have reference to the four-legged canines that run loose about us today. We had been given a list describing those who would have their part in the lake of fire, in this verse we have reference to this group, with the additional classification of *dogs*. We find Paul using this term in referring to a certain group of people in Philippians 3:2, *Beware of dogs, beware of evil workers, beware of the concision.*

We have an interesting reference in Deuteronomy 23:17,18 to dogs; *There shall be no whore of the daughters of Israel, nor a Sodomite of the sons of Israel. Thou shalt not bring the hire of a whore, or the price of a dog, into the house of the Lord thy God for any vow: for even both these {are} abomination unto the Lord thy God.* Evidently the reference here to dogs is employed in conjunction with the reference to Sodomites. In the eyes of God those who commit such sinful practices are classified as dogs. After all, this seems to have been the reason that God dispatched two special angels to the city of Sodom, because of the sinful practices of that place. In fact, the Jews would refer to the Gentiles as dogs. We are informed that the Jews in ancient time employed the term dog in reference to male prostitutes.

"But note how modern all these sins are, as well. Consider the amazing revival of acceptability in modem "Christendom" of homosexuality as well as sexual permissiveness in general, associated so commonly today again with drugs and occult paganism, not to mention idolatrous covetousness and even blatant idol worship. All show that John was writing in the context of the last days as much as he was of apostolic times." (Morris)

THE FINAL MESSAGE

Verse 16:

I Jesus have sent mine angel to testify unto you these things in the churches. I am the root and the offspring of David, {and} the bright and morning star.

This takes us back to the very beginning of the book; 1:1, *The Revelation of Jesus Christ, which God gave unto him, to shew unto his servants things which must shortly come to pass; and he sent and signified {it} by his angel unto his servant John.*

The fact is now accomplished, and the Lord speaks now in the past tense - *I have sent mine angel.*

We have not read the term *church* since we left chapter three and the letters to the seven churches of Asia. The church is not found during the time of tribulation. It is not referred to in the chapter which speaks of the millennium. It is only now at the conclusion of this wonderful book of visions that reference is once again made to the church. This is an open book, and its reading is encouraged in the churches.

While there will evidently be many "churches" on this earth at the time of the rapture of the true church, they will, evidently, unite together under the leadership of the false prophet, to form a super church. But this super church will be out of step with God and will feel the sting of His wrath just as the secular world of the beast will.

We are not for sure just what the phrase "*mine angel*" entails. There have, evidently, been several angels involved in the events which we have been studying about in the Revelation. Possibly there was one which was singled out that addressed himself personally to John concerning the things which he witnessed in the Spirit. Possibly it is this angel that John falls down before in verse eight.

Is this an indication that there is one special angel that is designated as the angel of Jesus Christ? Or, does this term simply imply that any angel which approached John to inform him of events taking place during the Revelation, would be considered the angel of Jesus Christ?

The last phrase is an interesting one which seems to point out to us the three-fold manifestation of the Deity of Jesus Christ:

I AM THE ROOT... OF DAVID... This speaks of the Creator. He is the Father of David.

AND THE OFFSPRING OF DAVID... This speaks of the term which we find in the gospel accounts applied to Jesus Christ as the Son of David. So, Jesus is here spoken of as the Son.

AND THE BRIGHT AND MORNING STAR... This speaks of light - of spirit. Our God has manifested Himself as Father in creation; as Son in redemption; as Holy Spirit in emanation in the church age.

The reference to bright and morning star is unique with this passage of scripture. Nowhere else in the Word of God do we find this title ascribed to our Lord.

The bright morning star heralds the arrival of the new day. What is unfolding to the people of God at this time is the greatest new day that has ever been witnessed. Those privileged to enter that society of the eternally blessed will certainly be experiencing a new day indeed!

It is also interesting to consider the reference here to David, which in turn is a reference to the people of Israel. Is this to emphasize that, although the church is the primary attraction at this time, God has not forgotten His covenant with Abraham. And so, the reference to this people in the concluding remarks of the Revelation as if to say They are still here!

Verse 17:

And the Spirit and the bride say, Come. And let him that heareth say, Come. And let him that is athirst come. And whosoever will, let him take the water of life freely.

The reference to the bride in this verse, is it speaking of the City, New Jerusalem, which we saw in chapter twenty-one is spoken of as the bride? Or, is it speaking of the redeemed that will indwell that city one day? Like the reference to the city as being the bride - while at the same time speaking of the redeemed, the terms are synonymous.

Some feel that this is an invitation directed to the Lord Jesus Christ Himself. He has made the proclamation that He was coming in verses seven and twelve. So, the Spirit and bride unite in appealing for His coming. From the rest of the verse, however, it does not appear that this would be the proper interpretation of this statement. Also, the Spirit that indwells the believer is the Spirit of Jesus Christ! They are not two separate persons as some would have us to believe.

The Spirit moves through the church reaching out to those who are outside of the church, inviting them to enter the church - and ultimately the joys of eternity.

The invitation reaches out to *WHOSOEVER WILL*. None are excluded from the invitation to know the blessings that may be known in the church and in eternity. Only the foolish would ignore this invitation!

That which awaits those who accept this invitation will be the "water of life", from which they may draw freely.

We have mention made in this chapter of the Tree of life, and now the water of life. Death, the last enemy, has now been destroyed (1Corinthians 15:26). All that come to this time and place will live for ever. Death is not mentioned because it will be unknown to this age and to this people.

Verse 18:

For I testify unto every man that heareth the words of the prophecy of this book, If any man shall add unto these things, God shall add unto him the plagues that are written in this book:

"It would be deemed an unpardonable offence for an ambassador to add words to, or to subtract them from, any royal mandate which he was commissioned to deliver. And if anyone in dispensing a physician's prescription, when the life or death of a patient trembled in the balance, were wantonly to tamper with it, what condemnation could be too severe? Yet we fear that the tendency of many in our day is to treat a message in this book far more lightly than they would any important official human document; and instead of sympathizing with the words before us, and adding their reverent "Amen," they would in all probability either condemn the severity of these words, or else pass them by as out of date and altogether effete. On this account we deem it needful, in approaching the close of our expositions, to look into these verses with special care." (Pul Comm)

The book is complete the way it is written! John, the beloved

Apostle, was the last living apostle when he wrote this book of Revelation. He was known throughout the Christian world at that time. Especially was he known by the seven churches in Asia, to whom he addressed letters. Anyone who would come forth with what he claimed was a new, or continued revelation would without doubt be met with rebuke and a solemn refusal to listen to what he had to say.

Those who have made claims to new revelations since this book was written - Mohammed - Joseph Smith - Mary Baker Eddy, and company, fall into the condemnation of this verse. There have been no new revelations since this book was written. John's writings were the last inspired of God.

The plagues which are written in this book that will be brought upon any who dares add to the Word of God should stand out as ample warning against anyone daring to tamper with the Word of God. Now it is true that the plagues which are referred to in this book happen during the tribulation of the last days, and those who have claimed to have a new revelation from the Lord, such as the above mentioned, have long since died. While they may never witness the plagues of the tribulation they will none the less know the judgments of an Eternal God, the same One who brought the plagues upon an ungodly people which are mentioned in this book.

Verse 19:

And if any man shall take away from the words of the book of this prophecy, God shall take away his part out of the book of life, and out of the holy city, and {from} the things which are written in this book.

When Moses gave Israel the Law from God, he warned them in Deuteronomy 4:2, *Ye shall not add unto the word which I command you, neither shall ye diminish {ought} from it, that ye may keep the commandments of the Lord your God which I command you.*

The Word of the Lord is not to be tampered with, either by adding to it nor taking away from it.

Those who would add to the Word of God are those who would claim new revelations from God.

Revelations which are contrary to the Word of God. Those who would take away from the Word of God are those who would change

544

it to suit their own liberal views. The so called "Good News For Modern Man" fits into this category. Other revisions of the Scriptures which have taken away the Virgin Birth; the cleansing by the Blood, etc., fit into this category.

The term *take away* could also be translated *cut off*, as both statements are from the same Greek term. To cut away any portion of the Word of God would be a vote by the offender that the Word of God is not inspired, and therefore not to be left alone as it is found recorded.

The warning which this verse gives to one and all is emphasized by the fact that they shall be removed from the book of life, and they shall never have an entrance into that holy city of God.

"Lest anyone still object that it applies only to the Book of Revelation, it may be noted, historically, that the various atheists and humanists, as well as the motley array of modernists, liberals, higher critics, and other pseudointellectuals in Christendom who have rejected or questioned, ridiculed or allegorized away the books of Daniel, Isaiah, Jonah, Acts, Peter or any other books of the Bible have also, invariably, done the same to the Book of Revelation, to the Book of Genesis, and the other books of the Pentateuch. The first and last books of the Bible have constituted a touchstone, as it were, so that the attitude of men and women toward these books always seems to determine their real attitude toward all the Scriptures." (Morris)

Solomon wrote: Proverbs 30:5, *Every word of God {is} pure: he {is} a shield unto them that put their trust in him.*

The term pure could also be rendered genuinely sincere. You can trust your whole eternity on the Word of God!

Verse 20:

He which testifieth these things saith, Surely I come quickly. Amen. Even so, come, Lord Jesus.

Again, we have the exclamation that He is coming again! The One who has declared these things is the same One who is also going to return to this earth which He left some nineteen hundred years ago.

The answer by John to this profound statement is the same answer which we too should offer at the promise of His return - even so, come, Lord Jesus. No more welcome event could happen to the people of God than for the Lord Jesus Christ to appear for His redeemed.

The words which we have been studying, not only in this Book of Revelation, but the entire Word of God, have come to us by the inspiration of the Holy Spirit. The Lord Jesus Christ who has inspired John to write these words proclaims that He will come again. Anyone who would write a book which was filled with so many awesome events, would surely not dare to return to the scene of which he wrote unless he knew that what he had written would happen just like he stated it. What the Lord inspired John to record for posterity will happen just as it is herein recorded. And the Author is declaring that He will return at the end of these events. He knows they will happen as recorded - so we too should accept their authenticity.

Verse 21:

The grace of our Lord Jesus Christ {be} with you all. Amen.

We now come to the conclusion of this fascinating book. It concludes in a way which is similar to its beginning; *Grace be unto you, and peace, from Him which is, and which was, and which is to come.* (1:4).

Paul begins his epistles in a similar manner. While this is the conclusion of this book, John sends his greetings to all who read it and anticipate the returning of the Lord Jesus Christ.

The *AMEN* declares So be it, to all that has been thus recorded. Whether we look back to the past twenty-two chapters of Revelation, or the past sixty-six books of the Word of God, the same "So be it" would apply.

• *What an interesting and fascinating journey!*

BIBLIOGRAPHY;

I borrowed comments from the following writers:

• F J Dake, Revelation Expounded, Dake Bible Sales, P O Box 173, Lawrenceville, GA 30245

• T Lahaye, Revelation Illustrated and Made Plain, Zondervan Publishing House, Grand Rapids, MI 49506

• H A Ironside, Revelation, Loizeaux Bros., Neptune, NJ

• C Larkin, The Book of Revelation, Clarence Larkin Estate, 2802 N Park Av, Philadelphia, PA

• Wim Malgo, An Exposition on Revelation, Midnight Call, Inc., P O Box 4389, W. Columbia, SC 2917 'i

• P Mauro, Of Things Which Soon Must Come To Pass, Reiner Publications, Swengel, PA

• J V McGee, Reveling Through Revelation, Thru The Bible Books, Box 100, Pasadena, CA 91109

• J McKeever, Revelation for Laymen, Omega Publications, P O Box 4130, Medford, OR 97501

• Henry Morris, The Revelation Record, Tyndale House Publishers, Wheaton, IL

• The Pulpit Commentary, WM B Eerdmans Publishing Company, Grand Rapids, MI

• C W M Turner, Outline Studies in the Book of Revelation,

ALSO, THE FOLLOWING:

Alford – Baxter – Berry –

Clarke – Eusebius – Gibbon –

Horton – Henry – Hislop – Hunt – Hastings – Haywood

Lockyer –

Milligan – Morgan – Olivier

Scott – Scofield – Seiss – Smith – Thomas – Watkinson –

Wordsworth – Walvoord – Vincent – Vine

Made in the USA
Middletown, DE
30 October 2023

41527660R00305